BOSTON,
THE GREAT DEPRESSION,
AND THE NEW DEAL

THE URBAN LIFE IN AMERICA SERIES

RICHARD C. WADE, GENERAL EDITOR

BOSTON,
THE GREAT DEPRESSION,
and THE NEW DEAL

CHARLES H. TROUT

NEW YORK
OXFORD UNIVERSITY PRESS
1977

To My Family

I have tried to fight the good fight,
to finish the course, to keep the faith.

Cardinal Cushing

Foreword

American cities had known depressions before; indeed, hard times had been a constant visitor throughout their long development. Hence, in October 1929, municipal leaders simply prepared for another bout. Belts would have to be tightened; budgets slashed; capital improvements postponed; and private charities encouraged to expand poor relief. After a year or two the worst would be over and a slow recovery would be the prelude to renewed expansion. This response to economic depressions had worked before; there seemed no reason to believe it would not again.

The Great Depression, however, proved to be quite different from previous ones. It was the first since 1920, when the Census Bureau announced that more Americans for the first time lived in cities than in the countryside. Moreover, it followed a decade of a prosperity that was based primarily on metropolitan growth. While farming was in continuous trouble in the twenties, urban areas enjoyed unprecedented expansion. The automobile created the first suburban explosion, home building boomed, new skylines sprouted everywhere, highways and telephones tied the "old" America to the "new." When the crash came, the cities felt it first and longest.

But the Great Depression was not only new in its special urban

dimension but also because of its length. Earlier ones, no matter
how harsh, were relatively brief; indeed, economists had created a
cyclical theory that explained both their causes and durations. Yet
the 1929 collapse continued, if somewhat abated, for a full decade.
Municipal resources ran out in the first few years; increasingly the
cities turned to Washington for help. Yet the Federal government
had no experience with this kind of problem. Slowly the Roosevelt
administration developed programs to shore up the nation's beleaguered cities. The scope and nature of that activity is described
and analyzed in an earlier volume in this series: Mark Gelfand's *A
Nation of Cities.*

Boston, The Great Depression, and The New Deal approaches the
topic from a different viewpoint. Instead of emphasizing Washington's response to economic crisis, it focuses on the impact of New
Deal programs on the economy, political traditions, and social life of
a single city. This approach provides a fresh perspective on the
whole period. Seen from the receiving end, the policies conceived
in Washington were not so radical or profound as most scholars
have believed. To be sure, by 1940, the balance of power had
shifted irrevocably in the nation's capital, but the texture of urban
life was not drastically altered. The New Deal might have produced
a revolutionary rearrangement in formal governmental institutions
and agencies, but it left most of the country's urban fabric intact.

These modest results were certainly not planned by New Deal
architects, who sought much greater change. Rather they stemmed
from local conditions. Programs developed in Washington had to be
implemented by municipal officials who tailored them to their own
needs, or at least their perception of these needs. "During the entire New Deal," Mr. Trout concludes, "policies from Washington altered Boston, but just as surely Boston modified federal programs."
"City government," he adds, ". . . exhibited a number of pre-
Depression traits throughout the thirties which . . . outranked the
changes." "Bostonians," he asserts, "were willing to clap for new arrangements with one hand only."

Perhaps it was the peculiarities of Boston that produced this result. After all, the city had enjoyed less than its share of the metropolitan prosperity of the twenties; its manufacturing facilities were old when not obsolete; its wharves withered; its key industries—textile and shoes—finally caved in; its unemployment was among the nation's highest; its high tax rate discouraged commercial investment; its business and labor leadership was not only conservative but also stodgy; and its political system was wonderfully corrupt. All this meant that when the Depression hit, there would be less resilience in the Boston economy than in those of younger and smaller cities.

Yet Boston was not without great resources. In 1929, it had the highest per capita retail sales in the nation, the third largest wholesale volume, the fourth greatest banking assets, and the highest blue-collar wages. If taxes were high, at least they were collected, providing the government with a higher per capita public income than that of any other municipality in the country. Less tangible but still important, was its pride in being the city that was at once the cradle of the American Republic and the Dublin of the New World. As hard times settled upon the Hub, the city fathers could draw upon these reserves.

The author is quite aware that all the world is not Boston and that it had characteristics that set it apart from other cities. Yet he carefully places its experience in a regional and national context. Hence his analysis transcends "local" history and suggests yet another interpretation of the thirties. The New Deal obviously looked different when seen from a local vantage point rather than from its Washington origins. What appeared to be bold innovation on the federal level was melded into local institutions and traditions often without an intolerable wrench.

But a large portion of Boston's business community found the New Deal threatening enough. Deeply conservative before the Depression, this community put up a spirited, though losing fight against what it considered, at best, socialism. Nor was the church hierarchy friendly. In a city that was three-quarters Catholic, its hostility made nearly every program contentious. Even labor had its

reservations though it was ultimately to become the primary benefi-
ciary of New Deal policies. Its old AF of L leadership distrusted the
incursion of CIO organizers and resisted the use of non-union workers on federal projects.

Despite these problems, the New Deal fared well at the polls.
Boston turned in majestic majorities for Franklin Roosevelt during
the entire period. Yet the Washington presence did little to alter the
politics of the city. The town had historically been Democratic, and
though it had local bosses, it had no monolithic machine. Personal
rather than party loyalties created the special quality of Bean Town's
political life. James Michael Curley was one of FDR's earliest supporters for the presidency, but he profited little from that. After
capturing the governorship in 1934, he was consistently defeated for
major offices in the second half of the Depression decade. High
turnover still characterized elections for neighborhood party offices,
and the two new mayors owed their success to Republicans and independents as well as to Democrats. The New Deal, in short, had
not transformed Boston's political system.

It would be an egregious understatement to say this volume is relevant to our times. The nation's general urban malaise, symbolized
by New York's brush with bankruptcy, is widely believed to en-
compass the next decade's most serious domestic problems. High
unemployment, cuts in municipal services, and mounting social tension recall the anxieties of the thirties. That most city officials now
look to Washington for hope and help, however, is a measure of the
change the New Deal wrought in an urban nation. Based on thorough research and written in an engaging style, *Boston, The Great
Depression and The New Deal* is a timely addition to the "Urban
Life in America Series," which seeks to illumine contemporary
issues by providing an historical perspective.

New York   RICHARD C. WADE
December, 1976   GENERAL EDITOR
                                    URBAN LIFE IN
                                    AMERICAN SERIES

Preface

Translux screens signaled Bostonians that an era had ended: in the autumn of 1929, the Great Bull Market collapsed. Soon, the shock waves felt by investors along State Street were rippling outward, and men with self-inflicted wounds staggered into Boston City Hospital to get themselves three meals and a bed. Women slept at night on hard benches in the Boston Common, and a member of the city council invited those who underestimated the seriousness of the crash to open their eyes to the jobless—to cigar makers and seamen, to truckers and longshoremen. Along the city's waterfront, he reported, skeptics could see, among others, a pathetic woman "in the evening of life, over there with her little bag, peddling cigars for ten cents apiece while the husband, willing to work, is at home." [1]

For more than a decade widespread unemployment plagued the City of Boston, and this study of the Great Depression's impact is concerned with several questions related to that experience. To put the matter most broadly, what traits did the city exhibit at the time of the crash, and to what degree did pre-Depression legacies endure? In an urban center acutely aware of ethnic differences, how did Irish, Italians, Yankees, Jews, and Negroes fare in respect to unemployment, housing, access to work relief, admission to labor unions, and entry into the courts of power? What were the consequences for municipal government as it attempted to relieve the poor, and what, too, were the political repercussions in Boston's neighborhoods? How typical was Boston and, through comparisons to other cities, what possibilities emerge for understanding the urban condition during eleven extraordinarily difficult years?

While several of these questions can be answered with precision, others that involve popular attitudes are decidedly trickier. Trade unionists, businessmen, social workers, clergy, Irish, Italians, Wasps—how did they react to economic upheaval, and how did the unemployed perceive their lot? What, indeed, was it like to be jobless in Boston? What solutions were expected from city government and how, in turn, did the people of Boston regard efforts to help them? What new ideological vistas, if any, were opened up to those who reeled under burdens which the Depression had so inexorably imposed?

Clearly, the Depression by 1932 had subjected American optimism to the supreme test. "I gues[s] every State and City is the same while these hard times lasts untill [sic] you are President," wrote an unemployed Boston Irishman to Franklin Delano Roosevelt, and "then people will see a change. When [I] wrote this letter to you I did not eat any thing for 2 days. I slept on a 10 cent flop where there is 500 men. [I]t is worse than an insane isylum [sic]." [2] And another told Roosevelt with simple eloquence, "I've reeled through Hell. . . . I've been down into the Valley." [3] But as the city groped for usable policies in the pre–New Deal years to emerge from "the Valley," and the time-honored virtues of self-help, individualism, thrift, hard work, and voluntary philanthropy were called into question, not all Bostonians cast off traditional outlooks at the same pace. As the diverse groups in the city reacted to the crisis of the old order, their responses defined Boston's capacity to invent solutions and to accept innovations from outside.

As early as August 1930, Boston's shrewdest observer of political vicissitudes, James Michael Curley, sized up what was happening to

his city and prophesied that the Depression would "make and un-
make in the United States in the next three years, Presidents, Senators, and Governors." "It is," he continued, "just as important to
every American as was the question of chattel slavery in 1861." [4]
True to Curley's words, the Boston electorate traveled new roads in
a quest for leadership. The most important led to Franklin Roosevelt.

With the inauguration of Roosevelt and the unfolding of the New
Deal, the mayor, the city council, and ward leaders were being
asked to adjust to untested intergovernmental relationships and to
the presence of strangers in the municipal power structure. Businessmen along State Street were confronted by unprecedented regulations, and labor unions looked to altered ground rules. Jobless
workers, wealthy Yankees from Beacon Hill, homeowners and tenement dwellers, the mighty and the lowly—in one way or another, all
were touched by policies emanating from the city on the Potomac.
The New Deal contribution demands assessment, and to this task a
major portion of this book is devoted. On balance, can it be said that
the Depression and the New Deal represented a great divide, that
they transformed visions and practices at the local level? What, in
sum, did the New Deal do to Boston?

But what, too, did Boston do to the New Deal? Perhaps more
than the Roosevelt administration could have anticipated, the city
which hosted federal programs also reshaped the experiments of
1933 and beyond. Certain characteristics evident on the eve of the
Great Depression persisted, and the course of events from 1929 to
1932 stimulated additional tensions in Boston. Consequently, the
programs of the Hundred Days were not greeted with unified re-
solve. Clashing objectives at the local level modified the New Deal.
When accommodations were made to local vagaries—and unavoid-
ably, many were—then so-called "federal" programs no longer retained their original appearance. As Washington's grand design absorbed qualities peculiar to Boston, parochial rivalries which
antedated the arrival of the New Deal were rekindled, releasing

forces over which Washington had little control. When the crucible in which the New Deal had to be forged is examined, what then are the implications for the Roosevelt record?

Over the protracted course of this investigation, unpayable debts have been accumulated, sometimes in surprising ways. Although it is usually assumed that at American Historical Association Conventions the befogged speak to the benumbed, the seminal idea for this book was nevertheless planted in one of those unbearably stuffy rooms. Way back in 1966, I heard Alfred B. Rollins, Jr., suggest the value of writing local histories of the 1930s. By moving away from the corridors of Washington, he intimated, a fuller sense of the New Deal's workings might be gained. Remarks made at an AHA meeting four years later by Otis L. Graham, Jr., were equally stimulating. It was Graham's hypothesis that when local obstacles are given more attention than they have thus far received, the New Deal will get higher marks than it has generally been accorded.

For unshrouding the mysteries of the National Archives, James Paulauskas has my special thanks, and other keepers of federal records have also supplied unfailingly helpful guidance. For the assistance rendered by the staffs of the National Archives' Social and Economic Division, the Franklin D. Roosevelt Library, the Library of Congress, and the Federal Records Center at Suitland, Maryland, I am grateful. Without the kindness of the Boston Public Library— its microfilm and government documents sections in particular—and the Littauer Center at Harvard University, this study could not possibly have been made. For providing special collections, I am indebted to Dr. Abram L. Sachar and the Goldfarb Library at Brandeis University as well as the staffs of the Baker Library of the Harvard University School of Business Administration, the Massachusetts Historical Society, Radcliffe's Schlesinger Library, the Robert Frost Library at Amherst, the Dinand Library at Holy Cross, and the Columbia Oral History Collection. Church libraries, labor organizations, and social agencies in Boston also have my gratitude. In addition, the libraries of the Phillips Exeter Academy, Harvard University, Mount Holyoke and Smith colleges, and the University of Massachusetts have all been of substantial assistance.

Bostonians who experienced the Great Depression—barbers and policemen, shop stewards and clerks, public officials and residents of Old Harbor Village—supplied vivid, informal recollections of the 1930s. Their willingness to share memories helped evoke a sense of the past as did nothing else.

My appreciation also extends to scholars who have freely given of their time—be it ten minutes or ten hours—in discussing aspects of the 1930s with me—Stephan Thernstrom, J. Joseph Huthmacher, Frank Freidel, David Brody, William Chafe, Harvard Sitkoff, John Chambers—and to those who have read the manuscript at earlier stages: Ann H. Barrie, Eric McKitrick, John Garraty, Bernard Barber and the late Wallace Sayre. Bruce Stave, Lyle Dorsett, and Bernard Sternsher offered valuable criticisms of an abridged version presented to the Organization of American Historians in 1972, while Kenneth T. Jackson's standards of precision, insistence upon comparisons to other cities, and grasp of urban history have contributed more than could possibly be conveyed in a passing note of acknowledgment. The aid given by Margot Stevens Trout at many levels has been sufficient to make me wince.

Although *Boston, The Great Depression, and The New Deal* is a story of hard times, it was written in a comparatively prosperous era made more so by generous financial assistance. Relatives, too often taken for granted, bailed me out more than once: Elizabeth and Sharp—my thanks. Richard Ward Day and the Phillips Exeter Academy helped with special munificence, and so did the Mount Holyoke College Committee on Faculty Grants.

Then, too, I wish to thank those who have helped with the preparation of the manuscript. Mary Mellor, Sandra Simpson, Emily Ranger, Barbara Bender, friend Margot, and especially Ann Brown Grassilli typed preliminary drafts, while Mary Frances Wall superintended the final copy.

Above all, there is William E. Leuchtenburg at Columbia University. More than a decade ago, he excited me about history in two lecture courses on America since 1877, and a memorable colloquium redoubled my determination to make history a life's work. In improving this manuscript, he wielded his scalpel with deftness and sensitivity. At the same time, the patient was allowed to smile once the ministrations had ended. His knowledge of the thirties, his sense of the historian's craft, and his unstinting encouragement during my bleakest moments have been inestimable gifts.

South Hadley, Massachusetts

Contents

BOSTON,
THE GREAT DEPRESSION,
AND THE NEW DEAL

1

Hub of the Universe

On September 5, 1929, Roger Babson, a member of the Board of Directors of the Boston Chamber of Commerce, conveyed bad tidings to businessmen assembled in nearby Wellesley. An economic debacle, he announced, was impending, and he counseled investors to "get out of debt and reef their sails." Not only would stock values evaporate, he predicted, but "factories will shut down . . . men will be thrown out of work . . . , the vicious circle will get in full swing, and the result will be a serious business depression." [1] Upon this bleak prophesy, Babson built a reputation as one of the most perspicacious observers of the American economy.

Babson, however, was not necessarily a clairvoyant: New Englanders in the 1920s occupied a splendid vantage point for picking up economic signals, and the signals were mixed. On the one hand, the six-state region upon which Boston's well-being in large measure depended had suffered both absolute and relative declines in manufacturing, had edged off in its percentage of the nation's population (especially the portion living in cities), and had also lost ground to healthier regions in its share of total personal income. On the other hand, New England still boasted considerable wealth. Ranking eighth in population among the nation's nine regions in 1929, the

3

Northeast placed third in virtually every significant category—in payments to the Internal Revenue Service, in the products turned out by its whirring mills, in its annual wage bill, and in its bank deposits. Still, Babson was worried—and properly so. Although the region had privileges, there could be no sloganeering about the limitless prosperity of the 1920s.[2]

Massachusetts, like the region to which it belonged, also presented a mixed picture. It, too, had inherited a substantial head start as a center of manufacturing, banking, and commerce. Both at the beginning of the 1920s and at the close, the Commonwealth contained more manufacturing establishments, provided jobs to a greater number of workers, produced more goods than the other five states combined, and paid out almost as much wages. But also like the New England region, Massachusetts' relative standing was eroded during the 1920s. While Rhode Island and Connecticut increased the number of wage earners in manufacturing, Massachusetts pared its industrial labor force from 695,000 in 1920 to 557,000 in 1929 (down to 481,000 in 1930), the largest decline not only in New England but in any of the forty-eight states. In the same decade that Connecticut nearly doubled its output, the total value of manufactured products in Massachusetts lost $1 billion, a shrinkage of 25 percent. Over a twelve-month period during 1928–1929, the number of boot and shoe establishments fell from 948 to 817, and textiles lost ground at a similar rate. The situation led President Thomas McMahon of the United Textile Workers' Union to say a few months later, "There is, perhaps, more destitution and misery in the mill towns of New England today than anywhere else in the United States."[3] Massachusetts, although a rich state by regional and national standards, was beginning to hurt in the years before the Great Depression.

Boston, with a population of 781,000, relied heavily upon the economy of Massachusetts and the rest of New England, yet the city also contained light manufacture with markets outside the region. While industrial productivity fell off during the 1920s, the 9 percent dip was 16 percent less than in the state as a whole. Diversification

accounted for the difference. Not one of the city's ten most important manufacturing occupations employed more than 4 percent of
the total labor force of 355,000, and not one engaged more than
15 percent of the 76,000 workers who, in 1929, earned their
living from manufacturing enterprise. Scores of small clothing
shops, many of them in downtown lofts off Washington Street,
turned out endless racks of dresses and suits. Although most of the
fabric which found its way into the cutting and sewing rooms was
produced outside the city, Boston also had its cotton, woolen, and
worsted mills. The home of the *Atlantic Monthly* and firms such as
Houghton, Mifflin and Little, Brown, the city rivaled Philadelphia
as a printing and publishing center. Industries that turned out finished boots and shoes or supplied stock and findings to other plants;
foundries and machine shops heavily oriented toward shoes and
textiles; and companies engaged in food processing also ranked
among the leading industries. Boston, then, contrasted sharply with
specialized manufacturing cities having populations above
100,000—places like Lynn within the Bay State, or Detroit, Cleveland, Milwaukee, and Akron to the west. Less than Pittsburgh, St.
Louis, Chicago, Baltimore, and Buffalo—urban centers also committed to diversified manufacture—Boston little resembled the proto-
typical industrial metropolis.

   With Boston's greatest economic activity concentrated in trade,
the city's nickname—"The Hub"—fit perfectly. Like New York in
the East, San Francisco and Los Angeles on the shores of the Pacific, Kansas City and Minneapolis in the nation's heartland, and
New Orleans in the South, Boston in 1929 was most of all a commercial city.[4] Handling a phenomenal 53.8 percent of New England's wholesale trade, some 3,700 firms employed 49,000 workers,
paid $104,000,000 in wages, and enjoyed net sales of $2.4 billion, a
volume which placed Boston, the nation's ninth largest city, behind
only New York and Chicago. From the luxury shops along Newbury
Street to the purveyors of exotica at Haymarket Square, retailers
also contributed significantly to the city's economy. Nearly ten thousand merchants, with a payroll of 66,000 employees and a wage bill

of $94,000,000, sold goods worth $672,000,000. While five cities surpassed Boston in total retail volume, the hometown of Filene's and Jordan Marsh exceeded all others on a per capita basis.[5] As a wool market, Boston occupied the preeminent position among cities in the United States and, in selected years, the volume pouring through the massive sheds on Summer Street topped even that of London.

A wooden cod, prominently displayed on the Speaker's desk in the State House on Beacon Hill, served as a reminder of the great fortunes Boston had once derived from the sea. Even in 1929 the city still claimed first rank among all the fishing ports in the entire western hemisphere. A fleet of some five hundred vessels annually unloaded cod, flounder, and mackerel for processing in the world's largest fish-freezing and storage plant. Fishermen, however, received diminishing prices throughout the 1920s, and by the end of the decade they had threatened to dump their cargoes rather than submit to the going offers of wharfside dealers.

Boston also declined as a port city in the twentieth century. Although shippers had been losing headway to rivals in New York and Philadelphia for over a hundred years, many attributed their immediate difficulties to rulings by the Interstate Commerce Commission on freight rate differentials and the failure to establish a competitive railroad trunk line that would attract New England shippers away from New York City, a situation about which Bostonians bitterly complained.[6] Ships using Boston Harbor suffered from what the industry called an "unfavorable load factor," meaning that vessels entered full to the gunwales but left with their holds half-empty.[7] The volume of cargo shipped through Boston fluctuated crazily in the early 1920s but from 1925 to 1930 the value of goods edged steadily downward and gains in passenger traffic, a relatively insignificant portion of the port's business, failed to compensate. Once the center of trade with Europe, the Port of Boston depended in 1929 on coastwise shipping for over half its business, and Boston's United Fruit Company handled the bulk of the remainder with its outposts in South and Central America. No longer did the harbor bustle with activity as it had in the nineteenth century when Brahmin merchants brought back silk from China, and when they accumulated the vast fortunes which they plowed into western railroad and mining adventures. The decaying grain elevators and crumbling wharves in East Boston and the abandoned hulks of once noble ships gave the harbor a sepulchral appearance.

Boston also employed a large number of salaried professionals in its remarkable financial, service, and medical organizations, which, in turn, provided jobs to thousands of subprofessionals. In the marble halls and oak-paneled offices of venerable institutions like the First National Bank of Boston and the National Shawmut, impeccably attired bankers husbanded more resources than any American city except New York, Philadelphia, and Chicago. Loans and discounts extended by Boston's national banks in 1929 exceeded those of every urban center save New York and San Francisco, and they more than equaled the combined activity of Detroit, Baltimore, St. Louis, Minneapolis, Cleveland, and Buffalo.[8] Along Milk, State, and Devonshire streets, investment houses tapped one of the richest securities markets in the world, and important life insurance companies such as John Hancock also headquartered in the Hub. Patients from a wide area flocked to renowned hospitals—particularly the Massachusetts General and the Boston Lying-In.

The city's banking institutions were at once Boston's blessing and its curse—a boon because they made substantial contributions to the city's tax levies [9] but a pox because they relied upon the resources of Brahmin families who insisted that their fortunes be withdrawn from aggressive entrepreneurial activity. As far back as the nineteenth century, Boston's moguls had devised conservative "spendthrift trusts" to protect the scions of wealthy merchants from taking business risks. As Frederic Jaher has put it, "Inheritances encouraged heirs to forsake business for other activities, and fostered conservative commercial practices by making Brahmin businessmen reluctant to jeopardize family fortunes of which they regarded themselves as stewards."[10] Estates were so firmly tied up by legal safeguards that they were said to be "beyond the reach of any power but the

Communist International." [11] Trust offices invested the money in downtown real estate, blue chip stocks, 4 percent bonds, and life insurance, but not in new industry. Said a Bostonian, properly critical of this cautious hoarding:

> It was as if the argosies of Venice had been realized and the proceeds placed with Shylock at 4 percent. Shylock took no risks and the Boston Bassanio, bored, spent his 4 percent in elegant living—to do him justice greatly promoting art, charity, public service—but the consequences were disastrous to a Venetian commercial supremacy. [12]

Fortune magazine expressed the opinion that the wealthiest Bostonians had left "their excellent and graceful trustees to dine annually upon champagne and terrapin and the memory of a vanished world." [13]

While the trustees supped, more reckless Bostonians found irresistible the Great Bull Market of the 1920s until, alas, the day arrived when no one wanted to buy. On October 23, 1929, relentless liquidation on the Boston and New York Stock Exchanges, as well as the Boston Curb Exchange, [14] reached epic proportions, and at the end of the session, said the Boston *Globe*, "the public was in a blue funk." The next day, in an even wilder performance, tickers in Boston and New York ran more than two hours late at the close, and trading on the Big Board reached a record volume of 12,894,650 shares. Bankers rushed to the offices of J. P. Morgan and Company to try to shore up the market. Half a dozen brokers collapsed on the floor and were taken to hospitals. The *Globe* reported that "the most pathetic scenes were witnessed in the customers' rooms of the brokerage houses where ruined speculators broke down and wept, while others congregated in small groups, stunned by the misfortune that had overtaken them." And the worst was yet to come.

Tuesday, October 29, 1929, established a record for shares traded (16,410,000) on the New York Exchange that would last for nearly thirty years. Crowds vied for space in the boardrooms of Boston brokerage houses along Devonshire Street, and an unusual number of women braved heavy cigar smoke to watch the ticker flash reports of fresh disaster. Assistant Secretary of Commerce Julius Klein took to nationwide radio and, in a performance that the Hoover administration would often repeat, assured his countrymen of the business structure's soundness, pleaded for a return of much-needed confidence, and stated that "normal purchasing power has not been appreciably impaired." The market made a modest comeback the next day, and then closed. Reopening on November 4 for a series of three-hour sessions, it ran up more losses before reaching rock bottom on November 13, another chilling day. "America lay back exhausted to marvel at its own magnificence," wrote Gilbert Seldes. "Nothing like it had ever been seen before; it was the record, millions of times more exciting and expensive than flagpole sitting. We had beaten the world again and the only question was what it would cost us." [15]

As the good citizens of Boston looked to the future, some unquestionably felt cushioned by the city's industrial diversification, by the clatter of its marketplace, and by its advantages over other cities in several important areas. Still, the 1920s had brought setbacks, and there were perils in the symbiotic relationship to a state where manufacturing had declined more than twice as precipitously during the 1920s as it had in the city. Reliance upon the economy of Massachusetts and the rest of New England would consign Boston to the peculiar fate of commercial cities during the Great Depression. When industrial output dropped, the impact would not be felt at once. Conversely, when economic revival took place elsewhere, it would always come in advance of recovery in the city. Indeed, the years ahead would underscore the Hub's inability to protect itself against the capricious world beyond the city limits.

For over two hundred years, Boston's population had been more or less homogeneous, but beginning with the Irish migration of the 1830s and 1840s, newcomers displaced the descendants of the *Mayflower* and the *Arbella*. Swarming principally into the thirty-five acres known as the North End (for location of the regions of Boston, see Map I), the Irish lived in unspeakable squalor. Moreover, they were greeted by the hostility of older Americans. But for almost forty years the newcomers at least were spared competition from other immigrants: not until the 1880s, by which time the Irish outnumbered old stock Yankees, did Italian migration become significant. By 1895, there were more Italians than Irish in the North End, and some 6,200 Jews (most of them from Russia) had joined them. Many of the Irish fled to the winding, narrow streets which climbed Charlestown's Bunker Hill—or they moved a few blocks away into the West End—or they escaped to South Boston, the peninsula jutting out into Boston Harbor. Meanwhile, still other Italians flocked to East Boston, a ferry ride away from the rest of the city, and thousands of Jews settled in Chelsea until a great fire dispersed them into Dorchester and Roxbury. Other groups poured into the Hub of the Universe until it could be said:

> The voices around Faneuil Hall are Italian voices and the silence of Copp's Hill is a silence of Yankee stones in a screaming of Levantine and Greek and the faces on Washington Street are Irish faces and the only race which remains now what it was when the Old South Church was building is the race of sedate and respectable pigeons which courteously steps aside on the paths of Boston Common to let the Lithuanians pass.[16]

The influx of immigrants touched off an exodus of Yankees into the suburbs while still others sought haven in the outlying regions of West Roxbury and Brighton, both technically part of Boston proper. In fact after 1880 the suburbs grew more rapidly than the city itself.[17] A substantial number of First Families, however, took refuge in the commodious town houses of the Back Bay where they looked on despairingly at the inundation.

Despite a reputation as an immigrant city, Boston was not altogether unique. By the time that the Immigration Act of 1924 all but halted the flow, Boston had joined seventeen American cities of over 250,000 people where foreign stock comprised more than 50 percent of the population. And of the ten largest urban centers, Boston contained a percentage of foreign stock almost identical with that of New York (71.5 vs. 73.3), while Cleveland (64.9) and Chicago (64.4) ranked close behind. This is not to say that Boston did not manifest variations: percentages in Detroit (57.6), Pittsburgh (51.1), and Philadelphia (50.6) more nearly approximated the big city average (53.4).[18]

If Boston differed from other cities, the main distinction lay in the composition of its population. Even in 1929, years after the major Irish migration had terminated, 20.3 percent of the entire city was made up of those born in Ireland or of those whose parents had once set sail from the Emerald Isle. Although no one could know for certain how many Bostonians claimed Irish kinship, the portion easily exceeded half the population. With the telephone directory listing a total of over five thousand Sullivans and Murphys alone, the city had been transformed into the Dublin of America. At the same time, Italians, Jews of Russian nativity, and especially Slavic groups were relatively less common. Moreover, with only 2.9 percent of Boston's population classified as nonwhite (2.6 percent Negro), Boston deviated from the big city norm (9.4 percent), a clear sign that most of the folk migration out of the South had stopped short of Boston.[19]

The Irish, then, had unquestionably gained ascendancy, but Boston's neighborhoods in the year of the crash nevertheless resembled a crazy quilt of nationalities. While considerable internal migration had led to a scattering throughout the city of older Irish, of Italians originally from Genoa and the North, and of some Jews, mainly those of German extraction, a high degree of residential segregation prevailed.[20] In a Jewish community of approximately eighty-five thousand, some fifty-five thousand made their homes in Dorchester, and fifteen thousand more lived in crowded sections of Roxbury where they intermingled in varying degrees with the more prosperous Sons of Erin. Low-income Irish comprised almost all of South Boston's sixty thousand residents and the thirty thousand inhabitants of Charlestown. Some ninety to one hundred thousand Bostonians

CAMBRIDGE

BRIGHTON

ALLSTON

BACK BAY

BROOKLINE

JAMAICA PLAIN

WEST ROXBURY

HYDE PARK

MAP I

Locations of Sections of Boston
Referred to in the Text

of Italian extraction clustered in East Boston and the North End in neighborhoods of remarkable solidarity. Over half the city's blacks could be found in the South End, although the migration of Negroes into Roxbury was well under way. In another area of high uniformity, thirty-eight thousand white Anglo-Saxon Protestants dominated the Back Bay and Beacon Hill.

Conditions of appalling inequality existed in these areas of the city where a high degree of ethnic uniformity prevailed. In the heavily populated North End, only a stone's throw from where Paul Revere had once flashed his lantern, population in the late 1920s had reached a suffocating density of 799 persons per gross acre, the juvenile delinquency rate hovered close to twenty-eight cases for every thousand persons, and 35 percent of employable workers held no jobs by April of 1930. At the opposite extreme, the Back Bay contained only 167 persons per gross acre, had but 19.9 juvenile infractions for every thousand persons, and managed to keep its unemployment rate at a mere 4 percent. The low-income West End, with its mixed Italian and Irish population, and South Dorchester, where wealthier Irish and Jews resided, provided another jolting contrast.[21]

Almost precisely four of every five Bostonians rented their housing, an extraordinarily high instance of tenancy which topped all major cities except New York, and once again substantial inequities prevailed. Negroes, for instance, although better off than blacks in most northern cities, were almost twice as unlikely to own their homes as Boston's whites. Then, too, several areas of pronounced ethnic segregation had reaped the unhappy legacy of the nineteenth century's balloon frame building revolution. As a partial consequence, Boston's per capita damage from fires in 1928 and 1929 exceeded losses in all major cities. Those who lived in the antiquated, wooden, multifamily structures in places like Irish Charlestown, however, had no monopoly on squalor. In the North End, where approximately nine of every ten families packed into brick tenements, only 81 of 5,030 rental units provided mechanical refrigeration, roughly half lacked a water closet in the dwelling unit, nearly three of every four apartments needed repair, and only one of every ten units had a tub or shower. The Back Bay, on the other hand, where Lowells spoke only to Cabots and Cabots spoke only to God, contained just 24 dwelling units that needed structural repair out of 9,000 in all, and only 14 apartments in the entire district lacked a tub or shower.[22]

Other social inequalities existed in Boston. In general, lower-class Italians crammed larger families into fewer rooms than any other group, and they tended to occupy the most dilapidated structures in the city. With food costs running high, the underprivileged suffered from malnutrition—especially in areas where mothers from non–English-speaking countries tried desperately to make ends meet. Furthermore, social workers discovered that Boston's Italian community, with an illiteracy rate some six times higher than the national average, was particularly prone to sickness, suggesting that low income was not the sole reason for failing health. Many non–English-speaking mothers simply did not know how to get the medical attention their families needed. In short, the greatest insecurity afflicted the poor, particularly the foreign-born. Even those families from non-Yankee stock who had gained more remunerative jobs in the 1920s had a much greater chance of slipping back into menial positions than did the native-born. And as the Depression intensified, the inequalities became ever more palpable.[23]

Ethnic consciousness abounded in Boston, not only in the day-to-day relationships between one person and the next, but in the myriad temporal and spiritual organizations to which the people of the city belonged. Even if far less noticeable than in the nineteenth century, when a howling mob had burned the Ursuline Convent in Charlestown, there could still be verbal harassment and physical combat between one racial or ethnic group and another. Porters and redcaps in South Station complained bitterly that white supervisors drove them like slaves, street-corner rumbles in the North and West Ends pitted Irish against Italians, and several Yankees, active in the Immigration Restriction League, had gloated when the 1924 Quota Act was passed. There could be little question that "Boston was very anti-English—very. So much so that when the Prince of Wales visited America . . . in the early twenties, and was on his way from New York to the North Shore, they didn't dare to bring him through Boston." [24] But on the whole, Bostonians appeared to solve intergroup feelings by retreating into segregated enclaves where they eyed outsiders with suspicion. As the Beacon Hill elite made their way to the June steeplechases at The Country Club in Brookline, or to the Harvard-Yale game ("*The* Game") in November, the sons of Italy played *boccie* in East Boston's back alleys. As the Ancient Order of Hibernians waved their signs in South Boston on St. Patrick's Day proclaiming "Erin Go Bragh," Yankee matrons chatted over tea at the venerable Vincent Club, or sat primly while Serge Koussevitzky majestically raised his baton over the Boston Symphony Orchestra. Virtual apartheid characterized the Boston Chamber of Commerce: by 1929 not a single important officership had been captured by a person with Irish blood. Moreover, few Irish names adorned the letterhead of the Boston Council of Social Agencies, the central body to which the city's charitable organizations belonged, and a number of firms excluded the largely Irish graduates of Suffolk Law, the city's night school, whose standards the Massachusetts Bar Association regularly deplored.

Yet in Boston's labor unions the Irish held a disproportionate number of elected positions, especially when deliberately segregated locals—Lithuanian Coat Makers, Italian Hod Carriers, Hebrew Butchers—are excluded from the count. Indeed, only 55 of 347 elective offices in nonsegregated unions went to Jews, Italians, French Canadians, or Negroes. And discounting clothing workers only 12 percent of union officials were drawn from these four ethnic groups, less than their numerical strength in the total work force would have suggested. [25]

The Boston Central Labor Union (BCLU), with which American Federation of Labor (AFL) locals in the city were associated, boasted a membership of close to sixty thousand men and women in

1929, approximately 17 percent of the labor force. Only a few thousand workers belonged to independent unions, most notably the Amalgamated Clothing Workers. With a share of organized blue-collar employees well above the national average,[26] and with experience dating back to 1878, the central labor body had given Boston a reputation as a strong union city. Locals in the building trades—carpenters, painters, and hod carriers, for example—accounted for roughly 40 percent of all BCLU members, and railway unions boasted the greatest number of locals. BCLU officerships were usually won by delegates from the heavily organized printing trades, the United Garment Workers, the Hotel and Restaurant Workers, the International Ladies Garment Workers (ILGWU), the Machinists and Sheet Metal Workers, the Bakers, the Barbers, and the United Textile Workers. Moreover, the International Longshoremen's Association and the Teamsters maintained active locals. For the most part, however, the preponderant share of the unionized labor force came from skilled crafts. Zealously bucking for better wages and hours, Boston locals staged nineteen walkouts during 1929, a number well above the norm for cities of comparable size,[27] and disturbances triggered by shoe, garment, and longshore workers were accompanied by violence. Over the years, Boston's unions had not developed the habit of silence, and they had meanwhile won wage rates considerably above state averages.[28]

In several respects, nevertheless, the AFL unions had miles to travel at the decade's close. Few municipal or federal employees were protected, scarcely a retail clerk in the city was enrolled, public utilities workers had no union, and less than 10 percent of the city's truckers paid dues to the Teamsters. A serious schism within the ILGWU in 1928 had weakened Boston's potentially most important organization, and scores of small, nonunion clothing shops existed. Shoe workers were hampered by a devastating combination of weak leadership and hostile employers, and ship workers submitted to company unionism. In addition, craft unions in Boston, as elsewhere, were built on the principle of exclusivity, and aggressive organizing campaigns were all but nonexistent. Although the BCLU regularly passed what it called "progressive" resolutions, almost all pertained to wages and hours, to workmen's compensation, and to urging consumer respect for union labels. Committed to pure and simple trade-union objectives, most labor leaders in 1929 were ideologically innocent.

To a considerable degree, Boston's unions were outgunned by the city's business community, which boasted a tightly knit structure and assumed a prominent public role. Far more than progressives like E. A. Filene, his brother A. Lincoln Filene, and Louis Kirstein, the Boston Chamber of Commerce and the tax and real-estate organizations associated with it typified the city's enterprisers. At the time of the crash, over five thousand businessmen belonged to the Chamber. With an annual budget in excess of $350,000, the organization constituted a powerful lobby, one which enjoyed impressive success in getting its way with the state legislature. Indeed, from 1914 to 1927, 73 percent of the positions taken by the Chamber had prevailed on Beacon Hill, and the group's stands were becoming more conservative as the twenties drew to a close. Presided over in 1928 and 1929 by Henry I. Harriman, chairman of the New England Power Company, the Chamber was gradually moving away from boosting Boston as a place in which to do business and toward serving as the special advocate of large corporations and trade associations. Stumping for reduced corporate and real-estate taxes, and opposing more than minimum spending by government at all levels, the Chamber's Municipal Finance Committee spoke out for fiscal conservatism. Moreover, the Chamber had shifted during the 1920s from its position in favor of a state minimum-wage commission to opposition, and it was also campaigning against workmen's compensation. Dedicated to the preservation of Boston's imposing economic assets, the Chamber was gradually isolating itself from the rest of the city. "The fact is," lamented a former president of the Chamber in 1930, "the business community of Boston has very little public spirit." [29]

Meanwhile, social-service organizations attended to thousands of less privileged Bostonians. Many of these associations, staffed by

Brahmins with a strong sense of obligation to the worthy poor and by the sons and daughters of the professional classes, dated from the Progressive Era. Indeed, a number of the head workers in the city's twenty-three social settlements affiliated with the Greater Boston Federation of Neighborhood Houses had received their initial training from Robert A. Woods at South End House. Following Woods's aim of "enlivening and uplifting humanity in all its parts," many were originally schooled in making the immigrant more presentable so that he would suffer less for his "uncouth exterior." [30] At the same time, emphasis was placed on immigrant gifts to America, and women like Eva Whiting White of Elizabeth Peabody House promoted so-called "racial pageants" on the Boston Common throughout the twenties—occasions when Chinese and Italians, Irish and Jews, would perform the dances and songs of their homelands. Russian choruses, presentations of "Little Black Sambo," kindergarten rhythm bands, readings by Khalil Gibran at Syrian-dominated Denison House, and the distribution of flowers and fruit to the elderly constituted standard activities.

Most settlement-house leaders during the twenties accepted poverty as an unpleasant fact of life. Social workers, according to the prevailing wisdom, should help their clients to achieve "spiritual adjustment . . . [for] that is what people remember and carry with them long after bags of coal and bushels of potatoes . . . are forgotten." [31] While "it is man's destiny to move forward," wrote Eva White, change must come gradually. "The reformer tends to be dogmatic," she declared, and social workers should be educators. "If more people could be taught the ancient Yankee principles with regard to how to use their money," she stated, "we'd have fewer heartrending cases coming up before us as social workers." [32] By and large, the twenties had brought no driving vision of means by which the causes of poverty might be eliminated. Rather, dealing with the effects counted for more.

At the same time, however, most head workers of the neighborhood houses belonged to other organizations which had also been established during the Progressive Era—the Consumers'

League, the Women's Educational and Industrial Union, the Boston
Women's Trade Union League, the Boston Housing Association, the
NAACP. The executive boards of these associations frequently over-
lapped and, not surprisingly, their causes were for the most part the
same—a Child Labor Amendment to the federal Constitution, state-
sponsored old-age and unemployment insurance systems, stricter
tenement and factory safety laws, protective legislation for female
workers. Links to liberal academics at Harvard had been forged, and
there were friendships as well not only with the more progressive
elements in the American Federation of Labor, but with a generally
liberal rabbinate. The city, then, contained a small cadre of less
hidebound elements, men and women who had somberly filed past
the Charlestown jail in 1927 to protest the execution of Sacco and
Vanzetti. These were the Bostonians who, upon discovering in 1929
that Harvard was paying its scrubwomen less than the Massachusetts Minimum Wage Commission allowed, issued strenuous
protests.

Still, the Yankee reformers' ranks in the year of the crash were
thin, a minority of a minority. The twenties had taken a toll on social
activism, and several organizations were in trouble, especially the
NAACP. Far weaker than in its early years when Moorfield Storey
had helped make the Boston Chapter a pillar of strength, the
NAACP in 1929 claimed a meager eighty-eight members. Remittances to the New York office fell drastically during the twenties,
and even a modest request from the parent organization led the
Boston director to complain of being "dragooned to a frazzle." [33]
Nominally led by a conservative Negro, Butler Wilson, and by an
all-white executive board, the Boston Branch paid little attention to
discrimination against the city's blacks. As one Negro, disgusted by
the NAACP's timidity, wrote, "I always thought Boston was above
the Mason & Dixon line but I see it has gradually slip[ped] a long
ways back." [34] Instead of paying heed to reports of this kind, the
NAACP concentrated what little energy remained upon legal defense funds for blacks in the South. Repudiated by William Monroe
Trotter, the militant editor of *The Boston Guardian*, the NAACP

had lost the confidence of moderate Negroes as well. In addition, settlement houses also were experiencing difficulties. Lacking funds, they were relying more and more on volunteers. And the Consumers' League, with a bank balance of $162 at the beginning of 1929, sensed an "appalling individualism" among college graduates of the twenties. The number one need of the hour, said a league member, was "a systematic campaign . . . to convince the younger generation" of its social responsibility.[35]

In Boston, the most predominantly Catholic city in the entire United States, the vast majority looked not to the institutional remnants of the Progressive Era but to the Church. With 73 percent of the population claiming allegiance to Roman Catholicism, Protestants despaired. Whether progressive or intractably conservative, Yankees might well have agreed with words written in 1928:

> Boston has been conquered and subdued,
>   Her monuments are meaningless; her dome
> That seems to shine in heaven's solitude
>   Is but a symbol of the Church of Rome.[36]

William Cardinal O'Connell oversaw the million-member Archdiocese of Boston,[37] and no greater genius for organization, no more worldly prelate, ruled any spiritual domain in America. In 1911, Pope Pius had given O'Connell his red hat, and by 1929, at the age of seventy, the still vigorous Cardinal had earned a deserved reputation for authoritarianism. "When I ask you to do anything," he had once told his parishioners, "trust me and do it." [38] While it would be erroneous to assume that when O'Connell spoke his loyal flock listened unquestioningly, he was nevertheless an imposing figure of remarkable power. The Archdiocese of Boston had become a model of rigid clerical discipline, as more than one uncooperative priest learned to his sorrow.[39] O'Connell set the tone, and the archdiocesan newspaper, *The Pilot*, while not officially under his control, generally echoed his views.

The son of poor Irish immigrants, Cardinal O'Connell had clawed his way to the top of the Catholic hierarchy. When not at his lavish home in Brighton, a showplace replete with private golf course, he resided at another magnificent estate on the ocean at Marblehead or journeyed to Caribbean watering spots during the winter. Derby hat, gold-knobbed cane, and an expensive taste in clothes stamped him as something of a dandy. Although he praised the American Federation of Labor and deplored those employers who, in the old days, had paid their men "the smallest pittance possible," O'Connell seemed at considerable remove from his working-class origins.

Indeed, the Cardinal during the 1920s expressed strongly conservative views. Actively embracing the Gospel of Wealth, he believed that "the rich man and woman of the United States have no fear of failing to enter the Heavenly Kingdom . . . so long as . . . [they continue] to be as warmhearted and kind as they are today." [40] Moreover, those who threatened the process of accumulation or fomented class antagonism topped the Cardinal's list of reprobates. To O'Connell, the hundred thousand members of the Holy Name Society acted as "bulwarks against anarchy, disloyalty, and disorder," [41] and his directives to clergy and laymen warned against the evils of socialism. O'Connell and most of the priests in his realm fought against the Child Labor Amendment, believing it to be an abhorrent intrusion upon the sanctity of the family, and the Cardinal also condemned liberal priests such as Father John Ryan of the National Catholic Welfare Conference in Washington. Holding feminism in contempt, O'Connell denounced the character, behavior, and dress of the "new woman" as more pagan than Christian. In outbursts of obscurantist rhetoric, he fiercely attacked modernism in all its forms. "What does all this worked up enthusiasm about Einstein mean?" asked His Eminence in 1929. "I never yet met a man who understood in the least what Einstein is driving at; and . . . I very seriously doubt that Einstein knows really what he means." [42]

Cardinal O'Connell equated social activism with Chistian charity. Poverty, he believed, resulted from an iron law which mortals could in no way affect, and he liked to remind his audiences that "Our blessed Lord said: 'The poor you have always with you.'" Drawing from this instruction, O'Connell concluded that "the complete abolition of poverty in this human life is a futile dream." Christ taught that the "philosophy of life is no pipe dream of universal riches"; rather, He looked to "a world in which there will always be the rich and the poor." [43] Furthermore, charity ennobled the giver. As O'Connell told St. Vincent de Paul Society workers, "If you have no material wealth you have the wealth of charity to which no billions of money can compare." Recipients should be accepting, putting their "humble faith in whatever God may send." Most of all, the poor needed to develop "the patience and perseverance to go along even in straitened circumstances." [44] In sum, William Cardinal O'Connell and, with few exceptions, the priests who assisted him with charitable enterprises, were not asking the Catholics of Boston to embark upon adventurous new paths.

Most Protestant churches, affirming that faith should be accompanied by works, also performed acts of charity through myriad service organizations. The Methodist Social Union, for instance, superintended Deaconess Hospital, and the Methodist Home Missionary Society sponsored a community center for Negro children and their mothers. Many faiths participated in the South End's Morgan Memorial–Goodwill Industries, and in fiscal year 1928–1929 more than $200,000 was paid to needy workers who repaired clothing and furniture for subsequent sale. In addition, the Congregational Missionary Society of Boston ran a summer fresh-air program and attended to the sick and elderly. "Our welfare secretary is like a fairy godmother," a minister stated in 1929 as he extolled his church's accomplishments. "It didn't take a prophet or a social engineer or a financial captain or a sociological expert or a civic reformer to do all this," he affirmed. All that was demanded, the clergyman added, was "love for needy folks, stick-to-it-iveness, and a bit of common sense." [45] For the moment, voluntary Christian endeavor sufficed.

In general, the Protestant clergy of Boston leaned toward conservatism. Dr. A. Z. Conrad of the prestigious Park Street Congregational Church, for example, called for the deportation of aliens, enthusiastically supported an anti-Communist crusade led by State

Senator Erland Fish, and regularly extolled the virtues of individualism. Under the restraining hand of Bishop William Appleton Lawrence, the Episcopal churches also displayed little zest for social action. Boston Unitarianism, once so closely identified with abolitionist fervor, had fallen into the hands of men who declined to speak on social issues, and Baptists such as the Reverend J. Whitcomb Brougher of Tremont Temple preached a fiery fundamentalism. Brougher, Conrad, and a number of others strenuously campaigned to uphold Prohibition, apparently seeing no contradiction between organizing massive "Dry" rallies at the Boston Garden and the stand against lobbying taken by the Massachusetts Federation of Churches. With Cardinal O'Connell attacking "dry fanatics," [46] the Protestants fought with added passion almost as if to compensate for the numerical supremacy lost to the dominant Catholics. "Prohibition," declared Dr. Conrad, "is anchored to the throne of God." [47]

While Prohibition tended to divide Catholics and Protestants, moral fundamentalism united a number of them. "What's the matter with Boston?" asked Heywood Broun in *The Nation*. "I think the answer is miscegenation," the fusion of puritanical Catholicism with Protestant neo-Puritanism. [48] Censorship had long been championed by the Watch and Ward Society, an organization that had given Yankees a means of getting at foreigners and had tried to institutionalize the Brahmin's social authority. [49] But in 1927 a Vatican campaign against immoral literature and an ensuing wave of censorship in Ireland had encouraged Cardinal O'Connell to mobilize his forces in consonance with Watch and Ward. City officials promptly joined the fight. Out went Dreiser's *An American Tragedy*, Hemingway's *The Sun Also Rises*, and scores of other books on the grounds of obscenity. "Alas! no actor today is at all likely to call Boston the Athens of America," said a critic. "If he came there with an Athenian play such as *Lysistrata*, he probably would be kicked out as O'Neill's *Strange Interlude* was kicked out." [50] Heywood Broun recalled the comic character, Little Johnny Boston Beans. "He wore horn-rimmed spectacles, knew long words, and read

Ibsen. Of course there never was a Johnny Boston Beans and there never will be. Even if he knew the long words he couldn't read Ibsen. The Watch and Ward Society wouldn't let him." [51]

Moreover, the honor roll of works "Banned in Boston" covered anything ideologically to the left of *Little Lord Fauntleroy*. Censors axed Upton Sinclair's *Oil*, John dos Passos' *Manhattan Transfer*, John Gunther's *Red Pavilion*, and Carl Van Vechten's *Nigger Heaven*. Sponsors of meetings on controversial social issues found it difficult to obtain public permits and, as Groucho Marx told the Harvard *Crimson* in 1929, "the Cabots and that crowd are so afraid of a left wing they won't go near one, even if it's on a chicken." [52] The comedian might well have included Cardinal O'Connell with the Reverend Conrad and the Cabots, for the Catholic hierarchy had usurped "the tradition of Puritanism, if not its blood." [53]

As Boston headed into what would be one of the most critical decades in its long history, the city enjoyed a number of advantages. Favored with commercial and financial activity greater than several cities with larger populations, powerful segments of the entrepreneurial community were flourishing. Although the industrial base had shriveled during the twenties, the cutbacks had hit textile and shoe manufacturers in particular, leaving other industries relatively unscathed—and Boston still added impressive totals to the value of products turned out in New England, one of America's three richest sections. Skilled blue-collar workers could feel fortunate. Often unionized and blessed with relatively high wages, they also had a diversified economy to buttress them against unemployment in a way that a specialized industrial city could not. In addition, Boston possessed a small but articulate cluster of men and women with a keen sense of social justice and the capability of adjusting to altered circumstances. And with a network of experienced private social-service and charitable agencies, the city seemed prepared in several respects to meet an emergency.

Nevertheless, Boston in 1929 also contained palpable liabilities. Despite the substantial economic lead over cities of similar size, the edge was being inexorably eroded. Confronted by layoffs as industries departed, the work force discovered that not all could be absorbed, at least not at the same skill level. Indeed, wealth was unevenly distributed—extremely so. While the Back Bay contained an American aristocracy, a virtual pariah class also dwelled in the city, especially in areas where recent immigrants resided. Glaring inequalities existed between skilled, unionized workers and the majority outside the AFL's more privileged crafts. And, too, business seemed much better organized than labor. Ethnic rivalries divided Bostonians, and it would have been hard to imagine in 1929 that the disparate population could patch up its quarrels to engage in common action. Furthermore, the city's progressive voices, diminishing during the twenties, were in danger of being drowned out by conservative refrains issuing forth from the Chamber of Commerce, Catholic and Protestant churches, and even from segments of organized labor and social-welfare agencies. On balance, the twenties had saddled Boston with inauspicious legacies.

As 1929 drew to a close, there were dim signs that an era was ending. Even as the Boston Shoe Manufacturer's Association pledged to fulfill President Herbert Hoover's "prosperity schedule" by maintaining wage levels, the stockholders of the Boston Manufacturing Company, the nation's oldest cotton textile firm, authorized directors to liquidate all assets. Crowds streamed into the Boston Garden to watch the Bruins begin their defense of the Stanley Cup, but patrons of the Boston Grand Opera Company, arriving for a performance of *Tosca*, found that the doors had been locked. Musicians packed their instruments, and chauffeurs stood in line to get refunds for their mink-coated, top-hatted employers from Beacon Hill. A few blocks away at the municipal welfare department on Hawkins Street, lines of a different sort were forming. For the first time in their lives, musicians and chauffeurs were on the dole.

2

On the Eve of the Great Depression: Politics Boston Style

Beneath the majestic dome of the state house which Charles Bulfinch designed in the late eighteenth century, another session of the Great and General Court of Massachusetts was being launched in 1929. "It is with a great deal of satisfaction," Governor Frank Allen was noting, "that we today observe the passing of the so-called 'almshouse,' and it is apparent that these institutions are gradually becoming a thing of the past." [1] Just a five-minute walk down Beacon Hill, at the neoclassical City Hall, officials were beginning their day—one like that of February 18, 1929, when a city council member from Dorchester rose to attack the Municipal Employment Bureau. "Unemployed men vainly seeking work loaf aimlessly around the filthy quarters of the Bureau all day long," he charged, "hoping to hear their names shouted by some employee peddling the few jobs obtained." "There is something rotten in Denmark," he concluded. [2] The men who would help guide Bostonians through the Great Depression were warming to new tasks; the mechanisms of government were about to face stern tests.

City government in Boston, much like its counterparts throughout the nation, derived its formal structure from a state-prescribed charter. Over the years, Yankee Republicans from rural Massachusetts, distrustful of Irish politicians in the city, had been largely responsible for voting through charter amendments by ordinary legislative act, and these amendments had diminished the power of local government. The governor, for example, was authorized to appoint Boston's commissioner of police and to select the city's licensing board. No other community in Massachusetts faced these limitations. While insisting that Boston pay the entire cost of operating Suffolk County, the state legislature left the cities of Chelsea and Revere and the town of Winthrop without obligation.[3]

Massachusetts exercised its most potent constraints on the city's autonomy, however, by controlling Boston's fiscal affairs. The General Court, for instance, annually set the tax limit, making Boston the only metropolis in America where the ceiling on total levies was established by the state—and Boston's sole recourse was to come on bended knee before the Joint Committee on Municipal Finance to plead for revisions. Although the city drew up its own budget, it had to obtain the legislature's imprimatur. Moreover, no debt outside a limit equal to 2½ percent of assessed valuations could be incurred without first getting the Commonwealth's approval. While Boston's voters elected the school committee, the state set the school budget except for the construction and repair of buildings. In addition, the Boston Finance Commission, a conservative five-member body appointed by the governor, conducted often mischievous, politically motivated probes of the city's fiscal affairs. Invariably dominated by rural and suburban Republicans, the "Fin. Com.," as the organization was popularly termed, served as an emotional rallying point for those who wanted to overturn Boston's servility to the state legislature. Indeed, the State House on Beacon Hill, with both its chambers controlled by the G.O.P. throughout the 1930s, sometimes resembled an island in the midst of a hostile empire. Like most American cities, Boston experienced a nettlesome insufficiency of home rule.

The city government which would have to negotiate with the state during the Great Depression was headed by a mayor and a city council of twenty-two members, one for each ward in Boston. By charter provision, the mayor enjoyed a considerable edge in any struggle between himself and the council, for he exercised a veto which could not be overridden. All appropriations originated with the mayor, save for the state-controlled school budget. The city council had the right to "reduce or reject any item" (a power of some consequence) "but without the approval of the Mayor [could] not increase any item in, nor the total of, a budget, nor add any item thereto, nor [could] it originate a budget." [4] Thus the mayor decided budget priorities, a power augmented by his ability to transfer funds through his appointee, the city auditor, from one department to another to meet current expenses. Moreover, the mayor acted alone in appointing the heads of Boston's thirty-plus municipal departments, a fertile source of patronage from which the city council was excluded.

The city council, however, also formulated policy, both through its expressly delegated authority and through the exercise of its latent powers. Entitled by charter to reduce or reject any item in the budget, the council also had the ability to force the mayor's hand by suggesting fiscal policies which His Honor could not politically afford to veto. Not only could the council mobilize public opinion on budgetary matters, but the ward representatives also had the authority to pass on all mayoral borrowing requests and to originate bond issues. In addition, the city council exercised its prerogative of initiating orders other than those directly concerned with finance. These orders, drafted as requests to the mayor, might plead for altered welfare procedures, or they might simply ask for information. But by the language used and information demanded, the council could make known its position on issues, including those of national and even international importance over which the mayor obviously had no jurisdiction.[5] Hailing from small geographic units, the councilors lived in proximity to the electorate, a closeness which allowed them to perceive quickly the temper of their constituents. "We are down in the trenches of life itself," boasted a council member. "We see the family in its happy times and also in its bad hours." [6] Capable of bestirring the mayor to action or guiding him away from policies of which the council did not approve, the body belied the popular maxim that once it had passed the budget, it ought to pack up and go home.

Unlike their counterparts in most major urban centers, the men at City Hall entered the Depression years cushioned by a relatively favorable fiscal situation. With over $70 million coming into the collector's office in 1929, Boston amassed total receipts above those of Cleveland, St. Louis, and Baltimore, all cities with larger populations. And on a per capita basis, the Hub—ninth in population—ranked third among the thirteen biggest cities in revenue collected from all sources.[7] Municipal government in Boston was costly, far too expensive according to real-estate owners: total expenditures ran ahead of all but the five largest cities in 1929, and per capita outlays put Boston at the top of the list.[8] Property owners, fuming at the nation's most severe urban tax rate, a levy based on per capita property assessments greater than any other city, displayed acute sensitivity to interest costs on a debt in excess of $100 million. But from an objective point of view, the debt constituted a relatively small liability. In fact, Boston's per capita obligation of $136 fell below every major city except Milwaukee ($108), Chicago ($92), and Cleveland ($57).[9] With 86 percent of its taxes collected on the 1929 due date, the highest percentage of the decade, and with its tax anticipation notes retired at the end of the year, Boston reached 1930 in sound financial condition.

Of the municipal agencies to which Boston's substantial assets would be funneled during the Depression, the Department of Public Welfare was most important—far more so than the relatively small Soldiers' Relief Department which cared for destitute veterans. That Boston had a tax-financed department at all is explained by Massachusetts' ancient insistence that its communities "relieve and support all poor and indigent persons lawfully settled therein whenever they stand in need thereof." To this end, the state demanded that every settlement establish a Board of Public Welfare to care for the unfortunate. In contrast, many American cities in 1929 had no tax-supported welfare system whatsoever.

While the Massachusetts legislature itself did not want to assume direct responsibility for the poor, it nevertheless pushed its cities to do so and, perhaps inevitably, the state gradually shouldered a portion of the costs. In the nineteenth century, the flood of immigrants produced the first major role for the state. Recognizing that its communities were deluged with transients, the legislature decided to reimburse the cities and towns for payments made to indigent persons who had resided less than five years in any one place. Then, in 1923, Massachusetts specified that its cities and towns assume the obligation of assisting mothers with dependent children under the age of sixteen. The mothers' aid statute specified that "the aid furnished shall be sufficient to enable them to bring up their children properly in their own homes." Moreover, the state pledged to recompense one third of the program's cost or, if the mother had no legal settlement, the Commonwealth promised to repay the full amount. And although Massachusetts had no old-age assistance law in 1929, the following year cities and towns were made to furnish "adequate assistance to deserving citizens in need of relief" who had to be at least seventy years old and have lived in the state for twenty years or more.[10] As generous as these provisions may seem when compared to other locales, the total expended directly by the Commonwealth for public-welfare purposes in all cities and towns annually amounted to less than half of what Boston alone paid out.

Since Massachusetts welfare laws placed the ultimate financial and administrative responsibility upon the city, it was largely up to the Overseers of the Public Welfare (originally known as the Overseers of the Poor) to care for needy Bostonians. Functioning as a state-chartered corporation since 1772, the Boston Overseers consisted of twelve unpaid residents of the city, selected by the mayor for three-year terms, who in turn elected a paid executive secretary charged with administering policies set by the Overseers. At the Chardon Street Temporary Home the Overseers sheltered and fed

destitute women and children, and they also operated the Wayfarers' Lodge for homeless, unemployed men. In addition, they
acted as the stewards of private charitable funds willed to them by
wealthy citizens, distributing the income according to the wishes of
the donors.[11] Despite a combined principal in excess of $1 million,
the private bequests held by the Overseers at the beginning of 1929
yielded only $35,000.

Above all, the Overseers superintended the municipal tax funds
allocated to the Department of Public Welfare, amounts which increased during the 1920s and surpassed those of most major cities.
Having paid out only $1,500,000 to 5,300 families at mid-decade, the
Overseers in 1929 aided 7,500 households at a cost of $2,500,000,
the largest welfare bill of any city except New York and Detroit. Although this sum represented less than 4 percent of the municipal
budget, it nevertheless appeared substantial by end-of-decade urban
standards. Indeed, for every person residing in Boston, the city
allotted more than twice as much to welfare as Detroit ($3.52 vs.
$1.69), over three times as much as New York ($1.08), and almost
precisely eight times what Chicago parceled out from its public
funds. Furthermore, the average monthly case load in Boston exceeded the absolute totals for every city but Los Angeles, and at the
same time Boston was able to grant a larger monthly allotment to
each case aided ($37.61) than all other cities.[12]

Welfare policies devised by the Boston Overseers in 1929 hinted
of an Elizabethan attitude toward the jobless. By making able-
bodied recipients labor in the city woodyard behind the headquarters on Hawkins Street, the Overseers upheld the principle that
one should work for what one gets. The requirement that relief
clients had to check in periodically at central headquarters, no matter how far away they might happen to live, suggested that the
Overseers were as interested in weeding out "chiselers" as they
were in conveniencing their recipients. By giving welfare families a
portion of their allotments in the form of grocery orders, the Overseers, suspicious that recipients would squander their money,
shared the national prejudice against 100 percent cash relief. Still,

long years of cooperation between the Overseers and private agencies made reasonably certain that the city's allotments would be supplemented if necessary. On the whole, the Overseers supervised a welfare system no more shaped by traditional outlooks than any other, and the city's commitment to aiding the poor was stronger than in most of urban America.

As Boston headed into the Great Depression, then, her institutions of government appeared to be relatively well-fixed. While Boston lacked home rule, especially in respect to financial matters, the constitutional ties between City Hall and Beacon Hill provided a formal structure for possible cooperation. And with a robust municipal budget underwritten by a dependable flow of receipts, it appeared during the 1920s that the state had not seriously handcuffed the men at City Hall. By making a public welfare system mandatory, the state had in actuality bequeathed Boston a fortunate legacy. Although the state had shown little inclination to bolster public welfare with significant monetary support, Boston had on its own developed a better-financed system than the rest of the urban United States. In addition, the state had provided Boston with charter arrangements which centralized power in the hands of the mayor, giving the office a high potential for action. The city council appeared to lack the capacity for bringing about a crippling deadlock with the mayor, yet it possessed enough authority to keep His Honor from becoming sluggish on the one hand or autocratic on the other. The structure of municipal government seemed admirably balanced; the relationship between city and state gave advantages to the state, but not necessarily to an intolerable degree. It remained for the city's political leadership, those who would flesh out the skeleton, to capitalize on the assets with which Boston was favored.

Malcolm Nichols, a Back Bay Republican, had only a few months left as Mayor of Boston when the stock market's collapse rocked State Street. Nichols, a former collector of the Port of Boston, was, when elected in 1925, the second Republican to win a mayoralty contest in the century. (To this day, Boston has never elected another.) That Nichols had managed a victory, even in the party's golden decade, smacked of the miraculous. Republicans, claiming just 33 percent of the city's registered voters, were at an overwhelming disadvantage.[13] Helped by a nonpartisan election system and a petition system of nomination, Nichols had proved that only when the field was swarming with Democratic candidates could a member of the Grand Old Party win a citywide contest.

The power of Boston Republicans had once relied not just on the wealthy Back Bay wards but on many newer immigrants as well. Claiming to be the party of sound business principles, and hence best able to provide job security, Republicans had lured newcomers, especially the Jewish community, French Canadians, and some Italians. Negroes, too, had been in the party of Lincoln, and Republicans had made headway by catering to anti-Irish feelings in all New Immigrant neighborhoods. But as the economy of Massachusetts slumped through most of the 1920s, desertions occurred at a more rapid rate in Boston than in the rest of the state despite the old guard's attempts to make accommodations with their ethnic allies.[14]

Defections taking place in the first half of the decade had reduced the major portion of the Republican contingent in Boston to Wards 4 and 5 (Back Bay and Beacon Hill), yet even these wards were not of one piece. Louis Liggett, owner of a nationwide drugstore chain, and his Boston ally from the South End, Charles Innes, both of them associated with a statewide Republican machine, dominated the less wealthy Ward 4. (For ward locations, see Map II.) To the Liggett-Innes faction, Mayor Nichols had close ties. In the city's wealthiest district, however, the so-called "Esplanade" or "Silk-stocking" Ward 5, where a potent group of Brahmin Republicans exercised influence far out of proportion to their numbers, party leaders looked upon Nichols with growing disdain.

The Ward 5 Republican committee showed decided nonparty characteristics: an ingrown group regularly swapped offices without bothering to wage more than token campaigns. In the protected setting of Ward 5 "the labor union and the hustings are unknown," ob-

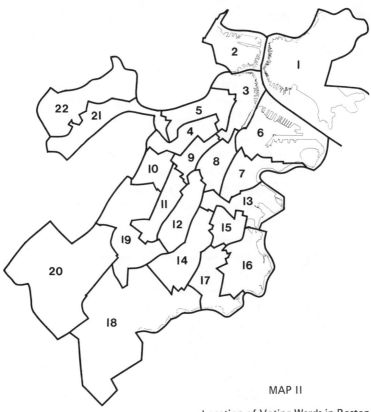

MAP II

Location of Voting Wards in Boston

Ward 1:	East Boston
Ward 2:	East Boston
	Charlestown
Ward 3:	North End,
	West End
Ward 4:	South End
Ward 5:	Back Bay
Ward 6-7:	South Boston
Wards 8-12:	Roxbury
Wards 13-17:	Dorchester
Ward 18:	Hyde Park
Ward 19:	Jamaica Plain
Ward 20:	West Roxbury
Ward 21:	Allston
Ward 22:	Brighton

served the *Transcript*. "Men hold offices there for long terms. Death is more apt to retire them than political defeat." [15] Henry Lee Shattuck, Charles Francis Adams, Christian Herter, Laurence Curtis II, and Henry Parkman, Jr. gave Ward 5 impressive leadership. Close links to the Speaker of the Massachusetts House, Leverett Saltonstall, to the Lodge family of Beverly, Sinclair Weeks of Newton, and to Eliot Wadsworth of the Boston Chamber of Commerce made this contingent an unusually formidable array. Although these old-stock Republicans were denounced by Irish politicians as "bluebloods," many Bostonians nevertheless accorded them a measure of deference, and they managed to exert considerable sway over state and national affairs in particular. To a lesser extent, they influenced municipal concerns. [16]

Still other Boston Republicans put their energies into the Good Government Association (GGA). Founded in 1903 by progressives such as Supreme Court Justice-to-be Louis D. Brandeis, the merchant prince Edward A. Filene, and the settlement-house pioneer, Robert A. Woods, the GGA, like the Boston Finance Commission with which it maintained close ties, attempted to bring to office men of unimpeachable integrity without regard for party affiliation, men who would put the public interest above private gain. Many "Goo-Goos," as detractors called them, also tried to curb the spending habits of Irish-controlled city government. Headed by George Read Nutter, the president of the Massachusetts Bar Association and an ardent defender of Judge Thayer during the Sacco-Vanzetti trials, the GGA had during the 1920s lost the progressive elements once led by Brandeis. Concerned mainly with structural changes, especially in municipal finance, GGA members seldom spoke for social reform. [17]

Having supported Mayor Nichols in 1925, the GGA repudiated him in 1929 for a number of reasons. The Association accused Nichols of keeping close company with the Liggett machine and of a tendency to appoint "poor men" to office. Moreover, the GGA charged that he was also scheming with James Michael Curley, the bombastic, powerful, and according to the Goo-Goos, corrupt, former Mayor of Boston. Nichols and Curley, the GGA alleged, were plotting to forge a quadrennial arrangement whereby the two men would rule Boston in the future by simply trading office upon the expiration of their respective terms. In addition, Nichols's zealous attack upon Eugene O'Neill's *Strange Interlude* and countless other works had made Boston the laughingstock of the nation, and the Mayor's obscurantism had aroused the ire of habitués of the Boston Athenaeum, the Brahmin citadel of intellect. Nichols also had offended Republicans with inhibitions against increasing the size, scope, and expense of government. By the time of the crash, Nichols had added a thousand new positions to the municipal payroll, hiked salaries by $3,000,000, accelerated short-term borrowing, and upped the city's funded debt. Nichols's attempts to realize "needed public improvements" included proposals for a $16,000,000 traffic tunnel to East Boston and a $5,000,000 court house for Suffolk County, both of which antagonized the GGA. Nevertheless, the Mayor's contemplated projects helped prepare the way for the large-scale works projects (with their concomitant deficits) which would become commonplace in the 1930s. Nichols, a mayor unafraid to tackle some of Boston's most conspicuous needs, appeared ahead of his time. The naysayers in his own party, however, were legion.

When economic activity slowed in the last four months of 1929, the Nichols administration began to use new but unavailing arguments to win acceptance of building plans which, with the exception of the East Boston tunnel, the city council had rejected during the summer. "It is correct policy to carry on public works when the most labor is available," Nichols stated in November.[18] However, few of the Mayor's fellow Republicans in the city advocated immediate work on the East Boston Tunnel, a project designed to spur development of the community across the harbor. Moreover, the city council, with nineteen of its twenty-two seats occupied by Democrats, showed that, in Boston, Republicans had no monopoly on a commitment to pay-as-you-go government. Before the year ended, the council, believing that it was forced to choose between welfare cuts and public works, dispensed with the Suffolk County Court

House proposal. One of the few Democrats on the council willing to support construction chided Nichols for his extravagant claims of success. Progress under Nichols, said the critic, is "a figment of the imagination now and probably will be for all future time." "Mal," he continued, "is the fifty-third card in the pack—a joker." [19] But with little backing from either Boston's leading Republicans or the Democratic city council, Nichols was hardly to blame. In opting for public works rather than direct relief (and this is what the council felt the choice to be in late 1929), Nichols would not be the last Mayor of Boston to take this position. [20]

In his final battles for public works, Nichols no longer occupied center stage. The Mayor sat as a lame duck, for in November of 1929 Boston chose his successor. Throughout the fall, public attention fixed on the Democrats who were, as usual, engaged in internecine warfare. Most especially, focus shifted to "the last of the political buccaneers, ungovernable, unmanageable, irrepressible, incorrigible, apparently indestructible." [21] James Michael Curley had returned from four years of charter-imposed exile.

Son of an immigrant hod carrier from County Galway, Curley had launched his career in elective politics in 1899 when he won a seat on Boston's old Common Council. This victory marked the beginning of nearly sixty raucous years of public service. From the very outset, Curley showed himself to be a keen student of the political craft, a man who learned his first lessons through exposure to the brawling ethnic politics practiced by Boston's quasi-feudal ward bosses, men like Patrick "Pea-Jacket" Maguire in Curley's home ward, the old seventeenth on Roxbury Neck. Indeed, the saying went that "Ward 17 children came into the world with clenched fists," and Curley was no exception. [22] A visit to New York City helped refine his political education, inspiring him to found his own Tammany Club in Boston. Dedicating his organization to the destruction of the old ward leaders, Curley by and large succeeded; Ward 3's redoubtable Martin Lomasney, "The Boston Mahatma," lingered on as an exception. From the time Curley resigned his seat in the United States Congress in 1913 to wage a successful mayor-

alty campaign, he increasingly became the center of all political
alignments in Boston. Voter identification polarized on a pro-Curley
and anti-Curley basis. That he should be elected mayor a third time
in 1929, therefore, seemed to thousands of Bostonians to be "as
much a custom and as necessary as baked beans and codfish balls for
Sunday breakfast." [23]

Curley's appeal to Boston's Democratic electorate was closely tied
to his personal attributes. Few ever mastered political oratory better
than he. Despite his limited education, Curley worked with characteristic energy to overcome his deficiencies. When the occasion
called for it, he could quote the famous works of literature and could
speak as a refined and educated man. As a political enemy noted,
Curley's theatrical language, always flamboyant, ranged from pure
Oxford to Dogpatch. [24] He had a gift for swaying masses of people
into frenzied ecstasy or uncontrolled rage, and he could be ruthless
or gentle within a matter of seconds. Toward women, he displayed
an invariable courtliness. To the Irish, he was a poor boy who had
made good, and tenement dwellers exulted vicariously at his flight
from the foul-smelling marsh gas which had polluted his boyhood
waterfront slum. Moving out to the elegant Jamaicaway, he purchased a seventeen-room mansion from a Brahmin, had shamrocks
cut in the shutters, and sent "a nose-thumbing in the direction of
Beacon Hill" where his mother had once scrubbed floors. [25] "Then,"
a friend recalled, "he would open the windows, and on Sunday
mornings he'd play all his Irish records. He'd play them at the most
ungodly hours and he'd play the hell out of them. . . ." Why?
Because he wanted "to be sure that everybody who could hear him
would know that there was an Irishman living there." [26]

But despite having left the inner city, Curley knew the Irish upon
whom he depended for victories, and thousands of them claimed
that they knew him. "Perhaps above all," a student of Massachusetts
politics has written, "he understood that the needs of the people had
changed; no longer illiterate immigrants, they wanted parks, playgrounds, schools, beaches, and hospitals rather than baskets of food
and loads of coal." [27] Curley obliged them; he liked to spend, and

when subjected to strong leadership, the city council proved more pliant than it did during the Nichols administration. In his two earlier terms as mayor (1914–1918 and 1922–1926) Curley had rivaled Caesar Augustus as a monumental builder, especially of projects which redounded to the benefit of lower-income voters. But toward those who still needed food and coal, he nevertheless manifested great compassion. "I have known what it is to be hungry," he wrote in 1929, "and I have known what it is to be cold, and if I have sometimes erred in response to the dictates of the heart rather than the head, perhaps I am not altogether to blame. . . . My sympathies and purse have been ever freely given to those who stood shivering in the shadow of adversity." [28] His critics called his appeal cheap demagoguery, but thousands of Bostonians were never so persuaded. As a popularizer of welfare on a grand scale, and as a man unintimidated by deficits, James Michael Curley had much to recommend as Boston neared the Great Depression.

Indeed, many of Curley's constituents apparently felt that his commitment to hard work and personal government was more important than his reputation for dishonesty. They were correct, and even his enemies conceded that though Curley was expensive, he got things done. Consequently, not every wealthy voter in Boston opposed him. While they believed that his methods produced "a kind of administrative wilderness," his ability to make bureaucracy responsive won him many staunch friends who at the same time were troubled by the allegations of corruption. [29]

Curley's notoriety dated back to the earliest days of his career when he had stood in for an acquaintance during a civil-service examination. "Pat couldn't spell Constantinople," Curley is purported to have said, "but he had wonderful feet for a letter carrier." Curley's attempted favor cost him a sixty-day confinement in the Charles Street Jail, an episode used against him in every campaign, though with counterproductive results. "How about the time you went to jail?" the ward heelers Curley had planted in the audience would shout. "I did it for a friend," Curley would reply. Each time he became mayor, he won the reputation as a purger, for he filled the vacancies with political allies who trooped endlessly into his office, no matter how menial the job they sought. His foes charged that he kept an Augean stable full of favored contractors, that his land sales were dishonest, that his administration paid no heed to the principles of sound finance. "A Great Dane," Curley later wrote, "always has a few poodles yapping at his heels." [30]

Boston furnished a perfect setting for Curley's talents. Like Curley, the city was Roman Catholic and Democratic. The preponderance of Irish voters occupied low- or lower-middle class status and in catering to this group, to whom "security and status [had become] ruling obsessions," Curley served as "the idol of a cult, arbiter of a social clique, and spokesman of a state of mind." [31] The Irish had first elected one of their own as mayor in 1885, and they solidified their hold on Boston politics thereafter. While it was not quite the case that "Puritans . . . surrendered even the privilege of resistance," the Irish takeover amounted to a remarkably thorough political revolution. [32] The native element was outnumbered and divided, and as long as Curley operated in Boston, he did not have to reckon seriously with Yankees. The Italian community, which might have become a force, lacked political and even social cohesiveness, torn as it was by Old World loyalties to specific regions of the homeland. A gerrymander in 1915 also fragmented Italo-Americans by putting the North, South, and West Ends within the territory ruled by Lomasney's Hendricks Club. Even by 1930 not one Boston Italian had ever served in the city council or the state legislature—nor had a Negro. Only in Dorchester's Ward 14 could Jewish voters regularly elect a city councilor, control a ward committee, or send one of their own number as delegate to the state Democratic convention. Green Power ruled in the Hub.

Nevertheless, ward leaders were a far less durable lot in Boston than in a number of American cities, a situation which Curley had helped bring about and from which he profited. While Democratic chieftains in Chicago almost never lost a contest, and while Republican bosses in Philadelphia seldom faced a serious electoral challenge, city councilors who tried to entrench themselves as ward leaders experienced difficulties.[33] In sixty-six ward contests held from 1925 to 1929 only thirty-eight of Boston's councilors received a majority of the votes cast. Those who aspired to keep their two-year terms were often disappointed, for in 1927 and 1929 thirteen incumbents were ousted, four decided not to seek reelection, and the combined turnover rate hit 38.6 percent. Unlike Pittsburgh, with only 5,000 registered Democrats at the decade's close, Boston listed 124,000 Democratic voters, 67 percent of the total electorate, and a near one-party system gave rise to keen competition. From 1925 to 1929 an average of ninety-one candidates vied for twenty-two seats, and in only five of sixty-six elections did a councilor run unopposed. Although ward committees tended to be more stable (and contests for state Democratic conventions more tranquil yet), the election of 1928 nevertheless produced committee races in ten of the wards. Moreover, the Boston Democratic Committee, in attempting to discipline feuding party members, proved a nullity in mayoralty elections. Sapped of its strength by internal quarrels, the city organization was unable to produce an alternative to Curley.[34]

James Michael, taking advantage of the relatively fluid circumstances, adroitly pieced together the city's best-run organization. Circumventing the majority of Democratic ward leaders, Curley relied on his own precinct captains, who, in turn, operated independently of the Democratic councilor and the standing Democratic committee in each ward. Paid off with positions at City Hall, Curley's workers were devoted. The ostensible ward leaders, in the meantime, were often left empty-handed by Curley's citywide machine. And although Boston's petition system of nomination might produce a host of Democratic mayoral candidates, this electoral device had an offsetting advantage: Curley did not have to dilute his assets in bruising municipal primaries.

In all, prospects could not have looked rosier for James Michael Curley in the late twenties. His work in 1928 on behalf of Alfred E. Smith (toward whom the Boston Irish expressed adoration bordering on idolatry) brought about détentes with the still-popular former mayor, John F. ("Honey Fitz") Fitzgerald, and with Martin Lomasney. That Curley would run in 1929 few cynics doubted, for one of his last acts prior to leaving office in January 1926 had been to double the mayor's salary to $20,000. Whether the economy flourished or floundered, James Michael looked like a winner.

Curley's formal candidacy in 1929 predictably awakened the Good Government Association to action, and GGA loyalists issued a call to the people "to rise in their might as their fathers did of old whenever the commonweal was threatened . . . *Delenda est Carthago.*" From what the GGA called the "decent wing" of the Democratic Party, the Association plucked Frederick Mansfield as its candidate, and rumors spread that Cardinal O'Connell would back him in order "to stamp out Curley and Curleyism." Mansfield, also a Roman Catholic, former American Federation of Labor lawyer, state treasurer, and president of the Massachusetts Bar Association, had been an unsuccessful gubernatorial candidate in 1916. Looking with favor upon Mansfield's virtual abstention from politics during the 1920s, the GGA pictured him as the honest Cincinnatus summoned, not from the farm, but from his law office, to do battle with the master politician. Counting on Mansfield to appeal to Republicans (the party failed to enter a candidate in the election), the Association also hoped to attract Independents, Yankee Democrats, and whatever other Democrats could be detached on the corruption issue. Making much of Curley's quest for a third term, Mansfield and his supporters asserted, "This is a Republic and not a Kingdom." After all, they argued, neither Calvin Coolidge nor George Washington nor John Hancock had been tempted by such a grandiose aspiration. "Is he greater than the others?" they asked.[35]

Curley warmed to the challenge. Ridiculing the GGA, "that select and exclusive body of social bounders in the Back Bay," he offered to bet the organization $5,000 that he would sweep to victory by seventy thousand votes. Delighting partisan audiences, he denounced the GGA's endorsement of Mansfield as "the most anemic effusion given to the public in the history of this organization." Curley promised positions on a new city-planning and development board to loyal women followers who would "supersede

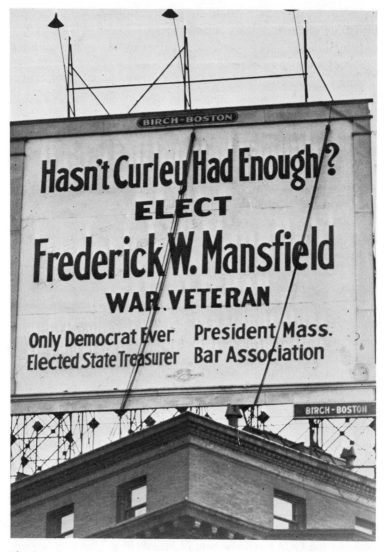

The fiercely contested mayoralty campaign of 1929 pitted Democrat against Democrat. Throughout the 1930s, internecine strife hampered efforts at a unified assault on the Depression. Boston University School of Communication.

ten bridge-playing individuals from Precinct 3, Ward 5, constituting the Good Government Association." Then, in "a characteristic bit of knavery," Curley put together the Women's Better Government League of Boston which issued a pamphlet identical in appearance to the GGA's traditional election-eve brochure. Substituting positive adjectives for the negative phrases, the women simply paraphrased the GGA flyer.[36]

Curley's more positive campaign appeal centered on a proposed fifty-year program for public works in Boston. Although he did not specify details of what should be constructed, he suggested that the City Planning Board be increased to a staggering 350 members and that it draw upon the best minds available, including those in the universities. "Work and wages," he said, "should be the fundamental issues in American political campaigns." [37] The "work and wages" formula touched off strong voter response and soon became Curley's principal slogan. While he did not convert the campaign phrase into a coherent program, he had taken official notice of growing unemployment and had made clear his preference for public works.

Mansfield, though regarded as a conservative, did almost as much in his campaign as Curley to move Boston toward a recognition that hard times were at hand. Recommending "unemployment relief through carrying out necessary public works," he also championed "adequate and liberal relief for the worthy poor," and pledged that he would not be "niggardly" in using city money. At the same time, Mansfield vowed "real municipal economy through wise expenditure," "not one penny for waste, graft, or impostors" on welfare, and lower taxes. He promised an administration that would contain "no bagmen and no favorites," but instead would construct playgrounds, gyms, streets, subway extensions, and an airport, without raising taxes. Honest government in Boston, said Mansfield, "will be not only worthy of the tercentenary of the foundation of our city but will give us a new deal." [38] However, Mansfield's "new deal" was unclear. His messages to the voters oscillated between pledges to spend and not to spend, his personality failed to excite enthusiasm, and even his backers at the GGA believed that he did not talk enough about issues.

Curley, in contrast, put his qualities as an indefatigable campaigner on display. With a minor Irish candidate also in the field, James Michael was able to charge that "Matador Mansfield" had sent out a picador to divide the Democratic vote, and Curley inveighed against his opponents "Amos 'n' Andy." Using sixteen bands, war veterans "of many nations," Indians in full regalia, and Irish dancers, he lured a turn-away throng of 30,000 to the Boston Garden. Mansfield charged that Curley was spending $750,000 on the campaign, much of it used to pay toughs to heckle Mansfield.[39] Undeterred, Curley staged his customary "Whirlwind Victory Tour" on the night before the election. Speaking for ten minutes in every ward to what the GGA privately called "the credulous multitude," [40] Curley was accompanied by an immense entourage complete with bands and searchlights.

Moreover, Curley picked up valuable assistance. The Boston Central Labor Union, accustomed to favors in previous Curley administrations, came through with an endorsement. With new construction at a virtual standstill, Curley's talk of work and wages undoubtedly was more credible to the BCLU than comparable promises by a candidate of the GGA. Also, key Democrats who normally held Curley in low esteem wanted a winner, a man who would return political favors in 1930. After four years of Malcolm Nichols, and with a Republican governor presiding over a Republican legislature, they preferred Curley to a mayor who would have obligations to the GGA. Consequently, Congressman John McCormack of South Boston, United States Senator David I. Walsh of Worcester, Martin Lomasney, and John F. Fitzgerald gave aid. At Lomasney's renowned Sunday-before-election meeting in Ward 3, the wall between the Hendricks Club and Curley's Tammany momentarily crumbled: the venerable Mahatma delivered a one-and-a-half hour speech for his longtime foe. "Honey Fitz" also served his former enemy and several times sang his famous rendition of "Sweet Adeline" at Curley rallies. While Frederick Mansfield had been essentially correct when he observed that the bosses hated Curley and he hated them, they did not, as Mansfield predicted, make James Michael "the most knifed man ever to run for office in [Boston]." [41]

When the voters decided on November 5, oddsmakers had installed Curley as a prohibitive 5-1 choice. The electorate returned for the bettors' favorite but by a margin of only 20,000 out of 216,000 ballots cast, well below Curley's prediction of a 70,000 vote plurality. Mansfield insisted on a recount, claiming that there would be "ghastly revelations of jobbing." While the recount amused some Bostonians by assuming a carnival atmosphere (Congressman McCormack offered a sports roadster to the person who came closest to guessing Curley's final margin), it reinforced the belief that when Curley ran for office, crookedness surely followed. To George Nutter of the GGA, the entire election confirmed his impression that "excitable" Irish, with no idea "of moral values in politics," had once more "defiled everything political—in standards, in methods, in cheapness and vulgarity." [42] In the end, the recount did not alter the Election Day verdict, and Curley had irrevocably captured his sixteenth office in twenty-one tries.

Fourteen of Boston's twenty-two wards had returned for Curley, and the election pointed up both class and ethnic considerations in the city's vote. Of the eight wards which Curley failed to win, all topped the city medians for income and housing rental: Jewish Ward 14 (by the slimmest of margins), Yankee Wards 4 and 5, and five districts with middle-class Irish and Yankee residents all supported Mansfield. East Boston, a lower-middle-class Italian area, backed Curley but only by a slim 6-5 edge. However, South Boston, Irish to the core and with comparable rentals, came in decisively for Curley. In two of the city's poorest neighborhoods, the Irish of Charlestown also backed the victor more heavily than the Italo-Americans of the North End. Moreover, the lowest-income wards, whether Italian or Irish, gave Curley a higher percentage of their votes than did their ethnic counterparts in East and South Boston. Ward 9, with a substantial Negro population, went for Curley 4-3. That margins in New Immigrant wards were generally smaller for

Curley than they had been for Al Smith in 1928 (East Boston, for example, had accorded Smith an 8-1 majority) confirmed that an Irishman in City Hall was suspect. The 1929 mayoralty contest also hinted by its unexpected closeness that a coalition of Republicans (mainly Yankees), middle-income Irish Democrats, and anti-Irish New Immigrants could conceivably thwart a candidate who made overt appeals to the blue-collar classes—to the poorer Irish in particular. That two Democrats could share the total vote so evenly, especially when the Lomasneys of Boston had tried to rally the electorate behind Curley, augured poorly for party harmony. Thus when Curley told his supporters that he had fulfilled his promise to "take Boston like Grant took Richmond," he had unwittingly made a sound analogy. The post-election mood resembled the bad feelings in the South after the Civil War. To win the city was one thing; to rule it might be another.

Prior to his inauguration in January of 1930, Curley gave few indications of the direction his administration would take. He denounced Nichols's Suffolk County Court House plan as too expensive. It would foist a "gross injustice" upon the taxpayers, he said. Yet anti-Curley forces, briefly encouraged to believe that Mayor Jim might opt for retrenchment, received a setback soon after when Curley stated that he would improve twelve hundred streets and seek $15,000,000 for the East Boston Airport. In the six weeks before his inauguration, Curley did not clarify his contradictory messages. Preoccupied by the cancer which would cost him his beloved wife within a year, the Mayor-elect, normally visible, withdrew behind the shamrock shutters.

At a distance from the Curley mansion, where the city's poor resided, other personal tragedies were unfolding. Increasing numbers of white females, among the first to lose their jobs, headed for the employment bureau of the Women's Educational and Industrial Union. Along Dudley Street in Roxbury a growing number of Negro males also faced Christmas without a job, even as their wives marched off to iron and clean. At the Wells Memorial Building, meanwhile, the Boston Central Labor Union received an unemployment insurance plan from the Socialist Party of Massachusetts. At nearly the same time, the Salvation Army was preparing 3,500 Christmas baskets, each designed for five persons, and other charitable organizations were also upping their Yuletide distributions to the needy.

Away from the low-income neighborhoods, external indications would not have prompted the Curley administration to plan extraordinary remedies. Crowds of Christmas shoppers surged through downtown streets, and on Christmas Eve thousands visited Beacon Hill to hear carols sung in a setting aglow with lamplight and candles. At the shrine of Father Powers in suburban Malden testimonies of miraculous healings lured over a million pilgrims (including Mr. and Mrs. Curley) in the last months of 1929, and reports of hysterical scenes captured headlines. Struggling to add *Lady Chatterley's Lover* to the long list of works "Banned in Boston," the Watch and Ward Society also vied for attention. In its "Annual Public Utility and Industrial Review," the Boston *Herald* predicted a year of healthy economic growth, and Bostonians listened to the radio as President Hoover's Secretary of the Treasury, Andrew Mellon, reassuringly stated that he saw "nothing in the present situation that is either menacing or warrants pessimism." Mellon looked ahead to "steady progress." At City Hall, a truck arrived with a floral tribute to James Michael Curley in anticipation of his inauguration. Shaped like a boxing ring, the florist's creation depicted the Mayor-elect towering triumphantly above his fallen opponents. A small sign on Curley's hat read, "Champion of Them All." [43]

3

Rehearsal for the Great Depression:
A City in Search of a Policy

No American city entered 1930 a *tabula rasa*. Rather, cities carried into the Great Depression their own particular economic practices, social structures, and political outlooks: prejudices developed over time imposed constraints. City dwellers, if the instance of Boston can be abstracted, nevertheless generated bountiful suggestions for mitigating business failures. Urban centers, after all, neither declared intellectual bankruptcy nor wallowed in all that was deliberately retrograde, pernicious, venal. Yet in the search for usable ideas each city was hamstrung by the identity which each had assumed. That urban administrations—James Michael Curley's included—would move uncertainly in their quests for workable solutions should have surprised no one. Shackled by what their pasts would permit, cities limited their responses within narrow, often predictable confines.

At Symphony Hall on January 6, 1930, James Michael Curley took the mayor's oath for the third time. The ninety-minute ceremony lasted fourteen times longer than the swearing in of James J. Walker in New York, and Curley aides insisted that this discrepancy fairly measured the difference in worth of the two men. Lacing his inaugural remarks with references to the colonial era, Curley reassured his listeners that as Boston entered its tercentenary year, the lessons learned by those who had braved the wilderness in 1630 would not be forgotten. "The problems that in our day bulk large are infinitesimal as contrasted with those in evidence in the days of the founders," he said, "and can be solved by the same methods in our days as in their day, namely, through cooperation and self-reliance." As he talked of communality and individualism, Curley glossed over the potential incompatibility of the two doctrines. The tension between "commonwealth" and individual striving, known so well to the Puritan divines extolled by Curley, would become the central dilemma for his administration.[1]

The Mayor devoted a substantial portion of his inaugural address to the faltering economy. Departing from those who were attributing unemployment to technological change or to fiendish stock manipulators, he asserted that joblessness, poverty, crime, and disease had resulted from the absence of "a sane economic policy." The solution lay in furnishing "work and wages to those in need of sustenance and employment." To this end, said Curley, "The city can do much, but private industry properly encouraged can do more, and to the promotion and encouragement of commerce and industry our effort should be directed." The Mayor's bow to private enterprise drew a salvo of applause, for in January of 1930 it was widely believed that the slump would be temporary and that business still possessed powers of self-regeneration.

In his first address, the Mayor also aligned Boston behind "the program of national planning inaugurated by President Hoover . . . to promote prosperity." [2] Terming the President's call for public construction "courageous," the Mayor expressed satisfaction that Hoover was pinning his greatest hopes for recovery to action on the local level.[3] Curley, as he had in his election campaign, again urged a Fifty-Year Plan to develop industry, commerce, and municipal construction. Boston would put its jobless to work on a golf course, new libraries, health units, and recreation facilities; the salaries and personnel of city government would be increased. By emphasizing long-range economic planning and city-financed construction as re-

Much like the icon screen of an Orthodox Church, Symphony Hall in 1930 is resplendent for the inauguration of Boston's central political saint, James Michael Curley. Boston University School of Communication.

storatives, Curley had placed himself in advance of mayors in several other cities.

Even as Curley promised Boston its own prosperity program, one with progressive overtones, he had not wandered very far into new pastures. Some of his objectives were clearly political. Upping the number of salaried municipal employees, for example, made his talk of planning suspect, for he was surely mindful that his army of campaign workers needed rewards. When he asked the state legislature in his inaugural address to surrender its power over Boston's tax limit and also give the city the right to incur 50 percent more debt, he may well have hoped for a bonanza such as his machine had never before enjoyed. Indeed, his talk about spending was most ambiguous. On the one hand, he wanted a $10-million hike in the debt limit for street improvements, yet in the same speech he vowed pay-as-you-go budgeting. In suggesting that Boston federate with its surrounding forty-three towns, in order, he said, to get the suburbs to share responsibility for inner-city services, he may well have hoped to extend his influence. A Cambridge official thought as much. "Metropolitan Boston," he asserted, "is Curley gone Napoleon." [4]

Whether politically inspired or not, public works for the unemployed, home rule, and metropolitan government all made sense. So did the decision to spend rather than retrench. Indeed, Curley's program, whatever the motivation behind it, seemed on target. National, state, and municipal government would work together; the business community and private philanthropy would supplement municipal efforts. Even the staunchly Republican *Herald* praised Curley for exhibiting "that boldness and comprehensiveness with which the President goes at things." The *Herald* added: "The Mayor is open to the charge, which is a compliment, of being a Hooverite, at least non-politically." [5] Part of the rub for ultimate cooperation, however, was that Curley's instincts ran strongly toward partisanship.

With his inauguration behind him, Curley barraged the city council with messages which both sought to implement and add to the major works projects outlined on January 6. Before the month went by, Curley had submitted a $7,500,000 package to be financed by borrowing, a sum equal to 90 percent of all the money the city could lawfully appropriate outside the state-imposed debt limit, and he had asked the Massachusetts legislature for permission to borrow $17,500,000 more. At the same time, Curley placed considerable emphasis on the approach to recovery so congenial to Republicans. On February 1, Curley asked the city council for a $25,000 appropriation to establish a Commercial and Industrial Publicity Bureau, an organization which would integrate the efforts of municipal government and local enterprises. At a Chamber of Commerce dinner, he invited "the new 400"—representatives of the business community—to cooperate with the Bureau and donated $5,000 out of his own bank account to dramatize the need for voluntary subscription. Curley told the Publicity Bureau to do all that it could to hold onto existing business and to attract new firms as well. "Faith without works," said the Mayor, "is of no avail." [6]

Recognizing that large projects would neccessitate heavy outlays for materials, thereby cutting into wages, and aware that start-up delays would be inevitable, the Mayor further diversified his attack by resorting to occasional make-work. The jobless would clean up Boston for the tercentenary celebration, he announced, and he set crews to sandblasting highways and washing them with acid. To spread the work, the Mayor approved the use of day labor instead of contract labor on all city projects and eliminated overtime, even though his decisions added 12 percent to costs. And during a February snowstorm the Curley administration had to respond to a crush of applicants who wanted shoveling jobs at $5 a day. When some thirteen hundred men crammed into every available inch of space at the Municipal Employment Bureau, unintentionally breaking doors and windows, the city hired a thousand workers, seven hundred more than would have been normal.

As snow shovelers rushed frantically for jobs, and as Curley launched his whirlwind search for remedies, unemployment worsened. No one knew how many were out of work, and estimates taken from February through April varied wildly, ranging from a low of 41,000 (ca. 11.5 percent of the labor force) to a high of 100,000 (28.5 percent). [7] But among Boston's poor, statistics were beside the point: on January 24, 1930, a destitute man toppled to the sidewalk in downtown Boston, dead from hunger. At Faneuil Hall Navy Yard workers rallied in protest of layoffs, and Harvard solved its problem with the state minimum wage commission by dismissing twenty charwomen rather than raise their pay from 35 cents to 37 cents an hour. The Boston Central Labor Union, cognizant of the mounting labor surplus, discovered that when a hundred striking bakers were locked out, jobless members of other unions stood in line to replace them. While the Musicians Union started a soup kitchen, the Typographers were setting up a relief fund for their unemployed members. In Boston, portents of the Great Depression came early, and before long the unemployed took to the streets.

The city's first full-scale unemployment disturbance broke out on March 6, 1930, when nearly four thousand men and women gathered at the Parkman Bandstand on the Common, the equivalent of London's Hyde Park. The Boston Council of the Unemployed, reportedly a Communist front, sponsored the demonstration. "We are determined not to starve," a spokesman insisted. Calling for work and wages, speakers gibed at the municipal, state, and federal governments for their lethargy. Governor Allen and Mayor Curley were denounced for ringing the Boston Common with police, and the American Federation of Labor was chastised for failing to endorse an unemployment insurance plan. When the group began to march on the heavily guarded State House (the Hall of Flags had been barricaded), police, many of them on horseback, charged. Blows rained down on the banner-carrying throng, yet only eight arrests were made.

Predictably, the police denounced the entire group as "reds." The disturbance had, indeed, been led by Communists, most of them from the Needle Trade Workers' Industrial Union,[8] and those who had been jailed, the police told reporters, were singing "a series of Communistic songs." To have attributed the upheaval solely to Communism within the NTWIU, however, was misleading. When a speaker asked the gathering how many needed work, hundreds in the crowd raised their hands. Moreover, the press noted that "all addresses were in moderation." The disturbances, mild in comparison to those in Detroit and New York, involved not just Bolsheviki but a large number of genuinely distressed workers.

Members of the Trade Union Unity League and the Council of the Unemployed cluster around a portrait of V. I. Lenin in March 1930. Repeated demonstrations by leftists, although never massive, signaled to Bostonians that a turbulent era lay ahead. Boston University School of Communication.

Throughout the spring of 1930, "unemployment riots"—as the newspapers called them—intensified, and Mayor Curley branded all public demonstrations as Communist-inspired. Accurately calculating that most Roman Catholics and Brahmins alike approved of a show of strength, and uneager for his administration to lose face, he took an ever more militant stand against "Red Roosters" during 1930. May Day and the third anniversary of the Sacco-Vanzetti executions in August again precipitated altercations between workers and the police. An October march on the national convention of the American Federation of Labor, meeting in Boston, brought out two hundred police, including a special "Flying Squadron" equipped with machine guns, bulletproof vests, and tear-gas bombs. The demonstrators sought to dramatize the need for unemployment insurance, and mayhem ensued. Workers denounced the assault on female pickets as brutal enough "to make Baron Münchausen laugh." One worker in the South End was charged with larceny for taking away a blackjack from a police captain. Curley, who had asked in July for "the application of the same character of courage . . . that made possible the firing of the shot heard around the world at Lexington" to "solve the problem of Communism we face today," demanded that the demonstrators, all of whom he erroneously branded as aliens, be deported to Russia.[9] Giving scant comfort to those who challenged the efficacy of capitalism, the Mayor urged labor to be patient.

At the same time that the unemployed were daily becoming more

Leftists at a Parkman Bandstand rally, Boston Common, March 1930. Boston University School of Communication.

At the Parkman Bandstand in early March 1930, Jack McCarthy of the Trade Union Unity League denounces police brutality against jobless demonstrators. As rallies of the unemployed in 1930 quickened, Bostonians realized that a depression—not a mere recession—was at hand. Boston University School of Communications.

evident, the Mayor was thwarted by the Republican-controlled state legislature. Curley, who had argued that the Greater Boston community would "sink together" if it did not "row together," watched a modest metropolitan government bill die in early February.[10] Several of his more important political appointments were blocked by the Civil Service Commission, and the General Court restricted the Mayor's fiscal maneuverability. Paring millions from Curley's street building and repair program, the Municipal Finance Committee allowed only $6 million to be borrowed outside the debt limit. The state also failed to provide public works which might have been of use to the idle men and women of Boston, and modest victories did not atone for the generally penurious outlook.[11] From the sidelines, Curley angrily watched as an Advisory Committee of the Massachusetts Department of Labor and Industries perfunctorily attempted to study unemployment, an undertaking that ranked with the old order's most appalling defeatism. Holding that it had been "practically impossible to secure any accurate measure" of unemployment patterns, the committee recommended the voluntary cooperation of private industry to get information and make large expenditures unnecessary. To spend money "on public works *after* business has fallen into a depression has been suggested many times," said the fact finders. "Yet under this makeshift proposal little has ever been done." [12]

Boston, then, would have to rely on its own substantial revenues, and Curley and the city council raised the tax rate $2.80 per thousand when they approved the regular city budget in April of 1930. Allowed by the state legislature to boost spending just 4 percent, a modest rise that nevertheless kept Boston's per capita outlays the highest in the nation,[13] the city officials watched cumulative welfare costs spiral to over $3,500,000 by the end of the year, up some 32 percent from 1929. Although able to maintain more adequate relief payments to its 11,000 clients (a 34 percent increase) than other cities,[14] Boston faced lengthening lines at the municipal welfare department and rising unemployment. Both developments signaled that far more aid and new approaches were needed.

Unable to get the state's assent for construction loans and locked into a budget set in April, James Michael Curley spoke out on what he would and would not do were he to have the free hand which, of course, he sadly lacked. These utterances, sometimes ambivalent and contradictory, revealed both the alternatives and the conundrums that major American cities faced during the second half of 1930. Moreover, the responses Curley's proposals elicited from various groups in the city would in part stake out the political boundaries within which the city's leaders would have to operate.

Repeatedly, Curley spoke against the "dole system." By "the dole," Curley meant not only public-welfare payments with no work demanded but any form of unemployment insurance. Drawing his lessons from what he regarded as England's negative experience of having spent in excess of $2 billion during the 1920s, Curley argued that an outright grant of money "saps initiative, and makes of a man a chronic loafer." Three decades of the dole in England, he pointed out, had accelerated "the disappearance of the type of Englishman that the world has known during the last five centuries, the domineering type," and had substituted "servile mendicants." Europe's health- and unemployment-insurance systems, he added, were nothing less than monarchical plots "for the continuance in power of royal blood." [15]

The Mayor's repudiation of direct grants to the jobless, whether federal, state, or municipal, drew overwhelmingly favorable notices. When in August Curley attacked the English system and asked for the reincarnation of the "spirit of the Pioneers," 10,000 delegates to a Knights of Columbus convention roared their approval. Moreover, the Boston Central Labor Union, like its parent, the American Federation of Labor, shared Curley's view that unemployment-insurance systems warranted no support. And when Congress proposed a $25 million appropriation for drought relief in Texas, the Boston Clearing House Association, a bankers' organization, termed the measure "a precedent for the uneconomic, soul-destroying dole" and charged that the legislation constituted "political interference" in local affairs. [16]

The Chamber of Commerce not only opposed direct relief but also procrastinated when asked to rethink its reason for being. In March of 1930, for instance, Andrew Peters—a Republican progressive and former mayor of Boston—had joined Curley in goading the Chamber. "Today is no longer the day of the individualist," Peters had said. "It is no longer the day of destructive competition but the day of constructive cooperation." Three months later, Curley announced that progress was being made: business leaders, the Mayor stated, had at last hatched a plan to eradicate unemployment. "The size and scope of the project . . . will draw the eyes of the entire country to Boston as a community that dares to go ahead when others hesitate," Curley declared, and Peters also expressed cautious satisfaction that the Chamber of Commerce was starting to budge. The details of the plan, however, were not spelled out until November, and they proved extremely disappointing: consumers, said the Chamber, should spend. In addition, the organization posted letters to its six thousand members, asking them "to quicken the end of this readjustment period by saving a job for some man and giving a new one to a worker now in the ranks of the unemployed." "Save-a-Job" schemes, however, every bit as much as buying campaigns without purchasing power, proved ludicrously inadequate and a far cry from the more collectivist message which Andrew Peters had formulated some five months earlier.[17]

Curley also asked employers not to cut wages, and he even hinted that "reprisals on the part of the public" could be expected if employers continued to reduce their payrolls. Wage cuts and layoffs, said the Mayor, were self-defeating, and he deplored the prevailing "psychology of fear." When companies ignored his message, however, reprisals were not forthcoming. The Boston Central Labor Union, in fact, took no action in November of 1930 when a delegate from the Hotel and Restaurant Workers pressed for strikes against firms that were chopping wages. Moreover, the Consumers' League was starting to discover sweatshops reappearing in Boston, yet its white-label campaigns were largely unavailing: when given free choice, customers bought candy whether or not employers paid female workers less than Massachusetts Wage Commission standards, and without regard for unsanitary production practices which included "finger licking and using saliva to separate the candy cups." While most employers tried to be more responsible than this, it was equally clear that when faced with a choice between paying dividends to stockholders and maintaining wages, dividends won nearly every time.[18]

Discouraged by voluntarism, but surely not in a position to disown it either, the Mayor meandered toward advocacy of federal assistance. In August, he was wondering whether the nation had the will to solve its problems. The United States in 1930, said Curley, contained "people on the borderland of starvation" while a small number possessed "the vast wealth of the country" with no apparent willingness "to contribute either money or thought to the relief of those in need." Unfortunately, noted Curley, the Hoover administration, "being an engineering one," was "still in the blueprint stage" and was substituting "a sugar-coated palliative . . . for a major surgical operation." Hoover, suggested Curley, should set up a federal commission to protect the workers of America, a commission empowered to limit hours, guarantee a "saving wage," and combat the evils of automation. The Mayor wanted Washington to sponsor public works, but in the next breath he disconsolately noted the shortcomings of slow and costly major construction. On the city's $3-million subway extension, where an extra shift had been installed, he confessed only 400 men were receiving a wage.[19]

Curley mixed radical rhetoric with older formulas. Coming before the State Federation of Labor, the Mayor railed against the hardships suffered by the unemployed who faced the impossibility of paying taxes or meeting bank charges. He said that banks were preparing "to take away the fruit of the workers' toil of a lifetime because of the industrial depression for which the worker is not responsible." He did not, however, urge the state to adopt mortgage moratoria or other banking legislation, and he went no further than to ask the banks to be merciful. Neither did Curley sustain any drive for tax reform to redistribute wealth, and in Boston of 1930—a city in which Cardinal O'Connell was lavishing praise on J. P. Morgan and in which property owners were incensed over a mild rise in the city tax rate—that idea would most likely have been opposed. But Curley nevertheless felt that "the wealthy capitalist, the educator, [and] the leaders of religious thought" might join with organized labor to develop a sound economic program for Boston and the rest of the nation.[20]

Consequently, in September Curley summoned what he later called his "Brain Trust" for weekly "unemployment conferences." This exceptionally able group, which included Karl Compton, the president of the Massachusetts Institute of Technology, progressive businessmen, labor leaders such as James T. Moriarty, and a sprinkling of professors gave Curley an opportunity to float trial balloons and win prestigious backing for his proposals. Meeting at the Parker

House for the first time on September 30, the conferees heard
Curley push for the universal establishment of the five-day week, a
$1 billion expenditure for the improvement of the Mississippi Val-
ley, long-range planning of public works programs, and the creation
of a Federal Industrial Planning Commission. He wanted the commission to be nonpartisan, to coordinate works activities, and to cooperate with city, state, and regional associations. By December
1930, Curley was convinced that "Federal planning would be but an
enlargement of present sound policy of city planning which in European countries not only enjoys government sanction but is compulsory." He hoped to stabilize industry by building up funds during
prosperous times which could be expended quickly during periods
of recession.[21]

Some years later, the Mayor looked back to 1930 and claimed that
Franklin Roosevelt had taken over a program which he, James Michael Curley, had devised. Eventually, Curley equated his Mississippi project with the Tennessee Valley Authority, the Federal Industrial Planning Board with the National Recovery Administration,
his Unemployment Conference with Roosevelt's "Brain Trust." Unquestionably, Curley had traveled some distance in his first year in
office. His pleas for a billion-dollar federal public works program and
his decision to endorse old-age pensions and public health insurance
were distinctly liberal. He personally visited President Hoover to
urge the Planning Commission, the Mississippi Project, and federal
cession of Governor's Island to the City of Boston for large-scale
public works projects on an expanded municipal airport. If Curley's
messages of 1930 are read selectively and if the advantages of hind-
sight can be excused, a case can be made that he advocated the
comprehensive use of national power. And yet to bind together
Curley's proposals into a coherent package is fatal to an understanding of a man who unblushingly combined voluntary "Build
Now" campaigns with praise for the outright statism of Mussolini.[22]

Curley, never very convincing as an ideologue, inched away from
traditionalism because of local political pressures and changing economic conditions. His advocacy of national solutions came at the

same time he struggled with the city council over municipal problems of a new variety. During this tug of war, the council insisted that Curley accommodate the jobless, but often in ways unpalatable to the Mayor. The council, in effect, was making clear to the Mayor of Boston that there were things he could not do—at least not without a fight.

Always the political man, Curley rightly suspected the sinister motivations of a council in which he had few friends, and they, in turn, properly suspected the Mayor. Curley disliked ideas for which he could not take credit, and he therefore denounced council suggestions as mere patchwork. Forced to counter with proposals of his own, he passed the buck to higher levels of government. Several councilors charged that Curley's new posture as a theoretician favoring federal activism constituted blatant temporizing. "It is all right for highbrows to meet at the Parker House," said John I. Fitzgerald of Martin Lomasney's Ward 3 in a reference to Curley's Brain Trust, "but what do highbrows know about the poor?" The Mayor countered that old formulas for dealing with the consequences of a wildly gyrating economic cycle were sorely outmoded. But Curley's most vocal nemeses on the council, men like Fitzgerald, John Dowd of Ward 8 (Roxbury), and Francis E. ("Frankie") Kelly of Ward 15 (Dorchester), would then roast Curley as a man who shielded "four-flushers" in chauffeur-driven cars while others suffered.[23]

In a dress rehearsal for the entire Depression decade, Curley and his volatile city council clashed in 1930 over a number of issues. The council insisted on more flexible attitudes toward tax collection and ordered that a proposed sale of property by the city for back taxes be postponed. In addition, the ward representatives asked that homeowners be granted an installment plan to pay off outstanding obligations. Yet Curley ignored the council's votes, possibly because his liberalism ended when payments to his administration would be delayed.

The council also desired control over the Municipal Employment Bureau in which Curley had placed political favorites. To gain public support, councilors blasted the policy which allowed contractors doing business with the city (Curley's "pet contractors," some said) to hire aliens (usually Italians) at only $3 to $4 a day. Instead, asserted Curley's opponents, the city should take on naturalized residents of Boston at the regular $5 rate. R. Gardiner Wilson, Jr. (Ward 17, Dorchester), one of just three Republicans on the council, wanted the Municipal Employment Bureau's director to have the authority to go to contractors "with a figurative gun" and "back these babies to the wall, and make them either hire citizens to do the work of the city or go out of business." In answer to those who asserted that an insufficient number of naturalized workers existed to fill the jobs, Wilson snapped, "If there was ever a public hearing in this hall to determine the fact that there are no able-bodied citizens available in Boston as laborers at $5 a day, they would need 10,000 to 15,000 men to rebuild City Hall after the riot was over." [24] Curley, however, showed little inclination to crack down on the hiring of aliens by enforcing an ordinance against the practice that had been on the books since 1925. The unnaturalized, after all, had to eat.

The anti-Curley majority on the council, indeed, feared any policies that centralized power in the Mayor's office. Consequently, the council decided on October 20, 1930, to upstage the Mayor by creating its own Special Committee on Unemployment, and a week later it asked Curley to provide places of registration for the jobless in all wards. The Mayor, instantly alert to changes that would give ward leaders more control, retorted that "no good cause would be served by advertising to the world that it was necessary to open up twenty-two separate places of registration for the unemployed of the city." The council requested that Curley direct officials to make municipal buildings available for use as sleeping quarters and urged him "to authorize the Overseers of the Public Welfare to serve food at such buildings during such emergency." Curley icily responded that an emergency condition did not obtain. Sounding more callous than he really was, Curley wanted to keep his own hands on the reins. But to the unemployed who would have to walk great distances to Hawkins Street, the debate must have appeared unseemly. Joblessness in Boston had become a political football.[25]

Despite mutual accusations, however, both Curley and the council were genuinely worried about the mounting welfare rolls. When the Mayor was forced to petition for a supplementary appropriation of nearly $1 million he was denounced as a profligate, but the councilors unanimously granted the extra funds. Similarly, the council turned with wrath on the Soldiers' Relief Department, charging that inconsistent rules compensated many veterans unjustly and compelled others "to come as paupers and beggars to the City of Boston."[26] The council advocated federal takeover of all payments to veterans, a step for which Curley was not prepared since federal money implied outside supervision over a department where his friends were safely ensconced. Despite the bitter recriminations, however, Boston's elderly and disabled soldiers received their stipends.

Curley and the city council also bickered over many aspects of welfare policy where the merits of their conflicting positions were anything but clear. The council, for example, scored Curley and the Overseers for their failure to adjust the scale of relief payments to the requirements of large families: the councilors voted an appropriation of $50,000 to be spent on shoes for the neediest welfare children so that they might attend elementary schools. Curley's city attorney held that municipal government possessed no such power, and he may well have been correct.[27] In defense of Curley, too, Boston spaced its welfare payments from $4 a week for a single person to $15 for a family with seven or more children. Thus it could be said that while the payments were surely not lavish, at least some attention had been devoted to family size. By the same token, the council berated the Wayfarers' Lodge for tolerating filth. "The pillows are black," a councilor asserted. "They should fumigate the building from top to bottom." Curley, in turn, wrote off the allegations to political frivolity. Here, too, there was some justice on both sides: the Wayfarers' Lodge was by no means mistakable for the

Ritz, but city-run institutions were not so bad that their lodgers were sleeping under newspapers for want of blankets, as was happening in Minneapolis. In Boston, at least, the Mayor and the city council were not at odds about whether there should be public welfare at all. Rather, the adversaries debated how the city could best run its program.[28]

The council and Mayor Curley also quarreled over the advisability of a public fund drive. In leading the fight to get Boston to resort to popular subscription for the benefit of the Public Welfare Department, Councilors Dowd and Clement Norton (Ward 18, Hyde Park) called upon city employees to contribute $1 million and assigned the business community a $2 million quota. The funds would be superintended by a committee appointed by the mayor consisting of industrial, commercial, and labor leaders accountable to Curley for the disbursement of the money. Congressman McCormack wired Dowd pledging support for the plan, and the council bought the proposal, noting that Cleveland had already raised $6 million and Chicago $12 million by public campaigns.

Curley, however, balked. He maintained that "the philanthropic element of the community . . . regardless of the promptings of heart and mind, are altogether too few and too poor to meet a situation of this character." In a letter to the council, Curley opposed the idea that city workers and employees of public-service corporations should donate any portion of their salaries to a fund for the unemployed. "Were the unfortunate required to wait for the collection of funds contributed by the charitable," said Curley, "the probability is that the money thus donated would be paid to an undertaker rather than to a purveyor of food." When, on November 17, the council again voted for a public fund drive Curley vetoed the proposal, scornfully pointing out that in a fifteen-day period, "the voluntary tender of . . . various industrial enterprises" amounted to precisely $770.02.[29]

The dispute over the fund drive had weighty political implications. If an organization of volunteers gained control of welfare money, power centralized in the mayor's office would be dissipated.

By advocating a relief campaign and by calling on the state legislature to provide money for the unemployed, Councilor Dowd and his allies intimated not very subtly that Curley had failed to develop constructive remedies. They compared him unfavorably to Mayor Walker of New York who had put large numbers to work on emergency street-repair projects. They praised fund drives in other cities, squabbled with Curley over whether breadlines did or did not exist in Boston, and pointed out that in spite of the Mayor's talk of massive public works, most had either failed to materialize or were too far off to be of use. Future projects, complained Councilman Wilson, "do not put coal in the cellar in the winter of 1930," and he predicted that without a fund drive Boston would witness the same spectacle as other cities, where "we now see on every corner men not selling apples but standing beside apples which they are trying to sell." [30]

The fund-drive controversy posed another vexing question, one which had begun to nag every urban government in the United States during the winter of 1930–1931: To what extent should municipal government run up deficits to finance relief? Boston had before it the example of Fall River, Massachusetts, which by July 1930 had found itself unable to pay its employees and a month later fell into the financial receivership of the state. Boston was acutely aware of Chicago's desperate circumstances where teachers went months without pay, a meager total of six thousand welfare recipients were averaging $9.09 per month, city and county workers were for a time compensated in tax anticipation scrip, and Mayor "Big Bill" Thompson suggested lotteries and Liberty Loans to raise money. From the standpoint of the Boston City Council, philanthropic donations would guarantee a continuation of relief payments and keep money out of Curley's hands as well. Furthermore, private gifts would enable the city to avert borrowing and reduce taxes. Curley, on the other hand, generally agreed with Congressman McCormack's view that government had been reducing debt too rapidly, thereby encouraging economic contraction rather than expansion. At heart, Curley was both a spender and a man who wanted no outsiders in control of welfare funds. While his motives may have been less than pristine, his brand of economics had much to recommend it. A city, after all, could for a time remain solvent while those who lived in its decaying neighborhoods had no work.

Far more than Curley, Governor Allen persisted in extolling the virtues of voluntarism. Piling committee on top of committee, Allen launched one of his most ambitious ventures of the year on October 26. Setting up an Emergency Committee on Unemployment Relief to act in consonance with President Hoover's recovery apparatus, Allen appointed James J. Phelan, a banker, to head a drive in Boston. Making "Shop Now for Christmas" appeals, the Allen-Phelan group also suggested that, as a way of creating jobs, railroads that entered Boston should electrify their lines. In addition, Allen and his committee endorsed the suggestion made by Colonel Arthur Woods, chairman of the President's Emergency Committee on Employment (PECE), that the unemployed could be helped if all Americans would "spruce up their homes" and if they would "make the little repairs that are needed." [31] Although Curley heeded Allen's request and formed a similar organization composed of fifty prominent men and women, the Mayor nevertheless reserved his warmest enthusiasm for the simultaneous announcement that he would seek a construction program costing $21,400,000, triple the authorization which he had been able to get from the state in 1930.

With the Allen approach to recovery not working, Democrats sniffed an opportunity to end Republican rule in the Commonwealth. But in settling on a candidate, Curley and a majority of the Democratic ward leaders carried their city council feud into state politics. In the gubernatorial primary, Curley backed his one-time enemy, "The Apostle of Sunshine," John F. Fitzgerald, and denounced Joseph B. Ely of Westfield, the choice of Martin Lomasney and Senator David I. Walsh. And when Curley accused Ely of being "an enemy of the Irish," nine Gaelic members of the city council rose to his defense. Curley, however, was undaunted. Even after Fitzgerald announced his withdrawal for reasons of health, Curley struggled to get write-in support for "Honey Fitz." The night

before the primary, a fistfight erupted in a Boston radio studio between Curley and several Ely supporters who branded Curley a
"bully, a bravo, a thug, a masquerading mayor, a moral and physical
coward, a blackleg and a jailbird." Curley returned the insult by
calling the State Democratic Chairman "the lowest, meanest, most
despicable person" he had ever known, a man who resembled the
Biblical figure who "went down from Jerusalem to Jericho and fell
among thieves." Ely won the primary, but it took a visit to Boston
on October 28 by Al Smith to patch up even temporarily the ruffled
feelings left over from the September imbroglio. At that, few political cognoscenti were fooled by Smith's emotional reception,
Fitzgerald's matchless rendering of "Sweet Adeline," and the presence of Ely, Walsh, and Curley on the same platform.[32]

In the 1930 election, Ely bested Governor Allen, but neither his
16,000-vote edge across the state nor his margin of 76,000 in Boston
could be termed stunning. Indeed, the Democratic gubernatorial
candidate in 1928 had carried the Hub by 91,000 votes. Although
the electorate also turned out United States Senator William Butler,
the conservative Republican's endorsement of Prohibition, his un-
popularity with organized labor, and his tendency to be "as mag-
netic as a clam," made him an easy target for the unexciting Yankee
Democrat from Fitchburg, Marcus Aurelius ("Mute Marcus")
Coolidge. Massachusetts now had two Democrats in the Senate, and
both were linked to Curley's opponents. While the party narrowed
the lopsided Republican margin in the lower chamber of the state
legislature from 155-85 to 139-100, and though Democrats swept all
major offices except the post of lieutenant governor, the turnover
was not especially impressive. After years of Republican rule on
Beacon Hill, explained Henry Shattuck to a friend, "a number of
barnacles are sure to be accumulated," and listless campaigning hurt
the atrophied party. So, too, did Prohibition: in the November 1930
referendum on the state's Baby Volstead Act, Boston voters rejected
enforcement of the Eighteenth Amendment by more than three to
one. And after the mayor of Boston, England, had left the Hub's
tercentenary celebration, he told his friends: "You can swim in

liquor there. You can drown yourself in it." [33] Whether Ely's condemnation of Allen for failing to disinter the emergency measures used in Massachusetts during World War I also registered with Bostonians is less clear. Having waged a negative campaign whose purpose had been largely "to protest, to reject, [and] to condemn" the party in power, Democrats exploited economic conditions but declined to elucidate coherent alternatives. The electorate had, in fact, traded one moderate-to-conservative set of officials for another, and in the process the fissure within Boston's Democratic party had widened.

During the first Depression year, several of the city's pre-crash characteristics had been brought into sharper outline. Boston had retained its ability to raise more revenue per capita and make larger welfare allotments than any other major city. Yet the relative insularity which this favored position allowed the city's leadership had to some extent dulled the capacity to make further progress. Taxpayers' organizations and the Chamber of Commerce had served notice that they would not go along with the Mayor's construction program for 1931, and ward bosses who for years had been on the outs with Curley displayed an eagerness to thwart the city's chief executive. Republican control of the Massachusetts legislature held firm, and the state had frustrated Curley's plans to speed public-works projects for the unemployed. Moreover, the new Democratic governor was on the outs with the Mayor of Boston. Prospects were therefore bleak that future relationships between City Hall and Beacon Hill would be much better than when Frank Allen had occupied the governor's chair. Although the question of whether or not the chronically poor should be supported by the Department of Public Welfare was not deemed a fit topic for debate, the will to finance indefinitely a soaring relief roster populated by the able-bodied unemployed was by no means assured: James Michael Curley believed that government had a responsibility to the jobless, but his enemies were not so certain. Curley's opponents, more than the Mayor himself, were pushing for decentralization of relief, and they saw that voluntary donations might serve their purposes well. And even as

A run on the Federal National Bank and the Boston-Continental Bank in December 1931 prompted a Roxbury theatre to dispatch this sound truck. Bostonians were urged to keep the faith. Boston University School of Communications.

Curley was reaching an impasse with the city council over how to finance and administer the welfare department most effectively, the Mayor was also discovering that his proposals for national planning and federal expenditures were generally being greeted either by silence or by derision. The spirit of self-reliance lived on among Boston's articulate elites, and a mayor whose motives were so widely suspected as were Curley's stood little chance of inspiring a broader sense of community.

Meanwhile, the city's poor eyed the deadlocks at City Hall, the municipal-state hostility, and the promises that were being made by Boston's notables. By the end of the year, only a subway extension at Governor's Square was furnishing emergency employment of any consequence despite the Mayor's boasts to the contrary. When the city's wealthy were asked to hire unemployed women to Christmas shop for them at 40 cents an hour, two hundred jobless showed up at a private emergency employment center at noon of the first registration day. "Pitiful in the extreme were some of their stories," the

New Year's Day, 1931. A throng of jobless men wedged close to buildings on Hanover Street wait for free meals. Nevertheless, Mayor Curley repeatedly denied that breadlines existed in Boston. Boston University School of Communications.

Mayor Curley and his son, George, break ground for a new Governor's Square tunnel. Curley, a monumental builder, preferred to make funds available to the unemployed through public works projects rather than voluntary philanthropy programs or the government dole. The *Boston Globe.*

Transcript reported, yet precisely four were placed.[34] Students at the Boston University School of Theology gave up a day's meal to raise a hundred dollars for the unemployed, but sums of this dimension must have seemed a mockery to the city's nine hundred cigar workers who wandered the streets looking for work.

What had been styled a "recession" at the time of Mayor Curley's inauguration had deepened into a depression, and the costs were evident in Boston through most of the year. At Christmastime the Mayor helped the Volunteers of America fit 1,600 poverty-stricken children with shoes. Manfully predicting a prosperous future, he continued to debate with his opponents—and even with himself— how a revival was to be accomplished. To the 11,000 families who depended on the municipal welfare department for their winter fuel, the need for an answer was fast becoming imperative.

4

"Build Now! Buy Now!"—Unemployment and Persistent Voluntarism, 1931–1932

On October 16, 1932, Harvard's Felix Frankfurter crossed the Charles River, addressed the Associated Jewish Philanthropies of Boston, and declared that the word "charity" had become obsolete. The entire social structure of America, he said, teetered on the brink of collapse:

> I think that the historian of the future will find new words behind the initials B.C. and A.D. I think they will connote, in addition to the great sacred weight those initials now carry, Before Crash and After Depression. For, ladies and gentlemen, I think we are in the midst of a social transformation.[1]

If, in 1930, Boston—like other American cities—rehearsed for the Great Depression, in 1931 and 1932 it was engaged in a more serious drama. Many of the lines spoken by Boston's leaders were unchanged; others were modified. Municipal government reacted to widespread unemployment by once again calling into question the old shibboleths about local responsibility and the adequacy of voluntary efforts, yet the sluggish response of state and federal government forced the city to look once again to its own resources. The city had to improvise, but improvisation alone could not put the idle back to work nor could it more than partially alleviate the misery of the jobless. Even so, by the time Frankfurter spoke of impending social transformation, a number of the city's more privileged leadership groups had still not cast aside their deeply ingrained belief that Boston's institutions, public and private, were the proper agents to handle unemployment.

In the two years prior to Franklin D. Roosevelt's election, Boston suffered negative economic changes that on the whole followed rather closely the patterns in the dozen other largest American cities. If, for the purposes of comparison, the 1929–1933 period is considered, the volume handled by Boston wholesalers tumbled 57.2 percent, a 2.8 percent greater loss than in the other cities with populations above 500,000, and the number of full-time employees engaged in wholesaling fell 45.9 percent, a decrease 10.7 percent more severe than elsewhere. The special weaknesses of shoes, textiles, and woolens in the Massachusetts mill towns had obviously hurt the city's merchants. Retailing, on the other hand, displayed more favorable patterns. While stores in other cities sustained combined losses of 52.1 percent, the sales figures for Boston's retailers dropped 44.4 percent. Yet in the vital area of manufacturing, Boston's figures resembled those of other major urban centers. Wages nose-dived 54.2 percent in the City of Boston (vs. 56.7 percent in other areas), the number of wage earners fell 39.0 percent (vs. 34.4 percent elsewhere), and the value of products made in Boston slumped 52.9 percent (vs. 56.6 percent in other large cities). When deviations from big-city norms are balanced out, Boston's combined economic activity from 1929 to 1933 had fallen off only one or two percentage points less than in other major cities. Blue-collar Bostonians found themselves in the anomalous position of suffering pay and job losses to a degree virtually as serious as their urban counterparts elsewhere, while at the same time they found themselves in a state and region which, though reeling, were not quite as sorely pressed as most others.[2]

Wealthier Bostonians with industrial empires reaching outside the city's borders, on the other hand, fared relatively well, and so did those with incomes dependent upon banking. Indeed, Boston's banks, servicing a comparatively fortunate region and propped up by the substantial trust funds bequeathed by the city's merchant capitalists, enjoyed liquidity throughout the early 1930s, save for a brief scare toward the close of 1931 when two of Boston's smallest houses closed, stranding hundreds of depositors. By mid-1932, however, Boston banks had actually increased their reserves at precisely the moment when houses outside New England were facing catastrophe, and the city's banks had also discharged in full their debt to the Federal Reserve. The reliability of the banking structure consequently protected some of Boston's most powerful men from the severe shocks that might otherwise have produced a strong reform impulse. Although executives cut their own salaries, the Yale Club of Boston closed its doors, and the Harvard Club (remaining open perhaps out of sheer perversity) established a job service to aid its five thousand members, the affluent Bostonian, on the whole, maintained his pre-Depression advantages.

In addition to retaining their social standing, most of those who spoke for the city's major business associations held onto their conservative, pre-crash attitudes as well. Chamber of Commerce directors, for instance, men like Edward French, president of the Boston and Maine Railroad; Frederic Snyder, a Boston wholesaler; and Sinclair Weeks, the Mayor of suburban Newton, made certain that the viewpoints of large corporations prevailed. Reflecting a belief that excessive statute-making in and of itself constituted a threat to liberty, the Chamber's stands tended to be negative: at both the state and federal levels, there should be no workmen's compensation, no mortgage moratoria, no unemployment insurance, no tax boosts, and no state regulation of business.

Boston businessmen much preferred the gentle appeals issued by President Hoover's Organization on Unemployment Relief (POUR) to coercive wages and hours measures.[3] Well received in Boston business circles, POUR allowed employers to do pretty much as they pleased while at the same time permitting them to boast that they had joined a national recovery effort. When, in the autumn of

1931, POUR's New England chairman visited the city to urge the maintenance of decent wages and to ask that businessmen not dismiss any more workers, his message was enthusiastically received. Four days later, however, the Building Trades Employers' Association mailed letters to unions suggesting that 25,000 workers accept pay cuts over the next eighteen months, and described the move as "simply a friendly overture" to stabilize the construction industry. While responsible employers extolled POUR's campaign against sweatshops, good will alone did not keep the unscrupulous few from gouging their employees. In the opinion of a local lawyer, Augustus Loring, POUR's lack of teeth was just as well. "Forced regulation," he said, "means regulation by the government, as in Russia." [4]

Similarly, the Chamber of Commerce and its affiliates looked askance at proposals that would have allowed the federal government to provide funds for public welfare. Holding that progressive United States senators like Robert M. La Follette, Jr. (Wisconsin), and Edward P. Costigan (Colorado) were dead wrong in advocating federal supplements to local emergency relief, directors of the Chamber supported Sinclair Weeks when he said, "Each community should look after its own unemployed." Weeks, in fact, preferred even municipal tax increases to Washington's intrusion, and another director, Roger Babson, thought that the national government could check unemployment if it gave companies taking back jobless men either tax incentives, direct bonuses, or monopoly rights. Moreover, the Chamber maintained close ties with the Harvard Business School and received scholarly backing for federal inaction from Dean Wallace Donham, who, in 1932, told the Boston Conference on Retail Distribution that if the national government had any role to play at all, it might pass a law to spread the work available. More than that it should not do. Boston's elites concurred. After a meeting at the Hotel Statler in February 1932, the Chairman of the New England Council, who was also heading the regional activities of POUR, reported to Washington that he had heard "no expressions, official or personal, in favor of federal appropriations for unemployed relief," but, "on the contrary, many were offered in opposition." [5]

Despite the professed enthusiasm for local activity, a growing number of Bostonians engaged in an ardent struggle to roll back municipal expenditures in 1931 and 1932, a campaign which brought together not wholly compatible allies. Small homeowners, for instance, urged a mortgage moratorium, called for a reduction of interest rates on loans, and sometimes advocated shifting the tax base so that larger bites would be taken from corporate dividends and from those in higher income-tax brackets. For obvious reasons, landlords, upper-income homeowners, and others with means who joined the antitax associations found these desiderata unappealing. In spite of the incongruities, the coalition held together with surprising cohesiveness: the welfare policies and public-works projects of James Michael Curley were targeted for defeat. [6]

As the assault upon government intensified in late 1931, Curley fought back. Singling out Alexander Whiteside, the leader of the Massachusetts Tax Association, for special condemnation, the Mayor derided the Republican attorney's forays to the State Board of Tax Appeals in search of abatements. In impugning the motives of Whiteside and his clients, Curley, in one deft sentence, got to the nub of the issue. "You must appreciate that government must exist in hard times as well as in prosperous times," said the Mayor. The attorney, Curley noted, recognized that the city had to give some relief to the idle, but he would not tolerate the expenditures. He believed that public construction might "have some psychological effect" on stimulating economic activity, but he opposed giving the city the money to undertake any projects. Curley blasted Whiteside's position as dole-oriented, a "fallacious and unsound" attitude toward government and the economy. [7]

In the spring of 1932, more than a year after the first noisy protests against local expenditures commenced, entrepreneurial groups drew together into a formal campaign specifically aimed at Washington's spending policies. The prospect of a $450 million bonus to veterans drove taxpayers' groups and structural reformers active in the

Good Government Association into a flutter of activity. Alarmed not only by the increased sentiment in Congress favoring direct aid to the unemployed, they also believed that Hoover's Economy Act had not reduced the wages of federal employees sufficiently, and they were further convinced that the enactment of a $375-million measure for public construction would unbalance the federal budget. To Boston's bewhiskered, unbeatable Republican Congressman, George Holden Tinkham, deficit spending signaled that "the American Republic is coming to an end." [8]

Over 30,000 Bostonians apparently agreed with Congressman Tinkham, and they rallied to the standard of the National Economy League (NEL), an organization designed to combat the federal government's alleged spending orgy. As the NEL mobilized throughout the country in 1932, Massachusetts became its strongest chapter, and Bostonians exercised a preponderant influence in the organization's executive committee. The noted explorer of the Antarctic, Admiral Richard Byrd of Number Nine Brimmer Street, Beacon Hill, served as the first national chairman, and Carl Dennett of the First National Bank of Boston and a director of the Chamber of Commerce succeeded him. [9] A spirited drive to enroll 50,000 of what an NEL spokesman called "the silent majority" in Massachusetts easily topped the quota, with half the enlistees at the end of 1932 coming from Boston. Enticing real-estate and taxpayers' associations, the NEL also proved attractive to the Elks, Kiwanis, and Rotary clubs as well as to insurance companies and the Chamber of Commerce. Henry Shattuck and his Brahmin compatriots donated a major share of the money needed for keeping the organization alive. Cabots belonged, and so did Cardinal O'Connell. Like many of the groups in Boston which had been designed to brake expenditures, the NEL also attracted Democratic political leaders committed to minimal government and, by definition, men who were anti-Curley. Inspired by the proposition that "every revolution has been due to taxation and fiscal policies," NEL members demonstrated that in Boston, older outlooks were not hastily discarded. [10]

As those not directly touched by unemployment made clear that they were ready for no extreme remedies, the first platoon of jobless workers was becoming an army. No one knew for sure how many, but American Federation of Labor surveys largely corroborated reports disseminated by state and federal bureaus: from July 1931 to December 1932 unemployment in all trades in Boston averaged 29.72 percent, almost precisely equal to the 30.17 rate reported by twenty-three other large cities. In numerical terms, the unemployed could not have been fewer than 90,000 to 100,000 through most of 1931 and 1932, and when combined with those who were underemployed, the figure skyrocketed to upwards of 130,000 to 150,000 in a work force of roughly 340,000. By December 1932 the rate of joblessness in the Hub, though slightly lower than that of New York and Chicago, had surged beyond levels recorded in Cleveland and Detroit.[11]

The Great Depression in Boston claimed its victims most unevenly and took its heaviest toll in areas that had been, on the eve of the crash, the most disadvantaged in the city. The 1930 figures for average income, rental costs, and population density acted as precise indicators of where unemployment hit with special savagery. Nativity and race also figured disproportionately in determining which areas were most afflicted. Negro workers in the South End and Roxbury—almost none of them in unions, over 70 percent of them unskilled, and with a tuberculosis death rate four times higher than that of whites—experienced an unemployment rate some 15 to 18 percent above the city average. Italians in the North End and East Boston, as well as the poorer Irish in South Boston and Charlestown, suffered comparable hardships. Back Bay Yankees, in contrast, enjoyed the lowest unemployment rate in the city throughout the Depression, and districts at a remove from the urban core—Brighton, Jamaica Plain, West Roxbury—also were relatively well off. Although Yankees and middle-class Irish were being added to the roster of the idle, their rates of joblessness tended to be four to five times smaller than those of the residents of the poorest wards.[12]

Not only were the ranks of the unemployed enormous but, in late 1931 and throughout 1932, workers who had managed to hold onto their jobs were also discovering that POUR's requests to employers not to slash wages or cut hours were being ignored. Unorganized workers were promised that the cuts would be of short duration, but as one Bostonian later recalled, the reductions "announced to be temporary soon proved to be temporary only in the sense that a new and larger cut was in the making." [13] Union leaders, faced with writing the cuts into contracts, normally asked the rank and file to vote their preference. Since reductions were deemed better than no pay at all, union members acquiesced to lower wages: the average weekly earnings of men's-clothing workers plummeted from 87 cents an hour to 62 cents (a decline which exceeded losses in Philadelphia and corresponded to setbacks in Chicago and New York), while wages in the building trades skidded from 12 to 18 percent, depending on a worker's skill. With the cost of living in Boston falling just 7.9 percent from 1931 to 1932 (only New York was a more expensive place to live), cuts of this magnitude affected real income with special severity.

Boston's unions tried to protect their members as best they could, but successes were few. While the number of work stoppages actually increased in 1931 and 1932, a rarity when compared to national urban trends,[14] the city's last strike of any size until the New Deal years occurred in late 1931, when longshoremen tied up the Port of Boston. Employers trucked in Negro strikebreakers, and an angry mob pelted them with rocks and bottles as the vans passed through Charlestown. When the strike ended, none of its major objectives had been achieved, and the longshoremen had inadvertently begun a pattern which would hold for almost two more years—a pattern of defeats. Although membership totals in AFL unions were by 1932 undiminished from the levels of 1929, a seemingly remarkable accomplishment and one which again was at variance with national tendencies,[15] the signs were clear that men were being carried on union books who were not paying their dues: the Central Labor Union lacked a quorum for some of its meetings in 1932, something that had rarely happened before, and at other Sunday afternoon sessions officers repeatedly expressed concern that affiliates were not paying their per capita tax. Organizing drives were out of the question. Instead, the BCLU tried to bolster its charitable activities and vainly asked the city to spread the work and stop using welfare recipients in place of organized workers in public buildings.

By and large, BCLU affiliates responded to horrendous unemployment without undergoing appreciable ideological change. While there were surely radical elements present in certain locals, especially in the garment trades, most BCLU locals stood four-square for capitalism. The secretary-treasurer of the Typographical Union, J. Arthur Moriarty, who also served as president of the BCLU, captured what appeared to be the prevailing outlook when he spoke at a pre–Labor Day rally on September 4, 1932. "[The wage earner] does not want charity, he does not want a noncontributory dole; he wants work and if he gets it he will be satisfied." Claiming that "in our fair city men are dying in alleys," Moriarty nevertheless concluded that industrial evils could be combated by moral suasion, an approach not much different from what POUR was urging.[16] And although labor leaders such as Moriarty and E. A. Johnson, the president of the Building Trades Council and a Republican, believed that government at all levels should expand public works, neither was speaking of a planned economy or of federal grants to the jobless.

Outside the ranks of the trade unions, a small group of Communists continued their overt and militant protests at the Boston Common, City Hall, and on the steps of the State House. Hoping to enlist Italian dock workers in the North End, to attract Negroes by a "campaign . . . against white chauvinism," and to detach sympathizers in AFL locals, the leftists had concocted a grandiose plan in 1931 for making gains in Boston.[17] Under the aegis of the International Labor Defense and the Boston Council of the Unemployed, demonstrators typically demanded jobs, direct cash relief of $15 per week, a mortgage moratorium, and an unemployment-insurance plan. And, just as in 1930, Mayor Curley told the Left to go back to Moscow. Massive police squadrons again moved in with clubs flying and made arrests for "carrying a placard," "making loud outcries in the park," or "speaking without a permit." [18]

However, the number of actual participants in 1931–1932 fell off appreciably from the demonstrations of 1930: police repression took its toll, and in a Catholic city the practitioners of Godless atheism encountered hostility.[19] Usually no more than fifty to one hundred gathered to sing the "Internationale" and to call for capitalism's overthrow. A demarcation line between activists and spectators was much more visible than had been the case in the first year after the crash, and counter-demonstrators far outnumbered the "Reds." Crowds gathered to see off Boston contingents destined for hunger marches to Washington both in 1931 and 1932, but each time the paraders set forth no more than seventy-five joined. Although 7,000 veterans showed up at a rally in support of the Bonus March on Washington in 1932, charges that radicals were using the veterans as a blind for ulterior purposes scared off participants. Organizers desperately held an "indignation meeting" at which they promised there would be "no rum, no vandalism, no unmilitary actions" during the trip. On June 5, the appointed day, a bugler sounded "Assembly" but only eight joined ranks to advance up Charles and Beacon Streets toward Kenmore Square. A Negro veteran commented, "We may need the bonus, but we're not crazy." Five months later, chants of "We want blood" and pledges to "punch Hoover and Roosevelt right in the snoot" mustered no discernible support.[20]

The Boston worker, then, did not take to the streets to plead for a revision of the system, but instead throngs milled outside the Municipal Employment Bureau in the Micawber-like hope that something would turn up. So few got jobs that on several occasions the city council chopped Mayor Curley's appropriations requests to maintain the Bureau. To a retrenchment-minded Republican councilor such as the Back Bay's Laurence Curtis, "The amount of work that office can do in finding jobs for people is very little in these times."[21] To Curley's Democratic foes on the council, the agency continued to be a haven for the Mayor's cronies, a "bull pen on Church Street" where "the champion whist players of the city" sent "the unfortunate unemployed on wild goose chases for jobs which do not exist." Whatever the reasons for the Bureau's rocky course, the odds against placing the idle were, in fact, so long that Hyde Park's Clement Norton suggested spending Employment Bureau funds on 60,000 quarts of milk for welfare children to still "the cry for bread, the primitive hungry cry of the race [which] rises from twenty million throats to a terrifying crescendo." Nevertheless, the unemployed who repeatedly endured the degrading experience of coming away empty-handed looked to alternatives other than the Left.[22]

That many job-seekers were thwarted was reflected by the phenomenal rise which took place in the municipal welfare load. From 1929 to 1932, as seen in Table 4.1, the number of families aided by the Overseers of the Public Welfare jumped from 7,463 to 40,672, and toward the end of 1932, Boston was assisting one out of every four of its unemployed workers. While no major city assisted so high a percentage of its jobless, the alarming fact remained that three out of every four without work had to fend for themselves. Daily the ranks were growing: the crush of unemployed that looked to welfare resources included fugitives from other parts of the nation, many of them enticed by the widespread rumor that New England still had obtainable work. Miners from Appalachia and the borax center in Death Valley came seeking jobs on the East Boston tunnel. Cowboys, seafarers, wandering boys, itinerant white-collar workers, and whole families added to the case load at the city-run Wayfarers'

Table 4.1 *. *Growth of Public Relief, Boston, 1929–1932*

Year	Amount to Boston Recipients	Families Aided	Active Cases at End of Year **
1929	$ 2,421,868	7,463	4,908
1930	3,578,158	11,478	9,087
1931	7,070,525	24,770	15,380
1932	11,930,587	40,672	28,168

* "Eighty-first Annual Report of the Overseers of the Public Welfare," *Boston City Documents*, No. 23, 1945.
** *City Record*, January issues, 1930–1933.

Lodge and at the Travelers' Aid Society. And in 1932 the New York, New Haven, and Hartford Railroad reported that trespassers headed for Boston had increased by roughly 200 percent.

Municipal government could boast of achievements in 1931 and 1932 even though it was taking care of slightly less than a quarter of the jobless in any one month. Of the cities with more than 500,000 people only Milwaukee and Chicago carried a larger monthly case load per 10,000 population. Welfare recipients in Boston averaged monthly payments of $39.36 in 1932, and while this sum represented a $6.80 decline from 1931, the outlays were 34 percent higher than in Buffalo, the second-ranked city. And throughout the 1929–1932 period Bostonians on a per capita basis continued to spend more for relief than the residents of any other major city. Compared to the urban record of the early 1930s, Boston was discharging its obligations very well indeed.[23] As a result, the city's more comfortable residents could rationalize their opposition to indefinite welfare expansion by pointing at what they considered to be lavish standards. Unhappily for the unemployed, the standards were not very high.

Those on relief, in fact, faced grindingly hard circumstances. Weekly allotments amounted to $10 for a family of four and $15 for a family of seven or over (plus coal) until June of 1932. Then, the city was forced to institute 10 percent cuts. Although recipients by the end of 1932 could go to one of eight offices around the city to file applications and receive their payments, they still had to check in and perform their make-work at central headquarters. Recipients also discovered in July of 1932 that the welfare department, yielding to angry taxpayers, was upping the required number of trips to four a week "as a further protection to the city finances." Few were exempted from "the House of Horrors on Hawkins Street," and those who could be seen there included "a man with one leg, who for six months has been sawing wood." Carfare to central Boston ate up a portion of the meager dole, the trips prevented the unemployed from seeking work, and reliefers seemed to be moving a step closer to permanent dependence.[24] Just the same, jobless citizens queued up for their weekly checks in lines which in 1932 took as long as eight hours to come to an end.

Moreover, the morale of reliefers could not have been lifted by the attitude toward welfare displayed by the Massachusetts Tax Association, the Boston Finance Commission, and by several members of the city council. In a vitriolic campaign to uncover undeserving recipients, these groups caricatured welfare clients as untrustworthy alcoholics or drug users, progenitors of hordes of children, as men who shamelessly sent their wives to collect relief while they sneaked work from private employers, and as Catholic Democrats who were trading their votes for the dole. The Overseers, responding to the pressure to unmask fraudulent claimants, checked local banks for unreported savings, submitted names to the Registry of Motor Vehicles to make sure that applicants owned no motor cars, and visited the homes of their clients' relatives to see whether assistance might be forthcoming. Unannounced visitations by social workers, in turn, led to the accusation that the poor were being treated "practically like dogs," and probers uncovered just enough instances of chiseling to stigmatize the city's unfortunate. Investigators, for example, turned up men and women who had used the names of deceased persons to collect checks, and one recipient listed a Lansdowne Street address which proved to be the center-field bleachers of Fenway Park.[25]

Despite the Public Welfare Department's opinion that "five trees do not make a forest and every rippling stream is not a raging torrent," Mayor Curley capitulated to the clamor for a special probe by the Boston police. Using vocabulary that incensed civil libertarians, the city's finest couched their findings with vague descriptions of alleged cheaters such as "possibly unworthy" and "case indicated fraud." The police estimate that at least 14 percent of all recipients prevaricated in making applications was, according to the Overseers, too high, but welfare department attempts to discredit the inquiry could not undo the incalculable damage. Defenseless reliefers had been branded as dishonest, parasitical, and without legitimate claim on public funds.[26]

As the savings of the unemployed and underemployed vanished, over four hundred private organizations were deluged by those seeking supplementary assistance. The Family Welfare Society, for example, found in 1931 that one of every three persons aided had no work; a year later, two of every three held no job. In 1929, the St. Vincent de Paul Society at one time or another had helped 3,206 families; three years later it served 8,433 in Boston proper. Like most private groups, the Society's case load increased while cash receipts dwindled, and fund-raising objectives had to be reduced. The Salvation Army, for instance, had taken in over $250,000 in 1929, but the goal was lowered to $150,000 in 1931 and 1932. At the end of the scheduled drives, the Army was considerably short of its objectives. Officials of the Associated Jewish Philanthropies witnessed a similar pattern: case loads zoomed and receipts plunged—$900,000 was easily raised in 1929, but campaigns to get $615,000 in 1931 and $600,000 in 1932 both fell short.[27]

With whatever money they had private agencies made a concerted effort to feed the poor. At first, charities obeyed the promptings of the President's Organization on Unemployment Relief that public feedings be avoided in order "to preserve the independence and self-respect of the unemployed." If it became necessary to dispense free meals, POUR continued, they should be handed out in private, a view which accorded closely with Mayor Curley's insistence that there should be no breadlines on the city's streets. However, it became increasingly difficult to maintain a distinction between food distribution which safeguarded privacy and the open spectacle of mass feeding. When, for example, a solitary evangelist opened a small shop on Washington Street in October of 1931 to dole out sandwiches and coffee, more than three hundred men lined up until Mayor Curley ordered the place closed. Students at Dorchester High School and the High School of Commerce rioted in protest of inadequate lunches in the spring of 1932, and they found it hard to accept the explanation offered by Eva Whiting White that they were embroiled in a situation no more serious than the disturbances following a Harvard hockey game. "Extra excitement that will take a student's mind off his work momentarily is just great," she said. "It's all just fun." The Family Welfare Society knew better, and in the summer of 1932 the agency curtailed summer vacations in the country for its clients, and instead concentrated on day picnics for undernourished children, "in order that they may be fortified for the coming winter." [28]

In August of 1932, when fishermen off the Grand Banks were dumping the largest mackerel catch in history because Boston markets were offering only half a cent a pound, it was no longer possible to mask breadlines in the city, or to disperse them as Mayor Curley had done earlier. Flocking to an immense hall run by the Volunteers of America, 8,000 Bostonians in less than a week proved valid the maxim of Councilor Norton that the poor man "cannot eat the clapboards, he cannot eat the house," by filing through to get four-cent suppers. When the Volunteers added penny lunches, the joyless queues lengthened week by week. Mayor Curley himself at last endorsed the operation and obtained a telegram of commendation for the project from Governor Roosevelt of New York. [29]

Penny lunches, however, were not what James Michael Curley wanted for the City of Boston, yet his quest for alternatives drew mostly blanks when he approached the state government. Although Joseph B. Ely, the first Democrat in sixteen years to occupy the governor's mansion, had made inaugural pledges to abandon pay-as-you-go financing and float a substantial bond issue for construction, he was immediately attacked by Republicans as a profligate who had gleaned his ideas "from listening to Amos 'n' Andy talking about millions." The GOP, however, need not have worried that Ely would take Massachusetts on a "Fall River ride," for after his initial six months in office he proved to be a cautious chief executive. In addition, Curley continued to face a recalcitrant legislative branch. Even though some forty of Boston's forty-three representatives to the lower chamber could usually be counted on to support bills giving the city the right to set its own tax limit and augment its borrowing powers, the solons on Beacon Hill in a wild final week of the 1932 legislative session swept aside a plan to lend $20 million to cities and towns, a 6 percent "soak the rich" tax on dividends from stocks and bonds, and a bill to transfer state highway funds to Massachusetts communities. Of twenty-two bills submitted by Curley to the Municipal Finance Committee for borrowing outside the debt limit, only one received approval, a minor measure for the Parks Department involving the paltry sum of $125,000. Only in sanctioning an $8,500,000 extension of the Huntington Avenue subway did the legislature appear to make a single exception to its gaunt program for Boston. However, the act stipulated that the city pay for the project.

Although Republican solidarity accounted for some of the sorry debacle, much of the responsibility rested with Ely himself. Ordering a $3-million budget reduction in 1932, the Commonwealth's first large decrease in thirteen years, Ely no longer championed spending as a restorative. Since economic maladies extended beyond Massachusetts, he argued, nothing could be "summarily settled by any legislative act of ours." Massachusetts, he blandly contended, had discharged its obligations in 1931. Therefore, he would wait for Washington to do the same, which, in 1932, was like waiting for Godot.[30]

Herbert Hoover, indeed, had demonstrated to Mayor Curley and Boston's jobless his inability to rescue the city from its miasma. Having come to the Hub on October 6, 1930, he had quickened few pulses. Speaking first to the American Legion, the President had dwelled mainly on patriotism and the glories of citizenship. In the afternoon, at the American Federation of Labor's national convention, which was also meeting in Boston, Hoover read his speech in a tired voice over an amplifying system that did not work. Only a third of the crowd could hear him as he denounced the dole as a limitation upon the independence of man, called for teamwork between labor and management to prevent strikes, and indicated that he would relax enforcement of the Sherman and Clayton antitrust acts. Concluding with his familiar paean to the genius of business and the American way, Hoover stated:

> We find inspiration in the courage of our employers, the resolu-
> tion of the nation that we shall build steadily to prevent and mitigate
> the destructiveness of these great business storms. It is this inspira-

tion which gives confidence for the future, and confirms our belief in fundamental human righteousness and the value of our American conception of mutuality of interest in our daily work.[31]

Although Hoover tried a good bit harder than his remarkably shrill detractors acknowledged, the mawkish views expressed in his Boston addresses changed little in 1931 and 1932. The crucial test for the United States, he believed, was "whether individuals and local communities continue to meet their responsibilities." Equally confining was his conviction that the arrogation of power to the federal government "can but lead to the super-state where every man becomes the servant of the state and real liberty is lost." [32]

As Hoover grudgingly assented to stepped-up activity, particularly in 1932, the resulting legislation proved of scant significance to American cities. Through his use or threat of veto, the President himself emasculated relevant bills, and Congress also displayed an antiurban bias. The Senate, for instance, overwhelmingly rejected Royal S. Copeland's motion empowering the Reconstruction Finance Corporation (RFC) to lend directly to muncipalities, a vote which appalled Curley and vitiated Eugene Meyer's claims for the RFC's flexibility. The RFC's subsequent record amply confirmed the Mayor's misgivings. Hoover's moratorium on the payment of international debts to stimulate trade failed to revive the Port of Boston, the Glass-Steagall Banking Act did not ease credit stringency, and Boston received not a penny from the Wagner-Garner Emergency Relief and Construction Act.[33] Passage of the Federal Home Loan Bank Act was of negligible value since its eligibility rules barred homeowners with either mortgages in arrears or with tax delinquencies from obtaining loans. Consequently, when 5,000 tax-delinquent homeowners had their possessions advertised for sale at the close of 1932, it was Curley's intervention and the generosity of Boston's banks—not the Federal Home Loan Banks—that postponed the auction.

Much of Curley's disgust at federal inaction stemmed from the Hoover administration's unwillingness to commit itself fully to public works. So little had been done on the $6-million Boston Post

Office after nearly two years of talk that Curley wrote Postmaster Walter Brown suggesting that he might turn loose a municipal cow to graze on the vacant site and provide Bostonians with "a real attraction" during 1931's Fourth of July celebration. Brown reported that "it is my opinion that the department should not be required to put up with your bull." Undaunted, Curley deluged Hoover and his cabinet with letters and telegrams counseling action, and on several occasions he traveled to Washington. His visits, however, convinced him that the nation's capital resembled "an old-fashioned wakehouse." Dismissal of federal employees, the absence of a Federal Planning Commission, and the revenue losses brought about by the "stupid and iniquitous Volstead Act" threatened to make the United States "a nation of beggars." Hoover, said the Mayor, did nothing but appoint commissions, and in August 1931 he noted that the President's latest organization listed two members who had been dead and buried for some time. "Something of a stupendous character should be embarked on now," he told the Inland Waterways Commission four months later as he sought money for Boston Harbor and as he reiterated his proposals for an "inland empire" in the Mississippi Valley.[34] When nothing colossal materialized, Curley flailed at Hoover's principal unemployment relief spokesman in Massachusetts, the ultraconservative Eliot Wadsworth, who was admonishing in early 1932 that more action from Washington might "put the damper" on local activity.[35]

By 1932, Curley had emerged as a national figure. His larger role derived from political activity on behalf of Franklin Roosevelt (see Chapter V) and from his position as chairman of the Resolutions Committee of the National Conference of Mayors. The Mayors' Conference in particular afforded him contact with men like Frank Murphy of Detroit and Daniel Hoan of Milwaukee, and together they endorsed the idea of a $500-million direct federal grant to the cities and a $5-billion federal bond issue for public works. When the 1932 mayors' session in Detroit adjourned, Curley headed a delegation to Washington to present resolutions to Hoover, but the President ignored the group, deputizing Vice President Charles

Curtis to receive the municipal executives. Trips to Washington, like his sorties to Beacon Hill, yielded an empty cup. Boston had to go it alone, and this it tried to do with élan.

With no aid forthcoming from the state or federal government, Curley had little choice but to turn to the voluntaristic approaches which he had repudiated even in 1930. In April 1931, the Mayor, who had previously opposed fund drives, created a special unemployment account into which municipal employees in higher wage and salary brackets were expected to contribute a day's pay. Curley himself gave $4,000, a fifth of his salary, and he purchased insurance policies on his own life that he estimated would provide Boston's poor with $45,458,527 in two hundred years. The need, however, was rather more immediate than that, and for the rest of the year receipts dribbled in: a newly organized Civic Symphony gave benefit concerts for the jobless, schoolteachers voted to donate 2 percent of their income for six months, and a wrestling match at the Boston Garden netted $5,000. On the eve of Harvard's annual clash with Yale, celebrants left parties early to come to Boston's theater district for midnight charity shows. But with relief expenses approaching a million dollars a month, the coins which the affluent dropped into the hampers proved wholly inadequate. Moreover, when President Lowell of Harvard agreed to turn over the university's stadium for a Thanksgiving benefit game between Boston College and Holy Cross (earlier, he had refused to transfer the Harvard-Army game to Yankee Stadium where the proceeds would have gone to charity), the gate receipts did not even match the guarantees to the two teams.

On December 1, 1931, Curley, who had been regularly vetoing city council orders for fund drives, gave in once and for all to the idea of a major philanthropic campaign. To dramatize the formation of an Emergency Unemployment Relief Committee headed by William Taylor, a member of the Overseers and vice president of the First National Bank, the Mayor orchestrated a full-scale burial of General D. Pression. An effigy, encased in a black pine coffin, arrived at Battery Wharf atop a municipal garbage truck bedecked with bunches of carrots, beets, and turnips. Workers lowered the

General onto the ferryboat *Flaherty* and Curley pushed him off. The Mayor reminded the audience that the grave lay "not far from the scene of the immortal Boston Tea Party" and that General D. Pression had been "well buried for all time." Two dozen chorus girls and a brass band led the multitude in a rendition of "Happy Days Are Here Again," the sirens of harbor craft sounded, and jets of water spouted skyward from city fireboats. The Mayor's attempt to exorcise demons by physical eradication, while not original, was vintage Curley. Once started, the hoopla never ceased.

Curley gave the Taylor Committee the responsibility of coordinating public and private relief, an assignment made difficult by the Mayor's insistence that the city be the sole recipient of proceeds from the emergency campaign. After several days of behind-the-scenes haggling, Curley backed down and allowed 110 private organizations one-third of the receipts, the remainder going to the Boston Welfare Department. Other aspects of campaign planning to raise $3 million proceeded harmoniously as the Taylor Committee consciously revived the organization and *esprit* of World War I's Liberty Loan drives. Even before the campaign opened, the 145,000 schoolchildren of Boston promised to take home written appeals to their parents, a thousand Boy Scouts enrolled to deliver 200,000 messages door to door, 5,000 volunteers signed up to solicit personally every residence in the city, and advertisers donated two hundred outdoor billboards to trumpet the theme, "We Have Shared." Aimee Semple McPherson, the "World's Most Beautiful Evangelist," who was appearing before packed houses of nearly 20,000 people at the Boston Garden, contributed from the proceeds of her sensational itinerant Gospel show: gifts totaled two cardboard cartons containing a few dollars' worth of food. She promised more, but nothing arrived.

At the campaign's formal opening at the Boston Opera House, Taylor summoned volunteers to save the American home by participating in a war against suffering and breadlines. "The curtain is risen," he declared. "Behold—an army of several thousand strong is here and ready to march forth." Another speaker perceived the

Over 1,000 Boy Scouts rang Boston door bells in January 1932 on behalf of the city's first unemployment relief campaign. Boston University School of Communication.

campaign as nothing less than an effort to keep Bostonians off "the highway to bolshevism and hoboism." As lights dimmed, the volunteers sang "The Star-Spangled Banner" while an electrical red, white, and blue flag flashed in the background.

Bostonians rallied to the cause, and though it took a week longer to raise the $3 million than the ten days allowed, on February 13, 1932, the mammoth campaign thermometer on the Boston Common burbled over. Taylor, in an outburst of pride, informed Walter Gif-

William Taylor and Richard Whitcomb flank the ladder that supports C. F. Weed as he tops off the unemployment relief drive's thermometer at the Boston Common. Youngsters from the Bouroughs Newsboys Foundation, partial beneficiaries of the 1932 drive, look on. The *Boston Globe.*

ford, chairman of POUR, that "the money-raising campaign was carried on without depressing the community" and that he saw "no noticeable unrest" in the city. "The matter of public and private relief," he added, "is well in hand." [36] But had each unemployed head of household been on relief instead of just one in four, the $3 million would have lasted less than three weeks. The welfare department, in fact, received only $1,896,235 as its share of voluntary donations throughout 1932, enough to support recipients for less than two months, and the fund drive had siphoned off money from the independent campaigns conducted by private agencies. And had the city employees not contributed $571,000 of the total collected, the campaign would have been an unmitigated disaster. [37]

Other attempts to stir the public into aiding the unemployed fizzled in 1932. The Taylor Committee's job-finding campaign, despite sending 150,000 letters to householders urging them to undertake repairs, and despite setting up neighborhood work centers, canvassing door to door, and holding block parties, found permanent positions for only 787 persons and temporary chores for 3,023 others. The total value of work actually located amounted to $3,576,806 in wages, roughly $44,500,000 below the target figure. Mayor Curley's sponsorship of additional events to raise money in 1932 flopped. Not even the appearance at a carnival for the unemployed of Boston heavyweight Jack Sharkey, fresh from lifting the world's title from Max Schmeling; Francis Ouimet, Boston's 1931 National Amateur golf champion; the Red Sox; the Braves; and Amelia Earhart; all on the same card, could lure patrons through the gates of Braves Field. [38] With the general public by and large failing to contribute, Curley—through forced exactions—extracted another $2,500,000 from city employees.

By instituting economies in government, Curley also turned up money for relief. In a dictum of May 5, 1931, he told department heads to practice the same degree of economy in municipal government as they would in their homes. A running debate instantly ensued over whether or not "Jimmie the burglar" had, in actuality, realized economies, and the city council peppered Curley with endless suggestions on how to protect the treasury's resources.[39] By having tax bills delivered on foot rather than paying postage, printing fewer documents, and canceling schoolboy hockey, Curley gave the appearance of a mayor in the throes of retrenchment. Unlike the powerful taxpayers' groups who wanted sizable budget cuts, however, Curley was saving on unessential activities so that he could spend more on relief and construction.

Curley's fertile imagination churned out literally dozens of building projects in 1931 and 1932. "I'd rather spend $100 million a year in keeping people at work than spend $100 for doles," he stated. But without appreciable state and federal help, and with the city council also playing a part in tying up or altogether scuttling Curley's requests, his undertakings turned out to be largely chimerical. The more important projects urged by the Mayor never escaped the drafting room of the City Planning Board. Between the approximately 60 million dollars' worth of projects formally announced by Curley in 1931 and 1932 and the actual realization of construction, there were discrepancies. Indeed, the sole ground-breaking of consequence (the $16-million East Boston tunnel) dated from the Nichols administration. The city council rejected a $5-million courthouse proposal after the state legislature had accepted it and the council also withheld approval of a $1,250,000 bond issue for airport improvement. A multimillion dollar extension of the Huntington Avenue subway, having gone through both the state legislature and the city council after two years of skirmishing, was scotched by the trustees of the Boston Elevated on the grounds that it would add to Boston's tax rate. For all of Curley's extravagant claims, he actually earmarked less for public works in 1932 than had originally been budgeted and little more than had been spent during an average year in the 1920s.

Having received no state or federal assistance worthy of mention, and with chinks developing in the city's philanthropic armor, idle workers were further menaced by conflicting perceptions of the city's fiscal condition. Advocates of retrenchment, including fourteen of the twenty-two city council members, pointed out that the

1932 tax rate, based on the second-highest per capita property valuations in the country and raised $4 to $35 (again the highest in the nation), had resulted in plunging revenue collections: 26.4 percent of 1932's taxes had not been received on the due date, some 6 percent worse than the median collection rate of the 195 cities with more than 50,000 people. With welfare expenditures exceeding budget estimates by approximately 25 percent in both 1931 and 1932, the lack of ready cash pushed the city into the money market to sell tax anticipation notes at an accelerated pace: $21 million in 1929, $30 million in 1931, and $45 million in 1932—some $6,500,000 more than that part of the budget under the mayor's control. Interest charges for short-term loans, the cost-cutters noted, had leaped from just over 1 percent in 1931 to 5.7 percent in February 1932, and for the first time in its history the city in 1932 floated long-term bonds to meet ordinary operating expenses.

Without minimizing the seriousness of these indicators, however, Mayor Curley and a minority of the city council had a stronger case when they argued that Boston had untapped resources which should have been unlocked. Debt service costs by 1932 had reached a plateau only 15.2 percent higher than in 1929, and the absolute per capita debt remained far below that of most major cities.[40] Tax anticipation notes were cleared up on their due dates, even as Detroit and Chicago defaulted. Interest rates on short-term loans, although briefly spiraling to dangerous levels in early 1932, dropped below 2 percent in the late spring and stayed there for the rest of the year, a certain sign that investors regarded Boston as an excellent credit risk. Even the normally gloomy Finance Commission boasted of "the exceptional financial standing of the City of Boston." [41] Most important, those who proposed to expand the function of government had a superior moral claim. Retorting to the argument that Boston was already providing more relief per capita than any other city, the advocates of government activism held that with a third of the population idled, pleas for budget-balancing were unconscionable. Moreover, voluntary efforts to bring about both recovery and relief had not worked. Bostonians who carried the torch for increased governmental activity had a difficult time, however, in winning over the thousands who were demanding fiscal restraint.

By the autumn of 1932, Boston was displaying a crisis of will. The political atmosphere was conducive neither to accumulating more debt nor to boosting taxes. Even had a greater number of ward leaders, businessmen, clergy, and social workers joined Mayor Curley in his pleas for federal intervention, augmented state aid, and greater municipal borrowing, there would still have been formidable obstacles in the way—the Massachusetts legislature, Governor Ely, and President Hoover. Organized labor was demoralized; the legions of unemployed were docile. Satisfied with the city's welfare expenditures and unwilling to jeopardize further the relatively favorable standing of the municipal treasury, Boston's elites clung tenaciously to the doctrines of voluntarism and local responsibility. So did members of the city council from wards as hard hit by unemployment as the West and North Ends, much of Roxbury, and parts of lace-curtain Dorchester. While Felix Frankfurter sensed that the nation stood "in the midst of a social transformation" in October 1932, the metamorphosis had not yet altered proper Bostonians. But to the unemployed who sent their children to the State Street area where they hunted pigeons for food, the perils of voluntarism were immense.

5

The Road to Roosevelt

On January 25, 1932, Franklin D. Roosevelt rendered a masterful political judgment which he could easily have applied to locales far from New England. "I really believe that Boston and Massachusetts Democrats will grow up some day," he observed to his Harvard '04 classmate, LaRue Brown, "but probably not until you and I are dead and gone." [1]

Clearly, though, Bay State Democrats held no monopoly on political feuds—not in a party which housed such power brokers as the Kansas City Pendergasts, Frank Hague of Jersey City, and Ed Flynn of the Bronx, while at the same time serving as the nominal home of urban liberals like New York's Robert Wagner and Detroit's Frank Murphy. Despite Roosevelt's waltz to victory in urban America—and in Boston, his majority was more lopsided than in any other large city—the election of 1932 proved in some ways unsatisfying. If the Boston story may be used as an aperture to big-city politics in 1932, three major points stand out. Despite the economic blitz of 1929–1932, municipalities retained in slightly modified form most of their pre-Depression characteristics. Secondly, the 1932 election failed to unite diverse elements behind a coherent ideology and almost certainly constituted no mandate for the New Deal. Finally, the particularism exhibited in 1932 would, in turn, ultimately limit New Deal accomplishments in the city.

Boston, long a Democratic stronghold in mayoral contests, had for years voted less predictably in national elections. Beginning in 1918, however, when Worcester's David I. Walsh was sent to the United States Senate, the party had strengthened its position. Aided by dissatisfaction with economic conditions and a strong dislike for Prohibition, Walsh in the mid-1920s gathered about him a coalition consisting of Irish and Yankee Democrats, labor leaders, and well-educated liberals, many of them Anglo-Saxon Protestants, from both major parties. In 1928 this same coalition surfaced throughout urban America in support of Alfred E. Smith, and in Boston bountiful dividends awaited the Democratic standard-bearer. While in 1920 the city had given only 36.3 percent of its total Presidential vote to the lusterless Democrat James M. Cox, in 1928 it returned a smashing 66.8 percent for Smith, enabling the "Happy Warrior" to carry Massachusetts by the narrow margin of 17,000 votes.

With the advent of the Great Depression, the Republican party looked even more vulnerable than it had in 1928, and a legion of voters in the Hub reserved for an Irishman the honor of retiring Herbert Hoover from public office. "Smitholatry," as *The New York Times* called it, ran "wide and deep" in Boston. In fact, the city's Irish electorate and Alfred Emanuel Smith could not have been more perfectly matched. Both hungered for recognition in a society that still viewed their Catholicism with suspicion; both readily sympathized with labor's right to bargain collectively, to earn decent wages, and to strike without fear of reprisals. Still, neither believed in federal action to improve the lot of the victimized. As one perceptive student of the New York Democrat has put it, "The extent of Smith's progressivism went only as far as to insure that the United States remained a mobile society where enough opportunity existed for future Al Smiths." [2] The Walsh coalition, like the man this alliance so revered, also lacked a "positive reform impulse," and substituted instead "a negative sort of discontent—with one hundred percent Americanism, with economic depression, and with Prohibition." [3] Distrustful of liberalism—which emphasized remote, long-term planning—and chary of government spending, the followers of Al Smith seemed generally suspicious of the world outside Boston.

For a number of reasons James Michael Curley, almost alone, stepped off the Smith bandwagon on June 13, 1931. Having worked assiduously for the New Yorker in 1928, Curley believed that his voter registration drive had opened the way to victory. For his assistance, though, Curley had received no booty. In addition, the decision to jettison Smith derived from a sagacious political reading: a Roman Catholic, after having lost so decisively to Hoover, had virtually no chance of being renominated. Most of all, the Mayor aspired to the leadership of the Democratic party in Massachusetts, but Walsh and Ely, both ardent Smith backers, thwarted him. By keeping the "Happy Warrior" from the Presidency, Curley could leapfrog his political rivals in the Commonwealth and establish a firm claim to higher office when his term as mayor expired. [4]

Curley naturally enough tried to avoid explanations for his rupture with the Smith forces which would have made him appear self-serving, and he later claimed to have told friends that the "Happy Warrior" had changed. "He had lost the common touch," wrote Curley. "Having discarded his brown derby for a tall hat, he had wrapped himself up in Du Pont cellophane and Morgan ticker tape." [5] But Curley, ever the artful, practical politician, found it just as easy to veer in more conservative directions if his own interests would be advanced. That the Mayor preferred the wealthy Owen D. Young, until it became evident that the conservative General Electric magnate had no realistic chance of winning, demonstrates that ideological incongruities troubled Curley not at all. Simultaneous to his courtship of Young, he maintained contact with Roosevelt and lauded the New York governor's "splendid exemplification of popular government in our country's largest commonwealth." [6]

On June 11, 1931, Curley docked in New York City after an eventful five-week foray through the courts of Europe. [7] By accident or design, he and Roosevelt found themselves on the same train between New York and Providence, and the two discussed politics. While the conversation remains obscure, Curley pledged his support and apparently mentioned the position of Secretary of the Navy as a fitting reward. Roosevelt is reported to have stated that he "knew of no reason why Curley couldn't have the post." [8] The two arranged to meet again on June 13 north of Boston at the Manchester-by-the-Sea estate of Colonel Edward House, formerly Woodrow Wilson's most intimate adviser.

The Manchester conclave brought together Republicans and Democrats alike, and while those in attendance indicated that "politics was taboo," the occasion turned out to be pivotal. Roosevelt and his aides-de-camp Louis Howe and Henry Morgenthau, Jr., wooed pro-Smith Senators Walsh and Coolidge, but they did not need to persuade Curley. As the conferees emerged to face a mob of newspapermen and newsreel photographers, Curley seized the occasion to endorse F.D.R., thus becoming the first big city mayor to declare his fealty. "We have been making history here today," he stated. "Franklin Delano Roosevelt is the hope of the nation." Although Senator Walsh for a moment stood by in ominous silence, he emerged with a strengthened determination to work for Smith, while Curley hurried back to Boston to publicize the Jovian qualities of his newly discovered leader. "If it means but one vote more for the election of Roosevelt," Curley told an audience three days later, "I should be willing to act as a ticket taker at the Democratic Convention, rather than as nominee for the office of Vice President." The Mayor very nearly went to Chicago as ticket taker, and Roosevelt was advised to stay out of the state because of acrimonious factionalism. [9]

By the time Al Smith visited Boston for a fund-raising dinner in January 1932, the Roosevelt candidacy was slowly taking hold. A message sent by F.D.R. "provoked a real demonstration," LaRue Brown enthusiastically reported to his friend. While Smith still had "a host of passionate admirers," continued Brown, "the hysterical outburst which has hitherto marked his showing himself to a Boston gathering was lacking." Rather than attributing Roosevelt's inroads to Curley's ardent politicking, Brown urged his classmate to disassociate himself from the Mayor of Boston. Roosevelt, however, declined to accept this advice.[10]

When the Massachusetts Democratic Committee announced the delegates to the party's national convention on January 26, 1932, no avowed Roosevelt supporter made the list. Although the state organization described its representatives as uncommitted, Curley immediately made known his intentions of entering a rival slate in the April preprimary, even before he had tested the allegiance of the delegation. Moreover, Smith's announcement on Febuary 7 that he intended to be a candidate, an event which created greater excitement in Boston than it did in New York City, convinced Curley that no reconciliation was possible. Indeed, the day after Smith's announcement, the Democratic members of the Boston City Council, save for four who were absent, unanimously endorsed Smith for the Presidency as "the greatest Democrat of all time." In addition, the two principal candidates, Smith and Roosevelt, were making venomous remarks about each other. As the *Globe* reminded its readers in commenting on the friction between Roosevelt and his predecessor as Governor of New York, "Neither Damon nor Pythias, whose beautiful friendship is recorded in the classics, ever succeeded the other in public office." Given no encouragement by Roosevelt to seek a compromise, it is understandable why Curley took a hard line. And with statements by Senator Walsh that it would be "ungrateful" of him not to support the "Happy Warrior," combined with the Mayor's own drive for power, there seemed little likelihood that a truce would come about—at least not at Curley's instigation.[11]

The chasm within the Massachusetts Democracy had not yet reached unbridgeable proportions, however, and the neutrality of several party members might have been preserved had Curley assumed a less bellicose posture. When LaRue Brown told Roosevelt that he would not win a single delegate in an election, the governor reacted with "manifest astonishment" and asked Brown to initiate a peace conference. Brown and Robert Jackson of New Hampshire, then Secretary of the Democratic Committee, brought together Ely,

Walsh, and the pro-Smith State Chairman, Frank J. Donahue, at the Hotel Lenox on March 10. Roosevelt's negotiators now had leverage, since, two days before, the New Yorker had swept to victory in the New Hampshire primary, and Senator Walsh was at the point of acceding to a request that at least two delegates favorable to F.D.R. be included. At that very moment, the telephone rang, Walsh picked it up, and visibly flushed. Curley had mischievously congratulated Smith on withdrawing, Smith had accused Curley of puting him "in a false light" with his friends in Massachusetts, and the Mayor had invoked the poetry of Sir Walter Scott to accuse the unhappy warrior of lying: "Oh, what a tangled web we weave,/ When first we practice to deceive." "That 'tore it,' " Brown later recalled. "Whether Mr. Curley's timing was fortuitous or intentional I cannot say. It was effective." [12]

With détente out of the question, Curley—aided by Roosevelt's son James—launched a signature drive to put delegates' names on the ballot.[13] Of necessity, the F.D.R. slate attracted second-echelon Democrats, all unknown except for Curley and James Roosevelt— and possibly James T. Moriarty of the Boston Central Labor Union, one of the very few members of that body to come over to the New York governor at such an early date. Smith supporters accused the pair of dragooning municipal employees, haranguing City Hall scrubwomen, and threatening the welfare department with a cutoff of funds in order to gather signatures. Smith's backers, in turn, repeatedly charged that Curley was using Roosevelt as a steppingstone to the governorship. Each time the Mayor denied the allegation.

With James Roosevelt frequently at his side, Curley toured the Commonwealth to denounce "Silk-hat Al" and to portray F.D.R. as a "modern Messiah," but on party primary day the electorate rejected Curley's bid. Boston elected delegates committed to Smith by a 5-3 margin, and Curley, in his own quest for a seat, carried only a single ward in Roxbury, an area of mixed ethnicity and lower incomes. Across Massachusetts, the average Smith delegate polled 141,920 votes to 38,540 for the Roosevelt slate. Letters poured into Albany attributing the setback less to a repudiation of the New York governor than to a vote against Curley. Furthermore, Roosevelt's lieutenants agreed with the verdict of *The Times:* the defeat had put "a chock under the Roosevelt bandwagon." Yet Curley had taken a candidate with whom Bostonians were not familiar, and, at least in his own city, the greatest Smith stronghold in the nation, he had detached three of every eight voters, almost all of whom had probably voted for the Catholic in 1928. Indeed, it is highly doubtful that Roosevelt would have done as well without Curley's leadership, and for a time he stuck with the Mayor, lauding his "magnificent" and "practically single-handed fight against the entire state machine." [14]

Smith's April victory reenforced Ely's obduracy. "So far as I am concerned, I have no second choice," he said as he prepared to leave for the Chicago Convention. "But if I am obliged to make a second choice, it will not be Governor Roosevelt." Charging that Roosevelt's strategists were guilty of "double-dealing" and "ruthlessness," he further accused them of "trying to circumvent the hopes of the people." [15] At Chicago, Ely was granted the honor of nominating Smith, whom he saluted as "a modern Andrew Jackson, a positive, virile, straight-speaking, plain-thinking statesman." "Now that the tide has turned, shall we turn him aside?" asked Ely. Roars of "No!" sounded through the convention, and the Massachusetts banner shot into the air as the organist played "How Dry I Am." Smith planted a kiss on Ely's cheek, and Herbert Bayard Swope, the newspaper publisher, said, "It's the greatest speech ever made in a national convention since Roscoe Conkling nominated Blaine in the Cleveland Convention." [16] On the first four ballots, Massachusetts held firm for Smith.

But on those same roll calls the Bay State representatives heard a hauntingly familiar voice from the adjacent delegation deliver six votes for Roosevelt. That voice belonged to Alcalde Jaime Miguel Curleo. Undeterred by his election setback, the indomitable mayor had gone to Chicago ostensibly to cheer for Roosevelt, and when the head of the Puerto Rican delegation was called home by illness in his family, Curley had replaced him.[17] Ely denounced his presence as "insulting to the Commonwealth" and "an undemocratic subver-

sion of the will of its voters," but the Credentials Committee found
the Mayor's papers in perfect order. Curley regaled the press with
lengthy recitations about his new constituents, prefaced his second-
ing speech for John Nance Garner as Vice President with a reference to "the beautiful island of Porto Rico" which he proudly represented, and responded to roll calls in a Spanish accent. As the
Massachusetts delegates watched in consternation when Roosevelt's
total moved beyond the two-thirds' requirement, James Michael
Curley savored the moment. Having been ostracized by the Democratic leaders in his own state, Curley quite obviously enjoyed
seeing them writhe.

James Roosevelt and James Michael Curley, rejected in the 1932 Mas-
sachusetts primary, arrive at LaSalle Station in Chicago for the Democratic
National Convention. The Mayor of Boston, seated with the delegation from
Puerto Rico, delivered his vote for Roosevelt as Don Jaime Miguel Curleo.
Boston Public Library, Print Department.

Electrified by Curley's audacity, the Mayor's supporters greeted him tumultuously upon his return from Chicago. Crowds slowed his train to a crawl as it moved eastward across Massachusetts, and his return to Boston resembled Lenin's arrival at the Finland Station. For city workers, the occasion was a command performance. As the Fire Department Band played "Wearin' of the Green" and "Tammany," Curley's entourage paraded to the Boston Common, where perhaps the largest gathering ever assembled in the Northeast to view a political leader awaited him. Hailed as "the greatest Roman of them all," he sniped at the Smith wing of the party and, in his best accent, revealed the discovery made by other island delegates that Spanish blood coursed through his veins.[18] The crowd thundered its approval. After years of fanatical attachment to Al Smith, the multitude that cheered the Mayor on the Common that evening, presumably many of them unemployed, appeared to have gone over to new heroes—Curley and Roosevelt.

Party regulars, on the other hand, were dismayed. Keenly disappointed by the rejection of Smith, with all its religious, ethnic, and ideological overtones, they nevertheless attacked Curley rather than Roosevelt, for, above all, eventual control of federal patronage in Massachusetts might very well be at stake. In Westfield, where 10,000 greeted Ely, a delegate held aloft a sign saying, "Under the Porto Rican Sway of Judas Myself Curley." Members of the Boston City Council charged that the homecoming of "Senor Jaime Miguel Staccato Obligato Curley" had been paid for by a misuse of the taxpayers' money. "Representatives of these foreign countries and islands," declaimed Councilor Kelly of Dorchester, had no right to a city-financed demonstration "to match the importance of the banana king of Porto Rico." [19]

The fracas left Franklin Roosevelt with unpleasant choices, and skillful maneuvering was demanded. Informed of the "intense bitterness" in Massachusetts by Felix Frankfurter, Roosevelt was urged to smooth things over with Ely. But Roosevelt thought the governor to be "an awful ass," a man who had "overstepped the bounds of decency at the Convention." [20] On the other hand, the New Yorker looked upon Curley as something of a clown, while realizing at the same time that " 'this fellow has won practically every time he runs for something in Massachusetts, and he can't hurt me.' " [21] When in mid-July Roosevelt's yawl, *Myth II*, docked at Marblehead, the nominee talked politics with Massachusetts leaders, Ely and Curley excluded. Soon after, Joseph A. Maynard, for eight years the Boston Port Surveyor during Wilson's Presidency and a friend of Ely's and LaRue Brown's, was named to the vacant position of Democratic State Chairman instead of Curley, and the Mayor humbly promised to be a "self-effacing" volunteer in the campaign. Still Ely balked, and although meetings with Farley and Roosevelt ended his formal holdout on July 31, the Governor's expressions of sadness over Smith's defeat and his reluctance to mention Roosevelt by name testified to his continuing obstinacy.

Curley, in contrast, made both ideological and tactical adjustments. During his months of campaigning in Massachusetts he had learned that however moderate Roosevelt might have appeared to the American Left, and even to many liberals, Boston's ward leaders generally felt menaced by the Democratic standard-bearer. As tough old Martin Lomasney put it to "Honey Fitz" Fitgerald in the pre-election months: "The man's a radical; he'll ruin the country. . . ." Accordingly, the Mayor showed less inclination to present Roosevelt as a progressive candidate than he had in the April primary, and Curley's first words to his constituents after Chicago assured them that the Democratic platform was "in no measure as radical as that adopted by the Continental Congress 156 years ago." [22] Moreover, Curley at last decided that with the state organization in the driver's seat, it would be better for him to adopt a low profile in Massachusetts and tour the country for Roosevelt. Thus, on September 1 he embarked on a month-long, 8,000-mile, hundred-speech trip. Boston newspapers buried accounts of the journey, which may have been just as well, since Curley's jeremiads against Hoover made him the *enfant terrible* of the Democratic party. [23]

During Curley's absence, the Ely-Walsh contingent ran almost no campaign at all, and a Republican drive picked up steam. Speakers

Franklin Roosevelt begins his 1932 New England tour with Mayor Curley at his side. Curley, *persona non grata* with most power brokers in his party, soon removed himself from the local campaign and toured the West on F.D.R.'s behalf. The *Boston Globe*.

at the opening rally for Hoover at Faneuil Hall castigated the prohibitive cost of bureaucracy in Washington, and the titans of Ward 5 contributed large sums to preach the Gospel of Economy, scorning "quack remedies having a superficial appeal." And while the Mayor of Boston sauntered through the West, the G.O.P. lured the Democratic State Committee into a discourse over which party more implacably opposed unbalanced budgets and the extension of government. In truth, speakers of both parties sounded not unlike Roosevelt himself in his Pittsburgh address of October 19, 1932, where he counseled fiscal restraint. Hoover's aides, buoyed by *Literary Digest* polls indicating a Republican victory in the Bay State, and by rumors that Senator Walsh had retired from the campaign, decided not to waste the President's time in Massachusetts.

Indeed, political soundings in Boston suggested that the turnout for Al Smith in 1928 might not be repeated. In the first week of October, the Boston Central Labor Union (BCLU) failed by a three-vote margin to endorse Roosevelt, as the Republican president of the Building Trades Council, E. A. Johnson, kept his powerful delegation in line, and a small contingent on the left cast ballots for Norman Thomas. Other disappointed Smith supporters, forming an unholy alliance with Republicans, disseminated literature attributing Roosevelt's nomination to an anti-Catholic campaign at the Chicago Convention. "Massachusetts needs prayerful attention from the high command," LaRue Brown counseled Roosevelt.[24] Some observers predicted that Democrats would cast a large protest vote "in honor of Al Smith," with Hoover and even Norman Thomas the beneficiaries. The impending arrival in Boston of Smith himself for a crucial Democratic rally on October 27 so vexed Curley that he bluntly stated his intention not to attend. Later, Curley changed his mind, but as a packed Boston Arena audience lustily applauded Smith, boos and catcalls greeted the Mayor.

To counteract the divisiveness, Curley instinctively turned to the machinations of a traditional urban boss. Described to Roosevelt as a man with "a fine American mind, a good Irish heart, and a clever Jewish head," the Mayor toured Czechoslovakian, Syrian, Polish, and Greek clubhouses and churches. Curley summoned department heads and told them that if Hoover were to win, city and county workers could expect to contribute 10 percent of their pay to welfare. He demanded that his top officials compel every municipal employee to register for the election, and he allegedly shook down City Hall workers for $10,000 by selling $1 Roosevelt-Garner medallions and a certificate of enrollment saying, "The Shareholders of America." Curley strong-armed private welfare agencies by threatening to deny the support of the mayor's office should any director publicly support Hoover. Other backers of the Democratic standard-bearer fought the charge of Roosevelt's alleged anti-Catholicism by circulating cards which read: "For the sake of your family ELECT ROOSEVELT—Remember the vicious attack made in 1928 on our Church by Hoover's hirelings." [25]

Machtpolitik Boston-style, however, acted as a less important force than the ravages of the Great Depression. From the desperate wards where unemployment ran between 35 and 40 percent came pleas for new leadership. On outer Tremont Street in Roxbury the newly formed Colored Democratic League impored black voters to forget the party of Lincoln. Several of the ethnic newspapers that found their way into the neighborhoods of the poor—the *Italian News*, the *Boston Dielli* (Lithuanian), the *Jewish Advocate*—filled their pages with tributes to Roosevelt, while the Syrian-American Club also stumped for the Democrat. At Our Lady of Ostrobrama Church, a center for Polish-Americans, jobless parishioners heard their priest argue that the party of high protective tariffs had failed. As Hoover faltered, an unemployed Irishman outlined what the next President of the United States should be like.

> I want him to be a man whose every thought and deed is for the well-being of ALL of his fellow men, the planter in the fields, the puddler in the mills as well as the plutocrat in his counting room; of EVERY American from the festering hovels of poverty to the perfumed ramparts of affluence. I want him to be a man the mere mention of whose name will click my heels together and snap my hand up in a salute to "My President!" [26]

In a city made desolate by joblessness, the Central Labor Union had second thoughts, and, on October 21, the AFL locals turned to a resolution which spoke of "the economic crimes against our people." By a thumping margin of 65–15, the delegates to the BCLU reversed the anti-Roosevelt verdict which they had delivered just three weeks earlier. "Labor as never before in its history needs friends in high places," the BCLU declared.[27]

In the final days before the election, the warring factions of the Democratic party, seemingly separated from the concerns of the poor, attempted to come together, and they did so at the lowest common denominator. While it is questionable how much any campaign performs an educative function, Boston, in need of guidance toward less parochial outlooks, was treated not to illumination but to clamorous attacks on Hoover. Thus, by eschewing affirmative appeals, Curley and Smith shared the same rostrum at the Roosevelt Rally in the Hub on October 27 despite their incompatibility. In fact, for all his reluctance to mention Roosevelt by name, Smith exceeded expectations by bitterly assailing Hoover.[28] Editorial endorsements followed his appearance, and more holdouts came over to Roosevelt, though not always with ease, as the case of Martin Lomasney demonstrates. At the forty-ninth Sunday-before-election convocation of the Hendricks Club, the normally unflappable West End leader appeared rattled. Lomasney implored his obedient followers to "forget the bitterness of the Smith defeat and vote for Hoover." When gales of laughter subsided, the Mahatma meekly explained, "After listening so much on the radio a fellow doesn't know where he is." Moments later, the word "Roosevelt" rolled off his tongue.[29]

On October 31, 1932, Roosevelt visited Boston. He arrived late, and some empty seats dotted the unheated hall where a restless audience had been kept waiting. His speech gave Bostonians one of their few direct exposures to a coherent argument for federal activism, and unsettled those critics who felt he had been vacillating.[30] Hoover and the 5,000 men in control of American industry had joined "the chorus of fear," stated Roosevelt, and instead of intoning dreary anthems, the government needed to assume responsibility for increasing purchasing power. "Grim poverty stalks throughout the land," he asserted. "It embitters the present and darkens the future." To arrest the Depression, Washington had to engage in "less fact finding and more thinking." "Immediate relief of the unemployed is the immediate need of the hour," he averred, and wherever local government failed to provide money, "the Federal Government owes the positive duty of stepping into the breach." Roosevelt also recommended the use of federal power to provide temporary work "in the national forests, on flood prevention, and on the development of water-way projects." "I decline to accept present conditions as inevitable or beyond control," he concluded. "I decline to stop at saying, 'It might have been worse.' " [31]

Roosevelt's eloquence evoked a prolonged ovation, and for an instant rescued the Massachusetts campaign from the spectacle of Democratic infighting, a good bit of conservative oratory, and from the diversionary issue of Prohibition.[32] Whether his Boston speech, coming in a wasteland otherwise innocent of serious political inquiry, prompted voters to give him the "liberal mandate" asked for by Norman Hapgood and a small group of progressives at the Boston City Club four days later is doubtful.[33] Democratic leaders had converted only at the last moment, and their reluctant journey into Roosevelt's corner smacked of opportunism no less than had Curley's initial discovery of the New Yorker. Moreover, it was by no means clear that the Boston Archdiocese's outspoken opposition to significant change had been overcome. "Collectivism is impossible in modern society," spokesmen for Cardinal O'Connell were saying. "You cannot build any government on legislation that strikes at the family, motherhood, and the Christian religion." [34] While many a jobless worker may well have considered the Archdiocese anachronistic, and while the words of the Boston *Pilot* surely did not preclude another Democratic landslide of dimensions reminiscent of 1928, the frantic last-minute efforts to inject a liberal punch into the campaign largely fizzled in Boston.

On November 8, 1932, Roosevelt triumphed. For all the prophecies of doom, he bested Hoover in Massachusetts and rolled up a stunning 101,000-vote margin in the city. Curleyites could hardly have asked for more: Hoover picked up only three wards; no city with a population above 500,000 gave Roosevelt a percentage of the total vote higher than the 67.1 percent harvested in Boston; and the Democratic plurality narrowly exceeded Smith's in 1928, both in the city and across the Bay State. Even the beleaguered cities of Detroit and Chicago accorded Roosevelt only 57.2 percent and 55.2 percent of their Presidential vote respectively, while Philadelphia, Buffalo, and Rochester all ended up in the Republican column. Moreover, in Boston, Roosevelt captured only a 1.6 percent smaller share of the total vote than did Joseph B. Ely in his gubernatorial race, whereas in most cities F.D.R. ran even farther behind local Democratic candidates. In every important particular, Bostonians reenforced the verdict of 1928.[35]

Yet any election reveals soft spots, and Boston was no exception. The returns indicated traces of the intraparty squabbles which had preceded the balloting, especially when the test of voter turnout is applied. Curley's feverish registration drive enrolled 5,500 more Bostonians than had been eligible in 1928, but 15,998 fewer went to the polls than in the Hoover-Smith contest. Across the nation, in contrast, 26.5 percent more people voted than in 1928.[36] The decline in voter participation showed up in the more well-to-do Irish precincts, and to a lesser extent among the lower-income Irish of South Boston.[37] The city's small Negro vote fell off very slightly, and at the opposite socioeconomic pole, the Beacon Hill–Back Bay electorate sat out in numbers proportionally larger than any other area of the city. Jewish, East European, and occasional Italian precincts alone resisted the tendency to stay home, and they, rather than the Irish, provided the net upward shift in the winning Democratic margin which allowed Roosevelt to garner a larger edge over Hoover than Smith had recorded in 1928. As it was, Boston gave Roosevelt the smallest increment over 1928 of any major city, a scant 0.3 percent compared to 9.8 percent for nineteen large metropolitan areas recently studied,[38] suggesting that the Great Depression produced less volatile results than when a Catholic had run for President. In addition, Republicans actually managed to add three more seats to their already substantial majority in the Massachusetts House of Representatives. But, at most, these deviations from 1928 represented no more than faint hints that trouble might lie ahead, especially should Roosevelt not conform to the moderate image he himself had helped to create during the campaign, an image made far more conservative in Boston by the Democratic State Committee.

Whatever the post-mortems, Bostonians readily agreed that the election had catapulted the premier Roosevelt enthusiast into an enviable position. "All hail Mayor Curley, the country's original Roosevelt booster," the *Italian News* proclaimed.[39] Speculation began at once about the appropriate political laurels which Roosevelt would bestow. The President-elect titillated the Mayor's imagination, thanking him for his "unflagging devotion to our cause" and adding, "When we return from Warm Springs you and I must get together to talk things over." [40] Curley's trips to Georgia, Washington, and Hyde Park kept rumors alive during the entire interregnum period, but by the time of Roosevelt's inauguration the Mayor was still empty-handed.

How to deal with the patronage demands of controversial urban bosses—the Ed Kellys, the Boss Crumps, the Curleys—was no easy matter for Roosevelt, and what to do about the Mayor of Boston had become even more puzzling by February 1933. At that point, Erland Fish, the president of the Massachusetts Senate, chaired public sessions at Gardner Auditorium which stigmatized Curley and his treasurer, Edmund Dolan. Investigating the Curley administration along the lines of Samuel Seabury's damaging probe into the affairs of Mayor James J. Walker of New York, Fish not only summoned conservative Republican organizations to testify, but he also opened the rostrum to anti-Curley Democrats. Frankie Kelly, for one, called the Mayor a "Santa Claus" who leaked city funds to favored contractors and built "antelope houses with the peoples' money at Franklin Park while people starved." [41] The Fish investigation prompted a flood of letters which complained to Roosevelt about the Mayor's supposed venality, likened Curley to Jimmy Walker, and argued that the Bostonian's appointment would discredit the new administration before it took office. Witnesses for Curley fought back, but the innuendos lived on. Under the circumstances, Roosevelt had little choice but to let Curley stew, while the Mayor's foes chortled over his discomfiture.

Yet the rebuff had serious consequences. It not only embarrassed Curley painfully, but also prejudiced the chances of success for the New Deal by hurting F.D.R.'s standing with the Mayor and his municipal appointees, the very people with whom the New Dealers would have to work. In addition, the rejection gave the Ely-Walsh contingent a chance to regain the momentum it had lost on November 8, 1932. Far from declaring politics adjourned, Democratic leaders squabbled more furiously than ever. As Roosevelt prepared for his inauguration, the local Democratic party still was divided. Therefore, no special prescience was needed to foresee that whatever patronage Roosevelt might ultimately confer, and whatever financial grants a new Democratic Congress might bestow, there would be strong political repercussions in Boston.

As Democrats jockeyed for power in the interval between Roosevelt's election and his inauguration on March 4, the Great Depression's toll mounted at a steady rate. Since Boston's aggregate payroll for those connected with manufacturing slumped less than 2 percent in January and February, it was not so much that the Depression struck the city with renewed ferocity as that it would not relent. Off to Hyde Park rushed James Michael Curley to urge the construction of cantonments for the unemployed, and well might be have done so: 110 Boston trade unions reported that 29 percent of their members had no jobs. Unionized garment workers could not enforce wage provisions in their contracts, and the AFL's Building Trades Association, calling for an emergency cutback to a twenty-four–hour week, repudiated striking plasterers who resisted the shortened schedule. But in many industries even twenty-four hours would have looked like a bonanza. National Biscuit Company employees were down to two days a week, and the number of partially employed continued to rise in all industries. Thousands canceled insurance policies that had been written by Boston firms, and several corporations ceased paying dividends. The atmosphere in the entrepreneurial community assumed a funereal quality.[42]

During the critical period when Boston waited for Roosevelt, municipal government operated under serious handicaps, some of which were traceable to the political ambitions of James Michael Curley. Since members of the city council firmly believed that Curley would receive an important federal appointment, the council presidency suddenly attracted a host of aspirants. Were Curley to go to Washington, the council president would become mayor. Debate between pro-Curley and pro-Ely councilors was so acerbic that expletives had to be deleted from the record. Hence, in its first sessions in January, the city council transacted little constructive business—still more evidence that the party of the New Deal in Boston had fallen into disarray.

Although not plunging into the abyss, municipal finances teetered at the brink. More than a quarter of the 1932 property tax had not come in by the time of Roosevelt's inauguration, and over 120,000 citizens still owed their 1932 poll tax. As a result, police missed pay days, firemen and other municipal employees beseeched the Central Labor Union to help them organize against Curley's forced contributions to the welfare department, and the daily pay of the city's snow shovelers was pared from $5 to $3.20. Moreover, the city council yielded to the pleas of real-estate owners that property valuations be slashed by 25 percent, and escalating interest charges on tax-anticipation notes—nearly three times the rate paid by Hartford, Connecticut—signaled that banks were beginning to question whether the city was, after all, an excellent credit risk. On the brighter side, municipal officials still did not have to face a situation as serious as many other large cities were confronting. Cleveland, approximately the same size as Boston, had over $60 million in taxes outstanding at the same time the Hub's delinquencies totaled $18 million. Whereas Detroit defaulted on debt due in February, Boston had not yet caved in. Nevertheless, the mood at City Hall was somber.

The idea that distress could be alleviated by voluntary efforts was severely tested during the winter of 1932–1933. As another emergency fund drive commenced, volunteers heard Owen D. Young say, "You cannot throw tea overboard in 1773 and fail to raise $5 million in 1933." Yet for all the bravado of the Emergency Relief Committee, organizers behind the scenes expected difficulties, and they were correct. Formerly sure-fire devices to raise money—holding a dance aboard the liner *Laconia* in Boston Harbor, for example—did not work. Two months after the drive opened, only $2,600,000 had been pledged, and officials of private social agencies as diverse as the YMCA, the Family Welfare Society, and the Permanent Charity Fund began to swing to the view that "public welfare agencies must bear the burden of relief for some time to come." [43]

As the emergency worsened, the prospect of help from the state government looked inauspicious. Not only had the election of 1932, and the harsh words exchanged thereafter between Joseph B. Ely and James Michael Curley, made cooperation next to impossible, but the Democratic governor rededicated himself to strict economy. Republicans also cautioned against "reckless extravagance." House Speaker Leverett Saltonstall, for instance, identified the "Forgotten Man" as the small homeowner, and advised salary cuts for state workers to spare the middle class from further taxation. Only in its decision to allow Massachusetts communities to borrow on titles held against taxpayers in arrears did the legislature offer assistance in any important particular.

With rudderless leadership at the local, state, and national levels, with no clear idea of what needed to be done, and indeed lacking confidence that anything would be done, a growing number of Bostonians agreed that action of some sort at least was imperative. Speaking at the Ford Hall Forum, the Reverend Arthur Kinsolving of Trinity Episcopal Church asked how the Saviour would have proceeded had He found 13 million unemployed, and the clergyman asserted that "even now Christ seeks to prompt those in authority to provide employment for the needy." When the columnist Walter Lippmann argued in the pages of the Boston *Globe* that Roosevelt should be given greater power over expenditures than any President had ever had, support came from unexpected quarters. Henry Shattuck—Brahmin, fiscal conservative, and long a guardian of the Massachusetts treasury—wrote in favor of Presidential spending. "The modern state," he said, "particularly in a time of emergency, cannot function with the required responsiveness and despatch if we hang on to the concept of legislative power handed down from colonial days." [44]

On a trek through Boston during the last weeks of Herbert Hoover's Presidency, no one could have missed signs of the Great Depression. Along streets lined by commodious residences in West Roxbury and Hyde Park, college-educated men "look[ed] foolish with new hoes, in January, out in front of . . . homes of their neighbors." In a vacant loft on Stuart Street in the heart of the downtown shopping district, the unemployed joined the Mutual Commercial Corporation, an organization which bartered labor services either for scrip or for unsalable goods. The corporation, reported the *Globe*, functioned like "a lumber camp or a coal industry or any other isolated industrial establishment" whose employees could not get to the cities to trade. Only a few blocks away, Harvard professors instituted courses for the unemployed at the Old South Meeting House, and Ethel Barrymore ate five-cent beef stew at the Volunteers of America's Washington Street cafeteria to publicize the need for contributions. Governor Ely could be seen canvassing the North End door to door to raise money for the unemployed (he collected $399), while James Michael Curley scoured the market district for funds. Cardinal O'Connell cabled $2,000 from his vacation retreat in the Bahamas, and the Harvard polo team staged an exhibition to benefit the jobless. But these were vacant gestures. Outside both City Hall and the Boston Welfare Department demonstrations reached epidemic proportions. Responding to hundreds of letters asking for joyful music to bolster morale, Arthur Fiedler of the Boston Pops visited the Boston Psychopathic Hospital for advice. The sensibilities of a grieving person, Fiedler was told, would be outraged by cheerful compositions. Play sad music, and the unemployed would feel they had "communed with a spirit that has known sadness so deep that [their] own amounts to little." Fiedler tried both the lilting "Overture" to *The Pirates of Penzance* and the lugubrious finale of *Symphonie Pathetique*. Neither seemed to help. In such a setting, the Greater Boston Federation of Churches directed that prayers be said for the President-elect. [45]

At South Station, at the ferry slips along Dock Street, and even at East Boston Airport, 6,000 people assembled for the trip to Washington and the inauguration of Franklin Delano Roosevelt. As Bostonians neared the capital, back home limousines were arriving at the Federal Reserve. Through the cloudy, cold night of March 3, police guarded the building while, inside, the city's most prominent financiers pondered whether Boston's banks, closed for the weekend, should be reopened. As reporters maintained their nocturnal vigil outside, the city seemed frighteningly still.

6

The Coming of the New Deal

Sometime past 2:00 A.M., just hours before the swearing-in of Franklin Roosevelt on March 4, 1933, the Executive Committee of the Boston Clearing House Association recommended closing the city's banks and imposing an embargo on gold. Across the wires to Washington, a telegram from the Central Labor Union sped noiselessly through the night, imploring the President to say something about wage cuts. At the *Globe,* reporters surrounded the teletype, waiting tensely for Roosevelt's words: "Only a foolish optimist can deny the dark realities of the moment," the President stated. "This nation asks for action, and action now." [1] The new order had begun.

Before heading back to Boston after the inauguration, Joseph B. Ely proclaimed the closing of all Massachusetts banks, and, at 4:00 P.M. on March 5, Roosevelt ordered a national bank holiday. Ely, speaking to worried Bostonians over the radio that evening, recalled the President's "vibrant and human declaration" of the day before. "Yesterday was cold and sunless; today has been warm and the sun shone. The weather typifies our feelings." Yet even as the Governor was telling the people of Massachusetts that "it is a patriotic obligation to remain calm," the Boston police were preparing elaborate defenses of every financial house in the city against attacks by irate depositors. "Stir the embers upon the hearth," Ely bravely continued. "Let the kettle boil upon the stove. Break bread and enjoy a good old-fashioned evening at home." [2]

In the Massachusetts legislature the next morning Ely sought an emergency banking statute which would "start us on the journey to more prosperous and contented times." Republican efforts to add restrictive amendments were shouted down. Heeding Ely's warning that "this is no time for legal quibbling," by 2:44 P.M. the Bay State legislators, in an unaccustomed display of unity and haste, had pushed through a law which sanctioned Ely's proclamation of March 4. The state banking commissioner was empowered to certify those houses which he considered sound, and, with only minor exceptions, the banks were to be open solely for purposes of deposit. [3]

During the emergency Bostonians pulled together. Prayers for Roosevelt and the safety of the nation were offered in Boston's Catholic churches and, at the direction of the Reverend Henry Knox Sherrill, an unprecedented corporate communion was held throughout the Episcopal Diocese of Massachusetts. Not only had Boston Republicans in the state legislature gone along with Ely, but the *Transcript*, normally an ardent advocate of laissez-faire, urged Congress to give Roosevelt "dictatorial authority" over the nation's banks. "The desperate temper of the people," said the *Transcript*, justified unprecedented remedies. [4] Despite the nearly total absence of shoppers, stores remained open, but instead of advertising merchandise retailers urged allegiance to Roosevelt. Uncle Eph, a fictitious Yankee rustic used in Raymond's Department Store ads, offered some typical advice:

> We're having an operation performed this week and while for a moment it is uncomfortable, the wound will heal quickly and conditions will be better than before, not like 1928 and '29. Surely we hope not coz those were the days in which the *disease was contracted*. Don't let's contract any more but keep a stiff upper lip, chin held high an poundeloutuvem an we'll kum out all rite. [5]

Bostonians followed Uncle Eph's dictum, responding with fortitude to their straitened circumstances. Food and fuel were rushed to welfare recipients, while at the other extreme Governor Ely confessed to reporters that on the day the banks closed he had "just enough for a shave." Hoarders disinterred colonial fractional currency, businessmen issued scrip, a hardware store took Boston Elevated tickets in lieu of cash, and several grocery stores accepted food orders on faith. "Lay aside the shutoff wrench!" Mayor Curley told the water department, and state institutions paid their employees in kind. On Sunday night, March 12, Bostonians gathered around their radios to listen to Roosevelt's first "fireside chat," and in a soothing voice the President assured them that the worst of the crisis had passed.[6]

When, on March 13, all banks in the Hub received permission from the federal government to unbar their doors, the President's words of reassurance seemed to have taken on a prophetic quality. Deposits surprisingly exceeded withdrawals, and encomiums were again lavished upon Roosevelt.[7] James Michael Curley extolled the "courage and vision" which had saved the nation from bankruptcy, and the Boston City Council passed a resolution praising "the summary, intelligent, and courageous action taken by President Roosevelt and Governor Ely." The council pledged "support and cooperation to the end that confidence and prosperity may be restored to our citizens."[8]

Conservative Bostonians were ecstatic over Roosevelt's first steps. The Economy Act of March 11, 1933—slashing payments to veterans, cutting back the wages of federal employees, and dismaying both groups—won enthusiastic commendation from Frederic Snyder of the Boston Chamber of Commerce. So, too, did the President's refusal to countenance a veterans' bonus, and Cardinal O'Connell, upon his return from vacation in the Bahamas, called F.D.R. "a God-sent man."[9] One of the Back Bay's most prominent Republicans, Henry Shattuck, wrote Senator Walsh that he thoroughly approved of the President's use of "broad and flexible powers," and he also lauded Roosevelt's ability to attack the Depression "in a broad national way rather than in a sectional way."[10]

When the Administration expedited passage of the Beer Bill, and Governor Ely signed a state measure legalizing beverages with alco-

With the coming of the New Deal, 3.2 beer flowed in Boston. Above, a drayman pulls up to the Commercial Brewing Company in Charlestown, his empty barrels soon to be filled with "Special Pilsner." Boston University School of Communication.

holic content of 3.2 percent, Boston celebrated as it had not done in years. Massive crowds surrounded the S. S. Pierce and Company warehouse on Brookline Avenue where "dignified matrons . . . and gentlemen in Chesterfield coats and derby hats" lugged away cases of ale, and "hundreds of Harvard and M.I.T. students arrived in sleek roadsters." Downtown cafés were jammed, and the sounds of Irish tenors reverberated from Charlestown to South Boston. Police looked the other way as revelers staggered homeward, having found

3.2 beer "interesting." [11] No move could have been more popular, and what would be known as "The Hundred Days" were just beginning.

"Our greatest primary task is to put people to work," Roosevelt had stated on March 4,[12] and in early April Bostonians saw in the Civilian Conservation Corps (CCC) the first tangible evidence that the federal government had committed itself to the direct recruitment of the unemployed. During the first six months' enrollment period, 18,000 youths between the ages of eighteen and twenty-five flocked to the Boston office of the CCC to enlist for work in the nation's forests. Providing the sons of families on relief with food, a barracks cot, uniforms, and $1 a day, the CCC also expected that recruits would send home $25 a month. To earn their stipend, the

Bostonians are taken by army truck to Fort Devens where they will begin their training as Civilian Conservation Corps (CCC) recruits. The *Boston Globe*.

CCC potato peelers at Fort Devens. Whether the young Bostonian at the right eventually warmed to the task is unknown. The *Boston Globe*.

young men had to cope with the hardships of a regimented life. After a rugged two-week conditioning period at Fort Devens, the corpsmen were transported in United States Army trucks to scattered campsites. Some lived in primitive tent villages; a few complained that veteran woodsmen pushed them beyond what their bodies, unaccustomed to physical labor, could endure. Most persevered, however, and the allure of six months in the forests continued to draw thousands of eager takers.

The pace of the Hundred Days dazzled Bostonians, and with lightninglike rapidity Congress rushed through additional legislation to sustain the unemployed. On May 12, 1933, Congress passed the Federal Emergency Relief Act, and ten days later the Federal Emergency Relief Administration (FERA), supported by a $500-million appropriation, came into being. Soon after, Roosevelt appointed Harry Hopkins to head the agency. Through Title II of the National Industrial Recovery Act (NIRA) of June 16, New Dealers attempted to stimulate recovery, and at the same time put the jobless to work on major public construction through Title II's spawn, the Public Works Administration (PWA). Congress entrusted the unprecedented sum of $3.3 billion to the cautious stewardship of Harold Ickes.

To those in municipal government, the CCC, FERA, and PWA had come none too soon, for in March and April, months when over 100,000 persons depended on public welfare and fully a third of the labor force held no jobs at all, the Boston City Council had repeatedly advocated 20-percent budget and tax reductions, and had slashed the wages of city workers. James Michael Curley had visited Roosevelt in both March and May, requesting that he lend cities money in anticipation of taxes, and after the Federal Emergency Relief Act was passed, the Mayor stated that the President was "the 'Moses' who will lead the people of America out of the land of darkness." [13]

Crews of FERA employees, most of them taken from municipal welfare lists, soon appeared in every corner of the city. Laboring for $15 a week, hundreds of women on sewing projects made clothing for the poor, and men removed old hulks and pilings from Boston Harbor. Grimy public buildings received needed scrubbings, public parks were weeded, and federal employees staffed recreation projects for the children of Boston. With over 4,000 indigent transients burdening municipal and private welfare agencies, the FERA established a center in Boston to which penniless seamen, vagrant children, and elderly tramps could turn for food and shelter. The 120,000 man-weeks of employment made possible in Boston by the FERA in 1933, although not impressive when set against the number of jobless in the city, nevertheless contrasted with the desultory approach of the Hoover administration. That more had not been provided, as will subsequently be seen, had much to do with local circumstances and not the New Deal. [14]

Five weeks after signing the Federal Emergency Relief Act,

Franklin Delano Roosevelt arrived in Boston. Thousands jammed South Station to greet the President, and tens of thousands saluted his caravan as it moved through the city on its way to Franklin, Jr.'s, graduation ceremonies at Groton. The reception was much more than a perfunctory turnout motivated by a desire to catch a glimpse of the nation's chief executive. The sense of motion imparted by the Hundred Days presaged better times for Boston's unemployed and underemployed work force, and Roosevelt clearly embodied their hopes. Whatever disappointment lingered on after Al Smith's defeat was not in evidence along the sidewalks of Boston on June 17, 1933.

Just one day before the President's visit to Boston, the National Industrial Recovery Act had been signed into law, and businessmen, too, were swept up in the New Deal's drive toward recovery. Heralded as the most comprehensive peacetime attempt to reorganize business in the history of the republic, the National Recovery Administration (NRA) aimed at bringing every employer under codes of fair practice governing hours, wages, and working conditions. The city's entrepreneurs entrained for Washington to protect their interests, and after six weeks of wrangling between business and labor, only the textile industry had enrolled, and New Dealers settled on a different strategy. Beginning in late July, employers were asked to sign the President's Reemployment Agreement (PRA) which established general guidelines for wages and hours. Commitment to PRA permitted the display of the Blue Eagle, the NRA's ensign of membership, and signified an intention to draft more detailed codes on an industry-by-industry basis. President Roosevelt was then to affix his signature, and the pact would become permanent. As the volcanic, bibulous head of the NRA, Hugh Johnson, explained to Bostonians at the Hotel Statler, the federal government would function as "a sort of Marquis of Queensberry . . . to keep the competitive struggle clean and leave as little human wreckage as possible in its wake." To those who thought the NRA repressive, Johnson commented, "Nobody ever heard Jack Dempsey complain of any hampering restrictions on his rugged individuality when Luis

James Farley exhorts Bostonians to adhere to the codes of the National Industrial Recovery Act. Boston Public Library, Print Department.

Firpo lifted him over the ropes into the typewriters, and he came back to floor Mr. Firpo four times in 40 seconds." [15]

On July 24, 1933, Roosevelt addressed his third fireside chat to the nation, calling upon employers to stage a "great summer offensive against unemployment." The normally crustaceous Chamber of Commerce at once picked sixty leaders, over 75 percent of them businessmen, to serve on the Boston Recovery Committee, and donated the second floor of its downtown building as headquarters for a massive enrollment campaign. Even the troglodytic president of the Chamber, Eliot Wadsworth, conceded that America was "in a state of mind to play the game," and that the experimental codes should be tried. A Kiwanis Club speaker believed the NRA campaign would be a "particularly thrilling . . . plunge into the unknown," and Boston's largest department stores immediately pledged full cooperation, the president of Raymond's saying, "We'll do our part and a damsite more [*sic*]." Emphasizing the precedent of World War I Victory Bond drives and the Boston Unemployment Relief Campaign of 1932–1933, and using many of the same techniques and personnel, the local recovery committee reported 10,000 employer pledges by August 1, the President's enrollment deadline. The Blue Eagle had become ubiquitous in Boston.[16]

In an effort to forestall infringements upon local autonomy, the Boston Recovery Committee redoubled its energies during August 1933 to demonstrate that business could, in fact, put its own house in order. The Dorchester Board of Trade, for instance, set up a "combat unit" headed by a general and colonels. To every theater in the city these soldiers of enterprise dispatched a Crusading Branch to give four-minute speeches touting NRA. Vowing cooperation, the Boston Central Labor Union, assisted by the Women's Trade Union League and the Consumers' League, helped make certain that employers were honoring PRA agreements, while clergy on "Rally Sunday" implored consumers to patronize only those stores 'that displayed the NRA emblem. "We must aim for the moon," said the rector of Trinity Church, "even though we hit the chimneypots." And the following day a thousand volunteers assembled in Faneuil Hall to hear Charles Francis Adams call upon Bostonians to unite behind the President. "This is a question of patriotism," he said, and indeed it seemed to be. Cannons boomed salutes on the Boston Common, and a squadron of airplanes left for Hyde Park to drop messages on Roosevelt's lawn heralding the drive's progress. The Boston Braves played an NRA benefit game against (appropriately) the Reds; an East Boston man, in a fit of heroic masochism, tatooed a Blue Eagle on his arm; and John McCormack led an "Over the Top" parade in Dorchester. The city once again mobilized as if at war.[17]

No one was unaffected by the New Deal. Tremors shook the business community when Roosevelt took the nation off the gold standard in April, and in the brokerage houses along State Street employees prepared detailed stock prospectuses as required by the Securities Act of 1933. Fortified by NIRA's Section 7(a), which guaranteed labor's right to organize for purposes of collective bargaining, unions in Boston began a resurgence. Textile and shoe manufacturers, beef distributors and the Boston Flour and Grain Exchange—all readied checks to pay the processing tax which the Agricultural Adjustment Act (AAA) demanded as a subsidy to farmers not to produce. At the Boston Housing Association (BHA) an exuberant staff worked late into the night, drafting slum-clearance proposals for submission to the Public Works Administration. In addition, the New Deal brought benefits to property owners: 3,000 applicants besieged the Home Owners' Loan Corporation (HOLC) on one day alone; bank accounts were now safeguarded by the Federal Deposit Insurance Corporation (FDIC). Never before in peacetime did so many people have to remaster the alphabet: FERA, PWA, CCC, NRA, AAA, FDIC, HOLC, and so on. Overnight, Washington had come to occupy a central place in the life of the city.

First the bank crisis, and then Roosevelt himself, had unquestionably made a number of conservative Bostonians see the world afresh. Albert Bigelow, Groton 'oo and Harvard '04, state senator and descendant of a famous textile family, though criticizing some aspects of the Hundred Days, muted his public statements about his former schoolmate. The same might be said of Eliot Wadsworth, also Harvard '04, and a political reactionary.[18] Speakers who flayed the selfishness of the moneychangers before rock-ribbed organizations like the New England Council drew not hisses but applause, as businessmen engaged in self-flagellation. Henry Shattuck, a supporter of Herbert Hoover and a dedicated opponent of government spending, confided to Republican Congresswoman Edith Nourse Rogers in June, "I believe that the President has done a remarkable job since he took office, and I believe that most people, regardless of party, think so too." [19] Even Episcopal Bishop William Lawrence chimed in. The clergyman, who for over half a century had been associated both with conservative economics and with implacable opposition to anarchism, urged his flock to "keep an open mind," "heed radicals," and "listen to reformers." [20] Nicola Sacco and Bartolomeo Vanzetti must have rolled over in their graves.

To sustain the enormous momentum generated by the Hundred Days, and to make the delicate, experimental new mechanisms work as they were intended, Roosevelt needed reliable assistants. Yet as he looked to the elected Democratic leaders in Boston, he could not have felt encouraged. Even as the President asked for unity, and even as the tempo of his programs accelerated, the bad vibrations of the Ely-Curley squabble, a feud which had been precipitated by the 1932 election, reverberated throughout Massachusetts. Lacking confidence in the mercurial Curley, and troubled both by the growing conservatism of Joseph B. Ely and by the questionable loyalty of the governor's partisans, Roosevelt eyed those who had kept aloof from the intraparty rift. Fortunately for the President, there were people in Boston he felt he could trust.

In a comfortable town house on Beacon Hill, on the night of November 5, 1932, the LaRue Browns, Andrew Peters and his wife, and Arthur and Helen Rotch had jubilantly listened to the election returns. Brown and Rotch, long associated with liberal causes, had been Roosevelt's classmates at Harvard (Peters had graduated in 1895). Coming of political age during the Progressive Era when Louis Brandeis had fought the traction magnates in Boston, Brown subsequently entered the Wilson administration as an assistant attorney general. A tireless worker for social justice, he had been active on behalf of Sacco and Vanzetti in the 1920s. Peters, a former Republican Mayor of Boston, had frequently involved himself in social work, and he had tried to rally the business community to new vistas after the crash. Capable of political ecumenism, he had for some time enjoyed a reputation among municipal reformers as a progressive—as had Helen Rotch. Mrs. Rotch, a Democratic Committeewoman for Massachusetts, had gone to the Chicago Convention as part of the Ely-Walsh delegation, yet her devotion to liberalism would instinctively make her loyal to the New Deal. Her husband, a Republican, had earned an enviable reputation as the New England Red Cross director during World War I, and he had contributed greatly to health services and to emergency relief drives in Boston thereafter. Twice Arthur Rotch had voted for the Democratic ticket—in 1916 for Woodrow Wilson, and now again for Franklin Roosevelt. "This may never reach you," Rotch wrote the President-elect, "but I could not help putting on paper how happy I am about your victory and how proud I am to have a clubmate [Harvard Club] as president." [21]

Over on Washington Street, the cer.ter of the retail district, the executive offices of Filene's Department Store buzzed with excitement over Roosevelt's election. E. A. Filene, considered the "Merchant Prince of Boston," and his brother, A. Lincoln Filene, were writing congratulatory messages, for neither man shared the business community's animus toward government spending, compulsory unemployment insurance, or other forms of federal activism. E. A. Filene, the more prolix of the brothers, had drawn heavy criticism in Boston by appealing directly to the jobless, implying that by backing Roosevelt they would, in effect, be voting themselves jobs. Although he told F.D.R. four days after the election that he was "not even secretly a socialist," he advised a cabinet appointment for Norman Thomas, believing that the gesture "would appeal to the masses and win their following." The struggle between "the best of the Old Capitalism and Socialism," Filene continued, would produce a synthesis, "the NEW CAPITALISM," and thus bloody revolution would be averted. [22]

The Filenes' principal executive officer, Louis Kirstein, also relished Roosevelt's triumph. Although a great admirer of Woodrow Wilson and Louis Brandeis, and a registered Democrat, he had during the 1920s supported Calvin Coolidge. When the Depression broke, Kirstein, like the Filenes, at first believed that businessmen were confronted by an internal problem which could be solved by unloading burdensome inventories, reducing prices, and bolstering purchasing power. Even in June 1932 he had stated that "if twelve experienced businessmen would devote themselves to . . . business conditions even for eight or ten hours at a stretch . . . automatically a solution . . . would unfold itself." [23] But by the autumn of 1932 his views had changed. Using the pages of the *Atlantic*, the esteemed Boston magazine which was published by Ellery Sedgwick, himself a friend of liberals in the Hub, Kirstein questioned those enterprisers who continued to claim special wisdom and the right to influence policy. The American habit of transmuting businessmen into masterminds, Kirstein stated, "carries its own measure of intoxication," but untrammeled plutocratic reign had to end. [24] His article shocked many of his friends in downtown Boston, and so too did his vote for Roosevelt. Yet to people like the LaRue Browns, Kirstein's service as one of the Overseers of the Public Welfare, his indispensable work on behalf of the Associated Jewish Philanthropies, his closeness to Felix Frankfurter, and his labors on behalf of West End House, Boston's oldest social settlement, stamped him as a man with a deeply developed commitment to a progressive outlook.

At 80 Boylston Street in the colonnaded Little Building, David K. Niles, whose parents had immigrated from Russia to the North End, presided over the Ford Hall Forum which, by the time of Roosevelt's election, had become not just a local but a national institution. For some twenty-five years, the Ford Hall Forum had sponsored almost every conceivable point of view and beamed its programs by radio throughout the United States. Since Niles assembled the participants, he had truly become the man who knew everyone. In Boston, he was closest to those who comprised the liberal community, and during the 1928 election he had worked out of the Democratic National Committee's headquarters in New York as director of the Progressive League for Al Smith. Four years later, he rallied progressive and independent voters for Roosevelt. Attempting to put a spark of liberalism into the Boston phase of the '32 campaign, he had mustered his friends for a late October trip to Groton to meet Roosevelt. At the same time, Niles orchestrated a progressive campaign for Joseph Ely out of Room 103 in the Hotel Lenox, and thus he had ingratiated himself to both the Ely and Roosevelt wings of the Democratic party.[25]

Niles's chief importance, whether volitional or not, was to be at the center of a third force in Boston politics, a force distinctly liberal and pro-Roosevelt, and one which transcended narrow partisanship. The informal group had no name, nor did it have any real constituency outside its own members. No one in it held public office, and almost as many independents and Republicans affiliated themselves as did Democrats. Nor did expectations of personal advancement play a part in holding together the circle in which Niles moved. Rather, the group's strength rested on bonds of friendship which had grown out of years of struggle for much the same causes—the American Civil Liberties Union, the NAACP, the Consumers' League, the Boston Council of Social Agencies. With few exceptions—and John Fahey, a newspaper publisher from Worcester was the most important—those of Irish descent did not belong. Distinguished Harvard professors were drawn into Niles's orbit (it could as easily be said that he was attracted into theirs): Arthur Holcombe and Zechariah Chafee, Jr. (government); Samuel Eliot Morison and Arthur M. Schlesinger, Sr. (history); and James Landis, Calvert Magruder, and Felix Frankfurter (law). Helen Rotch, Mrs. Lois Rantoul, Mrs. Francis Sayre, the LaRue Browns, Stella Frankfurter, Andrew Peters, Ellery Sedgwick, and a number of others added to the group's prestige. Although the Filenes were considered allies, neither brother was gregarious, a distinct liability among those who enjoyed conviviality and wit. Louis Kirstein also was associated, for he, Niles, and Frankfurter teamed up annually to raise funds for the Associated Jewish Philanthropies, just one of several interests which they had in common. Moreover, the group maintained ties with labor through Robert Watt, a man of great humanity and stature, who off and on had served as president of the Massachusetts State Federation of Labor.

Into this illustrious Boston galaxy a newcomer moved in 1932–1933. Like many of his new acquaintances, and like his father too, he was graduated from Harvard, was descended from a family whose name was linked with reform, had a faintly patrician aura, and appeared to be an ambitious politician. Like several of his new friends (and his father too), he had heard the Irish bosses of Boston ridiculed by Harvard professors—but his father had once told him that he could learn the political ropes from men like Curley. Moreover, like his father he enjoyed the company of people in academic and professional life, had the credentials to move easily into the Somerset and Boston City Clubs, and vacationed at places where people with "old money" could be found. Some might have wondered what a man with his background was doing in the Boston insurance firm of Obrion, Russell & Co., and why he frequently could be seen with James Michael Curley, but nevertheless James Roosevelt was marked as a man everyone wanted to know. As the new President looked to Boston, then, there were familiar faces and minds sympathetic to his.

It was fortunate for Roosevelt that there were in the Hub people upon whom he could rely, for the Curley and Ely factions were both convinced that the other side should have none of the rewards which the new administration was certain to bestow. Once again, the question of a major appointment for Curley was at the epicenter of the tempest over patronage, and Florence Brennan, for seventeen years a member of the Democratic State Committee, portrayed the Mayor as "a type who breeds turmoil," a man who should "not be placed where tact, diplomacy, and good balance are needed." [26] Other Boston Democrats campaigned to obtain a cabinet post for Senator Walsh, and Roosevelt received a petition with over 10,000 signatures opposed to Curley. The Mayor counterattacked. In a withering blast he denounced "a union of blueblood and blackleg representation" which featured "continuous character assassination by small errand-boy members of the City Council" and the "antics of scolds and scandalmongers." [27] Furthermore, Curley's allies, who repeatedly referred to him as "beloved" and "humanitarian," flooded the White House with denunciations of the old Smith following. Roosevelt, according to Curley's friends, was an ingrate for neglecting a man who had contributed more than $100,000 to the campaign and had even mortgaged his own home. Secretary of the Navy, Assistant Treasurer of the United States, Ambassador to Italy—each was coveted, each denied.[28]

On April 12, 1933, Curley finally learned of his nomination as Ambassador to Poland, and he rushed to Washington to confer with Roosevelt, his disappointment thinly disguised. In an angry fifteen-minute interview with the President, Curley was purportedly told that Poland was one of the world's most fascinating countries. "If it is such a goddam interesting place," the Mayor shot back, "why don't you resign the Presidency and take it yourself?"[29] Curley stalked out in a rage, and well he might, for there was little question that F.D.R. had led him to expect more and had then reneged. Roosevelt told the Press: "[Curley] feels and public sentiment feels—the Boston *Transcript* believes he should stay here in Boston during the emergency. There was much regret. We will have to withdraw his name." Curley composed himself, and put the unhappy affair in its most favorable light. To assembled reporters he lauded the President's "able, courageous, and humane leadership."[30] Back in Boston, however, Curley talked of himself as Roosevelt's forgotten man, and the joke traveled through the city that had he been appointed he undoubtedly would have paved the Polish Corridor.[31] Nevertheless, Boston newspapers which had either been hostile or had done nothing to advance his cause—the *Gazetta del Massachusetts*, for example—felt that the Mayor had been treated ungraciously. So did Curley, and he was correct.

Realizing that both Ely and Curley would be needed to implement the New Deal in Boston, the Democratic high command moved cautiously. Indeed, when Postmaster General James Farley came to the city on September 9, 1933, several key patronage posts had not been filled: no United States Attorney, no United States Marshal, no Immigration Commissioner, and no Postmaster for Boston had been selected to replace the holdovers from the Hoover years. State Democratic Chairman Joseph Maynard of suburban Waban had been named Collector of the Port of Boston, a choice widely construed to be a coup for the Ely-Walsh alliance, and Joseph P. Carney, a banker from Gardner in the central part of the state, had been designated the Collector of Internal Revenue. Carney had maintained neutrality in the Ely-Curley feud, and was considered to have been the choice of James Roosevelt. The President's son, in fact, made no bones about his own importance, as shortly before the Farley visit of September 9 he had stated that closeness "by blood and affection" to F.D.R. enabled him to judge best whether appointees would "measure up to . . . a fair standard of loyalty to the present administration." [32] Since Ely was beginning to see that the New Deal had, as he expressed it, the "power to destroy as well as to save," that in the NRA were the first signs that Roosevelt intended to "abandon the capitalist theory for the socialist state," and that the President had established no "fixed beacons to mark the course," he did not pass the test.[33] Neither did David I. Walsh. But at the end of round one it seemed even more doubtful that Curley passed inspection either, since not one of his men had won a position of any consequence.

In round two of the Great Patronage Bout, completed by the end of September, the Ely-Walsh contingent scored one more gain when Mary H. Ward, a Democratic committeewoman who had been for Smith at Chicago, was chosen Immigration Commissioner. The post of United States Attorney went to Francis J. W. Ford, Harvard '04 and a Catholic, and very likely LaRue Brown and David Niles were instrumental in his selection. In picking as United States Marshal Mayor John J. Murphy of Somerville, a city contiguous to James Roosevelt's Cambridge, the President rewarded a man who had been in his corner before the 1932 Convention (so too had Ford) and in this appointment Curley was consulted.[34]

Still, the pickings for the Mayor of Boston had been slim indeed, and his displeasure bordered on the apoplectic. Only two residents of Boston had been selected, and of these, Mary Ward was a foe. However, after Roosevelt had comforted Ely (the Maynard and Ward appointments) and catered to the liberal third force (Ford and Carney), he placated the irate Curley by authorizing him to approve seven assistants to Francis Ford. Moreover, he bowed to the Mayor's wishes in respect to the Postmastership, choosing one of his Boston political friends and an Irishman to boot.[35]

Roosevelt's dexterous tightroping between the contentious wings of the Democratic party had to be rated little short of brilliant, but to party regulars it smacked of contrivance. LaRue Brown later recalled that "Walsh was hurt. His recommendations were not carried out. Things which he regarded as his prerogative didn't happen."[36] At the same time, James Michael Curley also frowned as he watched the growing list of Bostonians who enrolled in the President's service.

As the Mayor kept his vigil, members of the Niles group traveled to Washington. John Fahey, a friend of both Niles and Maynard, assumed the chairmanship of the Home Owners' Loan Corporation. Felix Frankurter, who corresponded from England through most of 1933, kept the Roosevelt Administration's Brain Trust well supplied with his Harvard students, a group which newspapermen liked to call "the happy little hotdogs." During the humid summer months Louis Kirstein joined Gerard Swope of General Electric and Walter Teagle of Standard Oil in laboring tirelessly for the NRA's Industrial Advisory Board. Working in crowded, sticky quarters thronged with businessmen and reporters, Kirstein tried to mesh the conflicting desires of manufacturers, unions, and General Johnson into new industrial codes. In October, Kirstein chaired the advisory group, and, when he left Washington in December, A. Lincoln Filene came onto the board.

In the new offices scattered through Boston, Curley saw wielders of influence who had not previously been part of the city's power structure during his term as mayor. E. A. Filene headed the Massachusetts Recovery Board, which sought to coordinate the National Recovery Administration's drive for enrollees within the Bay State. Feeling himself "technically and spiritually with the President and NRA planning," Filene was joined by others who attempted to make employers and labor unions submit to codes toward which both groups were beginning to express reservations.[37] Over at the

Chamber of Commerce Building, a number of prominent Bostonians, including Andrew Peters and the banker Travers Carman, constituted an adjunct to Filene's organization. David Niles, who only two years before had been arrested for loitering during a Lawrence mill strike where he had gone to abet the union cause, served as the Massachusetts Labor Adjuster. And even though these men were unpaid and were engaged in a cause with which James Michael Curley sympathized, he did not like being upstaged.

Of all the agencies which sprouted in Boston during the Hundred Days, the Massachusetts Emergency Relief Administration (ERA) was of greatest importance to the unemployed, while, at the same time, it was becoming the most politically controversial New Deal appendage in the city. Not only did the ERA have the crucial task of approving projects which were to be funded on a matching grant basis by the Federal Emergency Relief Administration, but, in addition, the ERA's Emergency Finance Committee cleared all Public Works Administration projects submitted by the Mayor of Boston. Governor Ely, however, was boasting that Massachusetts had "never looked to the federal government to furnish it with revenue," nor did he "propose to do so." [38] Worse yet, the governor appointed the entire ERA board. The director, Joseph Bartlett, and his number one assistant, state treasurer Charles F. Hurley, thoroughly loathed Curley, a feeling which the Mayor heartily reciprocated. Bartlett and Hurley, both politically ambitious, made certain that their staff in Boston held no affection toward their rival. To complicate matters further, Hurley and James Roosevelt maintained a cordial friendship, and thus a bridge was built to the Brown-Niles contingent.

As the federal presence increased from 1933 on, the stakes that were being played for correspondingly shot up. In political terms, the new jobs that became available represented patronage and power. At the time of Roosevelt's inauguration roughly 10,000 Bostonians had been on the regular federal payrolls, but with the addition of emergency work relief the number nearly tripled within the next nine months. In socioeconomic terms, the jackpot was also high, for an evenhanded selection of federal administrators would be necessary to do justice to the diverse groups in ethnocentric Boston, a city where Harvard graduates sneered at those from Boston College and Suffolk Law, where the 200,000 Protestants and Jews eyed the 580,000 Catholics, and where the Italians of East Boston felt isolated. Most important, upon the effective functioning of the New Deal programs depended the welfare of the 300,000 people who at one time or another would be sustained by federal work relief during the Great Depression.

Throughout the Hundred Days, and in the first weeks beyond, most Bostonians had honeymooned with Roosevelt. Economic elites had shared in these feelings, and the very same ward leaders who had thought of Smith as "the greatest Democrat of all time" were now saying much the same thing about the President. Economic indices were rising and spirits correspondingly soared. Much of the excitement, especially for the thousands who still had no jobs and were relying on municipal welfare, as well as for organized labor, lay in anticipation of future results. Impressed nonetheless by the decisiveness of the Roosevelt administration, the plain people of Boston had accorded the President a welcome on June 17 that would have flattered the Emperor Titus upon his return from the sack of Jerusalem.

But at the same time the political script being written in the city during the summer of 1933 had the makings of an old-fashioned potboiler, and a changing cast of political characters sustained some of the drama over the entire course of the 1930s. Those who kept the plot alive included three mayors who sat during the New Deal period—Curley for the rest of 1933, Frederick Mansfield (January 1934 to January 1938), and Maurice Tobin. The fate of the New Deal in the city in large measure depended on their ability to get along both with the governors of Massachusetts and with the staffs that manned the burgeoning government agencies. The outcome for federal intervention also hinged on the mayors' skill at working effectively with a highly unstable city council which by 1940 had only one member sitting who had been elected prior to 1934.[39] Mayor

Curley having been amply introduced, it is appropriate to glance ahead briefly to Mansfield and Tobin.

Frederick Mansfield's friends called him "a sort of Cordell Hull among the Irish," "a quiet conservative gentlemen," while one of his detractors, James Michael Curley, thought him to be "as spectacular as a four-day old codfish and as colorful as a lump of mud." [40] In the 1933 election, Mansfield received the endorsement of the Good Government Association, a reward for his anti-Curley fight in 1929. A Yankee Democrat and a Catholic too, he had served as state treasurer during the governorship of David I. Walsh. In his race against five other candidates, including Curley's nominee, William J. Foley, Mansfield won the approval of Cardinal O'Connell and the cheerful acceptance of many Republicans. Mansfield's fiscal conservatism and his membership in the Ely-Walsh wing of the Democratic party augured poorly for his reception of Roosevelt and the New Deal. His feud with Curley meant that when Mayor Jim became governor in the 1934 election, there was little possibility of a tranquil relationship between the Commonwealth and its principal city. [41]

Mayor Mansfield did his utmost to fulfill his postelection vow "to redeem the fair name and credit of the city of Boston." Bostonians had a "patriotic duty to cooperate" with Roosevelt's "breathtaking venture to restore prosperity," he said. Nevertheless, "it must be remembered that national recovery will be hindered rather than helped if a municipality spends so freely that its credit is endangered." Mansfield battled for retrenchment, especially pay cuts for city workers: "Arouse yourselves, taxpayers! I am fighting this battle for you." Persistently trying to reduce the city's debt and favoring a regressive sales tax, he also waged "a holy war against Curley" during James Michael's mid-Depression reign on Beacon Hill. [42] As New Dealers scanned urban America for reliable friends, Boston looked unprepossessing under the tandems formed first by Mansfield and Governor Ely, then by the pairing of Mansfield and Governor Curley, and finally under the duo of Mansfield and Governor Charles F. Hurley, the selfsame political figure who, in 1933, was appointed by Ely to the Massachusetts Emergency Finance Board.

Maurice Tobin, a former Curley protégé, battled his mentor in the 1937 mayoralty and won comfortably. Like Mansfield in 1933, Tobin attracted the backing of Republicans and Cardinal O'Connell, as the familiar allies tried once again to eradicate Curleyism, with its reputation for spending and corruption. On election day, the Irish Democratic *Post*, which infrequently endorsed any candidate, printed a strong appeal: "Voters of Boston: Cardinal O'Connell in speaking to the Catholic Alumni Association, said, 'The walls are raised against honest men in civic life!' You can break down these walls by voting for an honest, clean, competent young man, *Maurice Tobin*, today." [43]

Tobin had campaigned for Roosevelt in the 1932 election and, unlike Frederick Mansfield, he evidenced modest predilections for federal activism. However, he so strongly craved fiscal stability that he outdid Mansfield in his pledges to run the city economically. [44] In the Mayor's Annual Address, both in 1939 and 1940, Tobin opposed large capital expenditures and disclaimed any intention of leaving behind "vast monuments of public works" or bequeathing "a heritage of monumental debts for later administrations." [45] Tobin and the governor at the end of the decade, Leverett Saltonstall, patched up the rift between the city and Commonwealth, largely because neither demanded much of the other, [46] and Boston's last Depression mayor kept up perfectly cordial (though often perfunctory) relations with Washington. An able administrator, Tobin gave Bostonians efficiency, but he offered them few vistas of the full potentialities of intergovernmental cooperation.

The dramatis personae who would have to make the New Deal work in Boston, then, represented a bewildering variety of social and political types who lived in a decade that placed upon them enormous demands. Out of the large cast there were some, like John Ihlder at the Boston Housing Association, who developed new outlooks congenial to the Roosevelt administration, while others never did. As 1933 drew to a close, Ihlder looked back over the first four years of the Depression and also tried to glimpse the future. An enthusiastic supporter of Herbert Hoover until the crash, a believer in individual initiative and private enterprise, he had gradually turned to Roosevelt. With the coming of the New Deal, Ihlder was convinced that America had found a great leader, yet "much of what he is doing calls for faith on the part of his supporters. Where it will lead us we do not know." Hoping that much of the Hundred Days legislation would be temporary, he was nevertheless prepared to accept a "permanent increase of governmental activity" if the economy failed to revive. "Apparently we have reached the end of an era," he wrote, and he welcomed "the great experiment upon which we are now embarked." [47]

As Bostonians sallied forth, however, they carried with them the sort of history that made it unlikely that many Ihlders would emerge. And to the extent that Boston was symptomatic of urban America during the Great Depression it would have been possible to have foreseen difficulties elsewhere. Elements of romance had been present in 1933 but spats with Washington would not down. Indeed, the antics of significant Bostonians had quickly divested the Roosevelt honeymoon of its initial ruddy glow.

7

Unemployment in the New Deal Years: A Test for Intergovernmental Cooperation

As the gavel banged to adjourn the United States Congress on June 16, 1933, exactly one hundred days after the remarkable special session had convened, several of the fifteen major bills enacted had already been implemented in the nation's great cities. Within a matter of days, all were undergoing their first trials. New Dealers had not only provided a comprehensive program for restoring prosperity but had also imparted a sense of urgency by the very swiftness of their actions. However, the legislation which men like Harry Hopkins and Harold Ickes would superintend relied heavily on the moral fervor, the social vision, and the competence of state and municipal officials. In cities with jarring ethnic divisions, and concomitant political antagonisms, the question of whether the New Deal's programs for the relief of the unemployed would work as charted in Washington had yet to be fully tested.

The Federal Emergency Relief Act which had been passed on May 12 placed substantial responsibility on the states. Half of the $500 million which Congress appropriated went for direct relief according to need, and FERA parceled out the remainder on the basis of a dollar of federal money for every three spent on unemployment relief by state governments. The new agency departed from the loan policies which the Hoover administration had favored, but Roosevelt nevertheless tested the mettle of local units by emphasizing the matching-grant features. Asserting that he did not intend federal aid to be preemptive, the President welcomed voluntary cash contributions to welfare organizations, and he expected projects to be designed outside of Washington.

Since Boston's relatively sound fiscal position ruled out the direct federal grants which a city like Detroit managed to obtain, FERA's impact clearly depended upon the responsiveness of the Commonwealth to the unemployment crisis: the more the state spent for public welfare the larger the federal matching grants would be. At the urging of Governor Ely, however, the legislature sat tight, and Washington relief officials were therefore convinced that Massachusetts abounded with skinflints. "I can see no possible claim on behalf of this rich state for any of the discretionary and unrestricted money," a field agent concluded during a September visit to Boston. The Commonwealth's unwillingness to match federal grants, he reported to Hopkins, "is deadly serious." "I hope it might seem like a joke in Washington," he added.[1]

And when the first modest matching grants arrived at the Massachusetts Emergency Relief Administration (called "ERA" to distinguish it from the parent organization in Washington), Joseph Bartlett, the Ely-appointed Democrat, revealed loyalties not to the central city but to suburbia. Even though Bartlett had promised in the summer of 1933 to follow an equitable formula giving cities and towns a third of what they had spent on welfare in April, May, and June, in practice he gave out the money in proportion to population. Bostonians, with an unemployment rate higher than that of the state as a whole, felt cheated, and Washington also believed the spirit of FERA was being subverted. As Hopkins's aide Robert Kelso put it, Bartlett thought that "his money belongs to Massachusetts, and how they spend it does not concern the Federal Administration."[2]

Part of Washington's skepticism, however, was inspired by Boston's tendency to play fast and loose with federal guidelines. Sixty percent of the money received from the Massachusetts ERA in

1933, for instance, was siphoned off by the Curley administration for regular subway, tunnel, and street-repair projects.[3] New Dealers, of course, had intended that the money be funneled into emergency make-work, yet city officials were quick to justify their illegitimate use of the funds. Washington, they suggested, was penalizing the thrifty states and rewarding the impecunious, and within the Commonwealth Boston was faring less well than other communities. The Mayor and his staff therefore felt entitled to solve their problems any way they could. Although accepting the principle of federal aid for relief, municipal officials—as with their parochial counterparts on the state level—rejected ideas basic to the New Deal.[4]

When the muncipal treasurer closed the books on fiscal year 1933, Washington had given the city $1,944,000, a sum which roughly equaled the expenses registered by the public welfare department over a seventy-day period. Expressed another way, the national government provided enough money to allow the transfer of close to 3,000 people from municipal welfare lists to federal jobs. Instead of expanding the city's commitment to relief, however, the savings were partly reflected by a $2.70 cut in the tax rate. This move lessened Boston's revenue take by almost $6 million, and a third of the reduction had come at the expense of the unemployed. Although James Michael Curley boasted that a "major surgical operation" had taken place (in contrast to Hoover's "homeopathic remedies"), the jobless had not been protected from the vagaries of state and local government.[5]

The Public Works Administration, devised as a stimulus to recovery through construction projects costing over $25,000, excited Curley and the city council far more than the make-work FERA, and they covetously eyed the unprecedented sum of $3.3 billion which Harold Ickes had at his disposal. Half a year after Roosevelt signed the public-works bill, however, Councilor Clement Norton angrily pointed out that Boston was the only city in the United States without a single man employed on a federal works project. Boston, in fact, received not a penny from PWA until 1935, when the city treasurer recorded a paltry $679,504 on the municipal ledger.

Beginning in July 1933, Curley announced lavish PWA undertakings which he said would start at once, but his plans were not realized: the State Emergency Finance Board, also under Ely's appointee Joseph Bartlett, stood in his way. Since the federal government paid only 30 percent of project costs (the missing 70 percent to be raised by floating expensive long-term municipal bonds), Bartlett gratuitously offered to protect honest taxpayers. He therefore scotched proposal after proposal, many of which the city council had endorsed. When the State Emergency Finance Board declined to approve the dollar total suggested by the Mayor for his long-simmering Huntington Avenue subway extension, Curley charged Bartlett with "willful obstruction . . . [of] the Federal Government." [6] Bartlett, though, had not obstructed the PWA solely because he believed in fiscal restraint. Rather, he knew full well that, to a man of the Mayor's background, federal money meant power, popularity, and patronage on a massive scale. Indeed, Curley's PWA shopping list suggested as much, for it included the kind of projects voters might notice in areas where his support was weak—new schools for West Roxbury and South Boston, and a highway from Hyde Park to Milton—and omitted them in wards where he was strong, such as the North and South Ends. Bartlett-Ely Democrats were not fooled, and they were determined that federal perquisites be kept out of the Mayor's hands. [7]

In the Mayor's unremitting struggle with his Democratic rivals, neither side came on as a paladin of New Deal liberalism, and Harold Ickes soon declared a plague on both their houses. Although Curley seductively urged that federally subsidized work and wages would promote economic recovery, he maintained the same attitude toward PWA as he had toward FERA: Boston should receive aid in proportion to its federal tax bill, and it should get its rightful share of the $3.3 billion earmarked by Congress for eventual distribution—$23,500,000. Yet this demand, followed by another for a rollicking $75 million, ignored pressing needs of the unemployed in cities that lacked Boston's welfare resources. Ickes, already troubled by Curley's tendency toward political manipulation of PWA, rapidly developed a low estimation of the Bostonian, a man who for over three years had advocated federal aid but then could not use it effectively when it materialized in a form slightly different from what he wanted.[8]

Meanwhile, the Ely-Bartlett accent upon budget-balancing harked back to an outworn creed, and an open feud between Ely and Ickes also revealed that the Governor would not accept new intergovernmental arrangements. When, for example, in August of 1933 Ickes announced the formation of a Federal Advisory Board to Massachusetts under ex-Governor Alvan Fuller, Ely exploded. In a telephone call to the PWA director, he insisted that both the federal government and municipalities "were creatures of the state." According to Ely, the Fuller board not only constituted an affront, but direct negotiations between PWA and the City of Boston, a prerogative upon which Curley insisted, also violated state sovereignty. "I don't like your tone, Governor," said Ickes to the petulant executive. "I don't like your policy," retorted Ely. Ickes hung up: his policy was intact, and his view of Massachusetts as a place of Byzantine intrigue was indelibly confirmed.[9]

Viewed from Boston, then, PWA must be considered the least effective of all the early New Deal programs, and repeated frustration attended municipal dealings with the federal agency well beyond 1933. Neither Mayor Mansfield nor Curley when he became governor liked the high interest charge on loans necessitated by PWA's matching grants. Delays in the receipt of the meager funds allotted to Boston in 1933–1934 irritated both Mansfield and the city council. Moreover, tripartite responsibility for formulation, approval, and financing of each project guaranteed complications: few states erected a more cumbersome obstacle course than did Massachusetts, a handicap in part attributable to the legislature's traditional control over Boston's debt limit. As proposals ran the gauntlet through municipal, state, and federal inspection (and back again), the odds against implementation soared. Furthermore, in the celebrated feud between Ickes and Hopkins in 1935–1936, Roosevelt sided with Hopkins's preference for make-work, as opposed to Ickes's affinity for major construction, and this decision, in turn, erased plans which the city thought had gained federal approval.

Yet 1936 marked something of a turning point for PWA. With the federal government upping its share of project expenses from 30 to 45 percent, the city council and the state at last agreed that Boston should seek a $5-million court house for Suffolk County. And with the Democratic National Committee, its eye on the 1936 election, intervening with Roosevelt, Boston obtained federal approval. The PWA, which had sent just $679,000 to the municipal treasurer from 1933 to 1935, dispatched $3,549,000 in 1936 and 1937. Combined with the bond issues floated by the city, work stimulated by the PWA in '36 and '37 reached $8,700,000, an amount almost exactly equal to the municipal public works department's average annual outlay. Although Mayor Mansfield stated in January 1937 that he planned "to be most conservative about future PWA projects," 1936 had been a vintage year.[10] In addition to the court-house project, sewers and water mains were laid, and Boston moved closer to its first public-housing project.

Probably no Boston venture in intergovernmental experimentation during the thirties demonstrated more vividly how so-called federal programs were transformed when they came into the local setting than did the New Deal housing program. While there has been virtually unanimous skepticism among historians about Roosevelt's zeal for low-rent units and urban renewal,[11] Section 202(d) of NIRA had nevertheless led to the creation of the PWA Housing Division. Authorized to construct low-cost units and to engage in slum clearance, the Housing Division ultimately built fifty-one projects, and Boston was one of the favored cities. Indeed, Boston had been singled out for a pilot project as early as 1933. Not until 1938, however, did South Boston's Old Harbor Village open its doors.

The unconscionable delay had been caused not by New Dealers but by dawdling at the local level. In 1934, for instance, the state legislature had failed to establish a municipal corporation in time to receive federal funds for slum removal,[12] and the Boston Planning Board had conditioned the receipt of federal loans on the proviso that ultimate "responsibility and control" be left in local hands. When former Governor Ely, acting as an attorney for large real-estate interests, blocked the government's eminent-domain proceedings, the state declined to pass legislation that would have allowed for land acquisition by the city. In addition, the Massachusetts Emergency Finance Board for a time failed to sanction the multimillion dollar project unless Washington footed the entire bill, and the city council caused further postponement by insisting that the Old Harbor Village site should not be exempted from municipal taxes, a position to which Mayor Mansfield also subscribed. Moreover, the PWA construction contract was awarded to Matthew Cummings, long regarded as one of Mayor Curley's pet contractors, and the site chosen was in Congressman McCormack's district on largely vacant land instead of on a location where slum units would be removed. The site, in fact, looked out across the Harbor to the breakwater and the Atlantic Ocean beyond, and it resembled anything but an urban slum.[13]

As apartments in the 1,016-unit project were assigned by the Boston Housing Authority, it became readily apparent that the truly poor and the non-Irish need not apply. Rentals were pegged at $22.15 per month for three rooms and $31.90 for five. Although the average monthly rental of all units ($25.65) fell $4 below the city median, Old Harbor Village was too expensive for anyone on municipal welfare. Indeed, a recipient at the top of Boston's scale of relief payments would have had to shell out over 50 percent of his monthly income for a federally subsidized five-room apartment. But this yardstick was academic, for welfare recipients, with the exception of those getting mothers' aid, were excluded. And, unlike the PWA project in neighboring Cambridge, tenants were required to be holders of a permanent job. Consequently, WPA workers were also left out. As Councilor Wilson put it, Old Harbor Village was not a "happy hunting ground for the poor."[14] And, in Washington,

Nathan Straus, the chairman of the newly formed United States Housing Authority (USHA), expressed strong dissatisfaction with Boston's transmogrification of national policies.[15]

When the USHA replaced PWA as the federal government's principal low-cost housing agency in 1938, Boston again transmuted New Deal intentions—although to a lesser extent than in the 1933–1937 period. Despite the fact that the USHA lent money to local housing corporations at 3 percent interest repayable over sixty years, a far more generous arrangement than under PWA, strenuous opposition came from the city's middle-income districts. Indeed, a nonbinding referendum in four wards led in 1938 to a decisive rejection of more housing for Boston.[16] At stake was a $24-million contract for low-cost units, and in October of 1938 the city council debated acceptance. Mayor Tobin, unlike his predecessor, Frederick Mansfield, proselytized for the USHA money, seeing "social significance" in the plans to house 4,500 low-income families. Opponents were reduced to stalling tactics and were outgunned.[17] Still, twice in 1939—and by a comfortable margin—the council voted that eminent domain should be held up until the public-housing question could be submitted to the entire Boston electorate. Only a ruling by city corporation counsel Henry Parkman, Jr.—to the effect that Boston had no power to put questions on the ballot other than those allowed by the state legislature—saved the day. Although USHA projects were reserved for poor families (income of tenants ranged from $672 to $1,490 a year) and replaced blighted areas of the city (92.6 percent of the 3,800 families moved by 1941 had resided in units with no central heating), Irish neighborhoods were again favored. Viewed from an ethnic perspective, in fact, USHA projects were no more democratic than Old Harbor Village had been.[18] Although of incalculable benefit to the families that were selected from the thousands of applicants, public housing in Boston stopped far short of what even the modest New Deal commitment might have allowed had there been no local impediments. Local resistance to change carried a price.

From November 1933 through 1940 the short-lived Civil Works Administration and its lineal descendants, the second Federal Emergency Relief Administration and the Works Progress Administration (WPA), were of far greater consequence to Boston than PWA had been, but the conflict among those who vied for control diminished not one iota. In general, the national government became so disenchanted with the elected Democrats of Massachusetts and their appointees that new recruits had to be enlisted, men more congenial to the New Deal. However, as Washington exerted stronger control and sought out somewhat different social types to manage work relief, the party regulars howled in dismay. Troubles began the instant Roosevelt and the Congress readied the nation for the terrible winter of 1933–1934 with one of the Depression's most remarkable crash programs, the Civil Works Administration.

On November 15, 1933, Mayor Curley and Governor Ely joined five hundred of their counterparts in Washington, D.C., to discover how Harry Hopkins proposed to spend $400 million and put 4 million men and women to work within three weeks. Hopkins gave answers almost too simple for great minds to grasp. Unlike PWA, CWA shunned an elaborate chain of command, and Hopkins informed Bartlett that his ubiquitous Emergency Finance Board was to act as the state CWA. In Boston, a CWA office under a state designee, Walter V. McCarthy of the Boston Overseers of the Public Welfare, was supposed to devise projects as speedily as possible. The proposals then went to Bartlett for a quick decision, and the city had only to transfer workers from relief rolls to federally subsidized jobs. A rigid formula specified population as the sole determinant of each city's manpower quota, and Boston's initial authorization came to 19,000 workers, 19 percent of the state's total. Furthermore, there would be no tug of war over dollar amounts. Outlays were calculated by giving a cash sum equal to one dollar times 75 percent of the number of people living in Boston ($585,000 for 781,000 residents), plus 25 percent of its previous year's welfare expenses (another $3,400,000). CWA expected the city to add 10 percent to the federal gift out of its own revenues to pay for materials. Despite the simplicity and apparent fairness of the procedures, CWA encountered tough going in Boston.

Curley muscled aside Walter McCarthy and selected Boston's first projects for the Bartlett board's consideration, but the inability of the Mayor and the state administrator to iron out differences had profound consequences for everyone associated with CWA. The Mayor's proposals to employ 5,000 men for a military airport project on Governor's Island and to put 1,500 to work on a strandway along Boston Harbor would, in Bartlett's estimation, have gobbled up an unacceptable amount of money for materials. After rejecting these schemes, Bartlett filled his quotas by turning to other cities and towns. Boston, as a result, came up short: in mid-December, when Massachusetts had filled not only the 97,000 jobs originally assigned by Hopkins but an additional bonus allotment that ran the total to 120,000, only 12,500 openings—10.4 percent—were given to the Hub. The city's rightful portion, according to the original CWA formula, should have been 19 percent, or 22,800 of the 120,000 places. Curley blamed the state director, who reciprocated by lambasting the Mayor, and Hopkins's field agents filed negative verdicts on them both, especially on Bartlett. As one put it, "His ideas are good and his thinking is sound, but he just can't get anything going." [19]

In the absence of a magical project to open up employment to thousands, Curley, and then Mansfield, whittled away at putting the jobless to work by devising lesser tasks. Seen in aggregate form, the short-lived CWA accomplished a great deal in Boston. Laborers excavated and regraded city cemeteries, reloamed and seeded the burying ground on the Boston Common for the first time in 179 years, and toiled on a double shift to begin recataloguing over 2 million books in the public library. Scores of workers helped to modernize the procedures of municipal government by devising a new poll-tax listing system, and still others filed property-tax records and consolidated the city's vital statistics. Large CWA task forces examined defective housing as a basis for future municipal planning and compiled a special unemployment census. Artists on the federal payroll designed health posters and painted murals in libraries and schools. By the time the CWA was terminated, the federal monetary contribution to Boston had been $3,974,000, only $300,000 less than the Public Welfare Department had expended in the same four-month period. While the sum almost exactly equaled the November 1933 estimate, it fell a million dollars short of the figure authorized in mid-December's bonus allotment. Had there existed a unified purpose at the state and city levels, and had this purpose coincided with that of Harry Hopkins, 10,000 additional Bostonians would have gotten federal positions.

Through the duration of CWA the persistent gulf between the city's legitimate quota of workers and the number actually on the job inspired sharp recriminations and excuse-making. Curley implied that the jobless preferred the dole to physical labor, a patently unfair insinuation, and ordered the removal of anyone who refused to join the CWA. The Mayor's defenders on the city council alternately blamed the weather—with three to ten inches of frost resisting penetration, they had a point—the unacceptability of $15-a-week jobs, and the CWA's failure to process applications twenty-four hours a day. Curley's foes, led by the noisy Francis Kelly, charged that at a time when the homes of council members were "being stormed . . . by these unfortunate men and women," the Mayor displayed more interest in PWA, where he could use his favorite contractors.[20] Moreover, the city's newspapers, thriving on conflict, shaped an image of CWA as an inept experiment by regaling their readers with accounts not of the agency's successes but rather of its failures: paint arrived at building sites but no one requisitioned brushes; men were sent to locations but no work existed; pay delays reached proportions where on one occasion Mayor Mansfield tried to placate forty outraged workers by giving them $45 out of his own pocket. And Washington also discerned "an almost unbelievable state of disorganization and maladministration" which "only drastic action and competent, aggressive leadership" might correct.[21]

For all the criticisms which the national government leveled—and

most were surely justified—Hopkins and his staff not only failed to
unsnarl the administrative tangle in Massachusetts but in some ways
added to the confusion. When Washington, for instance, discovered
that its directives were being countermanded, the national staff
threatened to cut off funds. Each time, however, the federal government backed off. Most serious of all, the CWA usually put its Massachusetts director in the situation of not knowing on Fridays
whether he would have funds to continue on Mondays, and wage
reductions and layoffs began only eight weeks after the first Bostonians enrolled in the CWA. Anything resembling careful planning
therefore became impossible, and the crude phase-out of CWA from
February to April compounded the uncertainty. Indeed, when national officials selected the date upon which initial work-force reductions were based (February 8, 1934), it happened by chance to have
been so frigid in Boston that foremen had kept nearly 20 percent of
the CWA workers at home. This meant, in essence, that me-
teorological caprice had short-changed the city by approximately
3,000 men and women. Despite Mayor Mansfield's protests, Hopkins passed the buck to the Bartlett board, which predictably refused to select a date when the full complement of laborers had
been on the job. Although local officials made grandstand plays for
popular approval by conveying the impression that they were trying
to shield local workers from the arbitrary decisions of distant bureaucrats, the case was not often one of the federal government
ruling too vigorously; rather, in the Bay State, it appeared in several
instances that federal power was not applied with sufficient firm-
ness.

Perhaps most of all, the CWA, supposedly a federal operation
from top to bottom, was at the mercy of local politicians with clashing interests, and inevitably the agency could not include every
group in Boston. Nor did it. No administrative offices of any consequence were given to those of Italian, French Canadian, or Central
European extraction, and Curleyites, even if Irish, were largely kept
on the sidelines. State Treasurer Charles Hurley, entrusted in January by his colleagues on the Bartlett board to make all appoint-

Left to right: Joseph W. Bartlett, Josephy P. Carney, and Charles F. Hurley. Described as "Available Democratic Candidates," the three anti-Curley cohorts helped torpedo successful intergovernmental cooperation. Boston University School of Communication.

ments, zealously built a following to the point where CWA was referred to as "Charlie's Workers Administration." Indeed, Hopkins's usually reliable field agent, Robert Kelso, alleged that Hurley had given over "to James Roosevelt the entire coverage of insurance which lies in the power of the State Treasurer to extend . . . and Mr. R. has accepted the same." [22] Though Kelso's report was unverified, the President's son unquestionably interested himself in the disposition of appointments and appeared to be drifting away from the Curley wing of the party. Moreover, Congressman John McCormack, who had accumulated a faithful New Deal voting record during the Hundred Days, played an augmented role in getting employment for his constituents in South Boston and Dorchester.

In fairness, Harry Hopkins had, to a limited extent, tried to skirt

When 5,000 unemployed Bostonians showed up at the Federal Building in downtown Boston one morning in April, 1933, other centers—such as this one—were opened to accommodate the overflow. The *Boston Globe.*

those Democrats associated in the public mind with electoral politics. Dipping into the ranks of Boston's progressives, he singled out David K. Niles to head an industrial and real-estate inventory project. Esteemed by James Roosevelt, popular with organized labor, and a force behind Ely's gubernatorial campaign, Niles aroused no controversy and acquitted himself admirably. But when Hopkins appointed Mrs. Lois Rantoul to head the CWA's Women's Division, Curley, Ely, and Democrats on the Boston City Council yelped in protest. To party regulars Mrs. Rantoul, a Republican who had long been active in the Women's Trade Union League and an acquaintance of Eleanor Roosevelt, appeared to be an intruder, a new type who had been foisted upon Bostonians from outside the traditional political network. Democrats served notice that adventures in nonpartisanship were unwelcome.

The situation in Boston gravely disturbed the CWA staff in Washington, and on several counts. Not only had politicking gotten out of hand, but the shadow of corruption also passed over the agency when, on February 7, 1934, a federal grand jury heard accusations that forged CWA work cards had been handed out to the unemployed by six Bostonians, including two state senators and a city councilor. (Four were eventually indicted, and jail sentences followed.) Furthermore, in early March, the entire State Civil Works Board expressed "dissatisfaction with the policies of Harry L. Hopkins," ostensibly an allusion to uncertain funding, and quit in a huff. Board member Charles F. Hurley, who shared Ely's states'-rights outlook, fired off his parting epitaph on the CWA. "We know conditions first hand in Massachusetts," said the future governor, "and were far better informed as to what course should be pursued here than the federal officials sitting on their swivel chairs in Washington." [23] In the next few weeks, Ely hampered work relief by tying up money which the national government sent to the Commonwealth and by stubbornly refusing to pay any more rent for CWA office space. Given the fourfold menaces of excessive politicking, corruption, administrative breakdown and the conservatism of those in control of work relief, field agents turned in reports which impelled Harry Hopkins toward drastic prescriptions. [24]

Soon after the New Dealers resuscitated FERA in the spring of 1934, Hopkins took steps to which he resorted only in Massachusetts and a few Southern states.[25] Washington made the Massachusetts ERA a direct branch of the Federal Emergency Relief Administration in the sense that Hopkins picked the state administrator, all executives were sworn in as federal officials, and only these men were allowed to handle the disbursements sent into the Commonwealth by the Comptroller-General of the United States. From then on through the end of WPA no governor or mayor of Boston ever touched a work-relief check. In addition, Washington was so thoroughly disgusted with the state's refusal to apply its resources for welfare purposes that the national government permanently halted grants for direct relief to the Commonwealth and its cities, with the single exception of aid to transients.

Under the new system, the key personnel were recruited from different social types, and by the spring of 1934 Hopkins had created a structure which operated at cross purposes with political life as it had existed in the Commonwealth prior to the New Deal. Curley, Mansfield, Ely, and the rest were experienced in the use of power derived from the capacity to win elections. A man like Curley was masterful in his use of patronage and in his ability to find money for improvements in closely contested wards. But Hopkins now held the trump cards: he appointed several Yankees who enjoyed comfortable economic circumstances and Irish who owed their selection not so much to ward politics as to engineering, law, and accounting courses taken at Boston College, Holy Cross, and Suffolk University. Hopkins's people, not party professionals, would distribute federal benefits. Moreover, what was fast becoming an important vote-getting attribute—namely, the ability to solve constituents' problems by serving as their intermediary with Washington—was being undermined. Not surprisingly, Hopkins's people created great animosity among local politicians.

Joseph P. Carney, the first state ERA chairman to step into the new system, was thought by Hopkins's trouble-shooters to be immune from political criticism in Boston despite leanings toward the

Ely-Walsh-Mansfield wing of the party. A resident of Gardner, Carney enjoyed the friendship of both James Roosevelt and Senator Walsh. When he was chosen in the autumn of 1933 as Collector of Internal Revenue, a position traditionally considered to be a fertile source of patronage, neither faction of the Democratic party had protested. In managing the revenue office, Carney had made no important enemies. Nevertheless, his position was unenviable. Not only did he inherit all the troubles which had caused the resignation of the Bartlett board, but he also faced the inevitable delays and confusion when workers were transferred from the CWA. In fact, from April 18 to 30 Carney had to shut down the ERA's operation completely in order to overhaul the administrative machinery, and workers were cast adrift without pay.

Then, too, Carney rapidly discovered from the yammering of Boston's Democrats that he could not expect them to support ERA appointees whose nonpolitical backgrounds very likely would have disqualified them from office under different circumstances. Lois Rantoul, for instance, drew heavy fire, and on April 27 she resigned her position as director of the ERA Women's Division. Although Hopkins picked her successor, he had been warned that choosing a replacement might be "a hot potato we don't want to touch." [26] In addition, Carney's Yankee assistants were targeted for removal. Roy Cushman of Melrose, for example, recruited from his position as chairman of the private Boston Council of Social Agencies, was described by "Honey Fitz" Fitzgerald as a suburbanite who possessed no knowledge of low-income districts in the city. Borrowing a couplet penned by John Boyle O'Reilly, Fitzgerald, angry over the rejection of an Irish political ally, pronounced a pox on Cushman and his Mugwump friends:

> The organized charity scrimped and iced,
> In the name of a cautious, statistical Christ.[27]

In July, Democratic headhunters forced the dispirited Cushman to resign, and the beleaguered Carney quit in October.

Carney's successor, Arthur Rotch, would head the Massachusetts ERA for fifteen crucial months. Like so many of Harvard's Class of 1904 from which Franklin Roosevelt had also graduated, he belonged to the Republican party. In Boston this was considered a sin from which even his liberal wife's position on the Democratic State Committee could not expiate him. An affluent Protestant Yankee closely identified with private social-welfare work, he made a perfect foil for the Fitzgeralds, Dowds, Kellys, Curleys—and the Boston Central Labor Union too. Whether using ethnic, class, or partisan standards, the politicians were convinced that Brahmins and suburban do-gooders had overrun the second ERA.

Rotch's performance during his first eight months on the job should have earned him popularity by any objective measurement. For two months, when Rotch was trying to establish his reputation, nothing seemed to work, but thereafter Boston's share of federal assistance gained remarkably. By June of 1935 the city's portion of all aid tendered to Massachusetts had reached 26.2 percent (vs. 16.3 percent in 1934), the nationally subsidized labor force in the Hub totaled nearly 28,000 men and women (vs. the 1934 low of 7,000), and cash receipts hit $1,700,000 a month (vs. $650,000, the nadir in 1934). Actors and artists, teachers and accountants, marble layers and ditchdiggers—all found a place in the ERA. However, from these heights, Rotch's fortunes plummeted. The birth of WPA in the summer of 1935 proved too much for the state administrator to manage, and by October and November a few seamstresses on sewing projects were all that remained of the federal work force in Boston.[28]

The blame for the disastrous setback to the federal works program in the Hub is traceable to a number of sources. With James Michael Curley at the zenith of his power in the State House, Arthur Rotch felt it necessary to screen every WPA foreman named by administrators in the cities and towns of the Commonwealth. His suspicions of Curleyites in Boston, however well-founded, slowed work relief to a pace resembling that of a lame snail. Furthermore, Rotch did not submit realistic requests for federal money: by the end of August

1935 he had asked that the Bay State's allotment for the next year be set at $300 million. As New Dealers waded through Rotch's demands, valuable time was lost.[29]

At the Boston WPA, an office largely confined to implementing what the state WPA had already decided, Colonel Thomas Sullivan also contributed to the dilatory beginnings of the new agency. Sullivan, a former city public-works commissioner and then a roadmaster for the Boston Elevated, miraculously endured as director of the local work-relief headquarters from September 21, 1934, through the end of the decade. Not until the late 1930s, however, did he earn a favorable word from Washington. The Colonel developed a reputation for wrangling with his staff, possibly understandable in light of the judgment made by a federal field agent that his subordinates were "totally incompetent" and that Boston had no one available with the proper credentials to do a serviceable job.[30] Tardy in devising projects, distrustful of outside advice, and a stickler for voluminous regulations, Sullivan inspired little confidence. Hopkins expressed the hope that the Boston administrator would get "off the reservation" and learn the WPA's procedures.[31] In time, he did, but not soon enough to save Arthur Rotch.[32]

Rotch had ultimate responsibility for the WPA in Massachusetts, and he was subjected to abuse. Nor could David Niles, who assisted Rotch through 1935, rescue him either, despite enjoying the confidence of Governor Curley, the Roosevelts (father and son), and organized labor. In the absence of another John Boyle O'Reilly, it made perfect sense for Rotch and Niles to bring in a man like Clifford Shipton of Harvard to head the WPA Writers' Project in the Commonwealth, yet such choices offended the typical Democratic politician in the Hub. Congressman McCormack called Rotch "a disruptive force in this state," termed him "arrogant," and added that he made it "difficult for the Democratic party to function with some degree of satisfaction." "There are some men that I will support right or wrong, and you are one of them," the South Bostonian told Hopkins," but Mr. Rotch—no." [33] The Governor, too, was "sore as Hell," Niles reported to Hopkins. "Curley took me for a

ride. He is ready to blast wide open," the Bostonian added, whereupon Hopkins made Niles his first deputy in the Hub, a minister
without portfolio.[34]

On December 1, 1935, with Niles handling most job requests and
treating directly with Governor Curley, the WPA, a half year behind schedule, at last began to function. For one woman who had
been picketing outside Arthur Rotch's headquarters off and on for
five months, pleading for the Works Progress Administration to get
under way, it was already too late. Three days after the agency took
on its first workers, a fellow protester wrote of her friend:

> She, weary with the battle, only a few days ago, just when victory
> crowned our efforts, lay down disheartened and weakened with the
> strife. Newspapers carried her obituary in a news column under the
> heading, "Jobless woman ends life by gas." When she was gone, the
> Government expended time, effort, and money to revive her lifeless
> clay, but she was now deaf to their call, and she, who had been ig-
> nored and forgotten in life, could not hear that she was wanted.[35]

But thousands of others survived to hear the sirens and gongs which
many Bay State communities sounded to herald the arrival of federal
pay. For the endless lines in Boston that patiently awaited their
money on the day before Christmas, Santa had arrived just in time,
and the WPA Orchestra accompanying the Yuletide play, *One Night
in Bethlehem*, had reason to perform with special gusto.

Even the $3,500,000 distributed in Massachusetts on December
23–24 did not quiet the criticism of Rotch and, in January 1936,
Harry Hopkins engineered a shake-up. Rotch departed, David Niles
moved into work-relief headquarters in Washington, and an out-of-
stater, Paul Edwards of New York, was named as the new director
of the Massachusetts WPA. In making the selection, Hopkins realized that there would be trouble. Accordingly, he warned his appointee to "take some bulletproof vests along" and assured him that
"we have . . . cemetery lots we can put you in." [36]

Edwards should have accepted the extra armor. Curley exploded,
the Democrats in the Massachusetts Congressional delegation belat-

edly submitted sixteen alternative names, and Colonel Sullivan of the Boston WPA declared, "It is a hell of a situation when they can't find a man in Massachusetts qualified for that job." An Irish member of the Boston City Council played to the Monday galleries by charging that the WPA was being staffed by "highbrows" who were driving to work in Pierce Arrows and Cadillacs and who had fewer brains than the "average immigrant . . . has . . . in his little finger." By March, Governor Curley was berating Edwards so relentlessly that one of Hopkins's field agents, in recommending the appointment of a local man, stated, "I don't think Paul can stand under the strain much longer." Nevertheless, Edwards hung on through most of 1936. [37]

Edwards arrived in Boston at the beginning of a national election year, and the pressures upon him to do right by the Democratic party were therefore especially acute. Congressman McCormack, Governor Curley, and State Chairman Joseph McGrath complained that important WPA positions were slipping away from the Bay State Democrats, "a situation," agreed James A. Farley, "which should not be permitted to exist." [38] Therefore, as part of the preparation for the 1936 contest, city officials were temporarily allowed to certify relief recipients for employment on federal projects. Although Hopkins acknowledged that "20,000 men [meaning WPA jobs] is very important in Massachusetts politics," [39] both he and Edwards tried to resist the conversion of the Works Progress Administration into a political agency. With the help of David Niles in Washington, who played a strong advisory role in processing appointments, Edwards and Hopkins exerted their best efforts to curb preelection manipulation. When all but two of the two hundred Boston Public Library workers dismissed in 1936 turned out to be Jewish, Edwards reinstated them. Moreover, he ousted four Boston delegates to the Massachusetts Democratic Convention from WPA posts because of their political activities, and in August he halted the practice of allowing the Boston WPA to select project supervisors. As Edwards cracked down, Democrats protested. Even Joseph P. Carney, normally temperate, asserted that most Catholic Bostonians of his acquaintance considered Hopkins's appointee to be "a Jewish gentleman from New York City . . . [who] has put a great many of his own people in peak places." [40]

During the ten weeks or so before the Roosevelt-Landon contest, attempts to make the WPA into a politically pristine organization broke down. Worried about the appeal of Father Charles Coughlin's Union Party to Catholic voters, and upset by some thirty months of frustration over appointments, Democrats hounded Edwards and began to receive satisfaction. By mid-September, Governor Curley was able to boast to James Farley that he had 2,200 project supervisors under control of the Democratic party.[41] Republicans like Sinclair Weeks and Henry Cabot Lodge, Jr., accused the WPA of propagandizing for the New Deal, and scored enough telling points to make Democrats wonder whether the agency had not become a political albatross.

In designating Paul Edwards, Hopkins had, on the whole, made a wise choice. Despite the animosity of professional politicians toward the out-of-stater, Edwards unquestionably made the WPA a more effective deliverer of work relief. His presence affronted Boston's Irish, but just as certainly there would have been the same kind of intraparty rancor that had swirled around Joseph Bartlett and Charles Hurley had Hopkins picked a man strongly identified with one of the city's Democratic factions. Brought in on a temporary basis with the express mission of untangling a seemingly hopeless snarl, Edwards had succeeded by the time of his quiet return to New York at the close of 1936. Yet there was a darker side. Edwards, as a nonresident of the Commonwealth, so obviously personified federal intrusion into local affairs that the criticism hurled against him was indistinguishable from an attack on the very principle of federal intervention. In addition, his relaxation of political safeguards toward the end of his tenure opened the way for ethnic discrimination in the selection of WPA workers. On balance, however, Edwards's year in Massachusetts was well spent.

After Edwards's exit, the WPA was turned back to Massachusetts administrators, and Colonel John McDonough, a man of unflamboyant competence, guided the WPA from 1937 through the end of the decade. Living just outside of Boston and a nominal Democrat, McDonough was as aloof from politics as anyone in the Bay State could have been. He had won a reputation for impartiality as Chief of the Inspection Division of the Massachusetts Department of Labor. Appointed to a major post on the State Recovery Board to abet the NRA, he had earned the respect of business and labor alike. Only in his inability to keep tabs on the ethnic composition of Boston's WPA work force did he prove deficient.[42]

Compared to the first three years of federally directed works programs, the period extending from roughly mid-1936 through, say, the autumn cutbacks of 1938, were halcyon days for the government experiment in unemployment relief. Colonel McDonough teamed well with his counterpart at the Boston WPA, Colonel Sullivan. David Niles rendered assistance from national headquarters, and coordination improved markedly. Furthermore, the successive defeats of James Michael Curley in the 1936 Senate race (by Henry Cabot Lodge, Jr.), the 1937 mayoralty (by Maurice Tobin), and the 1938 gubernatorial contest (by Leverett Saltonstall) removed a troublesome presence. Then, too, a steadier flow of money from Washington allowed the WPA to maintain a labor force which ranged from 22,000 to 25,000 Bostonians each month. With experience upon which to build and with more predictable resources, projects could be better designed. By 1938, in fact, the federal government was approving a phenomenal 99.3 percent of the proposals submitted from Massachusetts, and the WPA no longer dispatched Bostonians to the Cape Cod Canal for jobs which did not exist.[43]

When Mayor Maurice Tobin drove the final spike in the roadbed of the Huntington Avenue Subway on February 16, 1941, a decade after James Michael Curley first agitated for the project, the WPA and its predecessors had unquestionably accomplished prodigious feats. The Huntington Avenue project, costing just over $7 million and employing 2,800 workers at its peak, was the second largest ever undertaken by the WPA—only La Guardia Airport in New York City exceeded its scope. WPA cost the taxpayers of Boston

$10,500,000 through 1940 for materials and equipment. But city officials estimated that without federal money the $58 million handed out by the Boston Welfare Department during the same period would have been 70 percent higher, assuming that the municipal treasury would have had the capacity to disgorge such a prodigious sum.[44] From the day that Curley's tiny son Francis dedicated the East Boston tunnel—completed by CWA and the two ERAs—through the wartime defense projects of 1940–1943 sponsored by WPA, federal money gave Bostonians golf courses, underpasses, tennis courts, twenty-five miles of sewers, and one hundred miles of repaired streets. Concerts, plays, recreation programs, treatment of alcoholics, education projects for every age group, library modernization—all ostensibly improved mind, body, and spirit.

There is no doubt that the mayor of Boston and the city council wanted the money furnished by the Works Progress Administration. The council minutes abound with suggested projects, and scarcely a pothole which might have been filled by WPA laborers escaped the attention of the vigilant solons in City Hall. In 1940, council members filed over one hundred orders asking the agency to make alleys into thoroughfares in their wards. Suggesting schemes from rat control to new hospitals to a central filing system for the public welfare department, the city council never seemed to lack ideas; nor did Mayors Mansfield and Tobin. In 1937, his last full year in office, Mansfield said he had "consistently maintained" that federal assistance was imperative, and he frequently traveled to Washington for more money. Mayor Tobin also did his share of arm twisting, asking "Friend Jimmy" (James Roosevelt) for his "intercession" on any number of projects. Indeed, Tobin's interest in WPA earned him praise from Washington, a unique distinction for a mayor of Boston.[45]

It might therefore be argued that in the turbulent years of the Great Depression, the social and political rivalries in Boston, and the intergovernmental wrangling which was in part an outgrowth of these local tensions, did not count for very much. Federally subsidized work relief did, after all, go forward, and, calculated over the long run, the benefits to the city were immense. Nevertheless, local donnybrooks took a toll. Boston at no point received direct relief, and the state's unwillingness to spend for welfare diminished the size of matching grants. The city's CWA quota fell several thousand places below its legitimate share, and under the first FERA much the same thing occurred. The start of WPA was held up for six months, and when the unemployment compensation promised by the Social Security Act of 1935 was ready for distribution in 1938, Bostonians discovered serious delays: Governor Charles F. Hurley, it seemed, had loaded the Massachusetts Social Security Board with political hacks. Four to five years went by before the state and the municipality took significant advantage of PWA, particularly in respect to public housing. As federal programs absorbed local traits, bias in the selection of workers and the placement of projects became more acute—especially after the reigns of Arthur Rotch and Paul Edwards came to an end. Moreover, the mayors of Boston and the city council, the very men who wanted to mine the federal lode, hampered the operation of work relief. Infrequently unified in purpose, and often at odds with state and federal administrators, they repeatedly vetoed supplementary appropriations for the purchase of materials and equipment. By inflaming ethnic Boston's palpable distrust of natives like Arthur Rotch and outsiders like Paul Edwards, the city's political spokesmen kindled little enthusiasm for new arrangements. Instead of separating their blasts against those in charge of work relief from the social-welfare theories of the New Deal, men and principles were often lumped together.

Many of Boston's leaders also were inclined to support the President of the United States without accepting the philosophical consequences of the New Deal. However disparaging the mayors of Boston and the city council often were of the federal works agencies, Franklin Roosevelt was generally exempted from criticism. Whereas callous supernumeraries, Councilor Norton alleged, willingly sent the children of Boston to masquerade balls in the middle of winter "dressed in sunsuits and pillow slips," the President exhibited generosity.[46] Only by inference was Roosevelt associated with the coarser aspects of WPA—the politicking, the instances of corruption, the breakdowns. Even when the enormous reductions in the WPA labor force hit Boston in 1938, city-council president John Kerrigan informed the man in the White House that Bostonians regarded him "as their only salvation in this prolonged period of financial crisis and unemployment." "Your ear has ever been attuned to the cry of the poor and underprivileged," he continued. "Your heart has ever beaten in sympathy for them, and I know you won't fail them now." [47] It was one thing to admire the President's compassion, but quite another to sustain his vision.

The behavior of Boston's leadership during the Depression was simultaneously characterized by admiration for Roosevelt and failure to accept the ramifications of the New Deal as they encroached upon the fiefdoms of each individual. Rather than being liberated by new ideas, Bostonians retained a provincial outlook. Their own interests were always predominant—even as they accepted the money they so badly wanted. Like Potemkin villages, the physical accomplishments of the federal projects glittered, but behind the façades familiar structures of ideas and practices were still solidly in place. The view that the New Deal revolutionized federal-municipal relationships will not altogether wash. In Boston, at least, the so-called "New Federalism" too often looked musty.

8

The Jobless: Varieties of
Experience, 1933–1940

Day broke, yet for thousands of Bostonians the routines were unfamiliar. Stitchers no longer wolfed their breakfasts and rushed for their trains; the shoe shops had moved away and elevated stations were half-deserted at 6:30 A.M. While their husbands stayed home, Italian seamstresses walked from the North End to sweatshops on Kneeland Street where work had been promised. Earning 10 cents a dress, they accumulated $1.70 for fifty hours of sewing—and then the jobs gave out. But another seamstress, a West Roxbury woman of French Canadian descent, lacked even $1.70 and wrote a desperate letter to Eleanor Roosevelt:

> Pleading, asking you to help a single girl, good moral character. Pretending any longer I cannot do. They must be some one some where to help me. Where could we find abandoned farm, good enough to live in and do farming. With allowance from E.R.A. I could be self support and it would be a place to call home. Happiness to enjoy the beautiful sun, nature all so interesting.
> Handy at most everything.
> Good little fixer.[1]

For Bostonians, the Great Depression could be unpredictable and bewildering, and the diversity of experience was considerable. More than half the labor force never lost a day's pay; others found no job month after month, year after year. Between 1933 and 1940, depending on the year, approximately 70,000 to 110,000 employable workers (from 20 to 30 percent of the labor force) were idle. Of those without jobs, close to one-third became charges of the city welfare department, and another quarter of the unemployed, at most, were taken care of by federal work relief. During the eight-year span, some 40 percent of the jobless, on the average, were carried neither by federal nor by municipal agencies: savings tided them over, more fortunate relatives extended a helping hand, and private charity rendered assistance. There were instances of grave privation. At a Washington Street loft run by the Catholic Workers' Movement, for instance, men and women huddled next to a Franklin stove to keep warm and get a square meal, while down at Fish Pier idle workers waited for boats to return with unsalable scraps of cod. Yet the vast majority of the unemployed were confronted neither with homelessness nor with the need to beg along the streets of Boston. A handful of enraged workers—some of them Communists—participated in expressive acts of physical and verbal violence against a system which they perceived as unjust, but most faced their hardships with equanimity. When those on work relief filed into the Williams Memorial Building to pick up their paychecks, for example, it was not uncommon for one of their ranks to keep up morale by banging away at the piano, while others tap danced on stage.

There were those, however, without the resources or resilience to combat the Great Depression. At the worst, reported Martha Gellhorn to Harry Hopkins after a 1934 visit to Boston, "The picture is so grim that whatever words I use will seem hysterical and exaggerated." In the households of the unemployed, she witnessed "fear, fear driving them into a state of semi–collapse; cracking nerves; and an overpowering terror of the future." Moreover, she saw in home after home "the spectacle of a human being driven beyond his or her power of endurance and sanity." Convinced that the jobless workers in the Bay State had more intelligence than their counter-

parts in the Deep South, the agent noted that "the price of this intelligence is consciousness. They know what they are going
through." [2]

Others, too, viewed with grave concern the morale of those without jobs in private industry. Social workers, for example, noticed the
despondency, boredom, and planlessness of Boston's unemployed
and underemployed teenagers, and they saw much the same things
in the city's labor force over the age of forty-five. "Yet with all this,"
a team observed in 1934, "those will look in vain who seek in this
group an aggravated resentment against the existing social order." [3]
A most perceptive federal relief agent, Robert Washburn, was also
worried about the emotional flatness of idle workers in the Bay
State, a characteristic which he felt "applie[d] particularly to Boston." Doubting that the tangible results of federal projects could
compensate for a widespread feeling that relief had become a permanent way of life, Washburn believed that the government's
clients felt "absolutely no resentment" but "rarely any gratitude either." Deadened by too many months of disappointment, accepting
relief "as something to wrest a continued existence from," many recipients assumed the haggard appearance of chronic paupers. [4]

Throughout the New Deal years, the preponderant share of those
who became clients of the municipal welfare department and federal
work relief agencies lived in areas of the city that had been the most
depressed at the time of the crash. Theirs was not the Boston of
"well-scrubbed propriety and gracious leisure" or "prunes and
prisms." Rather, the unemployed came from "the Boston where
acres of ugly wood tenement houses line[d] the drab streets; where
ten dollars a month rent[ed] a three-room flat in a wooden fire trap
without heat, lighting, running water, or indoor toilet, where along
Mile End Road, on the dump, [were] the melancholy shacks of men
who . . . [paid] no rent at all." [5] More specifically, they were the
Italians of East Boston and the North End, the Irish of Charlestown
and South Boston, Negroes from the South End and Roxbury, and
the newcomers from Eastern Europe—Russian Jews and Poles in
particular—who were scattered throughout the city. And as Ta-

ble 8.1 demonstrates, the rate of unemployment during the Roosevelt years in the most stricken area, the Italian North End, reached harrowing proportions, a level 50 percent higher than the city as a whole and three times as high as its most fortunate district, the Back Bay. In the four most severely afflicted neighborhoods, where 160,000 people tried to eke out an existence, and where 1934 unemployment rates ranged from 38 to 43 percent, some 30 to 36 percent still held no jobs at the decade's close.

By the standards of urban America which existed on March 4, 1933, and by these standards alone, unemployed Bostonians who received city welfare payments might well have been envied. As the New Deal began, recipients of all forms of municipal relief were averaging $39.36 a month, a higher sum than existed in any other city with more than 500,000 people, and an amount that more than doubled the average expended in eight of the other twelve major urban centers.[6] Moreover, Boston accepted a higher per capita case load than any other large city except Milwaukee and Chicago, and also provided its jobless with a larger per capita share of tax revenues for relief than did any other urban locale.

After the initiation of New Deal programs, the advantages which Boston's jobless had enjoyed over the idle in other cities was narrowed and, in one important respect, was eliminated. The Overseers of the Public Welfare adopted a policy of granting small supplementary payments both to federal workers and to those with part-time private employment, and as a result of this tendency to spread funds in several directions the average client in Boston by March 1935 was getting only $26.47 per month. Municipal reliefers in cities where the federal government was spending relatively larger sums of money, in contrast, discovered that their local welfare departments could suddenly afford to be more munificent. In the spring of 1935, the municipal dole in Cleveland averaged $32.44 per case; Baltimore, close to the bottom of the list before the New Deal, averaged $32.89; and recipients in Detroit ($37.02) and Chicago ($43.74) fared substantially better than Bostonians. On the other hand, when federal payments in 1935 (excluding WPA) were added

Table 8.1. Unemployment by Selected Health and Welfare Areas, January 1934 and 1940, City of Boston [a]

Area (Ethnicity)	Employable Persons		Number, Percentage of Employable Persons Working on Government Projects		Number, Percentage of Workers Wholly Unemployed		Total, Percentage of Both Those Unemployed and Those on Government Projects	
	1934	1940	1934	1940	1934	1940	1934	1940
Boston	337,067	337,817	11,669 (3.5%)	22,283 (6.4%)	88,075 (26.1%)	44,868 (13.6%)	99,744 (29.6%)	67,161 (20.0%)
North End (Italian)	9,776	8,725	291 (3.0%)	987 (11.3%)	3,927 (40.2%)	2,186 (25.1%)	4,218 (43.2%)	5,205 (59.6%)
East Boston (Italian)	23,092	22,673	1,154 (5.0%)	2,556 (11.3%)	8,866 (38.4%)	4,354 (19.2%)	9,820 (42.5%)	6,910 (30.5%)
Negro Areas	9,965	11,803	NA	998 (8.5%)	3,378 (33.9%)	2,576 (21.8%)	NA	3,574 (30.3%)
South Boston (Irish)	23,091	22,868	1,526 (5.5%)	2,526 (11.1%)	7,496 (32.5%)	4,216 (18.5%)	8,757 (38.0%)	6,742 (29.6%)
Back Bay (WASP)	21,793	21,719	241 (1.1%)	609 (2.8%)	2,621 (12.0%)	1,419 (6.5%)	2,862 (13.1%)	2,028 (9.3%)

[a] Figures for 1934 have been taken from Boston Council of Social Agencies, "Social Statistics by Census Tracts in Boston," Vol. II, July 1935. pp. 9, 14. For 1940, census tracts have been identified in *ibid*. and computed from figures in U.S. Bureau of the Census, "Population and Housing: Statistics for Census Tracts, Boston" (Washington, 1942), pp. 26–41.

to municipal welfare expenditures, Boston's idle work force still took in higher monthly payments from public relief funds ($43.83) than the unemployed in any other municipality, and just four cities were handling a larger per capita case load than were Boston's combined municipal and federal agencies.[7] Nevertheless, few of the jobless on the city's dole or on federal work relief mistook the Hub for El Dorado.

From 1933 up to 1936 the word "relief" in Boston signified to roughly a third of the unemployed the municipal welfare department at No. 32 Hawkins Street. In an average week some 25,000 people, 7 percent of the total labor force, were given checks; and of the 25,000 approximately 19,000 jobless heads of families (76 percent) were fully able to work. Mothers with dependent children comprised 16 percent of the welfare clients, and those on Old Age Assistance accounted for the remaining 8 percent. Thus, most recipients were employable wage earners on so-called "dependent aid." Of this group, some 85 percent were under the age of fifty, half had been unemployed for over two years, and less than 10 percent complained of any physical handicap which would have kept them from working. Nearly 20 percent were aliens—that is, unnaturalized residents. Men on the municipal dole were not floaters, and most had searched for employment before coming to Hawkins Street. Several, in fact, had accepted loss of occupational status before going on the dole. A doctor had become a janitor, a wireless operator a chef, a meatcutter a furniture mover, a real-estate salesman a porter. Almost all of the dependent aid recipients were also registered at federal work relief headquarters, the Massachusetts Employment Office, and the Municipal Employment Bureau. Clearly, they were not shiftless.

From 1936 through 1940 the composition of the welfare roster changed. In September of 1936 the first fruits of the federal Social Security Act and the Massachusetts Old Age Assistance Act were harvested, and by the end of the decade the percentage of elderly welfare department clients had skyrocketed. The other significant modification, however, occurred more gradually than New Dealers had anticipated: in Boston, the Roosevelt administration's objective that municipal welfare clients be confined to the chronically indigent and unemployable was not completely fulfilled. Neither the WPA, which drew 90 percent of its workers from the city welfare pool, nor the unemployment insurance programs, whose allotments began in 1938, reached every jobless but able-bodied worker. Even in 1938 half the dependent-aid recipients on municipal relief were bread-winners capable of working, and two years later some 24 percent—3,800 men—were listed as employable. Nevertheless, by 1940 a decisive shift had taken place from mid-decade, when three-quarters of those on city welfare were capable of working. Of the 31,000 active cases handled in the last week of 1940, 37 percent were listed as dependent aid (vs. 76 percent in 1935), 13 percent involved Aid to Dependent Children (vs. 16 percent five years earlier), and 50 percent of the cases came under the heading of Old Age Assistance (vs. 8 percent in the mid-thirties).[8]

Those who arrived at Hawkins Street were affected by eligibility policies set in Boston, for Massachusetts permitted local control throughout the Depression, and the federal government made no move to change the city's standards. In the period extending from 1933 through much of 1935 the unemployed discovered a Draconian means test which had not been adjusted to make room for those who had suddenly lost their jobs. Rather, the Overseers of the Public Welfare, faced with an overwhelming number of applicants, continued to certify those who for years had been on the lower socio-economic fringe—men who rented rather than owned their homes, families without insurance, householders who had no relatives sufficiently well-off to take them in. For the new poor, Boston set eligibility standards at a stringent level, "forcing people to abandon their contacts and the neighbors they have known and their living standards . . . in order for them to qualify," as an observer from Washington noted.[9] While the decision to take care of the city's neediest cases was commendable, Boston's failure to spend even more for welfare and its reluctance to scrap Elizabethan standards were both overdue for correction.

Beginning in 1935, the rules were gradually made more flexible. Instead of holding to the ironclad requirement that real-estate owners could not get on the city dole, the Overseers of the Public Welfare responded positively to Mayor Mansfield's observation that the unemployed could not "eat their houses," and homeowners were gradually admitted to the relief roster.[10] ERA and WPA workers who had large families were often given supplemental aid, and some of the welfare department's clients who held part-time private jobs were nonetheless allowed to receive payments. In time, applicants were approved even if they held small life-insurance policies. Moreover, the welfare department's case workers ("visitors") were empowered to give emergency orders for food and fuel on the basis of what they found in the home, and with few exceptions those who needed dusty welfare coal could expect a half-ton a month during the winter. And, too, a Division of Nutrition and Medical Social Work, added in 1935, gave advice on diet and put reliefers in touch with dentists, doctors, and opticians at municipal expense. Welfare decentralization also proved advantageous: by August 1935, fourteen branch offices and eleven commodities centers convenienced recipients. Unquestionably these improvements contrasted favorably with the situation in a municipality like Philadelphia, whose progress toward liberalization was arrested when WPA dumped the chronically unemployed back into the city's lap and failed—as elsewhere— to impose coercive national guidelines.[11]

Nevertheless, Boston's jobless could not have felt that the city had ventured far from pre-Depression approaches. Even though the largest families received more money than they would have gotten as unskilled employees of both the second ERA and WPA, a year on municipal relief was dreadfully harsh. Except for minor alterations, the welfare rates from 1933 through the rest of the decade started with a payment of $4 a week for single men and women. Families of two received $7, and weekly allotments increased for each additional member up to a maximum of $15 for a family of seven. If a husband and wife had more than five offspring, they were granted no additional money. A family of four took in $10, some 32 percent less than the minimum standard of decency established by the state.[12] Women applying for children's aid faced the unaltered rule of having to sue their husbands for nonsupport; each September when school opened, welfare case workers discovered hundreds of children who had been kept home because they lacked adequate clothing and shoes. Noting the hardships suffered by recipients, a Republican moderate on the city council introduced a derisive order in 1937 asking that welfare families be granted an amount "more substantially in excess of the $40 a month now allowed by the city for the feeding and maintenance of each Park Department horse." [13]

Able-bodied recipients were required to report to welfare centers scattered through Boston where the men performed a variety of chores, few of which could have given them any sense of self-esteem. After trudging on foot or taking the Elevated (carfare was not reimbursed), some chopped wood, shoveled coal, or helped with the distribution of commodities to welfare families. Others lounged idly, because no tasks had been devised. The frequency with which recipients checked in varied according to the amount of aid allotted, and a householder on the $10 schedule had to show up four days a week. Others came daily, and thus had no time to seek private employment. Since many of these men labored side by side with parks department employees who were earning $5 a day for the same task, the blow to morale was substantial. Indeed, more than one member of the city council likened this incongruous situation to the antebellum South. "I was of the opinion that Lincoln freed the slaves," said a councilor from Roxbury, "but they are bringing them back to Boston under the guise of the public welfare." Even as late as 1940 some of the recipients still labored five days a week, and the city council deplored the "tendency to continue them on welfare work in perpetuity." [14]

Although city council members and Mayor Mansfield both were eager to devise alternative forms of work, scant progress was made. When a proposal came up to establish a farm on the property of the West Roxbury Veterans' Hospital where three hundred men could raise crops for the poor, the representative of this relatively prosperous district rushed to the protection of "thousands of young girls of high school age" who might be molested by "unregulated undesirables." Rather than make West Roxbury a "dumping ground" where homeowners would be threatened by men "roaming at large," the West Roxbury councilor suggested that "the soil along the Charles River could be profitably used for farming, because of its sandy nature." Despite the opposition, seventy-five men were taught the rudiments of farming on the hospital grounds. But when Mayor Mansfield, in his Annual Address of 1937, called upon the school department to retrain those on relief as compensation for "the almost complete breakdown of the apprenticeship system during the Depression," nothing materialized.[15] Innovation was left to the federal government onto whose projects thousands of welfare recipients were periodically transferred.

Almost never did these denizens of the lower depths become refractory, as few seemed to expect that the welfare department could possibly move beyond the standards of colonial almshouses in the midst of a savage depression. If clients felt anger, they did not act it out by picketing, and as far as can be discovered, they organized only on a single occasion. In 1936, a Welfare Recipients League came into being to protest a decision by the Overseers not to give reliefers a $5 Christmas bonus, and to denounce the requirement of four and five days of work for the pittance which they were paid. The organization, however, was short-lived. Moreover, the welfare force in general did not assert that they were victimized by local politics. Most apparently felt that the Overseers of the Public Welfare, the unpaid body heavily stocked with personnel drawn from private social agencies, was acting in a disinterested fashion and at a far remove from ward leaders and the mayor's office. Compared to the incessant controversy in which federal programs were embroiled, the municipal operation seemed placid.

The men and women who came onto federal work relief comprised some 15 percent of the city's unemployed at the beginning of 1934 and approximately 24 percent a year later. At the start of 1940, by which time Boston's unemployment rate had dropped just seven points below that of 1934, the WPA was sustaining 33 percent of the city's jobless—upwards of 22,000 people out of 67,000 that still had no private employment. During the peak days of CWA, the New Deal's unprecedented effort to complement municipal relief provided work for 16,000, the second ERA took on 21,000 a week at its maximum, and the WPA briefly reached a level of 28,000. From November 1933 through the end of 1938 federal clients received wages which totaled close to $70 million, almost $10 million above the average annual earning of Boston's entire industrial labor force in any one year during the same period, and 34 percent more than the cumulative cost of the public-welfare department to the city's taxpayers. The New Deal's aggregate contribution to those without jobs in Boston was obviously immense.

During the most productive six months of the second ERA (roughly November 1934–May 1935), and from February 1936 up to the autumn of 1938 under WPA, nearly 24,000 men and women set off for a typical day on federal work relief in the Hub. Uncle Sam's new legions arrived to work at thirty milk distribution centers and at commodities warehouses. Sandhogs burrowed underneath the city streets, completing needed subway extensions. Women traveled to mattress factories and canneries, to housekeeping assignments in the homes of invalids and to braille projects, while still others completed the recataloguing of the Boston Public Library. When a young clarinetist named Benny Goodman ushered in what would be the "Swing Era," the Boston ERA kept in beat by organizing a swing band. At the George Wright Golf Course in Hyde Park workers seeded fairways and greens and put the finishing touches on a spacious clubhouse, while another contingent of federal laborers carved out beaches along Boston Harbor and its estuaries. WPA nursery-school teachers brightened the lives of their young charges, WPA instructors taught the parents and grandparents of these tots in vocational education courses, and National Youth Administration workers paid their way through college by grading papers. Scores of men prepared a new WPA runway at East Boston Airport, others constructed the Commonwealth Avenue underpass across from the

Harvard Club, and a sizable work force repaired the tracks along which Boston Elevated trains made their way. This was no boondoggle. As the Boston *Traveler* put it, the work had "not been done by leaning on shovels, except to lean on them hard enough to push them into the earth and lift them to the torture of backs unaccustomed to such work." [16]

Reliefers who were shuttled off to federal work sites discovered a grand design unmatched by the public welfare department. Put to work on a variety of tasks, the white-collar unemployed aided their blue-collar counterparts. Dentists ministered to their fellow ERA-WPA workers; jobless salesmen drummed up work as they went door to door, explaining provisions of the National Housing Act, and obtained over $2,500,000 in owners' pledges to undertake repairs. Those with backgrounds in finance helped with payrolls, while FERA and WPA engineers undertook feasibility studies for additional projects.

Unemployed musicians, actors, and artists benefited from the innovative flair of both the second ERA and WPA and bolstered the morale of despondent audiences. Recent graduates of the New England Conservatory of Music sang in the community choruses, performed in the ERA-WPA Civic Orchestra (sometimes with Arthur Fiedler of the Boston Pops as guest conductor), and joined a number of smaller chamber groups. Singers entertained at hospitals, CCC camps, and at dedication ceremonies to mark the completion of projects like the East Boston tunnel. Combining with federal actors, the musicians created holiday pageants on the Boston Common and formed an opera company as well. And when WPA "opera on the dole made its bow in Boston," the *Globe*'s reviewer, despite his mild sarcasm, unwittingly revealed the potentialities of government-supported entertainment. An art form with a previously restricted clientele had been democratized:

> Footlights illuminating the W.P.A. production of Humperdinck's "Hansel and Gretel" flashed to the diamond horseshoe of the 400 and reflected to the orchestra circle the sheen of a celluloid collar on an Elevated motorman. . . . It was opera for the 4,000,000, and the

sign on the door warning "Drivers, Chauffeurs, Footmen not allowed to stand in the vestibule," might just as well have been draped, for the drivers, chauffeurs, and footmen were occupying seats of the master and the madame at 83 cents per chair.[17]

Actors, including those in Yiddish and Negro troupes, staged ancient melodramas and revived *Uncle Tom's Cabin*, while ERA-WPA artists painted sets for the federal theater presentations and murals for public buildings. Black actors won wide praise, and William E. B. DuBois's *Haiti* played to standing room only. The WPA production at the Copley Theater of Christopher Marlowe's *The Tragical History of Dr. Faustus*, presented without scenery in the mode of *Our Town*, held record audiences spellbound.[18]

Federal work relief, however, had not ushered in the millennium for the unorganized, unemployed men and women of Boston. Until 1936 much of the jobless labor force which looked to CWA, ERA, and WPA faced critical moments indeed. The periods of malfunction had dire implications for the unemployed, and federal officials knew it. As one of Harry Hopkins's trouble shooters observed in describing the second ERA under Arthur Rotch and Colonel Sullivan, when an agency became "definitely and blatantly bad," when incompetence itself constituted a menace, then the whole conception of federal intervention was converted into "an object of disapproval (if not disgust) for the unemployed classes."[19] This verdict was harsh, for it failed to acknowledge the accomplishments of federal work relief, and it overlooked the alternatives of either municipal welfare or nothing at all. Moreover, it was not true that no one expressed gratitude for his check. But the gloomy judgment also contained a strong element of validity. Thirty months of administrative shortcomings, pay cutbacks, uncertain funding, political shenanigans, and constantly shifting eligibility rules gave the national relief effort some unfortunate connotations.

Indeed, the poor discovered that federal work-relief agencies, as altered at the local level, could at their worst be heartless, inconsistent, and even venal. On the eve of the CWA's first enrollment, for instance, the jobless packed the city council galleries to shout down

Mayor Curley as he defended the decision to hire only those on public welfare or soldiers' relief. What about those "who are too proud to go on the Welfare . . . and were too young to go to the World War," a spokesman wanted to know. "Are you going to give them a gun and tell them to go out and kill somebody?" [20] The speaker soon had his answer. Despite an order from Harry Hopkins that the CWA divide its openings on a 50-50 basis between welfare recipients and those unemployed who had managed to stay off municipal relief, the Boston CWA for some time ignored the order. Victimized by the city's desire to reduce its welfare load and thus ease its fiscal plight, the new poor—many of whom had been waiting in severe cold for ten hours or longer—were turned away by the thousands. During CWA and the second FERA, angry and bewildered crowds gathered outside City Hall, not to call for an end to the agencies but to plead for faster and more equitable processing of applications.

Since tens of thousands of jobless men and women could not be absorbed by the national programs, and with the city's newspapers arousing suspicions that political chicanery was involved, the unemployed jumped to the conclusion that to be on federal work relief one needed friends. Each time that spasmodic funding reduced the number or hours of common laborers, while clerical and supervisory personnel retained longer weeks with no losses, the notion was clinched that federal relief was designed—as library workers put it—"to swell the salaries of politically appointed officials." [21] Even though the federal agencies encountered problems in their early stages that were far more complex than could be attributed solely to political conspiracy, a measure of partisan opportunism clearly existed. The perception that federal relief offices resembled political anthills would not go away.

Moreover, unskilled workers with large families who came onto the early federal programs earned smaller aggregate wages over most periods than they would have if they had been on municipal welfare. Although the first ERA and CWA paid $15 a week to common laborers (84 percent of the CWA force was classified unskilled), the second ERA set a $12 wage, $3 less than the public welfare department was parceling out to large households. While this suggested to a shocking degree that the New Deal treated the poor much as they had always been treated in Boston, the tendency of federal aid—unlike city relief—to ebb and crest was far more serious. The CWA, for instance, cut back to a twenty-four-hour, $12 schedule for common labor in mid-January of 1934, and both CWA and the second ERA slashed thousands of workers for short durations at other junctures. From April 18, 1934, to the end of the month, and again from October 26 to November 1 in the same year, the entire corps of unskilled never touched a shovel. Reduced compensation moved one laborer to complain that "for our Thanksgiving we will have the magnificent sum of Seven Dollars and Forty Cents with which to carry out our national custom of giving thanks as originated by our forefathers." [22] In addition, workers who had toiled a few months for one federal program were not assured that they would be taken on when the next commenced. The second ERA, for example, insisted that large families should have the inside track on available work, a morally defensible position. Nevertheless, the thousands who were dropped at the program's outset because they had not sired at least three children, suffered unexpected hardships, and six months elapsed before the ERA could hire men with two offspring or less. "It's just putting a premium on the village bulls," said a Hopkins aide upon visiting the city. [23] Municipal welfare, miserly as it was, at least spared its recipients comparable financial uncertainties.

Similarly, the early federal commodities program pointed up the dangers to the unemployed of administrative ineptitude and inadequate funding, difficulties made more poignant because rising food costs in Boston eliminated the crucial hedge against welfare checks and grocery orders whose cash value remained constant: whereas in 1932 Boston's food prices had tumbled 17 percent, New Deal agricultural policies, combined with droughts in the West, helped push prices up 33 percent from April 1933 through January 1935. Housewives in the Hub paid more for food than did shoppers in almost any other city,[24] and private organizations could not take up the slack. The St. Vincent de Paul Society, for instance, helped an average of 10,200 Boston families during each of the six years after Roosevelt's inauguration, but the 46,900 persons in these households received goods worth just $4.48 per annum. Yet even as the Family Welfare Society from 1934 to mid-1935 discovered malnutrition as the cause of rising illness among its clients, and as the unemployed deluged the ERA with urgent pleas for food, the agency could not make good on its promises to deliver beef and veal. Instead, Boston nearly drowned in cabbages. On December 7, 1934, 5 million heads—226 carloads—descended on the city, and, as *The New York Times* sarcastically noted, not a pound of corned beef came with them. Thousands of rotted cabbages were tossed into Boston Harbor, and a few days later 1,200,000 pounds of California prunes arrived. During the program's first nine months, 60 percent of all commodities consisted of potatoes and cabbage. Predictably, even these supplies were not dispensed in the neighborhoods of ethnic minorities: seven of the first eight distribution centers were placed in areas where Irish were heavily concentrated.[25]

As commodities programs matured, the unemployed discovered improvements. All but two of Boston's fourteen health and welfare districts had distribution centers by the time the WPA began operations in December 1935, and the commodities which the jobless picked up became ever more varied. ERA-WPA workers canned and successfully distributed 4,000 quarts of fish chowder a day,[26] and other government employees manufactured mattresses and made clothing for the city's poor. A more balanced supply of food arrived at the Surplus Commodities Division with greater regularity, and the WPA staggered handouts on an alphabetical basis to avoid the huge lines which had formed in the past. By 1938, Bostonians had walked away from outlets in churches, settlement houses, and municipal buildings with some 34 million pounds of food, 5 million quarts of milk, and over one million articles of clothing. Also by 1938 the caloric intake of the unemployed had neared three thousand a day, almost exactly equal to the standard maintained by pri-

vately employed workers averaging wages of over $1,500 a year, and
a food-stamp plan allowed any federal worker to participate if he
marshaled persuasive evidence of need. No one dined like Trimal-
chio, but neither did anyone starve.

Eventually, the frustrations of those who looked to the Boston
WPA in 1935, when Arthur Rotch and Colonel Sullivan could not
get the agency off the ground, would also be relieved, but at first
the unemployed felt the impact of an administrative wilderness, the
state's unwillingness to provide aid to its cities, and the skirmishing
between local politicians and the work-relief hierarchy. While the
unemployed cheered the new WPA minimum wage of $55 a month,
no Bostonian on relief received a check approximating this dimension until the very end of the year—and even in the first months of
1936 workers were still being paid 10 percent less than the maximum allowed by the President's announced scale. Teachers who
had been assured summer employment on education projects in
1935 were cast adrift. Five paydays in August could not be honored
without dropping 15 percent of all employees and placing the remainder on a stagger system. In a six-week period during September–October 1935, 24,000 laborers went on a twelve-hour, $6
week, yet local administrators nevertheless required the men to
show up each day, often for as little as two hours of work. The cut to
a $6 paycheck, a barely literate Charlestown resident complained to
Roosevelt, "is terriably humiating to Mother & Father to feed three
children say nothing about keeping a roof over head & trying to give
them nurishment to strengthen them for school." [27] Workers who
had received no pay for three weeks or longer massed in long lines
outside the Massachusetts ERA-WPA in October (the two agencies
operated under the same umbrella until December 1, when the
ERA officially passed out of existence), and picketed throughout the
rest of the year.

Next to hardships of this order of magnitude, the vicissitudes encountered by men and women on the government's white-collar,
professional projects seemed relatively inconsequential, although to
the complainants themselves they appeared serious. Musicians, for

instance, had difficulty in adjusting their temperaments and artistic ideals to regulations. While reviewers might rate performances as "decidedly fortissimo," [28] "solos" had to be sung by groups of ten because the rules stipulated that no soloists could be paid federal money. Moreover, it was almost impossible to form a large orchestra with the right combination of performers while at the same time honoring national eligibility standards. Aliens, single men and women, and more than one member of the same family were added in order to muster the proper number of violins, cellos, and horns. But when these liberties were taken with hiring guidelines to achieve orchestral balance, workers angrily informed on one another, and dismissals resulted. Considerable animosity was also vented on the Federal Audition Board. Endowed with extraordinary powers, the Board turned down musicians on the stated grounds of voice quality. However, the jobless charged that the auditioners were invoking artistic standards as an excuse for barring the elderly and that they also discriminated against Italians and Negroes.

Federal actors, for all their triumphs on stage, also suffered many of the same indignities, and, in addition, some of their efforts were repudiated as subversive or too risqué. Hours of rehearsal were wasted when local censors added plays like Molière's *Tartuffe* to the distinguished list of works "Banned in Boston." The Negro contingent successfully performed *Genesis,* the first play anywhere in America to be written, staged, and acted by ERA workers, but when they presented *Stevedore,* a drama depicting low wages and foul conditions on the New Orleans docks, officials displayed acute sensitivity to the social content. The company was packed off to nearby Saugus for a hastily scheduled presentation of *Macbeth,* which apparently fell within the parameters of ideological respectability. When dissident blacks placed a rush call to the Negro People's Theater in Harlem for replacements to stage *Stevedore* independently, eight ERA actors participated, an equal number of inspectors from the police department's radical squad viewed the proceedings, and an ERA timekeeper at the stage entrance jotted down the names of the mutinous cast. [29]

Not only did federal workers have to weather spasmodic outbursts of disapproval for alleged subversiveness (and by the late 1930s a few zealots on the city council were including *all* WPA employees as suspect), but segments of the unemployed blue-collar classes competed with one another in a most unpleasant rivalry. First, labor unions tried to wedge their jobless members onto federal projects. Belittling the qualifications of the unorganized and the unskilled, building trades workers in particular demanded that men in higher pay classifications be given first priority. By 1937 they had succeeded to the point where the Boston WPA was retaining 2,500 fewer unskilled workers than Washington was demanding. Thus, a number of the city's unions contributed to the misery of those who could not be taken on: the precious funds which the Boston WPA had at its disposal were being eaten up by workers who got the $94 skilled wage.

Moreover, the blue-collar classes were divided by harsh ethnic competition in which each group felt victimized. As a federal official had noted in 1934, Boston's ethnic hierarchy was especially rigid. Old Bostonians, he observed, regarded all but their own breed with suspicion, and "the Irish look down on the Italians, and so on, in order of immigration, to an extent that really colors all thought." [30] Jewish workers made incessant charges of prejudice against Irish and Italian supervisors. Women of Irish ancestry lambasted the Anglo-Saxon Protestants who superintended many of the WPA's projects (including "the sewing czarina in Boston") as "sanctimonious" and "autocratic." [31] Blacks also faced discrimination. Both the Urban League and the NAACP devoted attention to instances in which the WPA excluded Negroes from singing, writing, carpentry, and sewing projects, and they also complained about the type of work assigned to those who were actually hired. The WPA's tendency to place Negro females on the household workers demonstration program, for example, properly drew fire from both civil-rights organizations, because blacks had "performed this type of service for America ever since Colonial days." If the government continued to desist from training Boston's Afro-Americans for more dignified occupations, the secretary of the Urban League ominously stated, "there will eventually be . . . problems that we cannot now see." [32] Italians in the North End felt strongly, and with ample cause, that the Irish received all administrative plums and that Green Power invariably won competition with other ethnic groups in getting even menial positions. As one disgruntled Italo-American put it, the Irish element gouged "people who can't speak good English." "I want to say," he concluded, "that W.P.A. has bred more holdup or two-gun Petes of the old Western days than you can find in all the prisons of America." [33]

No program, of course, could have been administered with enough precision to have accommodated an absolutely just proportion of unemployed workers in each ethnic group, especially when ethnicity was ostensibly not a criterion for hiring. Nevertheless, it is apparent from Table 8.2 that Colonel Thomas Sullivan's work relief headquarters took care of the Sons of Erin, especially after Hopkins's hand-picked state administrator, Paul Edwards, left Massachusetts at the end of 1936. In the two health and welfare districts of highest ethnic segregation—Irish South Boston and the Italian North End—there was a clear discrepancy between the number of idle workers and the number actually taken onto government projects. On the other hand, the Italians of East Boston appear to have been treated equitably. Across the harbor, a greater degree of ethnic diversity and larger bank savings prevailed than in the North End, and there is no way of telling the extent to which the existence of a small Irish colony and greater Italo-American wealth distorted East Boston's figures. Negroes in the South End and Roxbury, however, were confronted with palpable bias as blacks discovered that federal jobs were much harder for them to obtain than they were for the Irish.

But in several respects the lot of federal workers improved after mid-decade as the WPA matured. Paychecks came on schedule, and for nearly three years wholesale layoffs ceased. Due in large measure to the WPA, fewer able-bodied men entered the municipal welfare centers, and a more complementary relationship between

Table 8.2. *Ethnic Discrimination on Government Projects in Boston, 1934 and 1940* [a]

	1934			1940		
	Fair Share [b]	Number on Projects	Discrimination Index [c]	Fair Share	Number on Projects	Discrimination Index
Back Bay (WASP)	334	241	−27.8	653	609	−6.7
East Boston (Italian)	1149	1154	+0.01	2225	2556	+13.0
North End (Italian)	494	291	−20.9	1676	987	−40.6
S. Boston (Irish)	1025	1261	+18.8	2171	2526	+14.0
Negro Areas	NA	NA	NA	1151	998	−13.3

[a] Calculated from figures in Table 8.1, and the statistical sources are the same. Because most of the health and welfare areas in Boston were geographically large, thereby producing ethnic diffusion, and because figures were not reported by ethnicity, it is impossible to trace other important groups on the federal projects.

[b] Defined as 11.7 percent of unemployed in 1934 and 32.2 percent of unemployed in 1940 (the citywide percentages of jobless actually on government projects).

[c] Defined as percentage deviancy from fair share.

city and national relief agencies was forged. Many of the laborers who had come onto the federal rosters during 1933–1935 had been powerless and confused, but as the years passed, the government's clients formed protective associations or combined with more vigorous unions—and the unions took up the cudgel for those who joined WPA or PWA. Moreover, the WPA's achievements in the second half of the 1930s must have engendered a greater sense of pride, and the landmarks which thousands of hands had fashioned in Boston were ineradicable. When the devastating hurricane of '38 ripped through Massachusetts, the federal workers waded into the debris with élan, earning substantial praise. Wildcat stoppages on project sites vanished; picket lines outside relief headquarters on Federal Street were uncommon. And since the reemployment rate of those who were separated from WPA in the cutbacks of 1938–1939 was lower for Boston than for other large cities, it was felicitous that the agency operated as well as it did.[34]

Whether feelings of gratitude when the federal programs worked effectively offset anger over malfunctions is conjectural, especially in the absence of a comprehensive study similar to E. Wight Bakke's classic investigation of New Haven.[35] Still, the unevenness of work relief adversely influenced at least the short-run attitudes of thousands of Bostonians toward government intrusion. Workers, for instance, chided "the ridiculously low wage the richest Government in the world expects men to accept without a murmur [sic]," [36] and they railed against the precariousness of each federal program. For those who stood ten abreast in interminable lines but found that promised aid had not materialized, anguish and even rage were inescapable.[37]

Months of fruitless job hunting could, of course, change expectations.[38] When a man was finally given work and brought home his first check, when his family could replenish its stores and perhaps even celebrate with some small extravagance, some degree of awareness of the source of this respite, however brief, surely dawned. Those who entered the CWA, ERA, and WPA labor force persistently made the point that they would "go to any lengths rather than apply to the [Overseers of the Public Welfare]." [39] "I do not want to be taken care of," said a Negro worker who had bounced from ERA to the Family Welfare Society, and then faced the municipal dole. "I want to work and support my home and family." [40] Like this man, the unemployed distinguished between work for Uncle Sam and chopping wood in the Hawkins Street yard. And even though a federal project supervisor acknowledged that "a job of endlessly wheeling dirt is the hardest thing to keep them going on," a great many tried—even in moments of direst adversity. A scene witnessed at Marine Park, involving this same foreman, suggests as much:

> It was bitter cold on the beach where the crew, many insufficiently clad and more than half without gloves, were wrestling great rocks into place to form a wall. "A lot of them are not used to the work—a couple were accountants, one a real estate man," said the supervisor. "How could I drive them as on a private job? One man came to me all taped up with a broken back. Was I to send him home without a job? I gave him light work. The real estate man first begged me for inside work, said he couldn't stand this, but when a cold day came and I got around to it he said he'd got used to it, and wanted to stay on it; that he ate and slept better than he had for years." [41]

Moreover, protests against the malfunctions which occurred from 1933 through 1935, and the outbursts which greeted the cutbacks instituted in late 1938 and early 1939, did not imply that the New Deal programs should have been scrapped. Rather, the outcries of the jobless suggested that work relief ought to have been expanded and made to operate without spasmodic interruptions. To the non-Irish unemployed, the programs needed less local control, but to the Irish, every administrative position ought to have been filled with an O'Callahan from South Boston. To those jobless not admitted to the ranks of the federal labor force, lack of places constituted the most basic grievance. Those on the payroll, on the other hand, ranked low wages and skill classifications as the most pressing issues. Judgments, then, depended on thousands of decisions which, in turn, were based on how well a particular program met an individual's situation. In this sense, the grateful unemployed resembled other elements in Boston—the homeowner bailed out by the HOLC, a businessman whose profits increased under the NRA, the union member with a new and favorable contract in hand, a depositor whose savings were rescued by the Federal Deposit Insurance Corporation. Conversely, the national work-relief programs earned specific animosities when they failed to do enough—not diffuse ideological reservations, of course, but the particular animus of one who was denied relief.

And when Bostonians complained they generally exempted the President of the United States. Roosevelt, they implied, had not been party to the local obstacles which had thwarted his intentions. Trade unions, not the President, had tilted the WPA in favor of skilled workers. When actors were sent home because another play had been banned in Boston, when the Bartlett-Hurley-Curley-burly had impeded work relief in its early stages, or when ethnic discrimination had occurred, Roosevelt had been at a far remove from Boston. Roosevelt, it was commonly believed, had transcended Boston's folkways: he had federalized work relief in Massachusetts and could be credited with the substantial aid which ran its way through the city's political gauntlet. Even the most brutal cutbacks in wages could be tolerated, said one worker, if only a cogent explanation could be provided. If a reason were given, the man stated, "it is more than probable that it would be accepted without question as we are, to a man, solidly back of our great Chief Executive, President Franklin D. Roosevelt, and are . . . thankful in the extreme for what has been done for us by him." [42]

Indeed, for those who had lost their jobs and come onto government work sites, the response to Roosevelt seemed rather less complicated than their views of the federal relief agencies themselves. Expressing the deepest affection, massive throngs spontaneously cheered the President's caravan as it moved through the city during the 1936 and 1940 campaigns. The President's visits to Boston were electric moments. His jaunty wave, the broad grin, and the con-

fident voice at Boston Common rallies were infectious. He clearly
cared for the people, and they for him. In his absence, they might
flirt with the prophets of the Left and Right which the Great Depression spewed forth—Father Charles Coughlin in particular. They
might continue to engage in street-corner brawls inspired by unabated ethnic rivalries, or march through the Italian quarter chanting "Viva Mussolini" after Roosevelt had departed; and they might
continue to measure national policy by their own personal well-being, understandably in an era of economic insecurity. But many of
those who had been sustained by federal paychecks at some point
from 1933 through 1940, a group which numbered at least 300,000
men, women, and children in a city of 780,000, did not miss the occasion to line the streets and shout their thanks to Roosevelt the humanitarian. Almost all could have joined the more quiet tribute
which a widow on a sewing project had once conferred: "Our debt
to you, Mr. President, Mr. Hopkins, and his associates can never be
paid. This work has been my salvation." [43]

But even as the Roosevelt administration extended its saving
graces to the unemployed of urban America, the poor retained
much in common with those who had always stood in need. For all
the outpouring of liberal humanitarianism, and for all the talk of a
welfare revolution, the stipends paid to both municipal and federal
workers were, without question, "terriably humiating." The burden
remained with the poor to prove their destitution; far too many
were excluded. Unfavored by job retraining, lacking a living wage,
and subject to both political manipulation and ethnic discrimination,
the unemployed were not so much principal actors as objects acted
upon. Boston's jobless, endowed with perhaps the most generous
program of public assistance in the United States, found the going
tough. To ask how their equivalents fared in other cities, it would
seem, is to answer the question.

9

Blue-Collar Boston: The Union Movement

To the tune of "Maryland, My Maryland" textile workers and waitresses, telephone operators and stenographers, garment workers and street railway carmen lifted their confident voices:

> Then rise as you ne'er rose before,
> Nor hoped before, nor dared before;
> And show as ne'er was shown before,
> The power that lies, that lies in you.
>
> Stand all as one till right is won,
> Believe and dare and dare and do,
> Stand all as one till right is won,
> Believe and dare and dare and do.[1]

The occasion—the twenty-fifth anniversary of the Boston Women's Trade Union League. The year—1929. Even though the melody was not always sung harmoniously, and the singers did not invariably "stand as one," the song lived on. During the Great Depression, blue-collar wage earners flocked to the standard of labor unions, rising as they "ne'er rose before, nor hoped before, nor dared before."

From the docks of San Francisco to the gates of Republic Steel, unions in the 1930s waged a struggle for social justice. Without the New Deal, it has been suggested, labor's resurgence would have been retarded, and union growth therefore may "serve as a useful litmus test of the New Deal record." [2] In America's great cities, moreover, union members gratefully backed Roosevelt and his social policies, many of which were informed by labor's left-of-center objectives. Labor, to complete the picture, supplied to the 1930s the swarthy juices of all that was exciting, progressive, humane. Labor and the New Deal were locked in a reciprocal arrangement to the benefit of both.

The Boston "litmus test," however, suggests rather different results. While distinctly more acidic than in the pre-New Deal era, the city's labor unions grew for a variety of reasons, not all of which had to do with the Roosevelt administration. Although more venturous than in the pre-Roosevelt years, the majority of the city's unions, too parochial to form a social vanguard, lagged behind. To those who have wondered why the New Deal at times appeared timid, the Boston story offers clues. If a supposedly indispensable part of the Roosevelt coalition held back, there could be no constituency for sweeping social change.

By national standards, Boston on March 4, 1933, was a strong union city. Roughly 62,000 men and women, 17 percent of the city's employable workers, were enrolled in some form of labor organization at the beginning of the New Deal. Indeed, from the day of the crash through Herbert Hoover's last hours in office, Boston's labor organizations exhibited somewhat greater staying power than unions in most of the nation. While trade union membership throughout the United States sagged by 13.6 percent, the number of dues-paying members in Boston unions, including independents such as the Amalgamated Clothing Workers, fell only 8 percent. Although membership in the Boston Central Labor Union, to which 85 to 90 percent of the city's organized workers belonged, dipped from approximately 60,000 to 54,000, a 10 percent loss, the number of workers enrolled in the Chicago Labor Federation plummeted from 105,000 to about 70,000 during the same period. [3]

In the union halls of Boston, however, few wore expressions of smugness, for despite the positive signs of organized labor's vitality, weaknesses appeared in the depths of the Depression which were more serious than the slight membership decline suggested. Thousands of workers carried on the lists as union members had lost their jobs, especially in the building trades, which comprised nearly 40 percent of the city's organized wage earners, and the BCLU's shrinking receipts testified that many were being counted as members who, in fact, had not paid their dues. There were Sunday afternoons at the Wells Memorial Building when the BCLU could not muster a quorum, several unions acquiesced when employers instituted wage cuts, and concerted organizing drives were out of the question. Most important, the AFL, catering mainly to skilled crafts, had not reached 83 percent of the city's labor force. In addition, thousands of workers, like those employed by the Bethlehem Ship Building Corporation's Boston yard, depended on company unions for redress of grievances, and the firing of those engaged in organizing activities was not uncommon. On balance, unions in the Hub had a world to win.

The first stirrings of spontaneous union organization began in Boston several weeks before President Roosevelt signed the National Industrial Recovery Act.[4] Teamsters Local 25 (the most important of the six International Brotherhood of Teamsters locals in the city)—$1,700 in debt, with only 335 paid-up members, and able to boast contracts with just sixteen employers—stirred even as the NIRA was being debated. Younger men displaced those who had served for years and issued a call for a mass meeting at the Wells Building. A thousand showed up, three times the number listed on the union register, and sound trucks dispatched to every corner of the city soon blared the news that the Teamsters were on the march. Fire fighters and federal employees, the ILGWU and shoe workers, upholsterers, bakers, and raincoat makers—all were simultaneously driving toward enlarged membership or were embroiled in walkouts to halt wage cuts. And the day before the President affixed his signature to the NIRA, the Central Labor Union sponsored

a meeting on the Boston Common dedicated to a new campaign to
enroll the unorganized.

Through the National Industrial Recovery Act of June 16, 1933,
the New Deal gave unionism a psychological boost, and in August
when the National Labor Board (NLB) was created, the federal government promised more concrete assistance. "Employees," stated
Section 7(a) of the NIRA, "shall have the right to organize and
bargain collectively through representatives of their own choosing,
and shall be free from the interference, restraint, or coercion of employers of labor." Stipulating further that no worker should be
"required as a condition of employment to join any company union,"
7(a) offered workers an implicit invitation—and no more than that—
to organize. To "consider, adjust, and settle . . . controversies" aris-
ing under NRA,[5] the President created the National Labor Board on
August 5, and the Boston Labor Board, serving as an arm of the
NLB, was packed with liberals.[6] To unions longing for positive help,
the steps taken by the federal government during the second half of
1933 seemed full of potential.

These developments spurred union activities in Boston that were
already discernible in nascent form prior to 7(a) and the NLB, and
by the end of 1933 unions in the city had added 16,000 members, a
gain of 21 percent since the beginning of the year and a level higher
than the 1929 peak. Roughly 23 percent of the city's total work force
were now in labor organizations. Delighted Teamsters officials credited 7(a) with allaying the fears of the hesitant, and their organizing
drive led to the enrollment of over a thousand drivers.[7] Men and
women who had either been in weak independents or had been
totally nonunion rushed to organize: candy workers, bakers, fishermen, seafood workers, butchers, telephone operators, and editorial
writers all displayed a new activism. Utilities workers, largely nonunion in early 1933 and paid $200 a year less than the state reckoned
as necessary to maintain a family of four ($767), obtained an AFL
charter and soon wrenched favorable contracts from their employers.[8] At the August convention of the Massachusetts Labor Federation, AFL officers called for an organizing drive to take advantage

of 7(a), and older unions—the ILGWU, the International Long-shoremen's Association, the Amalgamated Clothing Workers—not only enlarged their domains but also noted other positive developments. Dues were easier to collect, attendance at meetings soared, and the readiness of the city's unions to stage walkouts was reflected by a 36 percent jump in the number of strikes over the previous two-year period.[9]

While the New Deal's intervention in labor-management relations changed the climate in which unions operated, and therefore offered important encouragement, the NLB's direct contribution to increased union membership in Boston was slight. Vested with the authority to hold elections in which workers could choose their own representatives for the purposes of collective bargaining, the Boston Labor Board in fact oversaw balloting that led to certification of no more than two hundred union workers, most of them in the neck-wear trades.[10] The Boston Board also was authorized to block companies from dismissing men for union activity, but here, too, the NLB achieved minimal results: several companies refused to attend hearings and cavalierly evaded NLB orders. As the most serious cases started on a tortuous, time-consuming circuit from the initial union complaint until the matter ended up in Washington, employers coerced their men to join company unions.[11] In addition, a number of small furniture companies either moved in with nonunion shops or left Boston altogether in order to avoid unionization. Union growth may have had a debt to pay to 7(a) and the NLB for providing initial inspiration to organizing campaigns, and the more respectable employers may have been influenced to bargain with organized labor, but the evidence of direct 7(a) and NLB impact on membership gains in Boston was not forthcoming.

Afraid that the NLB was becoming a toothless tabby, and with Congress locked in debate over remedial legislation, the President acted. By Executive Order of June 29, 1934, Roosevelt replaced the NLB with the National Labor Relations Board (NLRB), which received authorization to do much the same thing the defunct NLB was trying to do all along—"investigate issues, facts, practices, or activities of employers or employees in any controversies," and provide for secret elections to determine bargaining representatives. This time, however, the new board promised to wield greater coercive power: the NLRB could subpoena documents and witnesses, use the circuit courts to enforce its decrees, and prescribe rules and regulations with the President's approval. Fines up to $1,000 or imprisonment up to a year or both would be meted out to violators.[12]

The direct consequences of the NLRB for union expansion in Boston were again limited, and in 1934 organized labor gained fewer than 4,000 new members in the Hub, a growth rate of 4 percent compared to national increases of roughly 12 percent. There were, of course, beneficiaries, and close to 500 new AFL members were added through representation elections in the autumn of 1934. Nevertheless, not a single election was held in the City of Boston from January through May of 1935, and workers were discovering that determined antiunion employers were not inhibited by NLRB sanctions. After nine companies in the upholstery trades had refused to bargain under 7(a), for example, the Furniture Workers Industrial Union struck. Men were locked out, and as the strike drew to a close, six of the employers refused to take back all workers identified as prounion. The NLRB ordered the men reinstated, the companies demurred, and the NLRB was unable to break the impasse. The cumbersome process of conferences and hearings in Boston, followed by hearings in Washington, gave those employers who had settled on an antiunion course every opportunity to stall. And even though the Boston Board seemed well aware of management's subterfuges, it was all but impossible to prove that a man had been fired for union activity.[13]

The growth of organized labor from mid-1933 through early 1935 derived from a number of considerations in addition to federal intervention. Like Chicago, New York, and San Francisco, Boston stood out as a center of well-established unionism when the New Deal arrived, and in these cities gains tended to be immediate and, for several months, impressive. Given an AFL structure upon which to build, organization of so-called Federal Labor Unions in 1934 proceeded at a rapid clip in the Hub.[14] Unlike states which had had little experience with unionism, Massachusetts boasted a Department of Labor and Industries with practiced arbitrators and able, even prounion commissioners. Not only were Boston's gains linked to an historical and political edge over unions in other places—Los Angeles, for instance—but two of the city's most heavily organized groups, building-trades operatives and railway workers, were clearly affected by the behavior of the economy. When economic indices took a pronounced upturn, as in the summer and early autumn of 1933, membership soared. When the economy sagged thereafter, reversals occurred. Brewery and Hotel and Restaurant Workers flourished with the repeal of Prohibition, but after the initial surge these unions tapered off. Disheartened workers abandoned the Boston Pattern Makers Association when they discovered that the sickness and disability funds in which they had for years been investing were exhausted, while the Boston Typographical Union, in contrast, maintained the loyalty of its members in the 1929–1936 period by paying out more than $300,000 in unemployment benefits. An ill-advised, poorly led strike could obliterate a union, as kosher butchers discovered in 1934; a well-timed stoppage, on the other hand, could bolster the victors. In short, variables quite apart from federal intervention influenced union growth.[15]

During the months when union membership was increasing most rapidly, the Boston labor movement's abiding concern lay with the blanket wages-and-hours provisions set forth in the President's Reemployment Agreement, and soon after as promulgated in the permanent NRA codes. During the NRA's formative months, most of organized labor focused on practical considerations—local wages, hours, working conditions, and job security. Several trade-union leaders, on the other hand, initially praised the NRA without resorting to arguments based on expediency or parochialism. To the leadership of Boston Typographical Union No. 13 the NRA provided an "alternative" to "violent revolution" and would check the "orgy of greed, avarice, and selfishness" which had culminated from "the so-called American system of rugged individualism." The Boston Central Labor Union, which seldom in the past had strayed from pure and simple trade-union objectives, pledged its "wholesome support to the fulfillment of the theories of the President of the United States in N.R.A." [16] Presumably those theories included rudimentary economic planning, achieving a balance between industrial and farm income, winning greater equality for all workers regardless of the geographical section in which they were employed, and obtaining justice not for unionized Bostonians alone but for all Americans. Thus, at the outset of NRA, self-interest and idealism coexisted.

Boston furnished a setting in which NRA benefits would appear relatively undramatic to important segments of the union movement. Despite pre–New Deal cuts, the city remained a center of high hourly wages, and the entrance rate even for common laborers topped that of most other urban centers in both the state and the nation. Weekly wages for men's clothing workers, though down 30 percent from 1930, bettered the average earnings of workers in ten of the other thirteen principal garment manufacturing centers. The union rate for machinists in Boston topped the going hourly wage in all other large cities; linotypers in the printing trades and motormen on street railways fared almost as well. Even in the bleak days of February 1933 the 70,000 employees in Boston's manufacturing establishments averaged $23.85 a week, roughly 14 percent more than the national industrial norm. Since virtually all of the NRA codes specified a minumum wage in the $13 to $15 range, organized labor did not, in general, express the view that deliverance was at hand.

The NRA in Boston could claim a number of achievements, but there was little question that the federal experiment looked more impressive to unorganized workers than to union members. Code wage rates usually represented an improvement to those without unions, unemployment was cut by approximately 10 percent, and though the NRA failed to drive out all the sweatshops which had so worried the Consumers' League in 1931 and 1932, industrial banditry unquestionably lessened. As a grateful nonunion laborer recalled, "The shoe workers which were held like 'Stalin Holds Russia,' felt the new life coming to them, as a man released from a dungeon, and finally being able to breathe the life God wanted us to live." [17]

A number of unions, however, their members already better fixed than unorganized workers, denied that federal intervention was helping. As unions and management attempted to work out codes regulating hours and wages, there was, in fact, a widespread sentiment that labor was "just the tail of the kite of industry." [18] When representatives of the Boot and Shoe Workers' Union, for instance, went to Washington for code hearings, they found themselves outgunned by management. Forced to accept a $14, forty-hour minimum, they subsequently discovered that the minimum was becoming the code maximum for both skilled and unskilled workers. Insisting that the codes be renegotiated, the shoe unions encountered the argument that if revisions were made, Boston's shoe shops would depart to cheap labor areas. When the code authority again rejected union demands John Mara of the Boot and Shoe Workers' Union concluded that "a purer example of Fascism could not have been concocted." Arguing that the regulations were written "by industry for industry through the help of government," Mara believed that the codes had drawn "an iron ring around labor." [19]

Restaurant workers, needle-trades operatives, and Newspaper Guild members made similar complaints, and with some justice. The average weekly manufacturing wage in Boston remained almost exactly the same from mid-1933 until the NRA's demise before the Supreme Court in May 1935, and the aggregate weekly paycheck was of greater consequence to workers than the improved hourly rate. Meanwhile, the cost of living increased, and real wages during the NRA period therefore dropped. A serious epidemic of noncompliance swept through Boston in 1934 and 1935, and disheartened unionists clamored for redress which in most cases they could not obtain from employers who flagrantly violated code provisions. [20] Even Robert Watt, the labor liberal who headed the Massachusetts AFL, attacked the NRA. Rather than emancipating the working man, he told the AFL convention at San Francisco in 1934, the NRA enslaved him. [21] Moreover, the 1934 state labor convention exuded an anti-NRA flavor. Asserting that the NRA had encouraged company unions, "thereby defeating the very purpose of the NRA," Boston electrotypers jammed through "a most vigorous protest to President Franklin D. Roosevelt." While delegates at the same convention turned thumbs down on an extreme resolution submitted by the Boston Typographical Union, one declaring that the New Deal had become "a 'raw deal,' a detriment to Labor," neither did they pass a motion lauding Roosevelt's "prompt action" which had accomplished "marvelous results." [22]

When the Supreme Court of the United States killed the NRA in May 1935, working-class reaction in Boston divided sharply between the more privileged elements of the union movement and workers who either belonged to the most vulnerable organizations or had no union at all. To E. A. Johnson, the conservative Republican head of the Boston Building Trades Council, the codes had not worked "so what we never had we will never miss." [23] But most would have considered this epitaph too morose, for many of those who had postured against the NRA during its life-span were dismayed by the events which followed in the wake of the Supreme Court decision. Union membership in Boston sagged 12.5 percent in 1935, and most of the loss occurred after the NRA was scuttled. BCLU officials stood by helplessly as the Massachusetts legislature sent a Child Labor Amendment to the federal Constitution down to a chilling defeat, teamsters were thwarted by lockouts in two separate strikes during June, and a Citizens' Committee on the Garment Industry found that shops which under the NRA had been paying $13 and $14 for thirty-seven and a half hours were, in the aftermath of NRA, paying $4 to $8 for weeks of forty-eight, fifty-four, and even sixty hours. When the Boston wage index dropped eight points from April through June of 1935, several unionists who had spoken harshly of the NRA recanted. As a warning to those employers who took advantage of the NRA's demise, for instance, the Boston Central Labor Union threatened a general strike, and garment workers staged wildcat stoppages against reversion to precode standards.

The tendency of the AFL unions to judge the NRA largely on the basis of immediate self-interest was duplicated in the reception accorded to national work-relief and recovery measures during the 1933 to 1935 period. There could be no doubt that federal pump priming was desired, and James T. Moriarty, president of the Massachusetts Federation of Labor, stated the case for action to a large rally of building-trades workers assembled on the Boston Common. "Massachusetts is now spending approximately $50,000,000 a year to pauperize its citizens through public relief," he said on June 15, 1933, "but I submit to you that it is just as easy to squeeze blood out of a stone as it is to extract prosperity from paupers. . . . Government work is the constructive answer." [24] Unions attached to the Building Trades Council, however, seemed to regard the federal government as just another employer rather than as the dispenser of emergency relief to destitute thousands, and their complaints were invariably self-serving. With over half the city's unionized construction workers out of a job in 1933–1934, the Building Trades concluded that a "fraud was being perpurtrated [sic]" whenever the CWA or PWA hired the unorganized. [25] Having built up an elaborate hierarchy of skill classifications and pay scales which rivaled the complexity of medieval guilds, labor leaders insisted that these differentials be preserved. The CWA, union officials asserted, was hiring a few skilled workers on each project but then was taking on assistants at 50 cents an hour. When a foreman belonging to the Operative Plasterers' and Cement Finishers' Association attempted to demote a nonunion plasterer to "a Laborer where he really belonged," however, he received "a punch in the jaw as compsnation [sic] for his . . . act." [26] At the Boston City Hospital project, claimed a Painters and Decorators local, nonunion men predominated by an eight-to-one margin. The installation of thousands of pieces of metal by unorganized workers on the hospital roof was especially dangerous, said the union, since at least half of the CWA building inspectors had no idea of what they were supposed to inspect.

This segment of organized labor kept up the attack in 1935, but the ultimate conclusions drawn about federal activism varied among even the building-trades locals. A vocal and growing minority, for instance, condemned the very principle of the New Deal's involvement in work relief and heavy construction under PWA. At a Boston conference with Arthur Rotch, David Niles, and officials from Washington in July 1935, representatives of the building trades scored not only the destruction of "100 years of hard work" to establish a living wage in the city, but also left the distinct impression that the federal government should withdraw. "These labor people are starting to raise Hell here in Massachusetts," observed one of Harry Hopkins's most trusted emissaries, who reported unions to be taking "the position that they will not work on WPA or PWA regardless of the wage rate." [27] On the other hand, criticism of all but the most conservative construction locals implied acceptance of government subsidies to the jobless, especially if a more vigorous works program were to emphasize heavy construction and were to honor union demands more scrupulously. The line between this position and outright repudiation of the national effort, however, often appeared thin: the insistence on unrealistically high wages and a virtual closed shop on PWA amounted to callous rejection of the nonunion jobless, who, after all, had a firm moral claim to federal assistance. This constricted view of New Deal intentions differed little from the blistering criticism directed at the NRA whenever it subverted union wage scales in Boston. In both cases, unions clearly put the immediate welfare of their own members ahead of national interests as defined by Washington.

Nevertheless, the Seventy-fourth Congress which adjourned in August 1935 had delivered an imposing legislative package, and a new situation was developing. Of vital importance to unions, the National Labor Relations Act was guided through to presidential signature by Representative William Connery (long recognized as the staunchest labor advocate in the Bay State) and Senator Robert Wagner of New York. Creating the second National Labor Relations Board as a permanent and independent agency, the Wagner Act reasserted the right of workers to form unions without harassment from employers. Empowered to hold elections to determine lawful

bargaining agents, the NLRB also spelled out "unfair labor practices" against which wage earners could complain without fear of
reprisal from their bosses. Not only did Congress provide a new
legal framework for unions, but it also passed the immensely popular Social Security Act, authorized the expenditure of $4.88 billion
in the Emergency Relief Act, and ratified the so-called Wealth Tax
bill. In some senses more spectacular than the legislative record of
1933, what came to be known as the Second New Deal had begun.

The Second Hundred Days, unlike the earlier installment,
sparked no instant resurgence of union growth. Losing 10,000
members in 1935, Boston locals recovered just 4,000 workers in
1936: the economy remained sluggish, and the momentum gathered
by employers during the last year of NRA could not be arrested.
The second NLRB's initial impact proved negligible, for in all of
New England the board held just two bargaining elections and settled only sixty-three unfair labor practice cases. Delays of up to a
year and a half occurred in processing union complaints (longer yet,
if the case was tried by an NLRB examiner), and despite the pro-
union attitude of the Boston Regional Board, few employers quaked
in fear. Indeed, a powerful firm such as the Bethlehem Ship Building Corporation discovered that it could evade the clear intent of the
Wagner Act for nearly half a decade by artful legal maneuvering. On
the other hand, employers who had to renegotiate contracts with
the most firmly established unions may have been inhibited by the
Wagner Act, for in bargaining sessions during the autumn of 1935,
older unions representing bricklayers, electrical journeymen, carpenters, linotypers, and street-railway men received higher wages.
Although it is impossible to know whether the Wagner Act played a
part, in general union wage scales for skilled workers went up in
Boston at the close of 1935.

In addition, public-works expenditures began to rise, and Harry
Hopkins took steps to silence unions in the building trades. On
August 22, 1935, he issued Administrative Order No. 15, stipulating
that on contract projects with private employers union workers were
entitled to first call. (The same order reaffirmed that 90 percent of

WPA day labor would be reserved for reliefers irrespective of union ties.) Within a few months, half the agency's work force belonged to trade unions. Moreover, the WPA, after six months of floundering, at last parceled out its first checks. Early in the morning of December 24, 1935, 6,000 men and women queued up at a municipal building in the South End. At 11:00 P.M., after standing for twelve hours with no food, the last in line got their pay. Presumably, there were union members among those who could now face their families on Christmas morning with money in their pockets.

The first days of 1936 also made clear to Boston's workers that the federal government was doing its best. The unpopular Arthur Rotch resigned in January as the state administrator of WPA, and in the next months the federal work force in the city jumped from less than 10,000 to 25,000 men and women. Rotch's successor, Paul Edwards, removed yet another *causus belli* when he exercised his discretionary power to raise wages on federal projects to a level 10 percent above President Roosevelt's announced schedule. Edwards thus recognized that pay scales in Boston had, over the years, crept ahead of the rates established elsewhere in the Commonwealth. And while 1936 witnessed scant additions to New Deal legislation, the single bill that affected organized labor had Massachusetts origins, thus demonstrating the advantage of having Democratic congressmen working in harmony with a Democratic President. David I. Walsh and Congressman Arthur Healey, whose district included Boston wards, cosponsored the Walsh-Healey Act of 1936. On any job where contracts with the federal government had been signed, the bill stated, minimum standards for labor had to be maintained. Although organized labor could applaud Washington's efforts, the union movement remained in low gear.

To emerge from the doldrums of 1935 and early 1936, unionists could ill afford to stand pat. In the wake of the Second New Deal, old line labor organizations were being pushed by developments taking place within the national movement, for at the 1935 AFL convention in Atlantic City the house of labor split apart. Unpersuaded that AFL President William Green and the craft unions were serving the interests of blue-collar America, men like John L. Lewis of the United Mine Workers (UMW) had called upon the AFL to devote itself to industrial unionism, and, more important, to signing up the unorganized in occupations previously bypassed. These commitments neither Green, the majority of the convention delegates, nor most Bostonians would make: the BCLU, the Massachusetts Federation of Labor, and almost every delegate from the Hub cast ballots against Lewis at Atlantic City.[28] Shortly after the 1935 convention, the Committee (later, the Congress) of Industrial Organizations (CIO) was formed, and at least four Boston unions— the ILGWU, the Amalgamated Clothing Workers, the International Typographical Union, the Hat, Cap, and Millinery Workers—were deeply affected, since their national presidents took part in the CIO's formation. Brewery workers, bakers, and hotel and restaurant workers were courted by the CIO almost at once. Among these Boston organizations, however, only the ILGWU and the Amalgamated gravitated into the CIO orbit when the AFL's Executive Committee read ten major unions out of the federation during the summer of 1936. The others remained pillars of the AFL, and at the federation's Tampa Convention in November the BCLU and the Massachusetts AFL voted for formal suspension of the rebels.

Although the loyalties of several decades were not easily shaken in the Hub, organized labor unquestionably felt the repercussions of the schism. The AFL utilities trades, for instance, had wanted to coalesce into a single union, but Green and the AFL had balked in 1935. In the aftermath of Atlantic City, a door opened to the Bostonians, and in 1936 they walked through. Gas, coke, and chemical employees joined District 50 of the United Mine Workers on September 4. Two days later, the men declined to march with AFL members in the city's Labor Day parade, for they were now attached to the CIO. New and militant organizations sprouted among WPA employees, and in May alone thirteen wildcat strikes occurred on federal projects. By autumn, these associations had either affiliated with the CIO or remained belligerently independent.

Unions at the core of the CIO movement launched the city's most spectacular strike of the 1933 to 1936 period during February and March of 1936. Forming a "living crusade" on the streets of Boston against some of the worst sweatshops of any eastern clothing market, the ILGWU and the Amalgamated Clothing Workers demonstrated what militant unionism could accomplish when the rank and file held together. In a major assault not only to win new contracts from companies in which the unions already held a precarious toehold, but to sign up workers in the nonunion fringe as well, the ILGWU and the Amalgamated mobilized 4,000 workers. Seeking closed-shop contracts, an increase to a $13 minimum wage in companies that had not been unionized, and a forty-hour week in place of the fifty-two hours most had been keeping, workers exhibited considerable courage in the face of determined employer opposition. Women in the needle trades engaged in hair-pulling melees with strike-breakers, and along Kneeland Street and Harrison Avenue workers hurled snowballs at scabs as they were being smuggled out back entrances by frightened employers. Police yanked men and women from the picket lines and spilled blood on Boylston and Washington Streets while the strikers, joined by Radcliffe students, avowed socialists, Consumers' League members, and professors, chanted, "The police are having a hell of a time to keep us off the picket line." [29] By April, solidarity had reaped rewards, for nearly every one of the Boston Joint Board's original demands was recognized. [30]

Although the boldness of the ILGWU and the Amalgamated failed to inspire many others to jettison the AFL, the militant tactics employed by the two unions presaged a number of changes which soon took place in Boston. Man-days lost from walkouts jumped 153 percent in 1936, and the atmosphere in the city for the first time seemed a bit closer to the blue-collar radicalism which had been so conspicuously absent in 1934. [31] Indeed, an unverified rumor that Leon Trotsky was hiding in the Hub, a tiny band of orators on the Boston Common, and sporadic outbreaks by renegade, non-ILGWU organizers in the needle trades had been almost the only manifestations of revolutionary consciousness. But in late 1935 and through much of 1936 the radical National Unemployment League was draw-

New Deal benefits did not always come on a silver platter. Gains for organized labor depended in part upon working class spontaneity. Militant female garment workers in 1936 are held back by hand-clasped police as scabs leave the Kneeland Street clothing shops. Boston University School of Communication.

ing three to four hundred people to weekly street-corner meetings with the slogan, "United we eat; divided we starve." [32] Fighting back against white hooliganism in Roxbury and the South End, many Negroes supported the International Labor Defense. Boston's WPA Lodge of the American Federation of Government Employees was expelled from the parent union for allegedly harboring Communists, and although the local called the charge "fantastic" it nevertheless castigated Roosevelt and the rest of organized labor for being too conservative. Even if it were true, as an officer of the Boston Central Labor Union asserted, that "25 Irish cops on horseback could drive all the Communists in this country out of [the South End's] Union Square in 15 minutes," it was evident that the rumblings on the left could not be ignored. [33]

In mid-1936, organized labor in Boston seemed poised for takeoff in new directions. Buoyed by more favorable economic indicators, confronted with a new brand of militant unionism, and apparently impressed by changes in both the WPA and PWA, BCLU affiliates made commitments from which they had previously abstained. At the Boston Common in July 1936, J. Arthur Moriarty of the BCLU joined speakers from the Communist and Socialist parties, the International Labor Defense, and the National Unemployment League to mark the twentieth anniversary of the imprisonment of Tom Mooney, the radical labor martyr jailed after San Francisco's 1916 Preparedness Day bombing. BCLU delegates at the state labor convention in August called for the unionization of all WPA employees, and they also declined to vote for a resolution favoring the national AFL's thirty-day ultimatum to all unions that were siding with the CIO. Moreover, Robert Watt of the Massachusetts AFL acted as spokesman for the leftist United Committee for the Support of the Struggle of Labor Against Spanish Fascism. When denied a permit for a meeting on the Boston Common, Watt blasted Representative Thomas Dorgan, Boston's Communist-baiting author of the Teachers' Loyalty Oath Act of 1935, Mayor Mansfield, and "a Fascist coalition of Carlists, generals, landowners, and capitalists." Unintimidated by William Green's warning to the BCLU not to support the Communist-backed committee, scores of workers carried signs in Boston's Labor Day Parade which said, "Defeat the Fascists and the Liberty League." Other banners called for an extension of WPA and PWA and for a five-day, thirty-hour week.[34]

Most important, the old-line unions took a significant and unprecedented step in August of 1936. With reason to be grateful for the strides made by the Second New Deal in Boston, worried by the nattering leftists, and uninspired by the Republican alternative, BCLU affiliates joined with the Massachusetts Federation of Labor in endorsing Franklin Roosevelt. Never before had the state organization put its official stamp of approval on a Presidential candidate. In addition, BCLU speakers appeared on the same platform with David Dubinsky and Sidney Hillman to launch a pro-Roosevelt campaign sponsored by labor's Non-Partisan League. Even though the

League attracted mostly Jewish and Italian garment workers while the Irish stayed home, the sound of workers booing the name of Alfred E. Smith, as happened at the League's opening meeting, was remarkable in a city which had once revered the New Yorker.

With Roosevelt's stunning 1936 landslide behind them, Boston's unions began to pick up members at a rapid clip. From 1932 to 1936, organized labor had registered a net gain of 12,000 workers, but during the second Roosevelt administration the city's unions added 45,000 men and women while the size of the labor force slightly decreased. Membership almost doubled in the seven years that followed the promulgation of the New Deal, as Table 9.1 demonstrates. Although the growth rate of locals in Boston trailed both state and national norms during the particularly volatile years of 1935 to 1938, the number of union workers paying their dues in the Hub nevertheless shot up by a robust 23 percent in that same period. The city had entered the Depression as one of the nation's major centers of unionism, and it emerged from hard times as an even greater stronghold of labor organization.

Boston's steeply rising union membership levels from 1937 to the close of the decade may be explained in several ways. Having exhibited renascent signs in 1936, labor was further bolstered by relatively favorable economic trends during the winter of 1936–1937. Aligning themselves with Roosevelt in '36, unionists may well have been encouraged by election results which all but guaranteed the continuation of prolabor policies in Washington, and labor officials entered the early months of 1937 apparently sensing that their hour had come. "There is definitely here in Boston a trend toward organization," an ILGWU official observed in February, "and we mean to take advantage of it." [35] When the Supreme Court ruled affirmatively on the Wagner Act's constitutionality in the spring, the setting for organization further improved. Indeed, the NLRB for Region #1, operating out of the Old South Building, was swamped with complaints of unfair labor practices, and the board handled nearly thirty times as many representation cases from mid-1937 through June 1938 as it had in the twelve months ending on June 30, 1936. [36]

Table 9.1*. *The Growth of Union Membership in Boston, in Massachusetts, and in the United States, 1932–1940*

	1932	1933–4	1935–6	1937–8	1939–40	1932–1940 % gain**
Boston: total union membership	62,340	80,647	74,717	97,553	119,572	95.0
Mass.: total union membership	155,342	239,001	224,561	264,374	307,250	105.8
Boston: number of locals	240	271	282	329	382	63.3
Mass.: number of locals	1,040	1,234	1,225	1,377	1,469	44.5
U.S.: union membership in millions, BLS schedule	—	3.05	3.95	7.75	8.96	213.7
U.S.: union membership in millions, NBER schedule	2.97	3.13	3.77	5.71	6.70	137.7

* Figures for Boston and for Massachusetts have been calculated from the *Thirty-Sixth and Fortieth Annual Directories of Labor Organizations in Massachusetts, 1937, 1941,* pp. 77, 99 respectively. Bureau of Labor Statistics (BLS) and National Bureau of Economic Research (NBER) schedules are found in Troy, *Trade Union Membership, 1897–1962,* pp. 1, 18. In addition to Troy's comments about the difficulty in measuring union statistics (the irreconcilability of the BLS and NBER figures is but one of many), consult Bernstein, *Turbulent Years,* pp. 769–771, 838–839n.; Derber, "Growth and Expansion,' in Derber and Young (eds.), *Labor and the New Deal,* pp. 3–44; and Troy, *Distribution of Union Membership Among the States, 1934 and 1953,* pp. 30–31.
** Percentages have been calculated by using the figures for 1940 rather than the aggregate statistics for 1939–1940.

At last able to bring recalcitrant employers to bay, the Boston Board was further strengthened when in January 1938 the United States Supreme Court ruled against the notorious "Bethlehem Plan" of employee representation at the Boston and Fore River (Quincy) yards.[37] The corporate giant soon entered into collective bargaining with the Industrial Union of Marine and Shipbuilding Workers (CIO), and other Boston firms could no longer depend upon injunctive remedies to maintain company unions. Successful organizing efforts elsewhere in the nation also seemed to inspire Boston's locals, and competition from the CIO prodded AFL affiliates to get moving.

Goaded by these stimuli, organized labor in Boston extended its scope considerably beyond that of the 1933 to 1936 period. Of the more than 150 new locals chartered after the coming of the New Deal, better than half were established in occupations already partly unionized. Yet the addition of one or more locals by nine unions which had existed in Boston prior to the New Deal transformed several of them from relatively weak organizations into more potent combinations, a process especially descriptive of the Teamsters: from a membership of 335 in 1933, Teamsters Local 25 had by 1940 built a sprawling fiefdom of 5,500 truckers, cab drivers, and warehousemen. Even more significant, whole new categories of workers who had been largely unorganized in 1933 belonged to unions in 1940: federal and municipal employees (including the first teachers' organizations), retail clerks, auto mechanics, taxi drivers, several groups of professional workers, and a host of others enjoyed representation at the decade's close. Union organization, both more intensive *and* extensive in 1940, displayed a slightly greater disposition to enroll non-Irish workers, at least as indicated by union election results. While the number of Irish officers rose 28 percent during the Depression decade (3 percent less than the total increase of all elected officials), the number of Jewish officers went up 36 percent while Italians gained 40 percent more positions than they had held in the early 1930s.[38]

Locals affiliated with the American Federation of Labor continued to represent the vast majority of unionized workers in Boston, while the CIO—except for the Amalgamated Clothing Workers—made only modest advances. Starting with a Massachusetts nucleus of 49 locals which had been ejected by the Executive Committee of the State AFL, the new organization claimed 218 locals in 1940, approximately 44 of them centered in the capital city. By 1940, one of every five to six union members in Boston was paying dues to the CIO (roughly 25,000 of 120,000 organized workers), but in the rest of the nation two of five unionized workers belonged to the AFL's rival. Of the 35 international unions and organizing committees which composed the CIO's domain at the end of 1940, just 19 had Boston locals. Some—the Amalgamated, the UMW's Gas and By-Product Workers, the Newspaper Guild—included workers who had been in unions prior to the 1937 to 1940 push. And of the CIO unions which were not lineal descendants of pre-1936 organizations, the only ones to enroll more than 500 members appear to have been the Marine and Shipbuilding Workers, the National Federation of Federal Employees, and the United Retail Clerks.[39]

Despite occasional breakthroughs, the CIO encountered a lack of opportunity in Boston. The city simply did not have the type of industrial structure which attracted this offshoot from the AFL. While the United Auto Workers staged massive sit-down strikes against the motor industry in Flint and Detroit, organizers chartered two small Boston locals composed of auto mechanics and body repairmen. The CIO enrolled tens of thousands of steelworkers in South Chicago, Gary, and Pittsburgh but had to content itself with a few sheet-metal workers at shipyards in the Hub. Instead of being able to attract large aggregates of blue-collar workers, the CIO turned to white-collar WPA employees and retail clerks. Perhaps sensing that the city's industrial structure would not be an auspicious setting for use of the CIO's most dramatic tactic, Sidney Hillman repudiated threats made by his own organizers and pledged to business leaders that "the CIO will not tolerate any disturbance or sitdown strike in the City of Boston." [40] Throughout the thirties, the CIO honored Hillman's promise, and CIO unions employed conventional weapons whenever they walked out.

Moreover, the CIO encountered tough sledding in Boston when internecine warfare broke out in earnest with the AFL. Having fared reasonably well in limited head-to-head competition with AFL units in 1937 and 1938, the CIO lost ground when the AFL mounted a determined counteroffensive in 1939 and 1940. In an especially vital election, the CIO was routed by Daniel Sullivan's Teamsters for the allegiance of 4,000 warehousemen, and the CIO's Packinghouse Workers, after an apparent victory during the so-called "Hotdog Strike" of 1939, watched several units defect thereafter. Longshoremen and shoe workers both resisted CIO overtures, several Newspaper Guild locals took AFL charters, and the ILGWU returned to its original home. Although the AFL fell short of its objective of driving the CIO out of Boston, the older organization extended no fraternal hand to what had become a hated adversary. A Boston delegate to the state AFL convention in 1940, still spoiling for a fight, accused the CIO of arrogantly "gazing into the pool of Narcissus." The Massachusetts Federation then voted a resolution which grandly asserted that the CIO was "not indispensable to the workers of this country." [41] With the tide running against the CIO, the delegates might well have added that the AFL's rival did not seem "indispensable" to much of blue-collar Boston either.

With the AFL maintaining hegemony over the preponderant share of organized workers, and with jurisdictional strikes relatively infrequent, Boston was spared much of the industrial conflict which broke out in other cities of comparable size. While Tables 9.2 and 9.3 indicate that the number of industrial disputes in the Massachusetts capital soared in 1937, Cleveland, Milwaukee, Pittsburgh, and St. Louis exhibited much higher rates of work stoppage. Labor was at times rambunctious in Boston: the ILGWU fought police and drove out strikebreakers in the heart of the city during 1938, and Teamsters Local 25 dismayed the NLRB and the Federal Mediation Service with repeated wildcat strikes. Nevertheless, the

Table 9.2 *. Number of Industrial Disputes in Boston, the State of Massachusetts, the Nation, and in Selected Cities of 500,000–1,000,000 Population, 1932–1940

	1932	1933	1934	1935	1936	1937	1938	1939	1940
Boston	17	22	16	16	17	46	34	NA	25
Mass.	76	157	112	110	111	277	123	NA	104
Nation	808	1,562	1,856	2,014	2,172	4,740	2,772	2,613	2,508
Cleveland	2	23	67	66	39	64	22	NA	56
Milwaukee	3	4	42	21	24	76	40	NA	17
Pittsburgh	10	17	18	17	16	99	44	NA	31
St. Louis	10	22	20	21	20	66	33	NA	43

* "Industrial Disputes," *Monthly Labor Review*, XXXVI (June, 1932), pp. 1297–1298; XXXIX (July, 1934), pp. 71–72, 80; XLII (May, 1936), pp. 1303–1306; XLIV (May, 1937), pp. 1226–1227; XLVI (May, 1938), pp. 1092–1103. Figures for all cities, 1935, do not include intercity strikes. Boston had three such disputes involving 759 workers at a cost of 5,508 man-days.

number of workers affected and the man-days lost through industrial disputes were slight when contrasted with most large cities, and in general the work stoppages in Boston proceeded with decorum. And while the vast majority of unionized workers won at least one pay increase from employers from 1937 to 1940, hourly wages relative to those earned by union members in other big cities slipped from the position enjoyed earlier in the decade. For all the momentous developments in Boston's union circles—membership advances, CIO incursions, jurisdictional warfare, increased strikes, wage gains—the pulse of organized labor beat a bit less rapidly in Boston than in most of urban America.

To New Deal liberalism in the city, the CIO made a solid contribution. Virtually all locals advocated expanded work relief and

Table 9.3 *. *Number of Workers in Industrial Disputes and Number of Man-days Idle in Boston and Selected Cities of 500,000–1,000,000 Population, 1934–1940 (1929–1933 Not Available)*

	1934		1935		1936	
	workers	days	workers	days	workers	days
Boston	4,200	58,611	3,694	29,127	7,226	63,504
Cleveland	30,727	428,956	28,490	538,022	13,918	124,926
Milwaukee	13,980	307,002	3,952	69,587	4,512	60,360
Pittsburgh	2,399	40,974	1,246	49,279	3,256	54,807
St. Louis	6,184	90,691	2,673	64,429	2,369	26,311

	1937		1938		1940	
	workers	days	workers	days	workers	days
Boston	9,644	71,337	3,872	32,316	7,665	111,023
Cleveland	20,531	259,693	4,895	55,049	7,778	107,659
Milwaukee	14,079	224,969	10,053	215,607	1,135	15,268
Pittsburgh	19,396	197,901	13,527	124,477	6,235	86,336
St. Louis	19,409	343,715	4,950	97,833	20,454	214,386

* Based on sources cited in Table 9.2.

public housing without insisting that union members receive preference. Almost all favored expansion both of the Social Security and Fair Labor Standards acts, and CIO unions also refrained from sniping at Roosevelt's programs for agriculture, his tax policies, and his efforts to curb monopolies. CIO unions gave wholehearted support to Labor's Non-Partisan League, for as a member of the Amalgamated Clothing Workers put it in 1938, "President Roosevelt's program is being opposed by the reactionaries of both parties." Politicians who had not kept pace with the liberalism of the 1930s, he continued, should be dumped. If it took a third party, an American Labor Party, to oust those who opposed the Roosevelt legislation, so be it. And although the Boston CIO never took this step, the union nevertheless made clear through its repudiation of Senator David I. Walsh that it was not enough to be an Irish Catholic Democrat and expect an automatic stamp of approval. Indeed, the CIO assumed something of a watchdog role over Roosevelt himself. "We will continue to support [the President]," said a delegate to the CIO's 1940 state convention, "as long as he will continue to support the New Deal." [42]

Several AFL locals, on the other hand, accumulated a more mixed record as they responded to Washington's moves. If put to a vote, probably no AFL chapter in the city would have repudiated the Social Security Act or the Wagner Act, and some AFL groups also advocated public housing, a thirty-hour week, and expansion of WPA and PWA. At the same time, however, unions affiliated with the Building Trades Council fell back on their old habits of construing New Deal programs in the narrowest terms. The Public Works Administration was viewed more favorably because, from 1937 on, union members made up almost the entire work force. But WPA, as construed by angry marble setters, for example, continued to be excoriated for filling its ranks with nonunion "incompetents whose tools comprise water pails and sponges." When skilled union members came onto federal work relief, they could not understand why they were being sent "to do work in a stable" where they "became violently sick with offensive odors." [43] Craft unions, then, clung to the idea of *sauve qui peut,* forced the Boston WPA in 1937 to classify 35 percent of its wage earners as skilled (the national norm was 25 percent), and thereby cost hundreds of jobless workers a monthly check. In much the same fashion, the Fair Labor Standards Act of 1938 attracted scant praise (despite its ban on child labor) because AFL workers already enjoyed wages higher than the 40-cent hourly minimum decreed by the bill. Teamsters Local 25, moreover, argued that the act's maximum forty-hour week would cost its men extra money. If a truck driver wanted to be on the job twelve hours a day, the union contended, he should have the liberty to do so.[44] And with William Green and George Meany of the national AFL pronouncing a murrain upon the Non-Partisan League, AFL locals in Boston turned down proposals to work for the New Deal through this political instrument.

The AFL unions were prone to much the same sort of illogical distinction that most of the city's elected Democrats were also making: Roosevelt the man was splendid but policies of which he had been the architect were either less beguiling or construed more narrowly. "Mistakes" had been made, a spokesman for the Cooks and Pastry Cooks told the state AFL convention in 1940, but they "were not the fault of Roosevelt." Yes, there had been "maladministration of some of the departments under our President," a delegate from the Bartenders and Hotel Employees agreed, but they had to be forgiven. Citing statistical evidence of union growth, it was possible to assert that "No other administration in the history of our country has given so much recognition to Labor as has President Roosevelt's." Accordingly, a majority of Boston's AFL delegates spurned an effort to endorse Wendell Willkie in 1940 and pushed through a pro-Roosevelt resolution.[45] It was fitting, however, that only the President's foreign policy received the convention's official imprimatur—and, typically, the resolution in support of assistance to the Allied Powers was coupled with a demand that more defense work be given to Boston. Countable as components of the Roosevelt coalition on election day, most BCLU affiliates sniped at the New Deal's total design once the ballots were cast. They were not authentic voices of liberalism, for they could muster no more than *ad hoc* enthusiasm for social engineering, economic planning, and redistribution of wealth.

Justifiable reasons abounded for this often limited behavior. From the trade-union point of view, certain aspects of the New Deal were fair game for criticism: the NLB and the first NLRB made little direct contribution to unionism; social security and unemployment insurance relied on regressive taxes; agricultural policies pushed up food costs; and by the decade's close the levels of economic activity in the city, less than in the state and nation, had not been restored to those of 1929. It may also have been the case that union officials detected in Roosevelt a greater concern for labor in the abstract than for labor organizations themselves, although it is not clear that Bostonians were especially aware of the President's ambivalence.

Local circumstances played a crucial part in shaping the AFL's lukewarm response toward federal policies of 1933 to 1940. Enjoying higher wage rates and a greater degree of union organization than the average city in 1933, labor in Boston at the very least expected to maintain its relative standing. Instead, its relative position declined, even as absolute advances were recorded. While this development alone could have accounted for feisty skepticism about the New Deal, labor leaders also took in generous dosages of conservative instruction from avowed friends to whom they looked for guidance: Cardinal O'Connell leveled withering tirades against Washington's novel policies; Joseph B. Ely found the Hundred Days dangerously socialistic; James Michael Curley was at odds with the Roosevelt administration for personal reasons; and David I. Walsh, never a Roosevelt loyalist, came out in the open in 1937 to say explicitly what he had long implied—the New Deal constituted a menace to American liberties. Finally, Boston had been an old union town, and the appearance of new organizations menaced the well-established crafts. Although the BCLU had long paid lip service to unionizing the city's blue-collar men and women, the CIO was viewed as an intruder despite its erratic successes in Boston. Since it was both easy to regard the New Deal as the progenitor of the unwelcome rival and tempting to yearn for the more tranquil days when the AFL had the field to itself, the clear majority of the city's unions viewed the assistance rendered to the CIO with a jaundiced eye.

John Kearney, business agent of the Bartenders and Hotel Employees and long a staunch Roosevelt supporter, took his fellow AFL delegates to task in August of 1940 for their unwillingness to support both the President and the social legislation which his administrations had promulgated. Speaking in a strong Irish voice, Kearney quickly got to the heart of the matter. "There has been no President ever to sit in Washington who knows the opinion and needs of our people better than President Roosevelt," he said. "Let me appeal to the delegates to subordinate their local disputes and be big men." Union members should not "confuse the great issue with our petty cases of certain specific things that were not done to please them," Kearney added. "Show you are a trade unionist! Subordinate your petty affairs!" [46] In Boston, that was easier said than done.

10

The View from State Street

From the cluttered alleys outside the decaying Quincy Market to the high-ceilinged offices along State Street, Boston's commercial and industrial enterprisers felt the Great Depression's fury. Aware, as one put it, that they could no longer live in a world where "Mammon and Moloch had become Gods," [1] businessmen—large and small—pondered reform. But just as the most destitute jobless, on the one hand, and the most privileged trade unionist, on the other, responded to both municipal and national reconstruction on a piecemeal basis, businessmen also exhibited self-serving tendencies. The matter, though, was more complicated than liberals would have had it when constructing their demonologies. "Malefactors of great wealth" surely existed, but all save the most pernicious among them could, on selected issues, be found on the side of progressive change. Nevertheless, enterprisers almost always tried to bend reform to their own provincial interests. Because the First New Deal in particular did not coerce with an iron fist, these efforts frequently succeeded. Urban businessmen, no less and possibly no more than other groups, helped convert legislation of the 1930s into a helter-skelter collage. Sometimes acting as outright adversaries of new arrangements between government and business, and at other moments trying to use government to serve their own purposes, businessmen limited what innovators could expect to accomplish in the city.

The business community had, in general, brought to March 4, 1933, a long history of opposition to federal intervention in the economy. During the Hoover years antispending sentiment, preference for voluntary approaches to relief and recovery, and a distrust of regulation had remained strong. Yet on Inauguration Day, 1933, Franklin Delano Roosevelt asked the nation to adopt "social values more noble than mere monetary profit." The President scored the "callous and selfish wrongdoing" of a materialistic civilization, and he described as a "sacred obligation" the need to "submit . . . lives and property" to "a common discipline." [2] To unite the discordant voices of Boston businessmen into a single anthem for change, however, was bound to be difficult, especially because so many had carefully rehearsed their lyrics before federal intervention took place.

The banking crisis of 1933 momentarily led the financial community to see the usefulness of energetic government, yet it is nevertheless striking that the instant the traumatic days of March 4–13 ended, important segments reverted to their habitual distrust of regulation. During the third week in March, for instance, Governor Ely attempted to bring the laws of the Commonwealth into harmony with the Federal Emergency Banking Act. In response, the Boston Clearing House Association and the Chamber of Commerce egged on Republican legislators, and Ely's proposals narrowly escaped defeat. When the United States Congress passed the Glass-Steagall Act of June 1933, the Chamber wired Roosevelt in protest of the bill's provision safeguarding bank accounts up to $5,000 through the Federal Deposit Insurance Corporation (FDIC). "Inefficient bank management should not thus be encouraged," said the organization, nor should "depositors and taxpayers in sections having had relatively good banking records . . . be penalized." Believing that the FDIC was costing the banks money and that depositors should have to absorb the expense, a spokesman for stockholders of the Federal

Reserve Bank of Boston denounced the new system as "unwise social policy," for it conferred "a large gratuitous benefit on a great group of citizens . . . without making them realize that someone has to pay for it." "We are being pitchforked into a nation-wide insurance system," the speaker concluded to a burst of applause.[3]

Regulation of the securities market, more than novel banking laws, had what a liberal Boston retailer called "a halting effect" on business attitudes toward the New Deal.[4] While it was readily acknowledged that firms should be required to publicize their assets and liabilities before floating their stock, the Securities Act of 1933 and the Securities and Exchange Act of 1934 were denounced as excessively drastic obstacles to corporate financing. The 1934 law in particular seemed menacing, for it separated underwriting and brokerage houses. If the two were kept apart, it was widely believed, neither could survive. In the opinion of Eliot Wadsworth and the Chamber of Commerce, the new legislation represented no less than a socialistic disruption of the capital market, and soon the Boston securities market was, in fact, shaken by a Securities and Exchange Commission (SEC) investigation of the Boston Curb. Joseph P. Kennedy, the first chairman of the regulatory body, returned to his native city on November 15, 1934, and attempted to assure the Chamber of Commerce that his agency was "not the death hand that some proclaim it to be." [5] Yet the next day at 3:00 P.M. the Curb Exchange, under threat of heavy penalties imposed by Kennedy's SEC, shut its doors. They would never open again. Although Kennedy's proselytizing mission was reported as having a soothing effect on businessmen, the SEC's crackdown in Boston bespoke a sterner federal policy. Even the city's larger corporations, most of whom traded on the more respectable Boston Stock Exchange, were made jittery by this display of federal coercion.

Meanwhile, the rousing first stages of the NRA campaign in Boston had stampeded 10,000 employers into signing the President's Reemployment Agreement (PRA), but the quantitative success did not necessarily mean that the city's businessmen had donned sackcloth and ashes. For one thing the PRA, whose temporary codes were widely understood to be unenforceable, made extremely modest demands: the $12 minimum wage for a forty-hour week was only half as much as unskilled municipal workers were making in Boston, and the $30 weekly minimum for skilled labor also fell below prevailing rates. Only the city's few sweatshop owners and employers of child labor were being asked to change drastically their customary practices. Moreover, the Boston Recovery Committee, the business-dominated organization which was charged with enrolling employers, made it perfectly clear that it would not stand for compulsion. When Congressman McCormack warned the Boston Market Terminal to cooperate or face total control, for example, the local committee intervened on the employer's behalf. "Our job is not to threaten," the recovery group announced. Instead, the committee insisted on voluntarism and called on business to solve its own problems "without howling for help from Washington." [6]

Even as the Boston Recovery Committee led a spirited drive to mobilize the city behind the NRA in August, entrepreneurial participation began to decline. More and more, James Michael Curley spoke for the NRA while business leadership, seemingly in inverse proportion to his waxing role, fell away. The Mayor publicly warned "obstructionists and slackers" not to "join behind the buzzard of despair," and in mid-September he declared a half-holiday so that businessmen and their employees might attend an NRA rally on the Boston Common. Schools let out, and pupils heard the Mayor laud the NRA and William Randolph Hearst's Boston *American*. In a demagogic speech, Curley denounced industry for having "absorbed . . . the wasted bodies of women and of little children . . . to build up dividends for the wealthy owners of mills and factories throughout the nation," and he then led Boston's youth in mass recitation of a Blue Eagle pledge. ("I promise, as a good American, to do my part for the NRA. I will buy where the Blue Eagle flies. I will ask my family to buy in September and buy American-made goods. I will help President Roosevelt bring back good times.") From then on, Curley stepped up his insinuations that all private enterprisers had arrayed themselves against reform. At a Columbus Day rally he reminded them that "when a bank fails in China everybody connected with it is beheaded." [7] Businessmen did not like this kind of talk, and, further, they did not care for the steeper demands placed upon them as code-drafting began in earnest. Sporadic "Buy Now" and enrollment drives in the autumn of 1933 fizzled for want of volunteers.

As Professor Felix Frankfurter of the Harvard Law School looked back at the businessmen's NRA campaigns of the summer of 1933, he claimed that they had never signified very much. In a partisan and sardonic letter to Louis Kirstein, he explained that "Republicans remain Republicans." Those "who threw up their hats for Franklin Roosevelt after March 4," he said, "resolved to go after Roosevelt at the earliest opportunity because his general direction would prevent his going back to the good old days." Frankfurter accused "the gang that owns the [Boston] *Herald*" of ordering staff writers in September to terminate favorable mention of the President, and he believed that "as early as August a lot of the big boys who had the Blue Eagles in their windows cursed Roosevelt and devised ways and means of circumventing him in their offices and in their libraries." [8]

While partisanship and anti-Curleyism contributed to diminished enthusiasm for the NRA, more important considerations were involved. Businessmen pointed out that economic improvement was insubstantial during the early months of the NRA, and their assessment was essentially correct. Although a sampling of Boston firms in December 1933 revealed that 65 percent enjoyed greater sales than during the last month of the Hoover administration and 51 percent boasted increased profits, the fact still remained that, a year after Roosevelt's election, half were no better off than they had been at the Depression's worst point. Businessmen emphasized the discrepancy between sales and profits, complained about the higher costs of labor and raw materials, and condemned the Roosevelt administration for giving encouragement to the union movement. Moreover, businessmen observed that the NRA had not stimulated heavy industry, and that only an inflationary monetary policy had brought even the appearance of prosperity. While the allegations made by the entrepreneurial classes carried a substantial measure of accuracy, Louis Kirstein also sagaciously noticed that owners "did not start the anvil chorus until they found that they really were going to be required to work under a code and also be forced to observe, like some others, decent conditions." [9]

At first, businessmen did not seem overly concerned about the matter of compliance to which Kirstein alluded. They had been told that E. A. Filene's State Recovery Board would do the policing, and that a regional group would act as another intermediary between alleged offenders and Washington. But, in September 1933, Hugh Johnson designated the United States Commerce Department, acting through a New England regional board, to superintend all agreements. When the emphasis had been upon the gentlemanly cooperation with a business-dominated state board, few complained, but when authority shifted, protests deluged Filene's office. Johnson retreated, and all compliance cases thereafter originated with a seven-member Boston Compliance Board composed of local business, labor, and consumer representatives. This was not to be the last alteration of the NRA's enforcement mechanism, however. The Boston Compliance Board remained in existence until the National Recovery Administration ended in 1935, but the local group's responsibilities and its lines of reporting within the NRA hierarchy frequently changed. In general, the Boston Compliance Board in 1934 simply routed cases to Washington, which then exercised fairly rigorous code supervision. In 1935, however, New Dealers returned to a decentralized scheme—one which left the powerless Boston Board in charge—and compliance totally broke down. Boston businessmen faulted both these tendencies, despite their contradictory nature.

In 1934 the local compliance board forwarded to Washington numerous applications for code exceptions and, through an unvarying form letter, repeatedly discovered that its petitions were rejected. Unless callous NRA factotums corrected their "appalling lack of comprehension" of local circumstances, the Boston Board pointed out, there would "along the Road to Recovery . . . be no milestones to record." [10] Joined by the Chamber of Commerce, which made it its business to act as an advocate for local firms, the Boston Compliance Board lashed out at what it considered to be irksome inconsistencies. The American Briquet Company of Boston, for instance, had to pay time and a third for overtime above thirty-five hours, while its competitors (fuel oil, coal, and coke companies) were entitled to work their men forty hours without the overtime penalty. Similarly, the Joseph P. Manning Company, a distributor of tobacco, had to maintain a forty-hour schedule while competing against wholesale grocers who were entitled to work their men a longer forty-eight hour week. The petitions of American Briquet and Joseph P. Manning were both denied, while Boston's kosher poultry dealers, accustomed to sweating their men eighty hours a week for $12, had no trouble in getting an exception to a new code which demanded $18 for forty-eight hours. Surveying the carnage, the Boston Board thought it saw a systematic pattern of injustices meted out by insensitive, distant officials. Washington, in turn, had a different perception. If a company like American Briquet or Joseph P. Manning received special dispensations, Pandora's box would open, and compliance would be impossible to obtain.

The shoe industry, perhaps more than any other, exemplifies what happened when Washington either succumbed to local pressures and bestowed special privileges, or when code enforcement was negligible. With small- and medium-sized shoe manufacturers violating NRA regulations more flagrantly than any other Massachusetts industry, larger firms demanded a remedy. When, in the spring of 1934, John McElwain, the conservative president of the McElwain Shoe Company, got Washington's approval for a fifty-hour week in his factory, other companies immediately followed suit. Furthermore, with unemployment increasing, some unions asked manufacturers to ignore the minimum-wage requirements in order to take on more men. With employers and unions both having an interest in circumventing the NRA, it is with small wonder that, of all complaints docketed with the Shoe Code Authority between

July 1934 and January 1935, 89 percent originated in Massachusetts. (The state contained a quarter of all shoe manufacturing in the nation.) A compliance drive in February to April, 1935, uncovered Boston employers who paid women stitchers as little as $1.10 for twenty hours, unmasked a Roxbury company which worked its men sixty hours a week, and found out that still other firms kept no time clocks, making piecework rates impossible to calculate. Companies that fled from Boston to northern New England to evade NRA specifications, as well as city taxes, sent work to the homes of Boston laborers in a reversion to one of the crudest of nineteenth-century practices.

Toward the end of NRA, compliance also broke down in other industries. When legal attacks jeopardized the agency's future, and rumors grew that the NRA would not be extended beyond the expiration date of June 16, 1935, compliance officials discovered acute demoralization. The "slow and lingering death" of NRA, a Boston Cotton and Suit Code administrator said, undermined "the efficiency of the code," and he advised that rather than extend the agency's life for a short period of time, it would be better "to go down . . . with the flag nailed to the mast." Discipline in 1935 had crumbled so thoroughly, a field officer reported, that even those employers who did not wish "to revert to the old policy of 'dog eat dog' " did "not see how the honest businessman was going to be able to continue." [11]

From the point of view of those who believed in New Deal recovery programs, the animosity of the textile industry must surely have been a sharp disappointment, for no manufacturing group had welcomed the NRA more fervently. Some three months before Congress passed the National Industrial Recovery Act, Henry Kendall, a textile owner and normally a conservative spokesman for the Boston Chamber of Commerce, had tried unsuccessfully to convince the New England Council that Roosevelt should have the power to create uniform labor laws. Only by fixing minimum wages and maximum hours, and by regulating night work and the employment of women, could the ruinous wage differential between northern and

southern mills be eliminated. Since New England textile manufacturers agreed with Kendall's analysis, the industry drafted a permanent code long before any other.

By the end of 1933, however, the city's millowners were clamor-
ing for revisions. Robert Amory of the Boston-headquartered
Nashua Manufacturing Company, in a blistering speech delivered to
the Harvard Economic Society on November 18, charged that work-
spreading decreased production and destroyed wealth. The NRA,
he said, defied natural economic law by increasing wages before
prices went up. Having made this theoretical pronouncement, he
added: "The more contacts I have had in Washington, the less I respect the theorists." Moreover, Amory was disturbed by the conflicting provisions of the wholesalers' and retailers' codes, by reports
from salesmen that the average housewife refused to believe that
goods with the Blue Eagle sewn in were of the same quality as
precode merchandise, and by a fear that the NRA would eventually
fix prices.[12]

Textile manufacturers also discovered that the NRA did not stabilize relations with labor. The industry suffered from the Great Textile Strike of 1934, and when the codes were revised in October of
that year, the new strictures included a lowering of the work week
from forty to thirty-six hours without lowering wages. Bostonians
joined other manufacturers in the rush to obtain court-enforced
orders restraining the NRA from putting this new schedule into effect. Furthermore, the industry held an abiding conviction that the
NRA had not eliminated the wage differential between northern
and southern mills, and that it had done "irreparable injuries to and
destruction of the business."[13]

If the NRA piqued textile manufacturers, the Agricultural Adjustment Administration drove them to the point of rebellion. Complaints of millowners and the Boston Chamber of Commerce alike
centered on the processing tax, a levy which cost owners 4.2 cents
for every pound of cotton that entered the factories. Almost no one
agreed with the Secretary of Agriculture, Henry Wallace, when he
stated that the processing tax had "nothing to do with the distress in

the New England textile mills." Protests against the AAA, claimed
Wallace, represented a "chiseling drive for special power" by men
who "haven't the guts of their grandfathers." [14] Wallace had a point.
Manufacturers, after all, were able to pass on part of the expense to
consumers, and the value of products turned out in cotton textiles
held steady in the Bay State during the AAA years. Nevertheless,
textile interests continued to balk: of the first seventy-six cases submitted by the AAA's New England field investigators for legal action
by Washington, seventy-three originated in Massachusetts. As an attorney for the Department of Agriculture ruefully confessed, "the
section around New England is a hotbed against processing taxes,"
and Boston became a principal arena of combat. [15] Indeed, few law-
suits have ever been more closely followed than the one filed on
April 23, 1935, in the United States Court of Appeals in Boston.
There, lawyers of former United States Senator William Butler, a
millowner and once a force behind Calvin Coolidge's political ascendancy, argued that the processing tax violated the United States
Constitution. Three months later, the Circuit Court ruled in Butler's favor, and Boston firms hastened to procure temporary injunctions against further payments. [16]

The United States Supreme Court struck down the NRA on May
27, 1935, in the *Schechter* case and upheld the Boston Circuit Court's
Butler ruling a year later, thus ending the Agricultural Adjustment
Administration and its dreaded processing tax. While the demise of
the AAA was marked by public celebration, the earlier death of
NRA produced a more complex response: many of the same men
who had undermined the NRA attempted to salvage the best features of the defunct codes. However, it took only a matter of days
for NRA regulations to crumble in Boston as compliance officers
were ordered to retreat from the field "in order to avoid embarrass-
ment or discouragement." [17] While it is impossible to know how
many of the city's businessmen opposed the NRA, a report issued
by the New England Council on almost exactly the same day that
the Supreme Court handed down the *Schechter* decision indicated
that businessmen looked forward to fewer regulations. Of 640 manu-

facturers polled, only 24 percent praised the regulations as having been helpful; the smaller the corporation, the larger the percentage that found the codes detrimental. E. A. Filene also thought that there had been no important modification of the businessman's outlook in the spring of 1935. "Instead of thinking of its opportunities," he said, "[business] has been thinking of its rights—like the monarchs of old who absolutely lost their thrones because they insisted upon their divine right to remain absolute." The titans of enterprise, he concluded, "went to bat and fanned." [18]

But the NRA also whiffed, at least in so far as the agency affected economic recovery in Boston. While the city registered percentage gains in manufacturing, wholesaling, and retailing from 1933 to 1935, improvement lagged behind national norms: the value of products turned out by Boston manufacturers, for instance, went up 18.4 percent, but the advance throughout the United States amounted to 30.2 percent; Boston's retail sales increased 14.6 percent, yet retail turnover elsewhere increased by a healthier 24.5 percent; wholesale volume in the Hub, up 24.6 percent, more closely approximated the national gain of 29.1 percent, but Boston's 1933–1935 improvement was less impressive than all but eight of the nation's twenty-five leading commercial cities.[19] Since Boston's relative economic standing slipped during the NRA years, it was understandable that businessmen did not grieve over the agency's passing. Few acknowledged that the unfavorable showing might have been worse had it not been for NRA, and there was reluctance to admit that 1933–1935 simply confirmed Boston's pre–New Deal economic trends. Indeed, most enterprisers scapegoated the NRA. Economic improvement, as business viewed it, was not sufficient to justify New Deal intervention. Ironically, the complaints against the regulatory state obscured a key point: the NRA never ruled with sufficient force to show what tough, centralized economic planning might accomplish in the city.

During the First New Deal period, businessmen also kept a close eye on government spending, and the National Economy League (NEL) afforded the organized means through which conservatives moved from Hoover's last days into scrutiny of the Roosevelt administration. Prepared for the worst, Boston's entrepreneurs nevertheless found much to praise in F.D.R.'s first month in office. Like Hoover, the President supported an Economy Act to pare the cost of the federal bureaucracy, and he, too, rejected the idea of a veterans' bonus. On March 15 he told the press that he intended to move cautiously in launching large works projects, and added that he was consulting with the Director of the Budget "to see if we cannot keep the appropriation for it—new money—down as low as we possibly can." Six days later, Roosevelt suggested that the first 250,000 CCC recruits could be paid by tapping funds that already had been appropriated for public works.[20] Interpreting the President's initial moves as a sign that he planned to save the United States by lowering expenditures, the Chamber of Commerce urged the City of Boston to conform to federal policy and reduce its budget by $15 million. Convinced that municipal, state, and federal spending were equally dangerous, the Chamber lobbied strenuously to restrain all three.

Roosevelt, however, had more positive programs in mind than his brief flirtation with economizing suggested. Even before his inauguration he had rebuffed Admiral Richard Byrd of the National Economy League in Boston, and the NEL and its allies then watched in anguish as programs like the Civil Works Administration pushed federal deficits to ever higher levels. When Byrd asked Louis Howe to get him money to support extra personnel for another polar expedition, Howe taunted the Admiral with the ironic rejoinder, "On account of the Economy Act [I] doubt if I can arrange for it." [21] Though a minor episode, the inconsistency between Byrd's request for funds and his activities in stirring up the business community against spending neatly symbolized the dilemma which troubled a good many Bostonians. Carl Dennett, for one, wavered between advocacy of budget cuts across the board and a momentary confession that he had come "to the reluctant conclusion that there is no satisfactory alternative to both federal grants and new taxation." [22] The onrush of New Deal programs in 1933, and the abandonment of the gold standard that same year, dispirited the NEL. Some members joined the more vigorous American Liberty League in 1934, while the most conservative fled to ultrarightist organizations such as the Sentinels of the Republic and the Industrial Defense Association.

In the diaspora which accompanied the NEL's decline, the major portion of its membership appears to have returned to the older business organizations in Boston, and these associations lumped together Curley (a man whose spending propensities most loathed), Roosevelt, and the President's son James in an unholy trinity. Since Curley had campaigned for Roosevelt in 1932, and since James made speeches on Curley's behalf in the 1934 gubernatorial election, it was not illogical for business interests to feel that the President approved of "extravagance and wasteful administrations." [23] Once again, local developments complicated acceptance of the New Deal. According to a popular rhyme,

> The King is in the White House,
>   Handing out the money.
> The Queen is on the front page,
>   Looking very funny.
> The Knave is up in Boston,
>   Picking up the plums,
> While the country alphabetically
>   Is feeding all the bums. [24]

So grave was the concern about the impact of anti-Curleyism and its potential effect on the 1936 presidential election that James Farley sent Joseph P. Kennedy on one of his many visits to his native Boston—this time to disarm the Democratic Businessmen's League. [25]

Yet local circumstances played a vital role in making business leaders look a second time at federal spending as a means of lightening municipal taxes. In 1934 the threat of a taxpayers' strike hovered over Boston, and it therefore was not possible to dismiss so lightly the "King . . . in the White House" and the money his administration was dispensing. Under the aegis of the Massachusetts Real Es-

Mayor Frederick Mansfield, a conservative Democrat, and one of his key supporters, the formidable William Cardinal O'Connell, pose at the dedication of a chapel on Franklin Street. The *Boston Globe*.

tate Owners' Association, hundreds of angry citizens marched from the Parkman Bandstand on the Common past the golden dome of the State House, and on to City Hall. Tremont Temple, with over a thousand seats, could not hold the crowds that met to consider non-payment of taxes. Speakers called for the creation of a new political party more responsive to their plight and advocated rigorous cut-backs in municipal spending. While the new party never material-ized, and few took the ultimate step of defying the city collector, the protests did not go unnoticed. Indeed, Mayor Mansfield took steps to economize at the very time that the outcries reached their most deafening peak.

Mansfield, however, pacified neither the Chamber of Commerce nor the Boston Real Estate Exchange, and the two organizations kept momentum by campaigning to have all plans for capital outlay borrowing submitted to popular referendum. According to the proposal, endorsement by two-thirds of those voting would have been necessary before the municipal government could commit itself to deficit spending. By the time of the 1936 election protesting taxpayers had succeeded in placing on the ballot in sixteen of the twenty-two wards a proposition to limit realty taxes, and the plan carried by a wide margin. While in no way binding, the referendum served warning that the accumulation of bonded debt would not be tolerated.

As an alternative to higher property taxes and rising debt, the business community commenced a modest shift in 1934 which then continued into the Second New Deal years. While never fully burying misgivings about the costly alphabetical work-relief agencies (FERA, CWA, WPA), and while never expressing affection for Roosevelt, the Municipal Research Bureau, one of the Chamber of Commerce affiliates, in August 1934 attempted to popularize federal grants as a means of reducing city taxes. The Bureau, strictly a private body which grew out of the defunct Good Government Association, thought that in all probability Boston could expect six more years of Roosevelt. Therefore, the organization reasoned that it made sense to take advantage of legislation already on the statute books. Businessmen, a field agent of Harry Hopkins reported, had converted to the idea "that people must be fed, clothed, and sheltered," and they recognized that assistance from Washington was "the cheapest way" to do it.[26] Yet three weeks later Hopkins himself came to Boston and felt it necessary to assail cost-conscious businessmen who were resisting federal support of the unemployed.

Hopkins was correct in doing so. Although the Municipal Research Bureau wanted federal money which had already been appropriated, the organization vowed to combat all new relief legislation.

Thus, the Research Bureau, and other businessmen's associations, barraged FERA and WPA with demands for a fair share of each new federal appropriation (with no strings attached) to save "disconsolate . . . honest, thrifty, backbone-of-the-community citizens" from losing their property while at the same time carping about inefficiency, waste, and the prospect of more of the same.[27] Even as the Municipal Research Bureau twice sent delegations to Washington in 1935 to get funds, the organization endeavored to curb borrowing which was needed to underwrite the maintenance costs of WPA and PWA. By 1938, the Bureau was stating that "federal aid is absolutely necessary," but in the same breath the organization repudiated federal work relief, claiming that "soldiering on the job" had made "a joke" of WPA. Although the Research Bureau spurned the Works Progress Administration, it recommended a direct federal dole to the unemployed as a suitable replacement.[28]

Ambivalent employers postured in nearly identical ways. As long as federal legislation had been enacted, businessmen wanted to derive maximum benefit, yet at the same time they argued that work relief menaced private companies.[29] Construction firms, for example, asked the CWA to award them contracts on either a cost-plus or a fixed-fee basis, and at a mass meeting in Faneuil Hall the Building Trades Employers' Association insisted they be empowered to recruit and supervise the entire PWA labor force. Costs would be reduced, jerry-built structures would cease, and engineering projects would no longer serve as "breeding places for communism and favoritism," the argument ran, if private firms played a greater role in the WPA.[30] The employers' stance, in essence, corresponded to that of labor unions that were also attempting to wedge their own men onto federal projects, but corporate hypocrisy showed an additional dimension. When, for instance, the ERA and WPA established centers which turned out clothing and blankets for Boston's most poverty-stricken families, textile owners issued a sweeping manifesto of protest. Yet the moment Washington contracted with Boston companies to manufacture thirty thousand sheepskin coats for the poor, the work was accepted with gratitude, and criticism of ERA and WPA was muted. Business wanted a slice of the pie, and in one of the most bizarre examples of business's two-faced stance, a wealthy constituent of Congressman Tinkham's simultaneously blasted the principle of federal work relief while asking that ERA and Civilian Conservation Corps laborers commandeer obsolete army tanks to clear acreage which he owned on the outskirts of Boston.[31]

Businessmen also directed barbs at the Public Works Administration during both the First and Second New Deal periods. The Chamber of Commerce, which had for decades opposed long-term municipal and state borrowing, saw danger in the requirement that to secure PWA grants the city would have to put up 70 percent of the costs (lowered to 55 percent in 1935). For Boston to participate the city's debt limit would have to be raised, an intolerable step. Whereas the Municipal Research Bureau temporized in its attitudes toward CWA, ERA, and WPA, it never wavered in its opposition to borrowing and heavy taxation for construction, and for years fought the Huntington Avenue Subway extension. Business exerted heavy pressures on members of the city council and the state legislature to consign all PWA undertakings to oblivion by refusing to permit bond issues.

And when the opportunity presented itself private interests directly thwarted the Public Works Administration, as in a notable fracas over the Boston Elevated in 1935. Some 50,000 residents of Roxbury and Charlestown had petitioned for the removal of aboveground portions of the El, and the PWA promised $10 million to support part of the estimated cost of $42 million. The city council approved multimillion-dollar borrowing, and on the final night of the longest (225 days) and most raucous legislative session in its history, the General Court handed Boston what Representative Christian Herter called a political blank check—unlimited authorization to finance the project. But within a week after the state legislature's move, the trustees of the Boston El balked. Stockholders were demanding restitution of $22 million for the scrap steel and were further arguing that acceptance of the PWA undertaking would add to the municipal tax rate. Since the terms of the Public Control Act gave the El the status of a quasi-public corporation, the trustees' vote against PWA aid was particularly galling. That an antispending elite could torpedo a project of social value to two of the city's most run-down districts was infuriating. That this same prejudice could deprive the unemployed of thousands of jobs demonstrated the extent to which a willful local-interest group could hamstring New Deal ambitions.

Large realty companies and mortgage bankers, in a fight equivalent to that staged by the Boston El's trustees, squared off against the PWA's Old Harbor Village housing project. Fearing that federal dwellings would compete with privately owned buildings, and especially chary of projects that might be constructed on vacant sites (rather than on land crowded with dilapidated tenements), the Massachusetts Real Estate Owners' Association in particular had campaigned against the PWA even in 1933. When the PWA filed condemnation proceedings on nineteen acres in South Boston in 1935, Harold Ickes warned that if landowners tried "to gouge the Federal Government on land prices, or holdups are attempted, the Government can withdraw and go elsewhere." Sinclair Weeks, president of the United-Carr Fastener Corporation, joined by real estate groups, challenged the constitutionality of the project by filing suit. Ickes countered by dropping the original site and taking another, one which included a considerable amount of unoccupied land. This time, former Governor Joseph B. Ely, acting as an attorney for realtors, filed a bill in equity in Federal District Court to restrain Ickes's eminent-domain proceedings. The Old Harbor Village project, said Ely, made it impossible for landlords to compete. John McCormack, unhappy with the delays, complained to President Roosevelt in October of 1935, whereupon F.D.R. told McCormack what the Congressman already knew: "Protests and demurrers were filed. Constant delays were encountered." By the time that the Boston cases were unsnarled in the courts, the original opening date set by Ickes for Old Harbor Village's first apartments was missed by nearly thirty months. Real-estate interests and banks were "still averse to the scheme" of low-cost housing as late as 1938, and not until the United States Housing Authority projects became a reality at the end of the decade did the Boston Real Estate Exchange issue a qualified approval. By then, considerable mischief had been done.[32]

These maneuvers against the PWA in the last half of the 1930s, while confined mainly to a limited group of business interests, were paralleled by other outbursts against the Second New Deal. Indeed, the higher taxes that were needed to underwrite federal programs were anathema. In the opinion of the Boston Chamber of Commerce, Roosevelt's move in 1935 to impose higher levies on corporations and to tax individuals in the upper income brackets constituted "an attempt to realize a vague and erroneous theory." By destroying incentive and crippling industry, continued the Chamber, the liberal Wealth Tax Act would return the United States "to the 'horse and buggy' days, a condition to which in other respects the administration has pointed with apprehension." [33] Moreover, the Chamber of Commerce held that the undistributed profits tax of 1936 was bringing "famine," because the government insisted upon "eating the seed corn" needed for private industrial expansion. By 1938 repeal of the tax burden imposed by Washington was ranked as the single item about which Boston businessmen were expressing unanimous agreement.[34]

Yet several other federal measures kindled flames of resistance. Bankers recognized that they were "living in another economic world" during the 1930s, as the Chairman of the Federal Reserve Bank of Boston put it, and scored the stricter margin requirements on collateral loans and the hike in reserve requirements demanded by the strengthened Federal Reserve in Washington.[35] New Deal tariff policies, unpopular in the pre-1935 years because of low duties on shoes and textiles and steep assessments against raw materials, were even less palatable later in the decade when Roosevelt shifted toward a series of reciprocal trade agreements. The one with Czechoslovakia, for instance, eased the import quota on shoes, and arrangements with Britain, Australia, and Argentina had an adverse impact on woolens and textiles. Troubles with unions led Boston

Front row, center: Joseph P. Kennedy, flanked by the conservative Democrat, Governor Joseph B. Ely and Kennedy's father-in-law, John F. "Honey Fitz" Fitzgerald, after a 1934 speech of reassurance to the Boston Chamber of Commerce. *Back row, second from left:* Former Governor Frank G. Allen. Boston University School of Communication.

firms to deplore Roosevelt's refusal to make labor organizations accountable for losses during strikes. And although the diversity of Boston's economy, with its many small manufacturing establishments, spared most companies from the stepped-up antitrust prosecutions of the late 1930s, and while virtually all firms of any repute paid more than the minimum wage specified in the Fair Labor Standards Act of 1938, neither move was hailed. Businessmen instead complained about Roosevelt's "uncertainty," about his frequent shifts of course, which, next to heavy taxes, were providing their most common grievances in the late 1930s.[36]

However, Boston's corporation executives manifested inconsistencies greater than those of the two Roosevelt administrations. Men who deplored federal benefits to the unemployed saw nothing wrong with taking loans from the Reconstruction Finance Corporation, and the very bankers who scorned PWA loans to the City of Boston competed to become the sole certifying agent for the Public Works Administration's 4 percent bonds. Real-estate firms and construction companies hailed the Federal Housing Administration's loans for repairs and for building new, private homes, but they stormed against low-cost housing in the decaying neighborhoods of Boston. Manufacturers trumpeted the blessings of laissez-faire, and yet in the late 1930s those who faced competition from Southern industry called upon the federal government to level out regional wage differentials, even if by means of wages and hours legislation. While accepting the principle of pensions to the elderly and unemployment insurance allotments, employers simultaneously complained about the social-security tax bite. Moreover, businessmen displayed a highly ambivalent attitude toward federal work relief. As a means of reducing municipal taxes, they approved; when federal taxes soared, they demurred. Sympathetic federal courts were deemed useful for special pleading against AAA and for blocking federal eminent-domain proceedings, but they were considered anathema when Roosevelt accomplished a judicial revolution in 1937. In succumbing to the natural instinct for self-preservation, Boston businessmen often opposed measures that were actually in their own interest.

As the forlorn business community awaited recovery that did not come, witnessed federal spending increases that appeared unstinting, and saw that it was more difficult to bend government agencies during the Second New Deal, there could be no growth in affection for centralized authority. Ill-prepared by ideological upbringing to accept intervention by Washington, and well-trained in early skirmishes against state regulation and municipal spending, the Boston businessman generally did not see activistic government as a remedy for his ailments—not at the beginning of the Great Depression, and not at the end. Far from inspiring a vision of America based on either national planning or sacrifices by the strong to assist the weak, the Depression made Bostonians more respectful of the wisdom that had guided them through the 1920s. To say that Roosevelt botched a chance to convert businessmen to less parochial attitudes would be to minimize the strength of the resistance which he faced.

In 1932, James Michael Curley had uttered one of his characteristic diatribes against the business community. "It is unfortunate," said the Mayor, "that environment and education never produced beneficial effect upon a Bourbon and from birth they are permitted one vision and one viewpoint." [37] Some years later, Frank Buxton, the editor of the Boston *Herald* who made friends with liberals while working for reactionary owners, dined with Felix Frankfurter and Joseph B. Ely. The conversation turned naturally to the man who had done more than anyone else to challenge the traditional attitudes of business, and Ely, by then a corporation lawyer in Boston, managed to voice a few kind remarks about Roosevelt. Wrote Buxton, "Joe is about the only man, if he now thinks charitably of the President, who regards him more kindly than in 1936. And I happen to know that Joe said he was out of his mind and should be under restraint." [38] It seemed that, once again, Curley's oracular powers had been confirmed.

Those in the White House were well apprised of the hostility in the Hub. Soon after Frankfurter's meeting with Buxton and Ely, for instance, the ardent New Dealer sent Roosevelt some brandied cheese which he had purchased at his favorite New England retreat. With special gratitude, the President's secretary responded, "We were terribly suspicious when we saw 'Harvard Club, Boston' and found food inside, but we all took a chance!" [39] The food was unpoisoned, but the suspicions were not unfounded.

11

The Great Depression:
Economic Change and Some
Social Consequences

As the orchestra struck up a final medley, Bostonians danced their last dance at Quincy House on September 14, 1929. For one hundred and twenty years the hotel had hosted visitors to the city. Sir Thomas Lipton, Porfirio Díaz, Samuel Gompers, John Philip Sousa, George M. Cohan—all entered its portals. And it was at Quincy House that a bartender named William Hogarty had won an instant's fame by breaking a bottle over the head of John L. Sullivan, thereby becoming the only man to knock unconscious the legendary bareknuckled heavyweight champion. There, too, "Honey Fitz" Fitzgerald had sung "Sweet Adeline" and prominent socialites had feted their daughters. Down crashed the wrecker's ball, even as blocks away the frantic clack of ticker-tape machines on Devonshire Street also sounded the end of a happier era.

Quincy House having been demolished, other Boston landmarks were soon to be either eradicated or transformed during the Great Depression. In offices where Lee, Higginson, and Company had once entertained the charlatan Ivar Kreuger, volunteers plotted emergency relief drives. Later, Boston Community Fund workers occupied desks jammed between the massive marble columns on the ground floor where bullish investors had once driven up the stock market. North of Massachusetts Avenue dozens of buildings were torn down to avoid paying taxes, and parking lots replaced a number of them. Town houses were locked up, for their owners had fled to the suburbs to escape ruination. "The day that Boston is in ruins," a wag had once written, "and the last dweller of the Back Bay passes into history, we are certain that he will enter eternity clutching in his hands a copy of the *Transcript*, with his glazing eyes fastened upon the latest news of Harvard, of Mrs. Jack Gardner's museum, the Arnold Arboretum, and the last nupitals [*sic*] of a Higginson to a Cabot." [1] But the *Transcript*, pronounced dead in 1941 at the overripe age of one hundred and eleven, was not around to instruct its Commonwealth Avenue readers—even had they stayed.

Not only had physical landmarks been reshaped, but several organizations, prominent at the beginning of the Depression, faded from view. When Dr. Francis Townsend, a relic of the Depression's volatile middle period, made his last visit to Boston in 1939, the National Economy League, which had battled his plan to give elderly citizens a pension of $200 a month, existed in name only. Hard times had also befallen the Chamber of Commerce. Teeming with more than 5,000 members in 1929, the Chamber boasted fewer than 2,000 eleven years later: the stagnancy of its headquarters, where businessmen lamented the municipal tax rate and federal controls, contrasted markedly with the hubbub at the Wells Memorial Building, where union leaders presided over an expanded membership. Penny cafeterias run by the Volunteers of America and the Salvation Army had been largely supplanted by federal commodities centers, and the "Fix It Now," "Buy Now," "Build Now" committees of the Hoover years had been consigned to the scrap heap.

Trying to prevent the many changes Boston experienced during the Depression, said a city council member, was "like putting women and children out in front in times of warfare or riot and saying 'Don't Shoot.' " [2] Indeed, a number of alterations occurred not through the exercise of volition, but through forces beyond the control of anyone in the city: the economy fell apart, housing decayed, demographic shifts took place, and ethnic groups were deeply affected. These transformations, however, discouraged the quest for a brave new era. Instead, a majority of Bostonians looked back to a world that had been lost.

Regional economic configurations added to Boston's hardships during the course of the decade. Although a federal expert had declared in 1936 that "if New England manufacturing is going into a museum along with the dodo, it will be a museum of belching chimneys and whirring machinery," his expectations were dashed.[3] The portion of New England's labor force engaged in manufacturing dropped from 43.1 percent in 1930 to 34.2 percent in 1940, and no area in the United States suffered a larger decline in the value of its industrial output. Although the Northeast continued to rank third of eight regions in per capita personal income, the margin of its lead over the rest of the United States was reduced.

Of the New England states, Massachusetts slipped more drastically than any other, and this development compounded Boston's woes. Only Vermont lost population at a greater rate, not one of the others exceeded the percentage declines suffered by Massachusetts industry, and in 1940 only Rhode Island had a more severe unemployment problem. While the value of personal income-tax returns approximately doubled in the rest of New England during the 1930s, the amount filed by Bay State residents went up at a pace roughly half that of the other states in the section. Although the total resources of Massachusetts banks edged up, the ten-year increase (roughly $55 million) was exceeded by Connecticut in both absolute and relative terms. Of the five other New England states, Connecticut, in fact, prospered most noticeably as Massachusetts declined.

Boston's economic recovery languished behind that of both region and state. Industrial wages, which nose-dived from $106 million in 1929 to $49 million in 1933, had come back to only $67 million a decade after the crash. Expressed another way, Boston's industrial labor force earned 37 percent less at the close of the 1930s than it had at the time of the stock-market collapse, while in Massachusetts the aggregate payroll for workers in manufacturing amounted to 28 percent less than 1929s wages. Moreover, the value of products made in Boston tumbled from $604 million in 1929 to the 1933 nadir of $289 million. By 1939 their worth had crept up to $413 million, still 32 percent under 1929's total and once again a less favorable showing than registered by the Commonwealth as a whole. While Boston's industrial labor force plunged from 77,000 to 57,800 from 1929 to 1939, a loss of 25 percent, the number of workers involved in manufacturing throughout Massachusetts dropped 21 percent, also less severe than Boston's decline. And while unemployment for all workers in the Hub stood at 19.9 percent at the end of the decade, the rate for the rest of the Commonwealth, despite the appalling shutdowns in places like Fall River and New Bedford, amounted to 16.8 percent of the entire work force. As Mayor Tobin noted in his 1939 message to Bostonians, hard times had left the city "struggling under burdens which are creations of an economic system that suddenly went askew." "It's a quick ride down the toboggan chute," he added, "but it's a long walk back." [4]

Major defense contracts eluded local firms in 1939 and 1940, for the federal government lavished its orders upon urban centers with a more substantial industrial base. Thus Boston failed to share the improved employment situation of other large cities. Indeed, all but Pittsburgh and Cleveland had a higher percentage of jobless workers than did the Hub in 1940.[5] Bank clearings, an important indicator of economic health, were snapping back faster than in New York but more slowly than in Philadelphia, Chicago, Pittsburgh, and Cleveland. New construction, a barometer of plant expansion, fell 55 percent from 1939 through 1940, and although manufacturers urged "more expansion, more speed" at the close of 1940, the lend-lease bill, signed the next March, affected the city precious little. One year after Pearl Harbor, the situation grew worse: shipping volume sagged 83 percent below 1940 tonnage, and more railroad cars entered Portland, Maine, than came to Boston. Although the city council importuned employers receiving government contracts to

Despite the stimulus supplied by the NRA and other Federal projects, Boston's social groups faced a sluggish economy all the way to the end of the Roosevelt years. The *Boston Globe*.

employ men on municipal welfare, there were, in fact, few opportunities for Bostonians to build the arsenal of democracy.[6]

Several components of Boston's occupational structure were also altered by the Great Depression. By 1940 the exodus of textile and shoe companies, especially acute during the two years of NRA, had all but ended. Whereas 8,000 Bostonians had earned their livelihood from the shoe and leather industries in 1930, ten years later only half that number remained. In 1930, 4,200 workers labored in textile factories, but a decade later their ranks had been pared by roughly 25 percent, and the city's clothing industry had discharged 30 percent of its employees. With manufacturing reversals in Boston running ahead of both Massachusetts and the rest of New England, industrial workers were shuffled into the wholesale and retail trades, which advanced 15 percent. Service occupations jumped even more.[7]

In only a few respects did Boston in 1940 have cause to take heart. As a fishing port, the city still occupied first place along the Atlantic coast: baskets which the Italian and Portuguese fleet unloaded for auction overflowed in the streets, and the value of the catch exceeded the pre-Depression haul. Banking activity kept Boston in fourth place among the nation's financial centers; more money, in fact, was deposited in the city's banking houses than had been the case in 1929. Then, too, wholesalers and retailers made an encouraging comeback toward the end of the decade: combined sales had returned to 89 percent of the 1929 dollar volume. And, on a somewhat lighter side, the Boston Bruins of 1939, with Captain Cooney Weiland, Dit Clapper, Eddie Shore, Ray Conacher, and Flash Howlett pacing the team, made money. Before capacity throngs at the Garden, the Bruins dispatched Toronto 3-1 in the Stanley Cup final, sending the crowd "into the screaming meemies for several minutes." Firecrackers popped, the band played "Paree," and champagne flowed. The Bruins had ended a ten-year drought, but most enterprises could not claim as much.[8]

Boston's faltering economy choked off the city's population growth, and for the only time since the United States Census was first taken in 1790 the number of people living in the Hub declined. Although the drop of 10,400 persons during the 1930s amounted to just 1.3 percent of the city's total (enabling it to hold its rank as the ninth biggest), Cleveland alone suffered a greater percentage decrease among the nation's fourteen largest municipalities. As Boston ebbed, metropolitan expansion was also retarded. Even though the sibling communities outside Boston's borders continued to gain in population at the expense of the parent, sharp advances which had been made in the suburban towns between 1920 and 1930 were largely arrested.[9]

Despite the superficial appearance that Boston's population remained stagnant, the Great Depression uprooted thousands from
their old neighborhoods, as Table 11.1 partly indicates. All areas
regarded by Walter Firey, Boston's foremost student of land use, as
"in-city" districts tailed off in population with the exception of the
Back Bay. Indeed, losses in the South End, Charlestown, and the
North End ranged from 13.4 percent to 29.2 percent. The overall
trend, as in the pre-1930 period, was distinctly centrifugal: of the
sections which jumped in population by more than 10 percent
(Brighton, Roslindale, and West Roxbury), all stretched far to the
West and Southwest of the urban core.

The figures supplied in Table 11.1, however, but dimly suggest
the internal migration which took place in the span of ten years.
Several areas in which the raw numerical totals might indicate an
unchanging population could and did undergo major upheavals.
With the exception of Beacon Hill and a few other streets in the
Back Bay, where the prestige value of the land was high enough to
keep residents from moving (despite strong temptations to exit), in-
town areas lost many of their wealthier denizens.[10] The moment
that displaced Yankees escaped from the high inner-city property
valuations and tax rates, newcomers rented apartments in what had
previously been owner-occupied homes. This development led to a
substantial increase of persons per gross acre in wealthier central
areas, particularly the Back Bay (see Table 11.1). And as these newcomers replaced the older residents along the western ends of Newbury Street, Commonwealth Avenue, and Beacon Street, the buildings were then occupied by families who were, in turn, escaping
from their own rapidly changing neighborhoods. Other dwellings
were either left vacant or razed, as suggested by the remarkable statistic that in the North and South Ends, with a combined population
loss of 18 percent, the number of persons per gross acre actually
jumped by more than 12 percent. Lured by low rents, victims of
hard times piled into decaying tenements in Charlestown and in the
North, South, and West Ends. Even though all these areas lost population during the 1930s, the density in occupied buildings reached

Table 11.1 *. Population Trends in Boston by Health and Welfare Area, 1930–1940 [a]

	1930 Population	1940 Population	± Percentage Population Shift 1930–1940	Persons per Gross Acre		1940 Percent of Households with over 1.5 Persons/Room
				1930	1940	
City	781,188	770,816	-1.3	112	94.5	3.9
* Back Bay	38,887	39,502	+1.5	167	202.8	4.8
Brighton	56,362	63,367	+12.4	79	72.5	3.4
* Charlestown	31,663	25,587	-19.2	256	255.1	4.1
Dorchester North	120,053	124,323	+3.6	109	103.0	2.2
Dorchester South	74,445	77,350	+3.9	78	69.2	1.2
* East Boston	59,242	56,928	-3.9	201	203.4	7.6
Hyde Park	24,498	25,192	+2.8	46	31.2	3.3
Jamaica Plain	44,542	37,294	-16.3	69	46.4	2.3
* North End	27,818	19,698	-29.2	799	924.3	15.8
Roxbury	105,790	107,002	+1.1	145	147.9	3.8
* South Boston	59,728	54,364	-7.3	214	196.8	4.6
* South End	60,506	52,442	-13.4	322	349.3	6.4
* West End	28,028	27,278	-2.7	334	369.7	4.5
West Roxbury [b] and Roslindale	47,414	57,754	+21.7	47	38.1	0.9

* Defined as in-town areas by Firey, *Land Use in Central Boston*, p. 276, with West End added by author as appropriately part of the core.

[a] Computations of Census data are from figures in Boston Council of Social Agencies, "Social Statistics by Census Tracts in Boston," II, July 1935, p. 5, and United Community Services of Metropolitan Boston, "Social Facts by Census Tracts," 1953(?). Persons per gross acre in 1930 are from Boston Council of Social Agencies, "Social Statistics . . . ," p. 6, and for 1940, data supplied by Firey, p. 173, are employed. See also, Boston Community Council, *The People of Boston and Its Fifteen Health and Welfare Areas* (Boston, 1944). Data of persons per room are from Firey, p. 173.

[b] Boston Council of Social Agencies reports from 1930 to 1935 incorporated Roslindale under the heading of West Roxbury. By 1940, the Council was separating the two. For purposes of simplicity, the two areas have been lumped together. Thus there is a slight discrepancy between the figures given here and those in Firey, p. 173.

the saturation point, and living conditions were appalling: the number of tenants jammed into each room of what the Census Bureau euphemistically called North End "residential units" exceeded by four times the citywide average.

These population movements altered the ethnic compositions of several neighborhoods. Some areas became even more highly segregated—the Italian North End, certain Jewish sections of Dorchester, and selected quarters of Roxbury and the South End where Negroes resided. Other districts swapped one highly concentrated ethnic group for another. Many of the eight thousand Italian North Enders who exited from their homes during the 1930s, for instance, spilled into the contiguous West End, where they replaced Irish families. Irish from the section of East Boston closest to Charlestown also tended to relocate, and here again Italians moved in. But in still other areas the ethnic solidarity which had helped forge a sense of community was severely threatened. No longer could a Frothingham depend upon the impeccable ancestry of his neighbors on Beacon Street, nor could an O'Sullivan in Roxbury be certain that an O'Leary lived next door.

Under the duress of job competition in an economy without enough work for all, and menaced by the disruption of neighborhood life, Bostonians manifested ethnic consciousness which appeared to grow in strength as the Depression wore on. This is not to say that the city's Irish had been noticeably reticent about expressing affection for the homeland before 1930, as any veteran of South Boston's St. Patrick's Day parade in the pre-Depression years could have testified. Nor is it to assert that class differences within a single ethnic group counted for nothing, as the conflict between the skilled unionized Irish in the building trades and their unorganized, menial brethren points up. But it is to say that the expression of group solidarity became more pronounced, and the city seemed more atomized than ever. Rather than producing an atmosphere in which all men could submerge their differences and work toward common goals, the Great Depression in Boston stimulated intergroup hostility, just as it did in cities like Muncie, Indiana, and Burlington, Vermont.[11] Neighborhood meeting places flourished—the Hibernian Halls, Polish-American Clubs, Ruggles Hall in Negro Roxbury, Catholic parishes—and all testified to ethnic affirmation. Some of this spirit was distinctly positive, for it built pride at a time when almost everyone needed a boost; some of this rejuvenated ethnocentrism, however, appeared cranky and defensive.

Italo-Americans, for instance, showed signs of estrangement from their adopted city. When Mussolini pillaged Ethiopia in 1936, 50,000 paraded through the streets of East Boston chanting "Il Duce, Il Duce, Il Duce," and a dummy of Haile Selassie was carried at the head of the procession.[12] Soon after, the Sons of Italy boasted 25,000 adult members and an additional 5,000 youngsters in a junior order. Through this organization, Boston's Italo-Americans converted into pro-Mussolini chauvinism the many frustrations which they had been experiencing—discriminatory hiring practices of private employers, lack of upward social mobility, exploitation by slumlords, and less than impartial treatment by work-relief officials.[13] Saddled with higher unemployment rates than any other group in Boston throughout the 1930s, feeling neglected and isolated, the Sons of Italy sought the "power, command, and 'glory' " denied them in the Hub by expressing ardent, pro-Italian sentiments.[14] Boston's Italo-American newspapers, with the exception of *Quaderni Italiani* which appeared briefly in 1939–1940, penned vigorous pro-Fascist editorials. In addition, the Benito Mussolini Club attracted followers, and while the Mazzini Society and the Lincoln Italian Club opposed Il Duce, their membership remained small. Instead of becoming more assimilated, much of Boston's Italian community manifested greater tendencies toward separatism.[15]

The low-income Irish in South Boston suffered many of the same indignities experienced by Italians. Rates of joblessness well above the city's average, inability to move upwards in the city's social structure, and the physical decay of their neighborhoods plagued the Sons of Erin throughout the 1930s. Hooligans attacked Negroes in the South End, and rumbles marred football games when South Boston faced teams composed largely of Italians. And like the Italian community of the North End and East Boston, "Southies" flirted with new prophets. In the mid-1930s, the Detroit radio priest, Father Charles Coughlin, created major excitement with his attacks against Roosevelt, intellectuals, Communism, the Federal Reserve System, and the WPA. As with the Italian community, the Irish were stirred by events abroad. Anglophobia had not vanished: Senator David I. Walsh's anti-interventionist stand won the solid endorsement of the Irish, while President Roosevelt's recall of Joseph P. Kennedy from his ambassadorship in London outraged the residents of South Boston, Dorchester, and Charlestown.

Communism, both in Spain and as State Senator Thomas Dorgan claimed it existed in Boston, gave Irish politicians an issue which they regularly exploited: from the mid-thirties to the close of the decade, the convulsions of a perpetual Red Scare seized the city. Suspects were haled before a committee of the state legislature and were asked whether they knew the meaning of "Boogwazzies" (bourgeoisie), or whether they planned "to liquefy the Church." [16] The Irish-dominated Boston School Committee, fired with enthusiasm for the crusade, also committed excesses, and the city council asked the federal government to investigate Boston's WPA and NYA. Harvard, too, was called a hotbed of radicalism. Perhaps it was. As an Irish member of the city council put it, "I want to ask what they expect of a university that teaches its football players how to dance." [17]

Both the Irish and Italian communities were overwhelmingly Catholic, and it is doubtful that any prelate in America remained as conservative during the 1930s as did William Cardinal O'Connell, the spiritual guide for roughly 76 percent of the city's population. While it cannot be assumed that every priest or every layman followed O'Connell's social teachings, especially in Italian parishes, the Cardinal nevertheless was a towering figure. At no point did he lose control of the priests under his dominion, and the Irish, to whom his messages were transmitted through the pages of the Boston

Pilot, generally adored him. A staunch advocate of Christian charity, O'Connell displayed spectacular ability to raise money for the Catholic Charitable Bureau and the St. Vincent de Paul Society.[18] Presenting himself as a friend of the worker, he admonished employers to follow the Golden Rule in treating their men. Given the institutional importance of the Catholic Church to the Irish, particularly in a decade when an already devout population turned to religion for consolation, there is no reason to suppose that O'Connell and his spokesmen were ignored.

O'Connell invoked blessings upon Franklin Roosevelt on Inauguration Day, 1933, expressing hope that the President would engage in "the conservation of America's highest ideals." By 1934, however, the Cardinal had taken the offensive. Seizing the occasion of a na-

Mayor Frederick Mansfield calls on Governor Joseph B. Ely on January 3, 1934. Before the year was over, the two would become ardent apostles of the conservative American Liberty League. Boston University School of Communication.

tionwide radio address from Faneuil Hall on July 4, he deplored leaders who "will dictate to us even against our will . . . [and] will rule us as if they had a divine right to rule." "That," said O'Connell, "is autocracy." Returning from a trip to Europe four months later, he softened but little. The President was "trying to do something," the Cardinal told reporters. "Perhaps I might say too many things," he added. To O'Connell, the government's legitimacy should be judged by the President's ability to check "popular uprisings . . . such as you see elsewhere." Father Robert Barry, Director of the Catholic Charitable Bureau, agreed. "The greatest job the Government has done has been in the stifling of possible disorder or protest," he stated.[19] And although the Church's desire to avert social upheaval might be regarded as desirable, the passion for order, obedience, and patience ran counter to even moderate reformist impulses.[20] To O'Connell anyone who aroused class warfare was an agent of the infidel, and he persistently scored "the drab uniformity of collectivism." [21] There could be no mistaking that his references were to Washington. In return, Roosevelt's inner circle looked upon the Cardinal as a powerful obstructionist.[22]

Not only did Cardinal O'Connell spice Boston with his flavorful panegyrics on domestic issues, but his enthusiasm for established institutions led to the logical next step of expressing himself on foreign affairs as well. Just as Socialists, Communists, and liberal Brain Trusters were threatening tranquillity at home, the Civil War in Spain seemed to His Eminence to be an instance in which Godlessness had arrayed itself against Christian order. When Francisco Franco's planes bombed and killed a thousand civilians in Barcelona on March 18, 1938, the Cardinal defended the Generalissimo as a fighter "for Christian civilization in Spain." The Loyalist government in Valencia, he added, was "nothing but piracy and communism gone rank," and he did his best to ban screenings in Boston of the pro-Loyalist film, "Blockade." [23] O'Connell, indeed, showed perfect consistency in backing Franco or in scoring Roosevelt's Mexican policies which he construed as anticlerical. Just as he believed that leftist gains across the ocean were menacing traditional government, he stumped for a teachers' loyalty oath in Massachusetts, supported the General Court in its 1938 hunt for subversives, stated that federal works projects were infected with radicals, and held that Roosevelt was destroying the Constitution and foisting socialism upon the country.

Although on occasion a contingent of more liberal priests made themselves heard, the bias of the church ran counter to change: clergy who exhibited a capacity for independent thought were generally kept in line. Father Jones I. Corrigan, for example, a Jesuit professor of economics at Boston College, regularly lambasted the Chamber of Commerce, declined invitations to speak against the Social Security Act, and lauded the Wagner Act. Unlike O'Connell, he did not believe that prayer alone held "the one great answer" to human avarice. When the chips were down, however, Corrigan heeded the Cardinal. Selected by O'Connell as his personal representative, Corrigan testified to a joint committee of the General Court in 1935 against the Child Labor Amendment. "Nothing redder ever came out of Red Russia," he stated.[24] Moreover, the well-known enmity between Cardinal O'Connell and the "Right Reverend New Dealer," Father John Ryan, forced Boston's priests to steer clear of the liberal National Catholic Welfare Conference. Contact with the radical Catholic Worker Movement was implicitly *verboten*.[25]

Toward the end of the decade, a number of Boston priests still were preaching against "modern women" and the ideas of Albert Einstein. Attacking Roosevelt's Supreme Court bill as a subversion of the Constitution, they also deplored the un-American experiments in "collective social domination" which, they contended, had inspired the President's assault upon the judiciary. To workingmen enticed by diabolical Communism, a strengthened Christian family life remained the principal answer. Fortunately, *The Pilot* told its 50,000 subscribers with a sense of relief, the Church was succeeding. The unemployed had been "little radicalized by that experience," and the devout had not fallen prey to radicalism's major sources—"students in the upper groups and professional groups."

Thanks to the church, said *The Pilot* in 1940, "the unemployed . . . are conservative." [26]

Boston's Negroes also received the full force of the Depression. Although the folk migration out of the South during the 1930s touched Boston less than New York and Indianapolis, and while the proportion of blacks living in Boston remained smaller than in other cities, the 13.5 percent increase of the black population in the Hub approximated that of most northern urban areas. [27] Competition for already scarce jobs intensified, and the axiom that Negroes are first fired and last hired in periods of economic hardship generally proved the rule in the Hub. As a jobless Afro-American complained to Eleanor Roosevelt with only a modicum of exaggeration, "I tell you my dear Hon. Lady—a dark colored person is by far more handicapped in the enlightened world than a *stone-blind white person.*" [28] The rate of black unemployment persistently topped that of whites (despite a lower illiteracy rate than that of the total white population, and just as much schooling). At the end of the decade, when unemployment in Boston still amounted to 19.9 percent, black joblessness reached 30.3 percent, a rate higher than for all groups except the Italo-American community.

In respect to housing only a few of the most miserable sections of Italian Boston fared as poorly as the Negro areas adjacent to the New York, New Haven, and Hartford Railroad, in the South End, and in Roxbury. Ten years of economic stringency reduced the number of homeowners among Negroes by 10.7 percent, while rental units occupied by black tenants jumped 32.0 percent. The median rental cost, nearly the same for blacks and whites in 1930, showed a greater disparity ten years later: in areas with the densest Afro-American population, monthly rent fell as much as $11 below the city median of $29.91, a telling sign that slums were developing.

Following much the same pattern as that of other low income groups, Boston's nonwhite population clumped together in more segregated neighborhoods, and, as a partial result, Negroes developed a heightened racial consciousness. When set upon by white toughs, the Negro was disposed to fight back; as Italians were drawn together by Mussolini's Ethiopian adventure, blacks were roused by the aggression against Haile Selassie's African nation. Economic insecurity and greater racial proximity both contributed to more tightly knit social organizations which, in turn, attempted to eliminate discriminatory hiring practices. Challenging the biases of private employers, supervisors of federal projects, and the city's trade unionists, groups such as the Urban League, the Basileus of Eta Phi Chapter of Omega Psi Phi Fraternity, and the Ebenezer Baptist Church extended their pre-Depression functions.

Afro-Americans also tried to gain control of the white-dominated NAACP and inject new life into the organization which, in 1929, had claimed only eighty-eight Boston members. Vigorous recruiting drives in the mid-1930s which attempted to "awaken the dead" succeeded, and by 1937 the enrollment of close to 2,000 members had at last included denizens of Roxbury in substantial numbers.[29] The shift of NAACP meetings in 1937 from the fashionable Twentieth Century Club to the Ebenezer Baptist Church, where the caterer was required to employ Negro waiters, symbolized the NAACP's new determination. Instead of focusing almost exclusively on extradition cases, defense funds for southern blacks, and a federal antilynching bill, as had been the case from 1929 to 1935, a beefed-up Local Liberties Committee fought against discrimination in its home city. Led by Mrs. Lillian Williams, the organizer of the NAACP's Junior Youth Chapter, Afro-Americans in 1937 marched through Boston carrying signs which called for jobs, and they also picketed stores which especially catered to black customers. Not since a pre-Civil War school boycott had the city's Negroes resorted to such visible tactics. In addition, the NAACP admonished junior-high-school guidance counselors who were advising youths to attend trade schools, staged voter registration drives, badgered the YMCA to halt discriminatory rooming practices, and called upon both public-service enterprises and government personnel officers to provide more jobs to blacks. The Dudley Theater, with 40 percent of its patrons coming from the black community, discovered what many another employer found out who refused to hire Negroes: a visit could be expected from an NAACP delegation and, as a last resort, pickets would appear. While the activism itself was more significant than the number of jobs gained, and although six of seven blacks still toiled in manual occupations, the NAACP had by the end of the decade won enough concessions to have averted a total catastrophe.[30]

From 1936 into the last months of 1939, the period of maximum vitality, leadership of the NAACP tried to steer "a middle course between radicalism and conservatism, so as to command the respect of the community at large."[31] But with Alfred Baker Lewis, Chairman of the Socialist Party of Massachusetts, serving as secretary, and with Negroes occupying more seats on the Executive Committee, Brahmin whites who had long supported the organization felt menaced. Tenaciously endeavoring to keep a white at the helm, the Old Guard turned back the challenge in November 1939 of Julian D. Rainey, Boston's most powerful Negro Democrat and member of President Roosevelt's so-called Black Cabinet. Ray Guild, a white Republican from Cambridge, narrowly defeated his black opponent in a meeting marred by considerable acrimony. Negro membership instantly plummeted, but the precedent for building what would become toward the end of the 1940s one of the strongest NAACP chapters in the United States had been set. Negroes had taken to the streets in affirmation of their claim to first-class citizenship, had responded to the NAACP and its voter registration drives, and, as will be seen, exhibited increasing political solidarity. The Great Depression, far from engendering defeatism, stirred the black community to new assertiveness. Thus Boston's Negroes in the late 1930s anticipated the emergence of civil rights as a crucial national issue during the presidency of Harry S. Truman.

The 85,000-member Jewish community, centered in parts of Roxbury, Dorchester, and Mattapan, came through the Depression much more handsomely than other non-Yankee groups. While not

escaping the curse of unemployment, Jews discovered that their
rates of joblessness fell below those of East Boston, the North
End, South Boston, and Negro areas. And, too, those who stayed
off relief lists, a recent study has suggested, enjoyed astounding
upward mobility, higher even than among Yankees.[32] The solid
brick apartments lining the streets of Dorchester deteriorated less
rapidly than the squalid wooden three-deckers in poorer areas of
the city, and crowding became less acute. Characteristics of
anomie which could be found in, say, the South End—high crime
and juvenile delinquency—were less severe.

The Jewish population seemed better assimilated than most other
New Immigrant groups. Except for a very few blocks, residential
segregation was not nearly so intense as in Italian neighborhoods.
Moreover, out of the streets where Jews lived came a number of
leaders who tore down the bars of once exclusive citadels. Whereas
Italian names were missing from those appointed as Overseers of
the Public Welfare and did not show up on the letterheads of the
Boston Council of Social Agencies, Jews broke through. Simon
Hecht played a significant part in social-welfare circles; Ben Selekman, director of the Associated Jewish Philanthropies (AJP), rendered important service to the National Labor Relations Board; and
still others assumed leadership in the union movement and the Consumers' League. While the appointment of Louis Brandeis to the
Supreme Court back in 1916 had touched off an explosion in the
WASPish Back Bay, those days appeared over. Brandeis, after all,
sat on the Supreme Court until 1939, and Bostonians proudly
claimed him as their own. David Niles, ascending from North End
poverty to high office in Washington, Louis Kirstein and other merchant princes of Boston, those who made phenomenal gifts to the
Associated Jewish Philanthropies—all could testify that, at least in
the Hub, the American dream was attainable by those of Jewish descent.

Nevertheless, the Jewish community at times conflicted with
other groups. Jews crossed swords with Irish work-relief supervisors, for instance, and they tended to be at odds with the majority

of Irish labor leaders during the AFL-CIO imbroglio. Boston Jewry
also rallied against Hitlerism and raised money for those who were
fleeing from Germany. Indeed, by mid-decade, those who were
speaking for the New Deal in Boston—Kirstein, Niles, Frankfurter,
Selekman, Rabbi Harry Levi—had begun to devote considerable attention to the refugee problem. Toward the Anglophobia of Senator
David I. Walsh and his supporters, the Jewish community could
have felt only antipathy. When Italians paraded through the streets
of East Boston shouting for Mussolini, Jews were aghast. With Cardinal O'Connell's pro-fascist stand on the Spanish Civil War and the
followers of Father Coughlin's Christian Front, there obviously
could be no compromise. These divergences from other groups
strengthened a sense of unity among Jews, one already deeply
rooted in their religious history.

In the city's synagogues, congregations heard messages rather different from those that echoed through the massive Holy Cross Ca-
thedral whenever the Cardinal made his appearance. Most rabbis
serving the Jewish community paid far more than pious lip service
to the needs of the unemployed, and the message entitled "Judaism
and Social Security," read in all temples on October 1, 1935, contrasted sharply with O'Connell's archdiocesan letters. Just as Isaiah
and the prophets of Israel had urged their people "to break the
bonds of wickedness and let the oppressed go free," "a fundamental
reconstruction of [the nation's] economic organization" was demanded. "According to an ancient Jewish law the well of water may not
be owned by an individual but must be owned and controlled by the
community," the rabbis continued, and this meant "that all enterprises that are essential to social life must be owned and controlled not by individuals and families but by society itself." [33]

Jews engaged in philanthropic endeavors understood that charitable activities constituted nothing more than a palliative. Having extolled those who had given $2,300,000 to the Associated Jewish
Philanthropies in the first four years after the crash, Dr. Selekman
went further. "The fundamental ills of our present social order lies
[sic] not in public or private social work," he stated, "but in a pro-

gram of economic and social planning." A "planned economy," he continued, ought to include unemployment and health insurance, old-age pensions, child-labor laws, a shorter work week, and a national minimum-wage law. Maurice Taylor, director of the Boston Jewish Family Welfare League, concurred. "The miserable policy of an inadequate dole," he announced, could provide no substitute for unemployment insurance.[34] Remaining in the vanguard of Boston liberalism through the end of the decade, Jewish spokesmen testified on behalf of the Fair Labor Standards Act, plugged for liberalization of the Social Security Act, asked for the extension of work relief to nonwelfare families, and rejoiced over the appointment of Felix Frankfurter to the Supreme Court.

It seemed fitting indeed that on the eve of World War II, when Franklin Roosevelt held his secret rendezvous with Winston Churchill to sign the Atlantic Charter, the President gave the Prime Minister one of the three neckties that had been sent to the White House by Louis Kirstein. Presumably, the tie came from Filene's store where John Roosevelt, the President's son, was employed from 1938 to Pearl Harbor. The gift to the President—hence, to Churchill—symbolically represented the support and affection which the Jewish community had bestowed upon the Roosevelts during the course of eight years.[35]

Just as Italian, Irish, Negro, and Jewish communities were physically and spiritually altered by the Great Depression, so were the Yankees of the Back Bay. Although least affected by unemployment, denizens of the city's wealthiest streets could see that all was not well. While the flight to the suburbs proceeded at a slower pace than in the immediate precrash years, those who exited lamented that Boston no longer stood at the Hub of the Universe. One refugee, who had escaped to Dedham, tried to summarize what he felt had happened to the city:

> The Hibernian horde overran us and we became more than a little rowdy. We indulged in frenzied finance and such like follies. We

burned a couple of innocent Communists. We entertained a Swede
named Kreuger and went off the deep end with the rest of the
country in the Indian Summer of 1929. We went Democratic.

Now we are pretty shabby. Our Colonial tradition is shiny at the
seams and frayed at the edges. We have holes in the pockets and the
seats of our trousers. We need a shave and a haircut. We need
fumigating. We are, in a word, what, to the urban yokelry of New
York, is a truly comic spectacle.[36]

But others stayed put, and those who on a Sunday morning set
out for the neighborhood's venerable churches—Henry Hobson Richardson's Trinity, Arlington Street Unitarian, the New Old South
Church—noticed the exterior changes. As the *Back Bay Ledger and
Beacon Hill Times* acknowledged in 1940, "Commonwealth Avenue
is a beautiful street in many ways; but it looks like a deserted village
in many block lengths, where house after house has been boarded
up, and the one-time residents gone." [37] Behind some of the oak
doors and stained-glass windows a Cabot or a Forbes may still have
dined in splendor, but while Paul Revere candlesticks adorned the
tables, the vista outside looked decidedly scruffier.

The travails of the wealthy in the Back Bay appeared minuscule
when compared to the struggle for survival that was taking place in
Boston's lower depths, but there is no reason to suppose that the
psychic ordeal was inconsequential. Threats to personal fortunes,
the changing face of the Back Bay landscape, and the feeling that a
way of life was vanishing inspired much the same sort of irascibility
characteristic of many blue-collar neighborhoods. The targets, of
course, differed. While jobless New Immigrants excoriated supervisors who had dismissed them from federal projects, property
owners clamored against the unrealistically high assessments that
were forcing them to sell their homes and businesses.[38] While the
Italian community compensated for its anxiety by joining ethnocentric organizations like the Sons of Italy, hundreds of Yankees dallied
with the Sentinels of the Republic, the American Liberty League,
the Minute Women, the National Economy League, and the National Committee to Uphold Constitutional Government. Especially

after the tempestuous term of Governor James Michael Curley had expired, Yankees generally found it hard to resist the conclusion that Irish politicians, in league with Franklin Delano Roosevelt, had made economic catastrophe far worse.

For all the unmistakable signs of defensive posturing among the Yankees, those active in Boston's settlement houses attempted in a variety of ways to build bridges to other ethnic communities. Although hampered by reductions in the number of paid workers, the affiliates of the Boston Federation of Neighborhood Houses recruited enough volunteers (including a number of former Bostonians who had left for the suburbs) to continue pre-Depression activities. During the thirties, most settlements again carried on their Americanization programs: English classes, citizenship courses, and trips to Boston's historic sites went on unabated. At the same time, the neighborhood houses perpetuated ethnic self-consciousness by evoking memories of the Old World: Syrian circuses, Italian *festas*, and balalaika orchestras persisted throughout the 1930s. Distribution of flowers and vegetables, baskets to shut-ins at Easter, needlework, sewing circles, leathercraft, children's theater, and summer camps in the country survived the Great Depression. Supplementing home, school, and church, settlement-house workers brought moments of pleasure to thousands of Bostonians.

Many of those engaged in urban social work spotted "gaps left by an imperfect social order," and the Federation of Neighborhood Houses concluded in 1934 that "the real goal in life is aimed at sharing and cooperation rather than individualistic grasping." The old-time sense of "comradeship," as social workers called it—people working together to achieve happiness—encouraged a number of individuals associated with the Boston Council of Social Agencies (BCSA) to accept new tasks.[39] As public representatives on the National Labor Relations Board and as members of the Boston Recovery Board during the NRA years, personnel from the BCSA assisted the New Deal. And when the Supreme Court jettisoned the NRA, settlement-house workers helped the Consumers' League with industrial surveys. On the lookout for sweatshops, the canvassers arrived at nearly identical conclusions: a replacement for the NRA had to be found quickly. At the Yankee-dominated Boston Housing Association, another BCSA affiliate, the staff worked unceasingly to expedite the construction of units by the PWA and, later, by the United States Housing Authority. Yankee social workers filled administrative positions in work-relief agencies; settlement houses gave over their stages to the Federal Theater and provided facilities for the distribution of surplus commodities. The days had vanished when the director of the Family Welfare Society could stand before the Women's City Club and say that " a crowd of homeless men and tramp families . . . would be attracted [to Boston] by the publicity of a large relief fund raised by private subscription." [40] Instead, at least some members of Boston's "untitled aristocracy" belied an observation made in 1930 that they offered "the most inhospitable soil conceivable for the planting of new economic, social, or moral ideas." [41]

Yankees discovered that attempts at brotherhood were not always welcomed. It was not so simple to fuse divergent ethnic types as when Denison House, in a 1933 skit, invited a tot named Nathan Hale ("direct descendant of the great Nathan Hale") to shake hands with the equally small Chinese girl, Virginia Wong Jayne. In less carefully controlled situations, Irish politicians leveled stinging rebukes at "bluebloods" appointed by Harry Hopkins. James Michael Curley, for instance, ever quick to spot a popular cause, chided the ERA for using Simmons College girls as field investigators. "I had thought qualification for ERA work was an empty stomach, not a college degree," he said. Moreover, the departure from accepted roles by female activists, always a significant element among Yankee reformers, at times ran smack into prejudices against women. As a city-council member said in response to a scolding from the League of Women Voters, "I think a woman's station is at home changing the babies, and that in so doing she will be doing far more for humanity than some of these organizations." [42]

These attacks were unjustified, but Yankees brought on others through their own doing. Joseph Lee, for example—a man who rendered important service to the park and recreation movement, and an outspoken opponent of Communist-hunting in the public schools—made the kind of unfortunate slip which partially negated many of the efforts of his colleagues. While serving on the Boston Housing Committee, Lee recommended a South Boston site for a PWA housing project. The inhabitants who would be displaced, said Lee, were merely "low-grade Irish, Poles, and Lithuanians." Stern rejoinders to Lee's comments about "white trash" were at once issued by Congressman McCormack, and State Senator Edward Carroll obtained a resolution in the General Court condemning Lee for his insulting remarks. "Does this Tory . . . realize that he is living in the United States and not in some European monarchy?" asked Carroll. "Does he dare to point scornfully at an honest workingman . . . [and at] honest people?" [43] Lee's error, though momentary, served as a reminder that the Irish still viewed "arrogant social workers" of the Back Bay with distrust. A number of Yankees reciprocated in spades.

Nevertheless, several ministers in Yankee areas of the city kept trying to reach out, and they reminded troubled parishioners of their social responsibilities to the less privileged. The majority of Congregational ministers broke new ground, and in 1935 they passed resolutions favoring public ownership and the right of workers to join unions. [44] And before the year was out a long-festering dispute among Boston's Unitarians came to a head. Younger clergy, determined to put their church in the forefront of reform, mustered sufficient votes to push through resolutions much like those adopted by the Congregationalists. [45]

But in still other Protestant churches the fresh winds of change blew more fitfully or not at all. By mid-decade, to be sure, Arthur Lee Kinsolving of Trinity Episcopal Church was prodding the Greater Boston Federation of Churches to interpret the Gospel as an instrument of reform. Jesus, said Kinsolving, had preached "a philosophy of crisis" which demanded that Christians strive "for [the] social justice implied in their religion." Yet, for Kinsolving,

social justice had limits. Viewing the contemplated veterans' bonus
of 1935 as a blow to the spirit of "self-reliance," he stated that "God
does not want weak-kneed parishioners." Warning against the
"something for nothing" attitude of those seeking relief from Washington, he deplored unbalanced budgets and centralized authority.[46]
To expense-minded municipal reformers who occupied his pews,
Kinsolving's messages must have sounded reassuring. Moreover,
most Presbyterian, Baptist, and Lutheran clergy either abstained
from taking positions on the great issues of the day, or else they
expressed dismay over what they perceived to be the socialistic
policies of the national government. "I have not come to preach
reform, for reform is not the primary task of the Christian church,"
said the new minister of Tremont Temple in 1935. "Salvation by
outward reform is bound to fail," wrote the minister of the South
End's Union Church, and he also warned of "illusions about being
able to 'save' the modern city simply by engaging in schemes and
movements." To certain Lutheran pastors, diplomatic recognition of
Russia and the Child Labor Amendment represented precisely this
kind of unwanted innovation.[47]

Eleven years of an economic system run amok had taken its toll on
Boston. Not only had the city lost ground to other urban centers in a
number of respects, but within its boundaries a sick economy had
exacted social costs. A dismaying rate of joblessness, housing decay,
internal population shifts, the disruption of community living patterns—Boston experienced them all. Judging from the cacophony of
voices that could be heard on an excursion through the city's neighborhoods at the end of the Depression, asperity had also resulted.
Aberrations of the spirit coexisted with a more positive cast of mind.
Ethnic rivalries remained strong—may, indeed, have intensified.
Not all the historical baggage which the city carried into the Depression was removed. Boston seemed divided into enclaves, sometimes
more rigid than before the crash. Moreover, intense expressions of

parochialism clashed with those who were to say, as did Franklin Roosevelt toward the end of his first term, that America needed "a program of one for all and all for one." [48] The Boston story suggests that the Great Depression had built up accretions which no political leader—municipal, state, or national—could have blasted away.

12

The Politics and Government
of Hard Times

By the end of the Great Depression, many of Boston's political monuments had been removed. In 1933 Martin Lomasney passed away, leaving behind not only an estate of $300,000 but almost as many legends of political success. Having once modestly boasted, "We don't tell 'em how to vote—we simply suggest," [1] the Mahatma in his last years was beginning to witness an electorate of somewhat more independent stripe. Less than four months after his death, a Yankee remnant disbanded the Good Government Association which for thirty years had warred against the Lomasneys of Boston. Several prominent figures who had been active during the First New Deal eventually moved to Washington—David K. Niles, John Ihlder of the Boston Housing Association, and Felix Frankfurter ranked among the most important. A few, like James Michael Curley's former municipal treasurer, Edmund L. Dolan, languished in jail. And John Dowd, the flamboyant city-council member from Roxbury, reached the end of the decade a fugitive from justice. Elected sheriff of Suffolk County toward the close of the thirties, he allegedly pocketed over $100,000 from the sale of prisoners' services and fled to escape the very cells over which he had been presiding.

At the same time that a number of familiar political leaders dropped from view, the tasks of municipal government also changed. In 1929, city-council members had devoted endless hours to questions like street paving, but after the advent of the New Deal the ward representatives acted as pitchmen for NRA enrollment campaigns, weighed the merits of public housing, debated PWA loans, and reached out for WPA allotments. Before the crash, the council had devoted minimal concern to the welfare department and had thought $5,000 an excessive annual appropriation for the municipal employment bureau. In the next decade, however, welfare costs drained Boston's treasury of not less than $100 million, and the federal government spent even more. Maurice Tobin very likely had some of these changes in mind when he observed that "the long continued depression has had its effect on almost every phase of our modern American life. Every branch and agency of the government, national, state, and municipal," he said, "has been vitally affected; so much so, indeed, that there has been a virtual transformation in the accepted conception of what should be expected of government." [2]

Yet ethnic Boston also carried historical legacies into the Great Depression, and eleven lean years failed to remove them all. Just as a number of social customs lingered on, several of the city's political traditions retained a life of their own. Other bequests from the past were modified, but not enough to allow an extensive overhaul of municipal government or to accept all the implications of Roosevelt's leadership. More than Mayor Tobin acknowledged, Bostonians sometimes poured old wine into new bottles.

Francis Skeffington, the fictional incarnation of James Michael Curley in Edwin O'Connor's *The Last Hurrah*, believed that Franklin Roosevelt's "celebrated impersonation of the Great White Father" had put the urban boss out of business. As another of the novel's characters explained to Skeffington's nephew, Roosevelt had "put the skids" under the old-time political leader:

> [Roosevelt] destroyed him by taking away his source of power. He made the kind of politician your uncle was an anachronism, sport. All

over the country the bosses have been dying for the last twenty years, thanks to Roosevelt. Your uncle lasted this long simply because he was who he was: an enormously popular man whose followers were devoted to him. . . . The old boss was strong simply because he held all the cards. If anybody wanted anything—jobs, favors, cash—he could only go to the boss, the local leader. What Roosevelt did was to take the handouts out of local hands. A few little things like Social Security, Unemployment Insurance, and the like—that's what shifted the gears, sport. No need now to depend on the boss for everything; the Federal Government was getting into the act. Otherwise known as social revolution.[3]

While O'Connor was largely correct that bossism had weakened by the late 1930s, he overestimated both the dimensions and causes of change. Although politics Boston style exhibited slightly more fluidity during the Depression than before, there were still strong continuities between the two decades. Secondly, the changes which did occur owed as much—and probably more—to local circumstances as to the New Deal. At most, trends evident prior to 1933 were no more than slightly accelerated.

The formal rules by which Bostonians played at politics survived the Depression unaltered. Ward lines were not redrawn, the non-partisan election law endured, and Boston's structural reformers—the Good Government Association's successors at the Municipal Employment Bureau, and Republicans such as Christian Herter, Henry Shattuck, and Laurence Curtis II—made no headway either. Despite repeated attempts to reduce the city council to eleven members, elect councilors-at-large and count votes through a proportional representation plan, all major reform efforts flopped. The Great Depression left no reconstructed electoral machinery in its wake.

At the ward level, pre–New Deal and post–New Deal elections also bore striking resemblances: both revealed astonishing and nearly identical turnover rates, and in neither period were most of the wards "bossed" in the classic sense that a behind-the-scenes puppeteer pulled the strings. In the three city-council elections held from 1927 to 1931, 25 percent of the incumbents lost their positions, while in the four contests from 1933 to 1939, an almost identical 27 percent were ousted.[4] Counting members of the council who decided not to seek another term, the cumulative turnover rate in sixty-six pre–New Deal ward elections reached 33 percent, while in eighty-eight post–New Deal races the combined turnover rate amounted to only a slightly higher 41 percent. While Chicago ward leaders almost never lost, and while Pittsburgh Democrats became more firmly entrenched by capturing control of New Deal work relief, Boston's politicians discovered that a ward boss could be licked.[5]

Despite the fact that only two of the twenty-two men elected to the city council in 1933 were still sitting at the end of the decade, the council's ethnic profile remained very much the same before and after the New Deal. Although in 1939 Italians broke the Irish stranglehold on the North and West Ends where Martin Lomasney had held sway, and although a second Jewish member of the city council sat from 1933 to 1937, some thirteen of the ward representatives at the end of the decade had names recognizable as Irish— one fewer than in 1929. Ward leaders came and ward leaders departed, but Green Power in Boston survived.

Few of the Irish ward sachems who came of political age during the 1930s, however, had ridden the New Deal gravy train into office, and even fewer stayed in power because they enjoyed a dependable monopoly of federal benefits. There were, of course, ways in which New Deal programs could bolster short-run political fortunes. William Galvin of Charlestown, for example, boasted to *The Saturday Evening Post* in 1941 that two of his brothers had received CCC jobs, that his ward had been designated a food-stamp area, that 80 percent of his fifteen hundred elderly constituents received government payments. Moreover, Galvin pointed out that the Irish, once excluded from posh federal jobs in Boston, had at last been recognized by the New Deal. Nevertheless, Galvin and his peers in other wards lacked the permanent headlock on federal patronage which would have made possible a conquest of indefinite duration. New Dealers, as seen in earlier chapters, had taken extraordinary—though not always successful—measures to keep federal benefits from being misused, and the advent of Roosevelt had put ward bosses like Galvin at the bottom of a new hierarchy overseen by a United States senator with a congressman next in line. Thus, Congressman McCormack played an active role in patronage, but in Boston friends of the New Deal often outflanked him. Down in the trenches, ward bosses were even further removed from erratically delivered federal booty.[6]

In addition to the particular way in which the New Deal operated in Boston, the persistent instability of municipal politics can be attributed to several local considerations. Heightened ethnocentrism, for instance, encouraged newcomers to enter politics, and demographic reshuffling altered the complexion of as many as six wards. Moreover, the Democratic party, having achieved an impressive 2–1 registration advantage over the Republicans in 1928, increased this lead until it exceeded 4–1 in 1938. The Democratic party had become too sprawling, too amorphous for its own good, and, throughout the thirties, Democrats monopolized all but three of the twenty-two wards. Competition for power in a virtual one-party system was acute, and Democrats jostled each other for the available offices. The nonpartisan election system encouraged a swarm of candidates to vie for city council seats: an average of 4.3 persons sought each seat in elections before the New Deal, while 4.5 contenders ran for each office in the 1933–1939 period. Without the threat of a second party to tighten the discipline within Democratic ranks, the party could not hold together.

Then, too, the austere backdrop against which Boston's elected officials staged their political tableaux also kept any would-be boss from becoming too comfortably ensconced. Not since the mid-nineteenth century, when the city fathers warily eyed the endless convoys of immigrant ships, had municipal government been confronted with so great a crisis. Property valuations fell 25 percent between 1930 and 1940, the most serious decline in the nation's thirteen largest centers, and the tax bite therefore had to be increased from $30.80 per $1,000 of assessed valuations in 1930 to

$40.60 in 1940, a hike which kept Boston's rate the highest of all major cities.[7] While exactly half of the other twelve cities of over 500,000 lowered their municipal debt during the Depression, Boston's increased: municipal interest payments jumped 37 percent between 1930 and 1940, and only New York, Buffalo, Los Angeles, and Detroit topped the Hub's $21 increase in per capita debt.[8] These developments reinforced the electorate's pre-Roosevelt inclination to throw the rascals out. Made anxious by unemployment on the one hand and soaring taxes on the other, constituents wanted solutions. As the Depression foisted somber new responsibilities on the city's politicians, few passed the tests imposed by an excitable electorate.

The machinations of James Michael Curley (O'Connor's "Skeffington"), the man who had broken many of the old ward leaders before the Depression began, added mightily to the uncertainties of local politics. Curley had built his following through personal appeal, and his workers seldom aspired to the city council. Neither the 1929 nor the 1931 ward election brought a majority of Curley loyalists into the council chambers, and he seemed not to care. Indeed, the Mayor saw obvious advantages to not building the strength of potential rivals. Instead, he rewarded his precinct captains with appointive offices in the municipal bureaucracy, and they helped him to his gubernatorial triumph of 1934. However, Curley's legions hustled mainly for Curley: neither his hated adversary, Frederick Mansfield, nor Maurice Tobin inherited his spear carriers. Rather, the last two mayors of the 1930s pieced together their own organizations out of Yankees and upper-income Irish. Unlike Chicago or New York, there was, in fact, no Democratic machine in Boston which one mayor blithely passed on to the next, and the city's Democratic Committee, reflecting the animosities between Curley and other party members, could not command any substantial degree of party discipline.

No single episode kept Democrats in greater disarray during the

1930s than James Michael Curley's two years in the State House. Commencing his reign in January 1934 with an inauguration-day punch thrown at his predecessor, Joseph B. Ely, he embarked upon a twenty-four month rampage. Fourteen thousand guests attended his inauguration party, and after a year in office he had spent $85,206 on taxis, flowers, meals, cigars, and excursions.[9] Yet more than what Leverett Saltonstall would call "squanderlust" (Curley's budgets were not out of line with national patterns), the governor's reckless political style and unrestrained partisanship became leading issues.[10]

"Curley moved across the Massachusetts landscape like a Latin Dictator," Francis Russell has observed. Accompanied by state police and military aides clad in garish blue uniforms with gold braid, the governor's careening limousine was involved in a number of accidents which earned him the sobriquet of "The Hit and Run Governor." When Curley attended a baseball game, howitzers made it difficult to miss his entrance, while at Harvard's tercentenary celebration a more modest trumpet fanfare heralded the arrival of the governor and his corsairs. As Curley swaggered in alumni booed, and Franklin D. Roosevelt looked on in icy silence.[11]

Variously styled a second Huey Long ("the late Louisiana dictator's twin"), "the very acme of Nero-like tyranny," a second Hitler, and "the Irish Mussolini," he "transform[ed] the State into a magnificent ward." [12] "Curley's regime is frankly racial beyond anything known elsewhere in America," wrote the respected journalist Louis Lyons, and "the nightmare of the corridors," the creation of sleepy hollows filled with dozing supernumeraries, began as soon as the former denizens of City Hall packed into the State House.[13] To choke off the investigation of fiscal chicanery which had gone on during his 1929–1933 term as mayor, Curley removed the chairman of the Governor's Council, and this pliant body proceeded to stock the Boston Finance Commission with James Michael's cronies. To render the Massachusetts judiciary more cooperative, Curley in 1936 devised a plan whereby judges over the age of seventy would be submitted to mental and physical examinations. If they balked, they would be retired. The move inspired one justice, the seventy-four-year-old Patrick J. "Silk Hat" Duane, to challenge Curley to a fight—with boxing gloves if the governor's budget permitted, he quipped.[14] Although Curley's proposal was thwarted by the state legislature, the episode topped off months of unseemly *hubris*.

Curley also displayed a finer side. His Inaugural Address, with its call for a state workmen's compensation fund, liberalization of the state minimum wage, toughening of protective legislation for women and children, a curb on antiunion injunctions, and government spending for "work and wages," represented, as Frances Perkins called it, "a conspicuously clear portrayal of major social issues . . . with many sound suggestions for meeting them." Throughout his tenure, recalled Eddie Dowling, the Governor "fought many a battle up there [in Massachusetts] in favor of the workingman." The judgment rang true, and, in a less formal way, Curley never lost his touch with the poor. Outside his Jamaicaway home it was not uncommon for over a hundred unemployed men and women to line up in the early hours of the morning in the expectation that the Governor would take care of them. Often he did. Yes, he was outrageous, but "the odor of sanctity," said Marion Frankfurter, was "so strong" that the Bay State needed "a shock or two." [15] Curley administered the jolt.

Nevertheless, there were rumblings in the wards that Curley's excesses in an age of hardship were indefensible, that his political style was anachronistic. In 1936, the year of the Democratic landslide across the nation, Curley competed with Henry Cabot Lodge, Jr., for a seat in the United States Senate and lost. Almost every ward gave Curley a smaller percentage than in 1934, and the most serious depletion of his tally occurred in Jewish Ward 14 where liberalism ran strongest. A year later Curley plunged into the 1937 mayoralty and still more decisive defeat, this time at the hands of Maurice Tobin. No longer in possession of the spoils of office with which to keep his workers in the trenches, he was thrashed by Leverett Saltonstall in the 1938 gubernatorial race. Saddled with a judgment requiring him to pay back $42,629 which a court said he had taken from the City of Boston in the early thirties, Curley watched the empire built on patronage and personal allegiance begin to crumble.[16] However, it did not vanish: there would be a half-dozen last hurrahs in the 1940s and 1950s. But for the purposes of attaining the kind of unity upon which ward politicians thrive, Curley's ambitions bordered on the disastrous. His losing statewide campaigns had left a vacuum which no one seemed big enough to fill.

The Boston story, then, undermines on several counts the notion that the New Deal changed local politics and destroyed bossism: the inability of most ward leaders to control elections characterized the 1930s as well as the 1920s. Furthermore, neither political party could monopolize power: unlike Philadelphia, Boston's Republicans were overwhelmingly outmanned; unlike Detroit, the city's Democrats were hopelessly split. Although the one person who might have established an entrenched machine, James Michael Curley, was thwarted in part because the federal government moved into the Boston picture with more force than in most other cities, he was also toppled by an electorate unwilling either to spend or to back his aspirations for state and national offices. When in later years Curley decided to run for mayor once again, Bostonians elected him despite O'Connor's thesis that the welfare state had supposedly rendered him obsolete. Unquestionably, Roosevelt and the New Deal made their mark upon intergovernmental relationships in the 1930s. They did not, however, recast local politics into unrecognizable forms.

Municipal finance, "the axis upon which the wheels of . . . government turn," as Mayor Tobin phrased it,[17] absorbed the attention of those who survived the electoral process, and city officials scrambled for ways to balance human needs with fiscal realities. While municipal government on the whole satisfactorily discharged its charter-imposed responsibilities, cautious juggling prevailed. For all the modifications that occurred, and for all the new avenues to Washington, city government played it safe in the Depression years.

Despite soaring taxes and rising debt, Boston was partly sheltered from the kind of experience that might have produced greater innovation and sacrifice. The total annual revenue collection, for instance, fell off just 4 percent from 1930 to 1940. Although four cities—New York, Chicago, Baltimore, and San Francisco—enjoyed increases in the same period, Boston maintained a strong relative position. The same might be said of property values. Even though Boston's valuations plunged alarmingly, the city's property base by 1938 exceeded that of Chicago, a municipality four and a half times larger. Taxpayers howled about the increase of municipal IOU's, but in ten years time Boston's unredeemed notes and bonds had risen from $114 million to only $127 million, thanks in part to Mayor Tobin's end-of-decade retrenchment. And even though interest costs were also affected as tax anticipation notes soared from $21 million in 1929 to an annual average of $45 million in the 1930s, the absolute per capita debt for Boston in 1940 ($166), although more than in St. Louis ($88) and Milwaukee ($62), had not reached the same plateau as New York's ($316), Buffalo's ($254), or San Francisco's ($236). Accordingly, investors considered Boston a decent credit risk and interest charges continued to be less steep than in the rest of urban America.[18]

These relatively favorable indicators, coupled with deeply embedded citizen preferences, immunized Boston against major change. The city had entered the Depression with the highest per capita cost of government of any large city, and it seemed quite enough to hold this rank throughout the 1930s. Even though the funds at the mayor's disposal from 1929 to 1940 dipped 17 percent, the drop was less serious than in eight of the other twelve largest cities.[19] Boston had resources that simply were not tapped, in part because a conservative state legislature would not permit new sources of revenue to be mined: the men on Beacon Hill refused sales taxes, levies on stock transactions, and taxes assessed against commuters. Twice the legislature rejected a monthly lottery, despite reminders that Harvard's first building—as well as Faneuil Hall—had been financed by this means. When in 1936 the legislature at last surrendered its power to control the tax limit on expenses incurred by municipal departments, no move was made to exact higher levies.

Moreover, comprehensive streamlining of municipal government fell beyond the reach of the city fathers, despite attempts by Mayors Mansfield and Tobin to revamp outmoded practices. Both tried repeatedly to consolidate the unwieldy structure of close to forty municipal departments, and each time either the city council or the state legislature turned thumbs down. Not even centralized purchasing was adopted: far too many political interests were at stake. When Mansfield's first bill to bring about departmental consolidation reached the state legislature, for example, Senator Joseph Langone of East Boston charged that the Mayor was using dismissals to oust Italian workers. "The word has been passed out, 'Get the Guinea,' " he declared.[20] Both Mansfield and Tobin favored replacing the venerable Overseers of the Poor with a single paid department head, but they got nowhere. Both men tried to stimulate enthusiasm for metropolitan government but the wealthier suburbs feared Irish rule and higher taxes, the same sources of alarm that had been evident as far back as 1874 when the city had tried to annex Brookline. At the same time a bill introduced in the state legislature to disgorge Chelsea, Winthrop, and Revere from Suffolk County was voted down, and the Depression ended with the antiquated county government intact.

Within the limits which a continued absence of home rule imposed and which local political traditions mandated, city government rearranged priorities. In 1929, for instance, welfare expenses consumed only 6.4 percent of all outlays controlled by the mayor and the city council. By 1933, welfare costs had zoomed to 35.8 percent of the mayor's budget, and they remained close to that figure for the rest of the decade. With fewer people able to afford private medical care, the Boston City Hospital carried new burdens. In addition, the Wayfarers' Lodge and the city's child welfare division needed larger transfusions of revenue. To meet these exigencies, and to make up for increased debt service which eventually consumed 12 cents of each tax dollar (a nickel more than in 1929), the city work force, a hefty 21,000 at the close of James Michael Curley's term in 1933, was trimmed to a svelte 12,500 by 1940.[21] City workers were periodically furloughed, overtime pay ended, a five-day week became the rule, and from April 1933 to January 1935 wage cuts saved the city $8,500,000. Meanwhile, the Department of Public Works took a drubbing: prior to 1932 more than 11 cents of every tax dollar had gone to the DPW, but by 1940 the department's share had tumbled to 7.9 cents. (In contrast, the Department of Public Welfare received 17.9 cents of every tax dollar, roughly a fivefold increase from the start of the decade.) City Hall as it looked in the Mansfield years symbolized what had happened to municipal upkeep: "Paint turned a grimy brown; there was darkness, gloom, and filth everywhere. The rich hangings in the Council Chambers were so dirty that you couldn't touch them without causing a dust storm." [22]

To be sure, some of the more inventive (and even unconstitutional) suggestions introduced for city-council deliberation failed—proposals such as a citywide health insurance plan, the construction of a municipal lighting plant, the imposition of levies on national corporations doing business in Boston. In keeping the nuts and bolts of government in working order, however, municipal officials deserved more credit than the electorate generally gave them. Seizing the advantages which Boston's tax-paying capacity afforded, and building on the seventeenth-century heritage that obligated Massachusetts communities to the destitute, the occupants of City Hall overcame enormous obstacles and maintained a welfare system, however austere, that acquitted itself rather better than its counterparts in most urban locales.

Municipal relationships with Washington, as suggested in Chapter 7, deserved lower grades. The city's 10 percent portion of FERA, WPA, and USHA costs boosted expenses: $1,100,000 was allotted in 1935, and in the last few years of the thirties the city's bill edged above $2 million. Rather than extolling the benefits, municipal officials often begrudged the outlay. Major capital expenditures for the heavy construction enterprises sponsored by PWA were studiously avoided, and officials with an ear to the ground heard conflicting reports from the electorate: four middle-income wards, voting in a 1938 referendum, returned a 30,685–14,170 verdict against expenditures for the USHA's low-rent projects, while residents of Charlestown, lower Roxbury, and South Boston instructed their city-council representatives through postcard polls and hearings to support public-housing units. Parochial and conflicting, these judgments were shaped by the same particularistic concerns that had kept municipal leaders guessing throughout the Depression: those who rented cared less about property taxes than those who owned; a ward with high unemployment might blame its representatives for penurious welfare checks while other wards insisted that their emissaries pare budgets to the bone.

As constituents semaphored mixed signals, the local superstructure sought additional clues about attitudes toward the New Deal. When Washington launched its rescue mission in the 1933–1935 period, Bostonians welcomed the vast sums of money but carped at other aspects of the Roosevelt program. The only clear tests of how the Roosevelt administration stood would come in the 1936 and 1940 elections. Alas, because many New Deal programs had been transmogrified once they entered Boston, national elections did not clearly test the same New Deal that the President had envisioned. Roosevelt's personality was always at issue and, by 1940, foreign policy had also obscured a clear reading of the electorate's ideological preferences. As in matters pertaining to local politics and government, however, it seemed that Bostonians were willing to clap for new arrangements with one hand only.

As the Roosevelt administration prepared to face the voters of Boston in 1936, the electorate which had to be cajoled was showing itself to be querulous indeed. At the beginning of the year Boston's progress toward economic recovery was faltering, and impatience mounted. Segments of organized labor refused to convert to New

Deal principles, and most of State Street, although seeing that federal work relief kept local taxes from an even more precipitous rise, displayed little affection for the New Deal. Far from being cut from whole cloth, Boston's political crazy quilt was stitched together from clashing patterns.

At the beginning of the fall campaign, no finely tuned Democratic machine stood ready to give assistance to Roosevelt. Anti-Curleyism was growing, and the Governor's WPA-approved scheme to build sidewalks along state highways—widely perceived as a consummate boondoggle—thickened preelection gloom. So, too, did the Suffolk Superior Court's ruling of September 9, 1936, that the municipal treasurer during Curley's most recent term as mayor had fleeced the city of $131,161.90. James Michael had become an obvious liability, and as he interspersed anti–New Deal polemic with quondam expressions of allegiance to Roosevelt, the President decided not to back him in his senatorial race against Lodge. Mayor Mansfield was continuing his open attacks on the Governor, calling him "not a Democrat" but "a Curleycrat." [23] Moreover, Joseph B. Ely, Curley's Democratic predecessor on Beacon Hill, endorsed the Republican nominee, Alfred M. Landon, and Senator David I. Walsh waited until October 20 to speak for Roosevelt. A number of ward leaders in the Hub also viewed the Second New Deal as leftism run riot, and Curley, ever the sensitive anemometer, urged James Farley in September to keep New Dealers like Rexford Tugwell, Frances Perkins, and Felix Frankfurter out of Boston. "The opinion of most persons," warned Curley, "is that they are communistic." [24] Messy as always, the Boston situation inspired predictions until the very last moment that Roosevelt would not carry the city by a margin sufficient to capture the state. [25]

Moreover, in 1936 a blazing comet reappeared in the Massachusetts firmament, and many Bostonians were beguiled. Father Charles Coughlin, the Detroit radio priest, had formed the Union Party and he appeared to be making inroads. Curley, always quick to associate himself with a front runner, offered Coughlin his secretary to help organize the Bay State, a loan which Coughlin soon

For all the hoopla over Roosevelt, the New Deal faced many threats in Boston. Father Charles E. Coughlin, the anti-New Deal radio priest from Detroit, leaves the State House with Governor Curley in August 1935, after receiving a standing ovation. *The Boston Globe.*

rejected. James Michael posed for pictures with Coughlin in June following a Boston speech in which the priest had stated that neither Roosevelt nor Landon was "worth a nickel—in fact, a plugged nickel." "One of them is a promise-breaker and the other is a dumb-bell," he added.[26] And when the Union Party designated Thomas O'Brien, the former district attorney of Suffolk County, as its Vice-presidential candidate, and some 40,000 Massachusetts residents responded to a sticker campaign to put O'Brien's name on the senatorial ballot as well, the threat seemed real enough.[27] On the raw, cloudy weekday afternoon of October 12, Coughlin lured some 30,000 cheering followers to Braves Field where he denounced the Roosevelt administration, and the city was widely regarded as the greatest stronghold of Coughlinism in the United States.[28]

Yet during the last weeks of the campaign Roosevelt's prospects took a turn for the better. For the first time since 1933 the economy sustained a pronounced upward movement which had begun during the summer, and the WPA, with state administrator Paul Edwards adorning his lapel with a Roosevelt button, was paying 25,000 Bostonians every week. Labor unions were once more picking up members. With Independents and CIO locals striding ahead, some of the moderate labor leaders in the Hub took more liberal positions, and Roosevelt picked up a valuable endorsement from the Massachusetts AFL. Moreover, Curley—his own senatorial campaign menaced by the Union Party entrant—finally lashed out at Father Coughlin's "mental irritations" on September 30.[29] Curley also began speaking for Roosevelt, even though the President was not reciprocating. Joseph P. Kennedy was brought in to reassure businessmen, and Cardinal O'Connell ordered local priests to tune off their radios while the Detroiter was on the air.

Roosevelt's appearance in Boston during the waning stages of the campaign also helped turn the tide. On October 21, 1936, just ten days after Father Coughlin's whirlwind visit, the President appeared before a surging throng of 125,000 on the Boston Common. Although not mentioning Coughlin by name, Roosevelt drew a bead on "rabble rousers," and he asserted that on the day after the election, "the American air will be cleaner and American democracy will be safer." State Chairman Joseph McGrath, ecstatic about the not wholly anticipated response, reported to Farley that "millions of smiling, happy Massachusetts citizens" had greeted Roosevelt, cheered him, wished him good luck, "and in many cases the older people gave him a very sincere 'God Bless You.' "[30]

Roosevelt crushed Landon in Boston, yet the percentage accorded him, handsome as it was, fell off from 1932: the President's share of the 1936 total vote slipped to 63.9 percent, down from his 1932 showing of 67.1 percent, and also less than Al Smith's 1928 margin of 66.8 percent. In contrast, every single one of the eighteen other cities where foreign stock comprised more than half the popu-

Roosevelt visits Boston, October 21, 1936. Part of the massive throng that turned out at the Common to greet the President, having trampled a female spectator, is pushed back by the police. Boston University School of Communication.

lation accorded Roosevelt a greater majority in 1936 than Smith had enjoyed. Only two of these cities (New York and Providence) gave Roosevelt a smaller share of the total vote in 1936 than in 1932, but neither dipped as much as Boston. While in 1932 only two of the eighteen other cities had assigned a higher percentage of their votes to Roosevelt than had Boston, four years later ten surpassed the Hub. Cleveland's Democratic vote, for example, rocketed from 50.1 percent to 65.1 percent, the highest of all nineteen except for Jersey City. As Roosevelt picked up steam in other cities, he lost momentum in Boston.[31]

The Union Party captured 8.3 percent of the city's total vote, the Coughlinites' strongest showing in any urban center.[32] South Boston and Charlestown, both low-income Irish districts, accorded the Union Party roughly 11 to 13 percent of their tally, and the radio priest's candidate, William Lemke, also lured more than 10 percent of the electorate in nine other wards.[33] With the important exception of East Boston, where Italo-Americans returned 12.4 percent for Lemke, most of these votes came from the relatively affluent Irish districts away from the inner city. Although the election took place at one of the few points in the 1930s when the city's economy was on a noticeable upbeat, and even though the Irish appeared to have been less agitated about Roosevelt's foreign policies than they would be in 1940, both concerns most likely added to Coughlin's turnout. In addition, hostility toward centralized authority in Washington—what the archdiocesan newspaper had called the "twenty thousand regulations . . . enacted since 1933"—undoubtedly contributed to the 26,000 ballots polled by the Coughlinites in Boston.[34]

With the passing of four years several of the local political difficulties which Roosevelt had largely overcome in 1936 were intensified. During the first four months of 1940, the President gave no firm indication of a desire for a third term, and in scenes reminiscent of 1932, Democrats chased new heroes. Congressman McCormack inclined toward Jospeh P. Kennedy until he learned in February that the Ambassador did not plan to run, and so it fell to James Farley, the President's disenchanted political mastermind, to command attention. "Monsignor Farley," said The New Republic, "whose middle name is not Aloysius for nothing, has the look of what people living in the rural areas of the Boston diocese call 'a city Irishman.' "[35] Irish in the City of Boston could not fail to approve. With anti–New Deal Senator David I. Walsh in the vanguard, the initial objections of Congressman McCormack to a pledged delegation were overcome: twenty-eight of the thirty-four delegates to the national convention had committed themselves to Farley by the end of February. And when Roosevelt appeared to slur his erstwhile friend's Catholicism,

Farley retorted with an appeal to which Bostonians could warm. "We must never permit the ideals of the Republic," he said, "to sink to the point where every American father and mother, regardless of race, color or creed, cannot look proudly into the cradle of their newborn babe and see a future President of the United States." [36] At the July convention in sweltering Chicago, one-sixth of Farley's votes on the first and only ballot came from Massachusetts.

Closer to the November election, Farley-Walsh devotees— without Walsh's formal approval—remained active, urging Bostonians to stay home rather than vote for Roosevelt. Other problems threatened the President's Boston prospects as well. Father Coughlin's Jew-baiting Christian Front endorsed the Republican standard-bearer, Wendell Willkie, and the priest's followers combed Irish neighborhoods in search of G.O.P. votes. An organization centered at Boston College, still smoldering over the President's court-packing plan of 1937 and his attempted purge of Congress the next year, believed the quest for a third term offered final proof of Roosevelt's dictatorial qualities. With the relaxation of federal control over the WPA, discrimination rates on work-relief projects for the non-Irish had climbed, and mutual animosity among the city's ethnic groups had intensified. To make matters worse, these indications of restlessness came in an economic setting in some ways less propitious than in 1936: while other cities were snapping back, Boston's pace of recovery was languishing. After eight years of Roosevelt's experiments, many wondered why.

Moreover, foreign affairs added to Roosevelt's problems. Anger at the President's ouster of the Italian Consul in the Hub abetted a Republican organizing drive in East Boston, and Italians tacked up "Willkie for President" signs in the North End. [37] The President's exchange with England of over-age destroyers in return for naval bases offended many Irish. Senator Walsh, holding fast to an isolationist line, was regularly harpooning the President and praising Ambassador Joseph P. Kennedy's disinclination to aid the British. Alarmed by these developments, liberals such as Margaret Weisman at the Consumers' League sent urgent requests to the Democratic

National Committee for speakers. "Featuring Yankee Democrats won't get the cause anywhere," she wrote. "We need some Reillys, O'Sullivans, McSweeneys in the picture." [38]

Republicans could at last attack with confidence, even in a city where registered Democrats outnumbered them by four and a half to one. Gradually accepting social security, unemployment insurance, and other features of the New Deal, Republicans generally presented a more moderate image than at mid-decade. Bolstered by the showings of Senator Lodge and Governor Saltonstall, Republicans also had in Wendell Willkie a far more energetic nominee than Alf Landon had been in 1936. Unlike Landon, who had stayed out of Massachusetts, Willkie traveled to Boston, where in April he drew a rousing ovation from the Chamber of Commerce. Six months later he stormed into the city for another highly successful reception, which included a cordial audience with Cardinal O'Connell. Willkie's promises to 35,000 listeners at Braves Field that he could restore prosperity and that "our boys shall stay out of Europe" elicited shouts of approval. Republican prospects looked bullish. [39]

But by resuming their quadrennial love-in, Democrats in the closing stages of the election patched up some of their differences and rallied. Maurice Tobin, the last mayor of the decade, campaigned for F.D.R., and so did Congressman McCormack. And James Michael Curley, who reminded the voters that he had been the first in the nation to endorse Roosevelt nine years before, told the Democratic State Convention in September that he still approved despite "personal disappointments experienced by me at the hands of the Chief Executive." [40] Once more, outside speakers were summoned, and though the Democratic National Committee neglected to send Reillys, O'Sullivans, and McSweeneys, New York Mayor Fiorello La Guardia wooed Boston's Italo-Americans on Roosevelt's behalf. In addition, the Massachusetts Federation of Labor came through with another endorsement of the President.

On October 30, when Roosevelt's train pulled into South Station, the President looked tired—with reason. Just the day before, he had stood by somberly while the first selective service number was pulled from a glass bowl. While heading for Massachusetts, the

President had learned of Willkie's stinging remarks about shattered promises. If Roosevelt were reelected, said Willkie, American boys would be fighting within six months. A stop-off at Worcester, where the President had endured Senator Walsh's presence on the same dais, could not have eased his state of mind. But, much as in 1936, Bostonians gave him a phenomenal reception. As the motorcade inched toward the Boston Garden, a multitude clogged the streets, and the President received a thunderous ovation when he entered the hall to deliver a national radio address. Flanked on the Garden platform by the city's Democratic leadership, the President equivocated. The Boston Navy Yard had never been busier, he stated, and in the next breath he praised Boston's native son, Ambassador Kennedy, who only three days before had returned from London, disgruntled by the destroyer-naval bases exchange. Then, in a remark that would later haunt him, the President replied to Willkie and reassured Boston's isolationists: "I have said this before, but I shall say it again and again and again: Your boys are not going to be sent into any foreign wars." A few sentences later, he urged 12,000 more planes for the British. Ignoring his Boston audience, he finished his remarks with a lengthy appeal to Midwestern farmers.[41] The speech was not very edifying, which may have been just as well. The politicians applauded, and the loyal throng, hearing whatever they chose to hear, roared.

On Election Day, the President again thrashed his Republican opponent, and this time Boston seemed more in line with national trends. From Roosevelt's point of view, the result in the Hub had some positive aspects. With the President's percentage of the total vote across the nation down 6.1 from 1936, and with his big city tally descending by roughly 2 to 3 percent, Boston slipped just 1 percent. In a personal triumph, Roosevelt romped home while all but one of the Democratic candidates seeking statewide office went down to a crashing defeat. F.D.R. had apparently been vindicated.

Aggregate tallies are one thing, however, and the separate components of the total are yet another. While Roosevelt's margins in Boston had fallen by only a few percentage points, the city's neighborhoods—as Table 12.1 demonstrates—fluctuated more markedly: of the major ethnic groups, only Back Bay Yankees held absolutely steady from 1932 to 1940, and they, of course, continued to oppose the President. The response to the New Deal had, in the main, been selective, shifting, seriatim. In Dorchester's Ward 14, for example, Roosevelt's staggering majorities among Jewish voters increased from a 5–2 margin in 1932 to a rollicking 10–1 in 1940. While Boston's Negroes inched ahead in their allegiance to the Democratic standard-bearer, low-income Italo-Irish neighborhoods began to fall away: although 71 percent of Wards 1–3 and 6–7 voted for Roosevelt in 1940, surely a robust showing, the President's margin had nevertheless ebbed from the 88 percent accorded him in 1932 and the 78 percent given him in 1936. Meanwhile, more affluent Irish and Italian voters defected to an even greater degree. Just as Boston's stable population figures masked substantial demographic change, so did Roosevelt's handsome margins obscure political realities. In Boston, no constant New Deal coalition existed.

In neighborhoods where Roosevelt generated an increased following, residents perceived that the New Deal had given them recognition and that their relative social standing had improved. These areas became much more politically active: the electorate in Jewish Ward 14, for example, doubled in size between 1932 and 1940, while the city's turnout advanced some 26 percent after the 1932 decline. With unemployment lessening, black voters turned a deaf ear when Republicans sent Jesse Owens, fresh from his Berlin Olympics triumph, into Roxbury. The gold-medal winner was cheered, but many who responded to Owens must also have joined "the largest crowd of colored people of Ward 9 and its environs" ever to squeeze into Ruggles Hall. There, a minister, speaking for the Democrats' cause, announced that "Lincoln is dead, and so is everything he stood for, as far as the Republican Party and the Negro is concerned." [42] A comfortable majority concurred. Other voters who stuck with Roosevelt could have cheered when Mayor Tobin, at the 1940 Jackson Day Dinner, praised the President as among "the most thoughtful men for the masses" to have served his country, a man who had extended "corporal works of mercy" to victims of the Depression.[43]

Despite the thumping Jewish vote, the percentages which Italians and Irish still delivered, the modest gains in Negro areas, and the constant levels attained in the Back Bay, national election results in Boston reflected several of the developments which had worried Roosevelt's campaign staff. While in 1928 the Democratic share of the presidential vote corresponded to party registrations, by 1940 the disparity between registered Democrats (80.3 percent) and the Democratic presidential vote (62.9 percent) had widened to 17.4 percent. Although every city in the nation with a population of over 500,000 gave Roosevelt a more substantial winning share in 1936 and 1940 than Al Smith had garnered in 1928, Boston alone dropped below its 1928 Democratic percentage. Boston's slump—the term "rebellion" would be too strong—represented more than a statistical aberration of having started the Depression years with a high Democratic presidential vote. The Roosevelt forces, in perceiving that all was not well, had not altogether missed the mark.

If Boston delivered ever smaller majorities to Roosevelt, it was not because the city was attracted to the political Left. Neither the portrayal of Communism as "20th-Century Americanism," nor the hanging of portraits of Washington, Jefferson, and Lincoln side by side with those of Marx, Lenin, and Stalin at Communist party rallies, enticed more than a meager handful. Bostonians rejected the Communist argument that Democrats and Republicans were "birds of a feather" wedded to an obsolete economic system,[44] and the mild flutter caused by the Councils of the Unemployed during the very early thirties, and again in 1935, was not sustained. The Socialist party's chairman, Alfred Baker Lewis, used his position in the NAACP to try to lure Negro voters, but had no luck. With only a slim following of academics and scattered votes coming from Ward 14, the Socialist party, as with the Communists and the Socialist Labor party, fell below 1 percent of the Boston total in 1936 and 1940. Those who ditched Roosevelt had not carried on a flirtation with the left.

Rather, defectors assigned their ballots to the Republican party in

Table 12.1. Presidential Elections, 1928–1940
Total Vote for Major Candidates; Percent of Total Vote in City of Boston; and Percent of Major Party Vote in Selected Wards [a]

Area and Dominant Ethnic Group	1928		1932			1936			1940		Shift in FDR's 1940 percentage vs. 1932
	Hoover	Smith	Hoover	F.D.R.	Landon	Lemke	F.D.R.	Willkie	F.D.R.		
City	87,445 (31.7%)	186,280 (66.8%)	78,097 (29.5%)	179,630 (67.1%)	85,789 (27.5%)	25,924 (8.3%)	199,504 (63.9%)	124,908 (36.5%)	215,244 (62.9%)		−4.2%
Ward 1 East Boston (Italian)	2,530 (17.8%)	11,691 (82.2%)	2,084 (14.3%)	12,617 (85.7%)	2,452 (14.0%)	1,432 (8.2%)	13,585 (77.8%)	6,621 (33.2%)	13,277 (66.8%)		−18.9%
Ward 3 North and West Ends (Italian)	2,060 (19.2%)	9,229 (81.8%)	1,765 (16.6%)	8,857 (83.4%)	2,672 (17.1%)	522 (3.4%)	12,395 (79.5%)	5,981 (34.3%)	11,457 (65.7%)		−17.7%
Ward 5 Back Bay (Wasp)	7,537 (59.5%)	5,128 (40.5%)	6,913 (64.5%)	3,806 (35.5%)	8,036 (58.6%)	514 (3.7%)	5,179 (37.7%)	10,095 (64.2%)	5,829 (35.8%)		+0.3%

Area and Dominant Ethnic Group	1928 Hoover	1928 Smith	1932 Hoover	1932 F.D.R.	1936 Landon	1936 Lemke	1936 F.D.R.	1940 Willkie	1940 F.D.R.	Shift in FDR's 1940 percentage vs. 1932
Wards 6–7 South Boston (Irish)	2,793 (12.0%)	20,510 (88.0%)	2,175 (10.9%)	17,784 (89.1%)	2,964 (12.8%)	2,462 (10.7%)	17,618 (76.5%)	6,327 (22.8%)	20,542 (77.2%)	−11.9%
Ward 14 Dorchester (Jewish)	4,727 (35.8%)	8,472 (64.2%)	3,979 (28.7%)	9,872 (71.3%)	2,238 (12.3%)	397 (2.5%)	15,602 (85.2%)	2,140 (13.7%)	19,789 (86.3%)	+15.0%
Negro Areas [b]	3,754 (41.4%)	5,309 (58.6%)	2,741 (35.1%)	5,089 (64.9%)	3,099 (30.7%)	589 (5.7%)	6,441 (63.6%)	3,536 (33.4%)	7,250 (66.6%)	+1.7%
Wards not shown in table	28.0%	72.0%	32.1%	67.9%	30.2%	9.4%	60.4%	41.9%	58.1%	−9.8%

[a] So that comparisons can be made in the text to the Clubb and Allen study of the 1928–1932 elections, the city percentage is given as a share of the total vote. Thus city percentages fail to sum up to 100%. Boston's insignificant minor party vote (Socialist, Socialist Labor, Communist) has not been used in calculating ward percentages, since only in Ward 14 during the 1932 election would inclusion of the left-wing tally make a difference of more than half of one percent. The three minor parties received 1,729 votes in 1928; 7,091 in 1932; 1,640 in 1936; and 1,855 in 1940.

[b] Black density was nowhere so intense in Boston as to constitute a foolproof index. Still, the votes from Ward 4, precincts 4–6, Ward 9, precincts 6–15 and Ward 12, precinct 1, serve as a rough indicator of Negro preference. All percentages calculated from "Annual Returns of the Election Department" for appropriate years, 1929–1941, except for Negro precinct vote where either the Globe (1928–1936) or the Herald (1940) has been employed.

sharply rising numbers. Italians in Wards 1 and 3 had given Hoover just 3,849 votes in 1932, but eight years later Willkie amassed 12,604. By 1940, the two wards had cut Roosevelt's share of the total by more than 18 percent. Ranking just behind, the Irish of South Boston tripled their Republican vote during the same interval and eroded the President's portion by 11.9 percent. Finally, areas away from the center city, ones likely to be of more mixed ethnicity and with higher incomes than those shown in Table 12.1 (except, of course, for the Back Bay), also moved closer to the G.O.P.[45]

Within the more prosperous areas of augmented Republican strength, grievances against municipal government ran strongest, and Roosevelt undoubtedly reaped some of the whirlwind. Wards with a disproportionately high frequency of home ownership and a mixed Irish-Yankee vote moved perceptibly toward Lemke and Landon, and by 1940 the Republican trend had become even more apparent. The issues of higher city and federal taxes animated these wards, and a growing number of voters in places such as West Roxbury, Jamaica Plain, Brighton, and middle-income areas of South Dorchester and Roxbury apparently felt that municipal welfare and the WPA were not so much legitimate rights bestowed by citizenship as expensive privileges which were bleeding property owners dry. In the four wards given a chance to vote on USHA housing through a referendum, all turned thumbs down. Furthermore, there seemed to be a connection in middle-income areas between defections from Roosevelt and forcible retirement of city-council representatives. Six outlying wards, in fact, ousted eleven councilors seeking reelection between 1933 and 1937, almost double the number that were retired in the remaining sixteen districts. Sentiment which repudiated government spending was apparently visited upon Roosevelt as well, and many could have agreed with the Back Bay's Henry Shattuck who, at the end of the decade, surveyed the deficits amassed by federal, state, and municipal governments. "Expenditures through borrowing which are painless today, but will give us a headache in years to come," Shattuck lamented, "are to my mind the most insidious poison. We are becoming a nation of drug addicts." [46]

A portion of the electorate may also have been stimulated by the way in which federal benefits were distributed. While Roosevelt's attacks on Mussolini unquestionably accounted for Italo-American rebelliousness, residents of East Boston and the North and West Ends received less than their fair share of WPA largesse, got no USHA housing, and were permitted no patronage. Relatively patient in 1936, Italians deserted in 1940. South Boston, in contrast, had received FERA and CWA openings out of all proportion to the percentage of the area's jobless workers, yet when Washington moved toward tighter control in April 1934 the area's favored position was weakened. So was the South Boston vote for Roosevelt which hit its low in 1936. As Washington eased its supervision of the Massachusetts WPA from 1936 on, "Southies" achieved an even more substantial lead in their percentage of federal jobs. And while areas in acute need of public housing waited for units to be constructed, South Boston's Irish attended dedication ceremonies for Old Harbor Village, by 1938 the single completed example in Boston of what a handsomely designed federal housing project could be. Clement Norton journeyed over for the opening, and he told James Roosevelt that "the rank and file, the crowd, love [F.D.R.]." Speaking to a sizable gathering, he said, "I'll kiss the ground Roosevelt walks on, in public, for what he has done for the underprivileged of this nation," and then Norton commented to the President's son: "10,000 people cheered as they cheered no other remark that day." [47] Two years later, South Boston halted the precipitous decline for Roosevelt. Without ruling out other sources of voter motivation, it appeared that, in poor neighborhoods, well-placed New Deal benefits could have an impact, and local politicians saw wisdom in claiming some of the credit.

However, applauding specific gains and voting in a consistently liberal direction were not always congruent. When the results in elections where local Democrats were running are compared to Roosevelt's turnout, the impression that Italians and Irish in the teeming neighborhoods of the urban core backed Democrats regardless of ideology is, in part, substantiated. And, to a slightly lesser degree, other areas of the city, except the more conspicuously liberal Jewish and Negro areas, revealed a similar tendency. Only in Curley's ill-considered races and in Paul Dever's shot at the governorship in 1940 did Roosevelt run ahead of the city vote cast for Massachusetts Democrats. Although it was not uncommon across the nation for Roosevelt to cling to the coattails of local politicians rather than the other way around, the showing in 1934 and 1940 of Senator Walsh, the most prominent anti–New Dealer in the Commonwealth, makes it difficult to describe Boston's politics as unusually liberal. Bostonians awarded Walsh a higher share of the tally than they were willing to give to the President, despite pleas from elements of the CIO that were calling for the Senator's defeat. Walsh, congressmen in the Eleventh and Twelfth Districts, and Democratic candidates for governor, in fact, chalked up a vote in South Boston and Charlestown that ranged from 71 to 88 percent, and these candidates persistently outpaced Roosevelt in Italian quarters of the city as well. Furthermore, these voting patterns were established before the city turned more of its attention to Europe and balked at F.D.R.'s interventionist policies. Political sages had learned that it was possible to snipe at the New Deal without fear of punishment. Indeed, they might even attract more votes by impeding projects destined for other wards than by rendering support.

National elections as conducted in Boston provided no emphatic directive to the preponderant share of ward leaders that their constituents wanted encores from the New Deal. When voters went to the polls, many peripheral issues must have weighed on their minds—the changes taking place in municipal finance, Curleyism, local improvisations upon programs which had been sketched in the nation's capital, foreign affairs, and even the question of Eleanor Roosevelt.[48] The habit of voting Democratic, developed before the Depression began, kept still other voters from changing their faith. Indeed, politicians in Boston must have eventually realized that the city had found a Democratic equilibrium of 60 to 65 percent of the vote in national elections, and higher than that in most Massachusetts contests.[49] Several of the very men who applauded

Mayor Tobin's testament to Roosevelt at the Jackson Day Dinner soon were pursuing James Farley with impunity, just as they had romped after Al Smith in 1932 and, for a time, as they had drawn close to Father Coughlin at mid-decade. Ward leaders learned that lopsided victories were attainable without paying homage to the New Deal, and they also found out that defeats might come with suddenness: Bostonians sustained their pre-1933 inclination to unseat incumbents in the wards for reasons often having little or nothing to do with the New Deal. With weak spots in the Roosevelt vote in 1932 more clearly verified in 1936 and 1940, local politicians discovered slackness in the long leash by which New Deal programs held them in check. Most could not wander off completely, but there was ample room to stray. The majority took the errant route.

Conclusion
Sicut Patribus, Sit Deus Nobis

How much can be claimed for the study of a single city? Ralph Waldo Emerson apparently felt that if the choice were right, universal truths awaited the beholder:

> This town of Boston has a history. It is not an accident, not a windmill or a railroad station, or a crossroads tavern, or an army-barracks grown up by time and luck to a place of wealth; but a seat of humanity, of men of principle, obeying a sentiment and marching loyally whither that should lead them; so that its annals are great historical lines, inextricably national; part of the history of political liberty. I do not speak with any fondness, but the language of coldest history, when I say that Boston commands attention as the town which was appointed in the destiny of nations to lead the civilization of North America.
>
> . . . In distant ages her motto shall be the prayer of millions on all the hills that gird the town, "As with our Fathers, so God be with us!" Sicut Patribus, Sit Deus Nobis! [1]

Emerson, of course, harked back to the founding experience. "Wee shall be as a Citty upon a Hill," John Winthrop had told the passengers on the *Arbella* in 1630, a "Citty" whose progress the whole world would be watching.[2] Three hundred years later, Boston com-

304

manded less attention than New York, Chicago, and Detroit. But when Emerson contended that Boston's "annals are great historical lines, inextricably national," he was on target. As Benjamin Labaree has noted, local history is "a means of deepening our understanding of national developments." [3] Indeed, an examination of a geographically restricted area may be as suggestive as glimpsing bits and snatches of experience within a larger extent of territory and, in the opinion of David Potter, is no less complex. "A microcosm," he once wrote, "is just as cosmic as a macrocosm." [4]

Quite obviously, no American city exhibited precisely the same set of characteristics which gave Boston its shape on the eve of the Great Depression. With the highest per capita retail sales in the nation, the third largest wholesale volume, and the fourth greatest banking assets, Boston—ninth in population—clearly enjoyed wealth to which other cities of comparable size could not pretend. Blue-collar wage levels also topped national averages, in part because Bostonians were twice as likely to belong to a labor union as the average urban worker. Boston's social composition also had atypical features: no major city had a smaller percentage of Negroes, and only New York had a larger percentage of those who were of foreign stock. Although containing a still potent Yankee remnant, as well as substantial Italo-American and Jewish populations, the city could well have laid claim to being the Dublin of America: more than half the population boasted Irish origins, no American city housed a larger proportion of Catholics, and Boston proved in 1928 that it had become, more than any other, a Democratic fortress. In addition, the government that served Bostonians had also developed distinctive attributes. On a per capita basis, no city collected more tax revenue, had higher property assessments, made larger annual expenditures, or ran a more comprehensive welfare program.

These traits, in turn, contributed to attitudes which no other city could have precisely recapitulated as the 1920s came to a close. Although the decade had been unkind to manufacturers, the city's economic base appeared well enough diversified to be depression-proof. Indeed, there was ample reason for businessmen to feel protected, confident, and even complacent. What had worked for their forefathers should work for them, and other groups exhibited similar smugness. Since Boston had the most generous public welfare system in urban America, a situation which admittedly said less for the Hub than it did about the nation's neglect of the poor, it was possible for the privileged to believe that the city had done for its indigent about as much as should be done. Since municipal government demanded more of the taxpayers than any other, citizens generally felt in 1929 that government had expanded to its utmost limits. The idea that new sacrifices might have to be made could not have won easy acceptance. Having stood virtually alone in rejecting Herbert Hoover in 1928, the city was inattentive to those who suggested that a quantitative victory was no substitute for qualitative change in the Democratic party: the ethnic enclaves which uneasily coexisted ought not to be aroused by introducing adventurous ideologies. With unionism better established in Boston than elsewhere but dominated by narrow crafts in the building trades, organized labor also rested on laurels which had been won in an earlier era. Exclusive and wage oriented, the city's unions harbored few zealots who were eying the unorganized. Buttressed by the cautious social doctrines of the Catholic Church, doctrines which meshed not only with most Protestant groups in the city but with the Brahmin-led Council of Social Agencies, Bostonians had constructed a tradition-directed edifice.

Yet each city bears certain resemblances to others. Commercial cities such as New York, Atlanta, New Orleans, and San Francisco, for instance, had economies not wholly unlike Boston's. Eighteen other cities with populations above 250,000 contained citizens more than half of whom derived from foreign stock, and nearly every urban center had its Irish, Italo-American, and Jewish quarters even if they existed in somewhat different proportions than in Boston. Few cities were spared the uglier side of ethnocentrism, and in each city a gulf existed between wealthy elites and the poor. A city such as Buffalo also had an effective public-welfare system, and urban governments in America throughout the 1920s inclined toward the expanded activities which had characterized Boston. Strong philanthropic traditions were surely not confined to the Hub, nor were progressive social agencies. Boston's tussles with the state legislature were not unusual, for every city to some degree was limited by a restrictive charter.[5]

Moreover, Boston enjoyed no unique immunity from the forces which ravaged the nation's great cities during the thirties. Until the very end of the decade, when an especially high unemployment rate propelled Boston toward the top of the list, the proportion of jobless workers kept Boston in a position midway between that of Detroit, Chicago, New York, and Philadelphia on the most serious extreme, and San Francisco, Cleveland, Milwaukee, and Baltimore on the other. A massive welfare burden that increased sevenfold from 1929 to 1940, fiscal difficulties which attended the rise in welfare costs, and physical deterioration of the city were predicaments familiar to urban America. Moreover, Bostonians saw during the course of the thirties the scenes which nearly every urban-dweller witnessed: transients swarmed into the city, Councils of the Unemployed appeared, Communists agitated among segments of the blue-collar class, endless lines formed at the municipal welfare department, Coughlinites and Townsend Clubbers proselytized. As in other cities, Liberty Leaguers championed conservatism while Labor's Non-Partisan League campaigned for liberalism. And, too, Boston questioned traditional assumptions about intergovernmental relationships, much as Minneapolis, Philadelphia, Los Angeles, and dozens of others had also done. Franklin Roosevelt registered substantial victories, and the federal government prominently intervened. For all of Boston's peculiarities, the city's course was, indeed, inextricably tied to the national experience.

From 1929 to 1932, Boston's pre-Depression traits stood out in sharper outline. While cities with less adequate resources and with less sophisticated welfare systems (or none at all) had to improvise, Boston could out of habit turn to venerable, well-heeled institutions. Convinced that Boston's advantages would carry the day, the city's elites clung tenaciously to voluntary efforts, resisted deficit spending, and infrequently evidenced a desire for grander approaches. Acute political rivalries made it impossible to launch large-scale public works, delayed the first emergency relief campaign a full year, and spilled over into national politics when anti-Curley Democrats supported Al Smith's candidacy rather than Curley's choice, Franklin D. Roosevelt.

And in the dreary months when Bostonians awaited the inauguration of a new President of the United States, no new spirit of cooperation emerged. With nearly a third of the labor force unemployed, and with those who held onto their jobs unable to fend off wage cuts, the political party that would be asked to implement the New Deal at the local level was in shambles. While Boston still manifested more ability to care for the army of idle workers than most places, the protection which superior fiscal resources had allowed the city fathers no longer existed: neither public welfare nor private charity had sufficient reserves, fund-raising efforts yielded near-empty cups, uncollected taxes menaced the city's solvency, and the plight of the unemployed was serious. At this critical moment, nevertheless, calls for retrenchment were being issued by a majority of the state legislature, several members of the city council, Governor Ely, Cardinal O'Connell, and most of the business community. Organized labor, on the other hand, was advocating public construction, private charities were saying that public welfare agencies would have to carry the burden for some time to come, and a small contingent of liberals was urging direct federal grants, unemployment insurance, and mortgage moratoria. The city expectantly awaited Roosevelt, but the nature of those expectations varied wildly. Bostonians had given no clear mandate for decisive change.

From 1933 to 1935, the programs of the First New Deal brought substantial benefits to Boston. The CWA and the first and second FERA poured in dollars and food, and at one time or another between the summer of 1933 and the autumn of 1935 federal paychecks sustained upwards of 20 percent of the city's total population. The HOLC prevented thousands of mortgage foreclosures, and the

FHA allowed homeowners to repair their dwellings. Sweatshops were driven out of existence by the NRA, and the abominable practice of employing children to work in factories ceased. Through Section 7(a) of NIRA labor organizations enjoyed new collective bargaining advantages, and the National Labor Board and its successor in 1934, the NLRB, also afforded protection to blue-collar Boston. Unions, as a partial consequence, chalked up solid membership gains. Personal bank accounts were now safeguarded by the Federal Deposit Insurance Corporation, and securities dealers had a clearer notion of the worth of corporations in which they were investing. While not the express result of a peculiarly urban set of plans, the achievements of the First New Deal helped beyond reckoning.[6]

Nevertheless, the First New Deal, hastily assembled to meet an emergency, contained deficiencies which might have been weeded out back in Washington had the times been less frantic. Both the funding and the eligibility rules of work relief oscillated, and the same difficulties obtained at headquarters of the Home Owners' Loan Corporation and the Federal Housing Administration. Washington lacked the power to enforce compliance with NRA codes, thereby demoralizing companies that tried to conform, and the small businessman rightly complained that the NRA favored large firms. Unwillingness or inability of the national government to rule with an iron fist also meant that the Boston Welfare Department could set whatever standards it pleased, thus in effect controlling who would get onto work-relief projects, and several outmoded practices might have been remedied had the Roosevelt administration intervened with greater force. Moreover, the AAA contributed to higher food costs, and the employed labor force, locked into NRA wage scales, discovered that real income gains were much less substantial than their hourly rates would have suggested. Millions of dollars were spent on streets during the First New Deal in Boston, yet not a single unit of low-cost housing was constructed. Although bankrolling the businessman, the Reconstruction Finance Corporation made no move to purchase municipal debt certificates or to finance slum clearance. On two counts, then, the New Deal fell short. Not only had the Roosevelt administration wielded insufficient power, but it had also failed to develop a coordinated urban policy.

If all of urban America were Boston, however, the history of the New Deal in the city, no less than in the states,[7] would have to emphasize that local obstacles hindered the implementation and public acceptance of Washington's programs. Plagued by an absence of cooperation with legislators and bureaucrats on Beacon Hill, Boston got a lesser share of ERA and CWA openings than it should have had. Indeed, equity was not achieved until 1934 when Harry Hopkins recruited Yankee progressives to run the ERA and decreed that state and municipal officials could no longer touch federal money. At that, Irish Democrats fumed at the presence of Mugwumps atop the work-relief hierarchy, and ethnic rivalries for available openings (there were never enough) remained intense. Organized labor warred with nonunion workers over hiring policies and wage rates on government projects; building trades locals repeatedly resorted to wildcat strikes against the ERA. In addition, the Public Works Administration suffered telling blows from large real-estate interests, homeowners, mortgage bankers, and a state legislature which looked askance at the agency's loan-grant arrangement. Under the incessant threats of the nation's most burdened property owners, the city council spurned several offers of assistance. Through 1935 the PWA fizzled because local support at high levels was not forthcoming. During hard times few could see beyond their own immediate interests. National programs which placed a premium on local cooperation, particularly for financial support, ran into difficulties in the Hub.

At a remarkably early date, then, an informal, unorganized, conservative coalition could be discerned in Boston. The fragile alliance of interests which had belatedly called for Roosevelt's election in 1932 had given no clear mandate for the programs of the Hundred Days, and after the legislation of 1933 was enacted it did not take long for detractors to appear. Toward the end of the year, disaffection grew as indices sagged. But to a greater degree the New Deal collided with habits of Yankee thrift ("pay-as-you-go government," it was called), a swarm of overextended taxpayers, and businessmen accustomed to laissez-faire. Entering a city which was at first eager for action, the legislation also came into the habitat of a conservative Catholic hierarchy and a number of cautious, parochial trade unions. The New Deal had to contend, too, with worshippers of Al Smith in the Walsh-Ely political orbit, and this contingent made up a majority of the city council. Having failed to block Roosevelt's nomination and resentful of James Michael Curley's association with F.D.R., elites clogged the municipal channels through which the New Deal would have to sail.

Moreover, specific policies of the first Roosevelt years did not mesh satisfactorily with Boston's economic composition. Dependent upon textiles, garment manufacturing, and food processing, Bostonians assailed the AAA's processing tax with special venom. Elements of the financial community, another mainstay of the city's economic structure, disliked federal competition in the home-mortgage market, felt that depositors should assume the carrying charges of the Federal Deposit Insurance Corporation, and drew a bead on Roosevelt's experiments with the dollar. When textile and shoe manufacturers discovered that the NRA pushed up labor costs without altogether eliminating the wage differential between Boston and the South, they resumed the exodus which had begun some years before. Moreover, the tempo of economic recovery in the Hub lagged behind both state and national norms during the NRA period. Importers scored New Deal tariff policies, and a number of unions revived their pre-Depression custom of siding with the manufacturer's plea for high duties. On the whole, local peculiarities dampened the New Deal's reception. Judgments of the New Deal were strongly related to a practical, understandable test: if a program hurt a specific group in Boston, it was lambasted by that group. The fact that this program might be helping other elements in the nation—southern millworkers, say, or western wheat growers—made little difference. Ad hoc discontents assumed considerable importance in building an atmosphere unreceptive to economic planning on a national scale.

There was, of course, another side of the coin. No legislative package as comprehensive as the First New Deal, even as some of it was transformed in Boston, could have antagonized everyone, nor did it. Except for PWA loans, the city council and the mayor's office asked for more federal money, not less. On the whole, this desire for funds offset a passion for greater local control of the money. The criticisms of those on work relief signaled a desire for the New Deal to plunge ahead with more ambitious designs rather than put an end to national projects. By 1935 several real-estate owners had begun to argue that federal grants ought to be accepted as a means of lowering city taxes. Those who received federal paychecks, held HOLC mortgages, got higher wages as the result of the NRA, or watched their labor unions flourish had clear reasons to be thankful. Only a few diehards in the business community indicated a desire to return all the way to the unregulated economy of pre-1929. Pictures of Roosevelt hung in the homes of Negroes in the South End, Jews in Dorchester, and Irish in South Boston. Social workers knew full well how great the suffering would have been had no CWA or ERA come along. Just as the First New Deal had awakened piecemeal criticism, it also gave rise to segmented praise. But on balance, skepticism about New Deal principles remained strong in Boston, and to be pleased about isolated aspects of the Roosevelt program was not tantamount to acceptance of greatly augmented federal power.

In the spring of 1935, however, a good many Bostonians engaged in reassessment. With the death of the NRA, wages dropped and hours were lengthened. The National Labor Relations Board in Boston adjourned its hearings; field agents of the NRA Compliance Board emptied their desks. In the meantime, sweatshops reappeared and union membership plunged. Other agencies ran out of funds: the HOLC for a time closed its doors, and the ERA was able to maintain little more than a skeleton work force at severely reduced wages. Reminiscent of March 4, when Roosevelt had taken his oath of office, attention was riveted on Washington and the "must" legislation which was making its way through Congress.

On paper, the agenda of the Second New Deal augured well for the city, but once again local hurdles thwarted its immediate prospects in 1935 and early 1936. Reduction of the loan portion of PWA aid encouraged a more vigorous pursuit of federal money, yet action by the state legislature torpedoed the most ambitious projects approved by the city council. Money was forthcoming for two major low-income housing developments, but suits against eminent-domain proceedings, especially numerous because of the small parcels of land that were taken in South Boston, delayed construction. The start-up of WPA proved too great an administrative load for the Boston and Massachusetts offices, and seven months after the WPA was slated to begin Hopkins purged state headquarters. Although wisely excluding local Democrats once again, he nevertheless reawakened fierce denunciations of the agency. From State Street, businessmen assailed the Wealth Tax Act as a confiscatory piece of class legislation and scored Roosevelt's tightened regulation of public utilities and banking. Moreover, the feud between Governor Curley and Mayor Mansfield poisoned municipal-state relations; Curley was taking potshots at the New Deal; Cardinal O'Connell was assailing socialists in Washington; Joseph B. Ely, a proven vote-getter, commanded a strengthened American Liberty League; Father Coughlin's star appeared to be ascending; and unrest in the Italian community expressed itself through massive rallies for Mussolini. Despite passage of the Wagner Act, weaknesses in the Boston economy until the summer of 1936 presented labor unions with an uphill struggle to recover their post-NRA losses. The local setting in which the Second New Deal would have to launch its operations was not propitious.

Just the same, a city of many divisions came through for Roosevelt in the 1936 election, although the slight decline in the Democratic percentage put Boston in the unique position of being the only large urban center to fall off from the levels of both 1928 and 1932. While the highly favorable vote for F.D.R. may in part be explained by his personal attractiveness (as distinct from programmatic aspects of the New Deal), by the immense Democratic registration which constituted a pre-New Deal legacy, and by Alfred M. Landon's drab campaign, no candidate could have lined up 64 percent of the electorate had his record been wholly unpalatable. Faced with an excruciatingly high tax rate which had jumped in an election year, confronted with the city government's operating deficits, and apparently convinced that a solution lay beyond local capacities, voters were not prepared to reject the lures dangled before them by Harry Hopkins. By mid-1936, the WPA—at last under way—was pouring close to a million dollars a month into Boston, and most of the council considered the direct grants essential, even while lusting after greater local control. To this extent, a revolution in municipal-federal relationships had been realized. In addition, the election took place when the economy was on a brief upbeat, and organized labor was making a comeback: the NLRB was consistently delivering pro-union rulings, the CIO was pushing older AFL locals into more advanced positions, and an unprecedented endorsement of a presidential candidate was forthcoming at the Massachusetts Federation of Labor's 1936 convention. The majority of Bostonians had not deserted Roosevelt, and they would not depart in 1940 either.

But from 1937 to 1940, as in the earlier period, Bostonians retained strong elements of distrust in their posture toward Washington. Although Roosevelt's foreign policy contributed to mutterings in Italian and Irish neighborhoods, the President's domestic policies continued to be judged one at a time: if they worked for a particular group, that group thought them fine; if they did not, they were subjected to withering criticism. Signs were few that a comprehensive ideological change had occurred toward social and political innovation. An organized overview of the New Deal failed to emerge.

Again, local developments impeded the effectiveness of federal programs during Roosevelt's second term. That Boston reached 1940 with the highest unemployment rate of any urban center except Pittsburgh and Cleveland did not help: the collapse of the Massachusetts textile and shoe industries (foreshadowed in the 1920s), the flight of businesses to escape the nation's highest big-city tax rate, the obsolete industrial equipment of America's oldest manufacturing region, the decay of wharf facilities, and the absence of the types of industry that could snatch the first defense contracts combined to load down Boston with ponderous liabilities. And as Washington eased control over the WPA, discrimination against the non-Irish increased—with concomitant ill effects. Italo-Americans in the North End, for instance, were receiving less than half the number of WPA openings to which their rate of joblessness entitled them, while South Bostonians got 14 percent more than should have been the case. No less than on federal work relief, public housing disproportionately benefited the Irish—and not the poorest Irish at that. An inadequate administrative apparatus in Massachusetts delayed the unemployment-compensation payments that flowed from the Social Security Act, just as years before the WPA had foundered for many of the same reasons. Moreover, the last two mayors of the 1930s, Frederick Mansfield and Maurice Tobin, both owed political debts to Republicans and conservative Democrats in good-government associations. Each man believed in retrenchment, and each exhibited the traits of a structural rather than a social reformer. While Tobin managed to work more cooperatively with Washington than either Curley or Mansfield had done, he did not approach Fiorello La Guardia of New York or Frank Murphy of Detroit as an expediter of national programs. During the entire New Deal period, policies from Washington altered Boston, but just as surely Boston modified federal programs. Washington made municipal government dependent upon monetary grants, and the Roosevelt administration also assumed responsibility for an enormous welfare clientele. The New Deal revised the context in which collective bargaining took place, and it tightened the strings on the business community. But the peculiarities of Boston gave New Dealers a constant headache, not so much because public notices were generally unfavorable, but because local leadership was not allowing the New Deal to put its best foot forward. This process, the localization of federal programs, frustrated the Roosevelt administration repeat-

Mayor Maurice Tobin, flanked by District Attorney Foley and Police Commissioner Timilty, prepare for a charity field day at Fenway Park in 1938. In Boston, voluntarism died hard. Boston University School of Communication.

edly. For those who would argue that the New Deal brought drastic change, the Boston story would give little comfort—not so much because of the nature of the New Deal, but because of recurrent obstacles at the local level. Boston during the Great Depression was, on balance, a city which feasted on the cake of custom.

Even as New Dealers superimposed myriad agencies on the City of Boston, a number of fundamental political characteristics were left intact. Turnover of ward offices remained high; ethnic clashes were severe; outsiders were distrusted; Green Power, or the domination of public office by Irish Catholic Democrats, persisted. Although political obituaries were written for James Michael Curley, he would soon rise Phoenix-like from the ashes: the New Deal had not destroyed bossism. With the exception of Jewish and Negro areas, it was easier to win votes for conservatives like Joseph B. Ely or

David I. Walsh than for Franklin D. Roosevelt, and campaigns at all levels continued to be waged less on questions of social experimentation than on the personality of local leadership, the issue of corruption, and the problem of municipal taxes. Throughout the decade, the Democratic party in Boston, precisely because of its faction-riddled nature, shied away from ideological issues. No significant political leader emerged to advocate redistribution of wealth or socialization of the economy, and even had one come forth, it is doubtful that he would have received a respectful hearing. Indeed, in a Catholic city, politicians knew that red-herring tactics would win votes, and the Left in Boston was at all times minuscule.

City government also exhibited a number of pre-Depression traits throughout the thirties which, in importance, outranked the changes: plans for metropolitan government were unavailing, little departmental consolidation occurred, proposed reforms of the election system were defeated, and Boston remained under the thumb of the state legislature. Municipal relief was decentralized and case workers were added, but an attempt to replace the Overseers of the Public Welfare with a three-man board staffed by professionals was thwarted. Eligibility rules remained harsh, the cash value of weekly allotments went virtually unchanged, and outcries against welfare expenditures were sufficiently shrill to raise doubts that the average employed citizen regarded the less fortunate as having a moral claim to public assistance. While the composition of the welfare list altered substantially (ADC and Old Age Assistance clients were added, while able-bodied unemployed were subtracted), the city was supporting as many employable men and women in 1940 as in 1930. And, in both years, those who were not physically broken were made to work for the cash they received. The Depression menaced the municipal treasury, yet Boston's revenues, expenditures, and long-term debt allowed the same relative standing to other cities over the span of a decade. From the viewpoint of the 36,000 employable Bostonians who even in 1940 had no job or any form of relief—either municipal or federal—the city might well have been advised to have spent more lavishly.

Labor unions, though boasting a memberhip twice as numerous in 1940 as in 1929, also exhibited several basic continuities. With few exceptions, labor leaders in the AFL pursued pure-and-simple trade union objectives, and, compared to other cities, unions declared relatively fewer strikes in the 1930s than in the 1920s, even as the absolute number of stoppages increased. Although the Irish grasp on elected union offices slipped slightly, as Italo-American and Jewish workers in particular recorded gains, the Sons of Erin continued to hold a disproportionate number of leadership posts. Industrial unionism, which flourished in so many cities and which, probably more than any other movement in the nation, gave Roosevelt's programs strong endorsements, registered relatively smaller gains in Boston. Consequently, Labor's Non-Partisan League never became an effective force in the Hub, yet at the same time the CIO was sufficiently robust to make the AFL organizations in an old union town resentful of interlopers: rightly or wrongly, some of the AFL crafts blamed Roosevelt and the NLRB for the CIO's incursions. Trade-union exclusivity in Boston persisted; ideological vistas were not greatly enlarged. Unions which had been thoroughly liberal in the early thirties—the ILGWU and the Amalgamated—remained that way, but they picked up few allies.

Institutions through which businessmen expressed themselves, even more than the labor unions, displayed a strong likeness to their pre-Depression counterparts. While Chamber of Commerce membership plummeted from 5,000 to 2,000, a number of equally conservative real-estate associations and taxpayers' alliances were organized in the thirties. And even as the Chamber lost dues-payers, its lobbying success before the state legislature fell by just 6 percent. In getting its way in two out of every three instances, the Chamber was able both to forestall regulatory legislation and to keep state spending at almost the same level at the end of the Depression as at the beginning. Stockholders of the Boston Elevated blocked the largest PWA project in the city, just as in 1932 they had thwarted the Huntington Avenue subway extension which had had both city council and state approval. Most of State Street lobbied against the corporate taxes to support federal budgets which had more than doubled since 1933, much as they had pleaded in the early thirties for Herbert Hoover to keep Washington in the black. Few in the business community believed that the government should disturb the organic nature of society by attempting to reapportion wealth.

To these views, Cardinal O'Connell would undoubtedly have said, "Amen," and so would most Episcopal, Baptist, and Lutheran ministers. The Jewish rabbinate, in contrast, had been liberal at the beginning of the decade and reached 1940 with its commitment to social justice unimpaired. And, too, both the Unitarian and Congregational Churches moved perceptibly away from conservatism on social issues. The Catholic hierarchy, however, instructed three-quarters of the population, and the Boston *Pilot* read very much the same in 1940 as in 1929. Anything which smacked of socialism was

Still jobless at the end of the decade, despite the herculean efforts of the New Deal, these men are hoping for employment in 1939 at the Charlestown Navy Yard. Boston University School of Communication.

denounced with fervor. Through charitable activities, the Church dealt with the results of poverty while failing to modify its position that the indigent were largely those who had fallen away from Christian precepts.

Eleven lean years, to be sure, brought gradual modifications to Boston. The Great Depression scarred the city's physical appear-

Although the New Deal encountered many obstacles in Boston, Roosevelt's personal popularity was immense. Boston Public Library, Print Department.

ance, diminished its importance as a manufacturing center, eliminated the wage lead which blue-collar employees had enjoyed over workers elsewhere, produced a population loss, and reshuffled the composition of several neighborhoods. The escape of the affluent to the suburbs persisted, but the exodus proceeded at a slower pace than in the 1910–1930 period. And as obdurate as many Bostonians had been about preserving the advantages which they had carried into the Depression, by 1940 the majority undoubtedly concurred that the city could not possibly be thrown back entirely on its own resources. United States Housing Authority projects (despite a 2-1 loss in a referendum involving four middle-class wards), social-security checks, and unemployment insurance won general acceptance. Heads of private social agencies, including those maintained by the churches of Boston, knew full well that the days had disappeared forever when voluntary donations to charity could be considered sufficient. Federal policing of business had become a *fait accompli,* and most acknowledged that some rules of the game were necessary. The imbalance that had existed between labor and management had been largely remedied—much to blue-collar Boston's delight.

Yet through most of the Depression Bostonians had lagged behind the New Deal. Had the New Deal been more radical than it was, the probability is that Boston would have trailed even farther behind. The power structure had accepted direct aid, but it had not always been equitable in dispensing the money which it had received. In programs demanding substantial local participation (e.g., NRA, PWA, the work-relief efforts), even greater heel-dragging occurred. When New Dealers asked that parochial outlooks be adjusted to the interest of the nation as a whole, few modified their customary behavior. Roosevelt achieved eye-popping election results, even in 1940, but behind the ballots there lurked little sentiment for a new social and economic bill of rights. The more philosophical aspects of the Roosevelt policies, as articulated by a man like Rexford Guy Tugwell, were not well understood. With only a few exceptions, the New Deal's manifestations were treated piecemeal and were perceived by individuals and groups according to their particular needs. There was nothing malicious or volitional about this. Rather, the local habits which had been apparent at the outset of the Great Depression were too encrusted to be removed in the course of the decade. The idea of a national or even a municipal communality of interest was seldom grasped. In the circumstances, the New Deal in a single American city accomplished as much as anyone could have reasonably expected.

As "Old Man 1940, laden with woes" bowed out, and "cherubic 1941 walk [ed] on the stage," [8] fires raged in London and Nazis were mining the mouth of the Danube. Soon, Bostonians were establishing a Committee of Public Safety, vaster in scope than the old emergency relief organizations of the early 1930s, the *Post* asserted. [9] Their fathers' faith having sustained them through times of trouble in the past, Bostonians looked to the future without flinching.

Notes

1. *Proceedings of the City Council of Boston,* Oct. 27, 1930, hereafter cited *"PCCB."*
2. (Name withheld by author) to Roosevelt, Feb. 1, 1932, Democratic National Committee State Files—Massachusetts, Franklin D. Roosevelt Library, Hyde Park, Box 264, hereafter cited "DNC-Mass."
3. (Name withheld by author) to Roosevelt, Nov. 2, 1932, *ibid.,* Box 272.
4. Boston *Globe,* Aug. 4, 1930. All *Globe* citations are for the morning edition unless otherwise noted.

CHAPTER 1

1. *The New York Times,* Sept. 6, 1929, and John Kenneth Galbraith, *The Great Crash* (Cambridge, 1954), pp. 89–90.
2. Harvey S. Perloff *et al., Regions, Resources and Economic Growth* (Baltimore, 1960), pp. 20, 24, 222–292.
3. Irving Bernstein, *The Lean Years: A History of the American Worker, 1920–1933* (Cambridge, 1960), p. 255.
4. The other cities with more than 100,000 people that may be properly assigned to this same classification in 1929 are Atlanta, Duluth, El Paso, Houston, Norfolk, Oakland, St. Paul, Salt Lake City, and San Diego.
5. The five with larger retail sales than Boston were New York, Chicago, Philadelphia, Detroit, and Los Angeles. Combined wholesaling and retailing in the Hub surpassed all rivals except New York, Chicago, and Philadelphia, more than tripled Milwaukee's total, and approximately doubled that of Baltimore and

Cleveland. *Statistical Abstract of the United States* (1932), pp. 790, 796–797. Also, Bureau of Business Research, Boston University School of Business Administration, "New England Statistical Abstracts," May 15, 1937.

6. In 1929 and 1930 an estimated 69 percent of all New England manufactures were exported by way of New York City. William Beer to Leverett Saltonstall, Nov. 28, 1938, Boston Chamber of Commerce Records, Baker Library, Harvard University, Drawer 2, 104–1, hereafter cited "Chamber of Commerce Records."

7. Boston suffered a 2 : 1 import-export imbalance which, in the mid-1930s, would reach an astonishing gap of 9 : 1. United States Department of Engineers, "The Port of Boston," typescript (Boston, 1938).

8. *Statistical Abstract of the United States* (1930), p. 270. Of the twelve Federal Reserve Districts, New York, Chicago, and Cleveland alone had more assets than the Boston Fed at the end of 1929. *Ibid.*, p. 248. Only this trio, plus Philadelphia, transacted more business than Boston. *Ibid.*, p. 256.

9. In 1932, for example, a single trust office paid $2 million of Boston's $67-million tax bill. "Boston," *Fortune*, VII (February, 1933), p. 36.

10. Frederic C. Jaher, "Businessman and Gentleman: Nathan and Thomas Gold Appleton—An Exploration in Intergenerational History," *Explorations in Entrepreneurial History*, IV (Fall, 1966), p. 10.

11. "Boston," *Fortune*, p. 35. The corporations spawned by the Great Families of Boston were, by 1929, no longer under their control. General Electric, American Telephone and Telegraph, and United Shoe Machinery serve as examples. New York banks floated the larger bond issues which Bostonians had once handled with ease, relegating Boston to a city of purchase. Moreover, the passing of Brahmin power is further revealed by contrasting the $636 million in assets held by the First National Bank of Boston ("new" money) and the $186 million in resources controlled by the Shawmut Bank ("old" money). And in the twenty-five years prior to the Great Depression, the only new firm of any consequence to be attracted to Boston was the Gillette Safety Razor Company.

12. *Ibid.*, p. 100, quoting Frederic J. Stimson. Also, Paul Goodman, "Ethics and Enterprise: The Values of a Boston Elite, 1800–1860," *American Quarterly*, XVIII (Fall, 1966), pp. 437–451.

13. "Boston," *Fortune*, p. 106.

14. The Boston Stock Exchange specialized in marketing New England securities while the Curb, founded in 1908, handled paper issued by firms located outside the region. The house specialties included minor oil and mining companies which had been unable to gain admission to major exchanges. In 1928 the Curb affiliated with the Boston Flour and Grain Exchange.

15. Gilbert Seldes, *The Years of the Locust: America, 1929–1932* (Boston, 1933), p. 10.

16. "Boston," *Fortune*, p. 27.

17. From 1920 to 1930, for example, Boston's growth index stood at 4.4 while the four rings around the city hit 22.6, 39.4, 12.9, and 20.1 respectively. Leo F. Schnore and Peter R. Knights, "Residence and Social Structure: Boston in the Ante-Bellum Period," in Stephan Thernstrom and Richard Sennett (eds.), *Nineteenth-*

Century Cities: Essays in the New Urban History (New Haven, 1969), pp. 247–257.

18. Bruce Stave, *The New Deal and the Last Hurrah: Pittsburgh Machine Politics* (Pittsburgh, 1970), p. 4. Stave's table of ethnicity, from which these figures are drawn, places the percentages of foreign stock of only three cities—Los Angeles (36.8), St. Louis (35.1), and Baltimore (29.1)—below the big city average (53.4).

19. Pittsburgh, Cleveland, and Detroit had nonwhite populations 1.5 percent below the national average for large urban centers. New York's nonwhite percentage (5.0) came closest to Boston's, while Philadelphia, St. Louis, Los Angeles, and Baltimore ranged from 11.4 percent to 17.7 percent respectively. *Ibid.* Out of Boston's 781,000 people, 200,000 were native-born white; 229,000 were foreign-born white; and 329,000 were listed as foreign-born or of mixed parentage. By numbers (and percent of total population), Boston's foreign stock included 159,000 Irish (20.3), 91,000 Italians (11.7), 82,000 classified as "Canadians and Others" (10.5), 68,000 Russians (8.6), 38,000 non-Russian Slavs (4.9), and 21,000 Negroes (2.6). *Fifteenth Census of the United States: 1920—Population*, III, Part I, pp. 1098–1110.

20. Boston Council of Social Agencies, "Social Statistics by Census Tracts in Boston," July, 1935. Pinning down the movement of peoples within a city presents considerable difficulties to which this study is sensitive but does not attempt a definitive answer. Stephan Thernstrom was on target, however, when he noted that "the city's demographic stagnation was more apparent than real" in the post-1920 period. Thernstrom, *The Other Bostonians: Poverty and Progress in the American Metropolis, 1880–1970* (Cambridge, 1973), p. 10.

21. *Fifteenth Census, Population,* III, Part I, pp. 1071–1111, "Social Statistics by Census Tracts in Boston," July, 1935; and United States Bureau of the Census, "Population and Housing: Statistics for Census Tracts, Boston, Massachusetts, 1940." To arrive at 1929 conditions, figures have been interpolated.

22. *City Record*, June 29, 1935, pp. 889, 893–894. These social statistics were derived from the Emergency Relief Administration's real property inventory of 1934 and have been adjusted in the text to approximate the situation in 1929. Also, *ibid.*, July 13 and 17, 1935.

23. Jerome S. Bruner and Jeanette Sayre, "Shortwave Listening in an Italian Community," *Public Opinion Quarterly* (Winter, 1941), pp. 640–656, and Stephan Thernstrom, "Immigrants and Wasps: Ethnic Differences in Occupational Mobility in Boston, 1890–1940," in Thernstrom and Sennett (eds.), *Nineteenth-Century Cities*, pp. 125–164.

24. William S. Braithwaite, Columbia Oral History Collection, No. 345, p. 198, hereafter cited "COHC." Also, *The Black Worker*, April 1, 1930, and William Foote Whyte, "Race Conflicts in the North End of Boston," *New England Quarterly*, XII (December, 1939), pp. 623–642.

25. Ethnic classifications based on names are, of course, susceptible to error, but leaving out the segregated locals, it was approximately the case that only thirty-six Jews, nineteen Italians, four Negroes, and seven French-Canadians held union offices. Computed from Commonwealth of Massachusetts, *Twenty-Ninth Annual*

Directory of Labor Organizations in Massachusetts, 1930 (Public Document No. 15, Labor Bulletin No. 160), pp. 23–35. Underrepresentation in trade-union hierarchies also reflected hiring discrimination, a particularly acute problem for Negroes and Italians.

26. National trade-union membership for 1929 has been estimated at 7 percent of the total labor force and 11 percent of all nonagricultural workers (vs. Boston's 17 percent). Leo Troy, *Trade Union Membership, 1897–1962* (National Bureau of Economic Research, New York, 1965, Occasional Paper 92), p. 2.

27. In contrast to Boston's nineteen disputes, St. Louis had twelve, Cleveland and Pittsburgh each had eleven, and Milwaukee had only one. "Review of Industrial Disputes in the United States from 1916 to 1932," *Monthly Labor Review*, XXXVI (June, 1933), p. 1298.

28. Boston's union rates in most occupational categories topped those of other Massachusetts cities by 10 to 15 cents an hour. Commonwealth of Massachusetts, *Annual Reports of the Department of Labor and Industries of Years Ending November 30, 1928, 1929* (Public Document No. 104), 2 vols. Massachusetts, in turn, was a high-wage state by national standards.

29. George Read Nutter Diary, Massachusetts Historical Society, XXV, May 23, 1930, hereafter cited "Nutter Diary." Also, Lawrence Jones, "Legislative Activities of the Greater Boston Chamber of Commerce: A Study of Representativeness and Effectiveness of a Business Lobby," unpublished doctoral dissertation, Harvard Graduate School of Business, 1960, pp. 17, 48, 53–56, 82–83, 146.

30. Robert A. Woods, *The Neighborhood in Nation Building* (Cambridge, 1923), p. 46, and Eva Whiting White, "Elizabeth Peabody House and the Immigrant," *Immigration*, III (February, 1912), pp. 240–244.

31. Ethel Ward Dougherty, "The Adventure of Spiritual Living," in Richard Clark Cabot (ed.), *The Goal of Social Work* (Cambridge, Mass., 1927), p. 87.

32. Eva Whiting White, "Technique and the Development of Students in Social Work," in *ibid.*, p. 180; *Herald*, Oct. 2, 1929, clipping in Eva Whiting White MSS., Schlesinger Library, Radcliffe College, Scrapbook VII; and unidentified clipping dated 1929 in White MSS., Box 1, Folder 6.

33. Butler Wilson to James Weldon Johnson, Jan. 18, 1929, NAACP Records, Boston Branch, Library of Congress, Box G-88, hereafter cited "NAACP-Boston."

34. (Name withheld by author) to Boston NAACP, June 9, 1924, NAACP-Boston, Box G-88.

35. Minutes of the Executive Committee Meeting of Feb. 11, 1930, Consumers' League of Massachusetts Records, Schlesinger Library, Radcliffe College, Folder 15, hereafter cited "CL-Mass."

36. Quoted in M. A. DeWolfe Howe, "Boston from Within," *The Saturday Review of Literature*, IX (November 19, 1932), p. 250.

37. The archdiocese included several metropolitan towns, and its numerical strength in Boston amounted to roughly a half million people.

38. Charles J. V. Murphy, "Pope of New England: A Portrait of Cardinal O'Connell," *Outlook and Independent*, CLIII (October 23, 1929), p. 319.

39. O'Connell exiled young Francis Spellman to an obscure parish in Newton during

the 1930s. Spellman, immensely popular in Boston and marked as a rising priest, was regarded by O'Connell as a threat to his sovereignty. See Cardinal Spellman's obituary, *The New York Times*, Dec. 3, 1967.

40. Murphy, "Pope of New England," p. 319. O'Connell's *Recollections of Seventy Years* (Boston, 1934) fulsomely praises those who, like himself, had been able to rise in economic standing.

41. Murphy, "Pope of New England," p. 288. When O'Connell made this remark in 1924, President Calvin Coolidge stood approvingly at his side.

42. *The Pilot*, April 13, 1929, quoted in Paul Boyer, "Boston Book Censorship in the Twenties," *American Quarterly*, XV (Spring, 1963), p. 12. Typically, *The Pilot* supported O'Connell, stating that "If this wonderful theory [of Einstein's] is too far away from the average human being, what is the good of it?" Quoted in *ibid.*

43. *Globe*, Dec. 15, 1930.

44. General Council Minutes, Dec. 13, 1931, St. Vincent de Paul Society Records, 294 Washington Street, Boston.

45. Reverend E. J. Helms, "Expanding Methods of a City Church," *The Missionary Review of the World*, III (July, 1929), pp. 501–504.

46. *Globe*, Jan. 13, 1930. Not every Catholic sided with O'Connell in advocating repeal. John Dowling, a major figure in public-welfare work, chaired the Boston Association of Catholics Favoring Prohibition and termed the linking of Catholics to repeal an "intolerant insult." *The New York Times*, Oct. 1, 1930.

47. *Globe*, Jan. 13, 1930.

48. Heywood Broun, "It Seems to Heywood Broun," *The Nation*, CXXIX (October 2, 1929), p. 345.

49. Boyer, "Boston Book Censorship in the Twenties," pp. 3–24. "As the Watch and Ward Society lost confidence in itself," says Boyer, "the idea of coercive social control became increasingly appealing." An authoritarian elite thus imposed "a rigid social conformity." *Ibid.*, p. 15.

50. Walter P. Eaton, "New England in 1930," *Current History*, XXXIII (November, 1930), p. 170, and " 'Athens of America' No Longer," *Literary Digest*, CVIII (November 15, 1930), p. 23.

51. Broun, "It Seems to Heywood Broun," p. 345.

52. Quoted in Boyer, "Boston Book Censorship in the Twenties," p. 12. For a list of the sixty-eight titles excluded in 1929, see *The New York Times*, Jan. 24, 1930.

53. R. L. Duffus, "Things That Make Boston What She Is," *The New York Times Magazine*, Feb. 16, 1930.

CHAPTER 2

1. Commonwealth of Massachusetts, Senate Document No. 1, Jan. 3, 1929, in the Henry Lee Shattuck MSS., Littauer Center, Harvard University, Drawer 7, hereafter cited "Shattuck MSS."

2. *PCCB*, Feb. 18, 1929, pp. 66–67.

3. Chelsea, Revere, and Winthrop made up 17 percent of Suffolk's geographic expanse and contained 10 percent of its population. A critic noted that "Boston is

the lion of Suffolk County and pays more than the lion's share of expenses." In 1929, these costs topped $3 million. Arthur Bromage, "Boston and Suffolk County," *The American Political Science Review*, XXIV (February, 1930), pp. 140–143.

4. "Amended City Charter of 1909," *Boston City Documents, 1929*, No. 36, pp. 21–43, especially p. 22.

5. On occasion, the council strayed far outside its proper realm, so much so that a staid councilor from the Back Bay called upon the members to halt their "vaudeville performances . . . designed to entertain the Monday matinee audience." In 1932, a councilor noted, the body had forgotten to congratulate or sympathize with Gandhi, Von Hindenburg, and Mussolini, though it had taken sides on Irish elections, expressed fealty to Al Smith, advocated payment of a bonus to veterans, and repudiated the Eighteenth Amendment. *PCCB*, April 4, 1932, pp. 127–128.

6. *Ibid.*, Jan. 4, 1936, p. 543.

7. Revenue receipts on a per person basis came to $100.31 in Boston, compared to the national urban average (146 cities) of $69.32. Los Angeles ($137) and New York ($106) headed the list of cities with more than 500,000 people; Philadelphia ranked closest to the national norm; and Baltimore ($55) and desperate Chicago ($30) ranked at the bottom. *Statistical Abstract of the United States* (1931), pp. 233–235.

8. Municipal government cost Bostonians $82.66 per person, well above the urban standard (146 cities) of $55.84. Los Angeles ($81) approximated Boston, with Detroit ($76) and New York ($74) close behind. Buffalo, Pittsburgh, Cleveland, and Philadelphia came next, all in the $60 to $69 range. St. Louis ($46) ranked last of the thirteen largest cities. *Ibid.*, pp. 233, 240–241.

9. In contrast, New York ($224), Philadelphia ($225), and Pittsburgh ($194) had far more ponderous per capita debt. The national average for 146 cities amounted to $139.63, some $3 above Boston's. *Ibid.*, pp. 233–242.

10. Commonwealth of Massachusetts, *General Laws* (Tercentenary Edition, 1932), I, Chapter 118, pp. 1435–1436.

11. Several donors of the private funds specified that the gifts be given to Protestants only. Others provided for the "standing chaplain of the almshouse" and for "the purchase of tea, coffee, chocolate, and sugar for those persons who, in the providence of God, are, or shall be reduced and obliged to take shelter in the almshouse, after having lived reputably." Needless to say, the City Law Department had difficulty in adjusting these quaint wills to a more modern era. "Sixty-fifth Annual Report of the Overseers of the Public Welfare," Jan. 1, 1929, in *Boston City Documents* (1929), pp. 5–17.

12. Chicago recipients, for instance, averaged the pathetic monthly sum of $7.95 in 1929, and those in Milwaukee took in only $11.93. Buffalo, generally regarded as having an advanced public welfare system, extended $29.67 to its clients. By turning down thousands of applicants, Detroit was able to average monthly payments of $37.26 to all recipients and maintain second rank to Boston. Emma

Winslow, *Trends in Different Types of Public and Private Relief in Urban Areas,* *1929–1935* (U.S. Department of Labor, Children's Bureau Bulletin No. 237, Washington, D.C., 1937), pp. 72–85, 96–100.

13. Based on voter check lists for the 1928 state primary in "Annual Report of the Election Department," *Boston City Documents*, No. 11 (1929).

14. J. Joseph Huthmacher, *Massachusetts People and Politics* (Cambridge, 1959), especially Chapter 5.

15. *Transcript*, June 30, 1930, clipping, Shattuck MSS., Drawer 25.

16. In accepting literature satirizing the Brahmins, it is easy to miss the clout of this elite, for "no group which has as many banking, business, and political ties as the Massachusetts aristocracy is suddenly going to be without power." Duane Lockard, *New England State Politics* (Princeton, N.J., 1959), p. 119.

17. The distinction between a structural reformer and a social reformer has received detailed treatment in Melvin G. Holli's *Reform in Detroit: Hazen Pingree and Urban Politics* (New York, 1969), especially pp. 23–55.

8. *PCCB*, Nov. 25, 1929, p. 403.

19. *Ibid.*, Jan. 4, 1930, pp. 428–429.

20. "The question of direct relief versus public works projects that later became a national concern," William V. Shannon has written, "were already an issue in Boston throughout the ostensibly prosperous 1920's." Shannon, *The American Irish* (New York, 1963), p. 214.

21. Joseph Dinneen, *The Purple Shamrock* (New York, 1949), p. 322.

22. Francis Russell, "The Last of the Bosses," *American Heritage*, X (June, 1959), p. 22.

23. *The New York Times*, Sept. 9, 1929.

24. Michael Ward to James Roosevelt, Nov. 15, 1938, James Roosevelt MSS., Franklin D. Roosevelt Library, Hyde Park, Box 20. Curley was unquestionably the finest entertainer in a city which both relished and expected rhetorical hyperbole from its politicians.

25. Russell, "The Last of the Bosses," p. 21.

26. Eddie Dowling, COHC, No. 532, p. 433.

27. Murray B. Levin, *The Alienated Voter: Politics in Boston* (New York, 1962), p. 5.

28. 1929 Campaign Circular, Shattuck MSS., Drawer 24.

29. Dayton McKean, "Patterns of Politics," in James Fesler (ed.), *The Fifty States and Their Local Governments* (New York, 1967), pp. 243–244, and Jerome S. Bruner and Sheldon J. Korchin, "The Boss and the Vote: Case Study in City Politics," *Public Opinion Quarterly*, X (Spring, 1946), pp. 18–21.

30. Robert R. Mullen, "Poor Old Boston," *The Forum*, CIII (May, 1940), p. 234; Russell, "The Last of the Bosses," p. 24; and James Michael Curley, *I'd Do It Again: A Record of All My Uproarious Years* (Englewood Cliffs, N.J., 1957), p. 80.

31. Shannon, *The American Irish*, pp. 187, 203.

32. Murphy, "Pope of New England," p. 285.

33. It cannot be assumed in every case that the city councilor bossed the ward. John

I. Fitzgerald, for instance, ran as Martin Lomasney's captive candidate in Ward 3, and no one in South Boston could ignore "Knocko" McCormack's clan. But the city council elections furnish a useful tip-off as to whether or not a boss's constituents were accepting his nominee. Unfortunately, the Boston Election Department ceased reporting ward-committee elections after 1930, but contests for state Democratic delegate provide strong clues about political tendencies in the wards and were reported. For the hardiness of Chicago's ward bosses, see Harold Gosnell, *Machine Politics: Chicago Model* (Chicago, 1937), pp. 27–50, and for Philadelphia consult John F. Bauman, "The City, the Depression, and Relief: The Philadelphia Experience, 1929–1939," unpublished doctoral dissertation, Rutgers University, 1969, especially pp. 265–314.

34. All computations have been based on "Annual Report of the Election Department" for appropriate years, 1926–1930.

35. *The New York Times*, Aug. 19, 1929; Dinneen, *The Purple Shamrock*, p. 162; "Hasn't Curley Had Enough?"—campaign pamphlet in Shattuck MSS., Drawer 24; *Transcript*, June 29, 1929; and Nutter Diary, XXIII, Sept. 10–16, 1929.

36. Curley, *I'd Do It Again*, p. 201; *Herald*, Sept. 20, 1929; *Globe*, Oct. 2, 21, Nov. 1, 1929; pamphlets in Shattuck MSS., Drawer 24; and Nutter Diary, XXIII, Oct. 30, 1929.

37. "Curley to the Voters of Boston, 1929," Shattuck MSS., Drawer 24, and *Globe*, Sept. 15, 1929.

38. "Hasn't Curley Had Enough?" in Shattuck MSS., Drawer 24; *Globe*, Sept. 15, Oct. 2, 1929; *Sunday Globe*, Sept. 29, 1929; and *The New York Times*, Oct. 20, 1929.

39. Curley later filed personal campaign expenses of $2,598 compared to Mansfield's $3,000, the legal limit. *Globe*, Oct. 30, Nov. 2, 20, 1929.

40. Nutter Diary, XXIII, Nov. 12, 1929.

41. *Post*, Nov. 3, 1929. Curley also received the Democratic City Committee's approval with few present at the meeting. Mansfield charged, with justice, that the session had been rigged. *Globe*, Oct. 2, 1929. Having once called the committee "a collection of chowderheads," Curley had most likely not modified his opinion. Shannon, *The American Irish*, p. 210.

42. Nutter Diary, XXIII, Oct. 9, Nov. 1–2, 1929.

43. WEIU News Service, Appointments Bureau Releases, WEIU Records (Radcliffe), Box 9; Minutes of the Boston Central Labor Union, made available to the author through the kindness of Lawrence Sullivan of the Greater Boston Labor Council (AFL–CIO), hereafter cited "BCLU Minutes"; *Globe* for December, 1929; and *ibid.*, Jan. 1, 6, 1930.

CHAPTER 3

1. All quotations from the Inaugural Address are from *PCCB*, Jan. 6, 1930, pp. 1–5.

2. To have said in January 1930 that Hoover had a program may have been stretching the point. The Federal Reserve eased credit, and Hoover counseled modest federal expenditures for public construction. Primarily, the President relied on

persuading business not to cut wages, on cajoling consumers to buy, and on the activities of local government. Harris G. Warren, *Herbert Hoover and the Great Depression* (New York, 1959), pp. 114–119.

3. *Christian Science Monitor*, Jan. 7, 1930, clipping, James Michael Curley Scrapbook No. 12, Dinand Library, Holy Cross College, Worcester, Mass., hereafter cited "JMC-SB."

4. *Post*, Feb. 11, 1930, clipping, JMC-SB, No. 16.

5. *Herald*, Jan. 7, 1930.

6. *Globe*, Feb. 28, 1930.

7. In July, the American Federation of Labor pegged Boston's building-trades unemployment at 45 percent (6 percent above the urban norm) and reported that 11 percent of all other workers had lost their jobs (5 percent below the national urban average). "American Federation of Labor Employment Reports, July 1930–December 1932," Records of the President's Organization on Unemployment Relief, National Archives, Drawer 374, hereafter cited "PECE-POUR."

8. The NTWIU, along with the fur workers, had for some time been the center of Communist party activity in Boston, and Communist organizers who had been active in the New York City fur and cloak industries were spotted at the Boston rallies. Bernstein, *The Lean Years*, pp. 136–141; Philip S. Foner, *The Fur and Leather Workers Union* (Newark, 1950), pp. 313–320; and Federal Mediation and Conciliation Service Records (hereafter cited "FMCS"), Federal Records Center, Suitland, Md., Dispute File 170-5521.

9. The arrest lists printed in Boston newspapers during 1930 show that in twenty-five so-called "Communist riots," the proportion of foreign-born demonstrators exceeded only slightly what one would anticipate in a city where nearly one-third of the population was of European nativity.

10. *City Record*, Jan. 25, 1930, p. 99, and *Globe*, Feb. 5, 1930.

11. The state legislature passed a bill suspending Civil Service Commission rules for sixty days, thereby allowing Boston's hiring officials to give preference to unemployed men with more than five children, but the state continued to insist that veterans be given first call. An Old Age Assistance Act emerged, but eligibility began at age seventy for those who had lived in Massachusetts for twenty years. The legislature modestly expanded aid to mothers, approved Curley's special $3,100,000 subway project, and allowed the city to increase its regular budget by $2 million. *Globe*, Feb. 1–May 30, 1930.

12. "Special Report of the Department of Labor and Industries," *Massachusetts Legislative Documents*, House No. 1278 (January, 1931), pp. 21, 54.

13. Only Milwaukee (by 35 cents), Buffalo (by 24 cents), and New York (by 14 cents) raised their 1930 cost payments over 1929's by more than Boston. Boston's per capita payments went up $4.42 to $87.08, a total some $40 more per person than St. Louis. Philadelphia cut its payments in 1930, the single big city to retrench. *Statistical Abstract of the United States* (1932), pp. 218–219.

14. Per capita welfare expenditures in Boston, 1930, placed the city behind only Detroit and were more than double the relief outlays in Buffalo, the third-ranked city. The monthly average payment to recipients of $42.12 topped all cities, with

Detroit ($36.48) placing second. Winslow, *Trends in Different Types of Public and Private Relief*, pp. 72–85, 96–100. Also, "Annual Report of the Overseers of the Public Welfare" for 1929 and 1930.

15. *City Record*, July 19, 26, 1930, pp. 815–816, 845, and Aug. 16, 1930, p. 1264.

16. *Globe*, Jan. 29, 1931; *Evening Globe*, Aug. 19, 1930; and *City Record* Aug. 23, 1930, p. 1415.

17. *Globe*, March 8, Sept. 2, 7, and Oct. 10, 25, 1930; *Herald*, Sept. 2, 1930, clipping, JMC-SB, No. 36; *City Record*, July 19, Aug. 27, 1930, pp. 815–816, 1460; and *PCCB*, Nov. 24, 1930, pp. 350–351.

18. Some employers paid the same hourly wages and therefore claimed to be doing their part. Meanwhile, they reduced hours. AFL employment reports (PECE-POUR, Box 374) reflect increasing percentages in the last half of 1930 for part-time employment in Boston. Seldes, *Years of the Locust*, pp. 48–50, 89–94; Consumers' League Executive Committee Minutes, Oct. 21, 1930, CL-Mass., Folder 15; *City Record*, Aug. 2, 23, 1930, pp. 904, 1417; and BCLU Minutes, November, 1930.

19. *City Record*, Aug. 16, 23, 1930, pp. 1261, 1263–1267, 1417–1418.

20. *Ibid.*, Sept. 2, 1930. *Globe*, Aug. 5, Sept. 2, 1930.

21. *City Record*, Dec. 20, 1930, pp. 1970, 1976.

22. Mussolini appealed to Curley not only for his attempts to stop "the mad march of anarchy, Bolshevism, and Communism," but also for the massive building programs which had reduced unemployment in Italy. *Globe*, Oct. 28, 1930, and *City Record*, Oct. 18, 1930, p. 1696. On the whole, Boston's Italian community liked the tribute. *Italian News*, Oct. 17, 1930, clipping, JMC-SB, unnumbered.

23. *PCCB*, Oct. 20, Nov. 10, 1930, pp. 308–310, 333.

24. *Ibid.*, July 7, 1930, pp. 226–228. With monotonous regularity, the council passed orders to terminate employment of the unnaturalized foreign-born. At one point, the council even asked Curley to give $50 rewards to those residents who reported job-holding aliens "while 75,000 citizens of Boston walk the streets seeking that sort of employment." *Ibid.*, July 21, 1930, p. 240.

25. *Ibid.*, Oct. 20, 27, Nov. 10, 1930, pp. 306, 316, 328; and *Post*, Oct. 21, 1930.

26. *PCCB*, April 14, 1930, pp. 134–135.

27. When the city council assumed a neo-Luddite position by ordering that no machinery be used on public-works projects, Curley replied that he favored a federal law to curb automatic machinery but correctly feared "that the courts could construe it as unconstitutional." *Ibid.*, Oct. 27, Nov. 10, 1930, pp. 318–319, 329.

28. *Ibid.*, Oct. 27, Nov. 10, 1930, pp. 322, 329, 334, and Raymond L. Koch, "Politics and Relief in Minneapolis During the 1930's," *Minnesota History*, XLI (Winter, 1968), pp. 153–154.

29. Curley to City Council, Dec. 5, 1930, in *PCCB*, Dec. 15, 1930, p. 362. In December, Curley reported that two nationally known concerns had pledged 10 percent of their receipts from one business day to the city. One gave $0.76, and the other donated $93. *City Record*, Dec. 20, 1930, p. 1989.

30. *PCCB*, Dec. 15, 1930, pp. 367–368. By the close of 1930, Pittsburgh's unemployed had received approval to sell apples without a license. For $2, an idle

worker could obtain a box of roughly a hundred apples, which he then sold at 5 cents apiece. New Orleans in December of 1930 carefully screened the jobless, and the fortunate were allowed to buy "Louisiana's golden oranges," as newspapers called them, at $2.70 a case. The fruit was peddled on the streets—two for a nickel. Councilor Wilson was correct when he implied that Boston had not reached quite these extremes. Stave, *The New Deal and the Last Hurrah*, p. 33, and Roman Heleniak, "Local Reaction to the Great Depression in New Orleans, 1929–1933," *Louisiana History*, X (Fall, 1969), pp. 296–297.

31. *Ibid.*, Oct. 27, 1930. PECE has accurately been called "an organ of exhortation for the American way" and "an endless correspondence mill." Alfred Romasco, *The Poverty of Abundance: Hoover, the Nation, the Depression* (New York, 1965). This description would fit Allen's committees with equal accuracy.

32. *Globe*, Sept. 10–17, Oct. 29, 1930; *Post*, Oct. 29, 1930; Ray Kierman, "Jim Curley, Boss of Massachusetts," *The American Mercury*, XXXVII (February, 1936), p. 143; and Robert K. Massey, Jr., "The State Politics of Massachusetts Democracy, 1928–1938," unpublished doctoral dissertation, Duke University, 1968, pp. 65–97.

33. Shattuck to Damon Hall, Nov. 10, 1930, Shattuck MSS., Drawer 25, and *Globe*, Sept. 26, 1930.

34. *Transcript*, Nov. 29, Dec. 1, 8, 1930, clippings, unnumbered scrapbook at WEIU headquarters, 264 Boylston Street.

CHAPTER 4

1. *Globe*, Oct. 17, 1932.

2. All calculations are based on *Statistical Abstract of the United States* (1933–1935) and "Statistics of Manufactures, 1920–1938," *Massachusetts Public Documents*, 1938, No. 36, pp. 3, 20. Although manufacturing employment in the Bay State dropped 20.9 index points, the loss was less serious than in such key places as New York (−26.8), New Jersey (−27.0), Pennsylvania (−24.5), and Illinois (−31.9).

3. Exceptions must be noted. The Filenes, Louis Kirstein, and P. A. O'Connell, the president of the E. T. Slattery department store, for example, were convinced that the power of government over business had to be enlarged.

4. Memorandum from W. J. Barrett to the Cotton Textile Institute, Jan. 18, 1932, PECE-POUR, Box 377; *Globe*, Oct. 23, 1931, and April 4, 1932.

5. H. C. Knight to Walter Gifford, Feb. 24, 1932, PECE-POUR, Drawer 371.

6. From 1920 to 1932, the city's population increased 20 percent, net debt 50 percent, the cost of government 56 percent, and the property tax levy 81 percent. Since Curley sat longer as mayor during this period than anyone else (six years), the blame fell on him. *The New York Times*, Dec. 4, 1932.

7. *City Record*, Nov. 30, Dec. 1931, pp. 2011, 2135–2136.

8. Tinkham to Henry Shattuck, April 30, 1932, Shattuck MSS., Drawer 10.

9. Admiral Byrd, brother of Virginia's conservative senator, Harry Byrd, maintained residence in Boston during the entire Depression. A towering hero, Byrd was ac-

corded a tumultuous reception in the Hub when he returned from the South Pole in 1930. *City Record*, June 28, 1930, pp. 705, 707.

10. National Economy League, Press Release, typescript, Shattuck MSS., Drawer 10.

11. Department of Commerce, Bureau of the Census, "Unemployment Returns by Classes—Special Unemployment Census, January, 1931"; "AFL Employment Reports, July 1930–December 1932; and U.S. Department of Labor, Children's Bureau, "Monthly Relief Bulletin," all in PECE-POUR, Drawer 374.

12. Boston Council of Social Agencies, "Social Statistics by Census Tracts in Boston," II, July, 1935, especially p. 11, and U.S. Bureau of the Census, *Negroes in the United States, 1920–1932* (Washington, D.C., 1935), pp. 301–306, 454–455. For a detailed analysis of unemployment in Boston, see Chapter 8.

13. Charles W. Morton, "Lean Times in Boston: Depression and the Drys," *The Atlantic Monthly*, CCXI (February, 1963), p. 48.

14. Eleven strikes took place in Boston during 1931 (vs. nineteen in 1929 and nine in 1930), and seventeen broke out in 1932. Only New York, Chicago, Philadelphia, and Pittsburgh topped Boston in the number of stoppages, and of these four cities only Chicago experienced more strikes in 1932 than in 1931 (twenty-three vs. twenty-one). *Monthly Labor Review*, XXVI (June, 1933), p. 1298.

15. Union membership in Boston at the end of 1932 was reported at 62,340, perhaps two thousand more than in 1929. Trade-union membership in the United States went down from 3,442,600 to roughly 3 million during the same period. *Thirty-Sixth Annual Directory of Labor Organizations* (1937), p. 77, and Troy, *Trade Union Membership, 1897–1962*, p. 1.

16. *Globe*, Sept. 5, 1932.

17. "Open Letter," April, 1932, National Recovery Administration Records, National Archives, Box 1086, hereafter cited "NRA Records."

18. *Globe*, Jan. 20, Feb. 5, 10–12, 25, March 5, May 1–2, and Oct. 5, 1931, and Feb. 5, April 30–May 4, 1932; *Post*, May 1–2, 1931, and May 1–4, 1932.

19. The crushing psychological effect of unemployment on many workers also would have served as a deterrent. For a discussion of this possibility, see Chapter 8.

20. *Globe*, Dec. 2, 1931, April 19–20, June 3–6, 1932, and *Post*, June 3–6, 1932.

21. *PCCB*, Aug. 8, 1932, p. 288. More than in 1930, snowstorms touched off virtual hysteria. Crowds as large as ten thousand descended on the Municipal Employment Bureau to shovel at $5 a day, and on occasion the entire mob was turned away, having been told that the sun would take care of the snow.

22. *PCCB*, March 28, Aug. 8, 1932, pp. 115–116, 287, 290.

23. Winslow, *Trends in Different Types of Public and Private Relief in Urban Areas, 1929–1935*, pp. 72–85, 96–100, and Searle F. Charles, *Minister of Relief: Harry Hopkins and the Depression* (Syracuse, 1963), p. 11.

24. The Overseers had, in 1931, refused an explicit city-council request to subsidize carfare, and the trustees of the Boston Elevated Railroad had turned down pleas to allow reliefers to ride at reduced fares. At the close of 1932 these policies still obtained. *PCCB*, Nov. 23, 1931, and June 20, July 11, Aug. 3, 17, 22, Oct. 10, 31, 1932.

25. *Ibid.*, May 4, 6, 1931, pp. 181, 209–215, and Feb. 1, 1932, p. 50; *City Record*, Aug. 27, 1932, p. 943; and *Globe*, Aug. 12–31, 1932.

26. *PCCB*, April 13, 1931, p. 162, and *Globe*, Aug. 12–31, 1932.

27. Society of St. Vincent de Paul, *Annual Reports . . . September 30, 1930–September 30, 1938*, and Barbara Miller Solomon, *Pioneers in Service: The History of the Associated Jewish Philanthropies of Boston* (Boston, 1956), pp. 125–130, 183.

28. "Resolutions of the Committee on Administration of Relief to the President's Organization on Unemployment Relief," Oct. 16, 1931, PECE-POUR, Drawer 412; *Globe*, Oct. 6, 1931, July 20, 1932; *PCCB*, March 7, 28, 1932, pp. 92–109; and *Traveler*, March 17, 1932, clipping, WEIU Scrapbook, WEIU headquarters.

29. Curley to Roosevelt, telegram, Aug. 29, 1932, and a draft for a message to Volunteers of America in Roosevelt MSS., "Private Correspondence, 1928–1932, James M. Curley," Record Group 12, Roosevelt Library, Hyde Park; *PCCB*, Aug. 22, 1932, pp. 297–298. In Dallas, the Chamber of Commerce served the jobless 36,000 pounds of red snapper, while the Junior League and the Salvation Army operated the kind of soup kitchen that was visible almost everywhere but Boston. Robert C. Cotner *et al.*, *Texas Cities and the Great Depression* (Austin, 1973), p. 123.

30. *Globe*, Sept. 19, 1931; *Evening Globe*, Jan. 6, 25, 1932; and "Address of Joseph B. Ely to the Two Branches of the Legislature of Massachusetts, January 6, 1932," Senate Document No. 1, Shattuck MSS., Drawer 2. Ely did favor some form of unemployment insurance but the legislature turned down two different plans.

31. *Globe*, Oct. 7, 1930.

32. *Ibid.*, Feb. 13, June 23, 1931.

33. The $300 million made available to the states could be obtained only upon application of the governor. Ely had stated in late 1931 that "Massachusetts will be able to take care of herself so far as financial arrangements are concerned," and he wanted no more than "the advice and information of the federal government." Ely to H. C. Knight, Sept. 12, 1931, PECE-POUR, Drawer 412. Ely never budged from this position, and the Commonwealth received not one nickel. *Globe*, Jan. 9, 1933.

34. *The New York Times*, June 25, 1931; *Globe*, June 26, Dec. 11, 1931; *PCCB*, April 27, May 11, Dec. 14, 1931, pp. 169, 195, 456–457; and *City Record*, July 25, Aug. 1, 1931, pp. 947, 989, 993.

35. *Globe*, Jan. 22, Feb. 11, 1932. According to Wadsworth, the surest prescription for economic health was the medicine of hard work and thrift. "There's plenty of prosperity now," he told the bemused Boston Council of Social Agencies on January 21, 1932. "The automobiles are still running, as you may notice, and the movies are still full. We can handle the problem locally and we will do it."

36. Taylor to Gifford, Feb. 25, 1932, PECE-POUR, Drawer 412. Also, *Globe*, Feb. 1–15, 1932, and *Post*, Jan. 25, 1932.

37. However inadequate, Boston's maiden effort compared favorably with the first

campaigns in New York ($18 million in six weeks) and Philadelphia ($10,250,800 in a year) when population differences are taken into account.

38. Only twenty-two thousand turned out for the six-hour athletic festival, which raised just $25,000 for relief. In contrast, a nonphilanthropic doubleheader between the Braves and the Phillies in May had drawn a crowd of 51,331. The following day Rabbit Maranville's tenth-inning single disposed of the Brooklyn Dodgers, giving the Braves temporary possession of first place. In lockstep with the city's fund-raising effort, the Braves rapidly slumped.

39. *Globe*, May 6, 1931, and *PCCB*, June 15, 1931, p. 241. Curley's enemies charged that he deliberately manipulated budget figures by instructing his department heads to submit inflated estimates which he could then chop, thus appearing to be an economizer rather than a profligate who spent $198,000 entertaining "English Dukes, German Counselors, and Chinese Generals." *Ibid.*, April 13, 1931, pp. 154–161.

40. Seventeen of the thirty largest cities had per capita debt greater than Boston's $164.90, and nine had obligations of more than $200 per person including New York, Philadelphia, Baltimore, Pittsburgh, and San Francisco. *Statistical Abstract of the United States* (1934), pp. 214–215.

41. *Globe*, Feb. 1, 1932.

CHAPTER 5

1. Roosevelt to Brown, Jan. 25, 1932, DNC-Mass., Box 261. Brown had served as Woodrow Wilson's Assistant Attorney General and had long been associated with liberal causes in the Hub.

2. Jordan A. Schwarz, "Al Smith in the Thirties," *New York History*, XLV (October, 1964), p. 328.

3. Huthmacher, *Massachusetts People and Politics*, p. 148. William Shannon, too, calls the Boston Irish "rebels, not reformers." Although his description pertains to the turn of the century, it applies to the next generations as well. Shannon, *The American Irish*, p. 200.

4. Massey, Jr., "The State Politics of Massachusetts Democracy," pp. 39–42, 56–64, and Curley, *I'd Do It Again*, pp. 231–232. Boston's newspapers interpreted Curley's switch to Roosevelt as both a calculated gamble to get at Governor Ely and as an expression of the Mayor's natural combativeness. "He was born, not with a silver spoon, but with a wooden ladder in his mouth, which he proceeded forthwith to climb." "Bob Washburn Says," *Transcript*, July 13, 1931.

5. Curley, *I'd Do It Again*, pp. 231–232. Smith's position as president of the Empire State Building, his directorship of several corporations, and his intimacy with John Raskob made plausible Curley's allegations.

6. Curley to Roosevelt, telegram, Jan. 30, 1931, "Private Correspondence, 1928–1932, James M. Curley," Record Group 12, Roosevelt Library.

7. High points included a visit to his ancestral home in Galway, a tumultuous welcome in Boston, England, the laying of wreaths at the tombs of unknown soldiers

in Paris and Rome, a short-wave radio broadcast from the Eiffel Tower, presentation of a blackthorn shillelagh to Mussolini, a papal audience, intervention in a dispute between Il Duce and the Pope, and the drinking of a sufficient number of toasts to leave no doubt about his wetness. Of the trip Curley later wrote, "Members of my party kissed the Blarney Stone, but I did not think this ritual necessary for myself." *I'd Do It Again*, p. 214. Even in hard times, Curley was continuing a tradition associated with urban bosses: the European grand tour was a *sine qua non*.

8. Dinneen, *The Purple Shamrock*, p. 179.

9. *Salem News*, June 15, 1931, clipping, JMC-SB unnumbered; *Globe* and *The New York Times*, June 14, 1931; and *City Record*, June 20, 1931, p. 757. In contrast to Curley, bosses such as Frank Hague of Jersey City backed Smith, Kansas City's Pendergast machine favored Senator James Reed of Missouri, and Chicago's Nash-Kelly machine supported a native son, the conservative banker Melvin J. Traylor. Stave, *The New Deal and the Last Hurrah*, p. 18. In Curley's case, he had "hustled on the Roosevelt bandwagon when it was the only wagon in sight." Nutter Diary, XXVIII, March 21, 1932.

10. Brown to Roosevelt, Dec. 6, 1931, and Jan. 16, 1932; Roosevelt to Brown, Jan. 25, 1932, DNC-Mass., Box 261. "To see an honoured name like Roosevelt linked with Curley," said another member of Boston's elite, "is nauseating." Nutter Diary, XXVIII, March 21, 1932.

11. *PCCB*, Feb. 8, 1932, pp. 65–66, and *Globe*, Feb. 8, 1932.

12. Editor's note in Elliott Roosevelt (ed.), *F.D.R.: His Personal Letters, 1928–1945*, I (New York, 1950), pp. 274–275, and Massey, Jr., "The State Politics of Massachusetts Democracy," pp. 112–113, based on a 1967 interview with LaRue Brown, now deceased.

13. Curley later claimed that he put up a slate of delegates at Roosevelt's request. *I'd Do It Again*, p. 233. Others, like Ed Flynn of the Bronx, remembered it differently. See *Personal Letters*, I, pp. 274–275. Even in March Louis Howe told Roosevelt that the Smith boom was a mirage. Only too late did he and Roosevelt suspect that "Curley's interest was parasitic." Alfred B. Rollins, Jr., *Roosevelt and Howe* (New York, 1962), pp. 326–327. The suggestion has also been made that Roosevelt was blinded by paternal pride in son James's participation. The young Roosevelt had taken up residence in Cambridge and was employed as an insurance executive in Boston. James M. Burns, *Roosevelt: The Lion and the Fox* (New York, 1956), p. 132.

14. Roosevelt to Curley, April 28, 1932, DNC-Mass., Box 261. The 3 : 1 statewide margin dismayed Louis Howe, who feared that the momentum gained in other primaries had been broken. Rollins, *Roosevelt and Howe*, p. 327.

15. *Globe*, June 20, 27, 1932. Ely's charges derived from a short-lived attempt by the New Yorker's strategists to eliminate the two-thirds rule. See Burns, *Lion and the Fox*, pp. 134–135.

16. *Globe*, July 1, 1932. Smith himself told Ely that he had not heard such sterling oratory since 1920 when Bourke Cochran nominated him at San Francisco.

17. *Post*, June 28, 1932, cited in Massey, Jr., "The State Politics of Massachusetts

Democracy," p. 125. The *Post* story is only one of many which persist in Boston, including a version which claims that the missing Puerto Rican was locked in his hotel room.

18. *Globe* and *Post*, July 5, 1932; *The New York Times*, July 5, 7, 1932. Curley stretched the theme of Spanish descent to unimaginable lengths. He found that an Irishman had steered Columbus's flagship to the New World, said that "Curley" meant "courageous" in Spanish, and asked the Superintendent of Schools to offer Puerto Rican geography and history so that Boston children might learn of the island's "soft tropical beauties." *City Record*, July 16, 1932, pp. 781, 785.

19. *Globe*, July 4, 1932, and *PCCB*, July 11, 1932, p. 252.

20. Memorandum of a telephone conversation, Frankfurter and Roosevelt, July 2, 1932, in Max Freedman (ed.), *Roosevelt and Frankfurter: Their Correspondence, 1928–1945* (Boston, 1967), pp. 74–76.

21. Quoted by Eddie Dowling, COHC, No. 532, p. 323.

22. A. D. Van Nostrand, "The Lomasney Legend," *New England Quarterly*, XXI (December, 1948), p. 453, and *Globe*, July 5, 1932. An exasperated foe once said of Lomasney that he was "a socialist on Tuesday and Thursday, while on Wednesday and Friday he sets his face like flint against any scheme having the slightest socialistic flavor." John D. Buenker, "The Mahatma and Progressive Reform: Martin Lomasney as Lawmaker, 1911–1917,"*New England Quarterly*, XLIV (September, 1971), p. 404. For Roosevelt's problem in establishing liberal credentials on the national level, see William E. Leuchtenburg, *Franklin D. Roosevelt and the New Deal, 1932–1940* (New York, 1963), pp. 9–13.

23. "I am confident that under the leadership of Franklin Roosevelt," Curley told an audience in Seattle, "the people will be able to consume something more pleasant and wholesome than embalming fluid." In Portland, Oregon, where the American Legion was holding its national convention, Curley poured ice water out of his hotel window on Legionnaires who were chanting "We want Roosevelt" at 3:00 A.M., and created a well-reported furor when he excoriated Hoover for his "brutal and arbitrary methods" in shooting down Bonus Marchers "like dogs in the street." *Seattle Post-Intelligencer*, Sept. 11, 1932; *Portland Oregonian* and *Medford Mail-Tribune*, Sept. 13, 1932, clippings, JMC-SB.

24. Brown to Roosevelt, Sept. 7, 1932, DNC-Mass., Box 265. As far back as the Massachusetts preprimary, Martin Lomasney had set the tone for vicious attacks on F.D.R. In a statement that ranks with some of Boston's most offensive oratory, the Mahatma commented: "Roosevelt was an actor, and his hobbling into the Democratic convention on crutches to nominate Smith was all part of the play. All the time he was dealing with the Heflins and the Cannons . . . to put the knife into Smith. Are we who licked the know-nothings going to be quitters?" *Post*, April 25, 1932, quoted in Massey, Jr., "The State Politics of Massachusetts Democracy," pp. 120–121.

25. Joseph Reder to Roosevelt, Nov. 9, 1932, DNC-Mass., Box 280; cards in *ibid.*, Box 275; *The New York Times*, Oct. 14, 18, 1932; *East Boston Argus-Advocate*, Oct. 1932, clippings, JMC-SB, unnumbered; and *Globe*, Oct. 1–21, 1932.

26. (Name withheld by author) to Roosevelt, Nov. 2, 1932, DNC-Mass., Box 265.

27. BCLU Minutes, Oct. 21, 1932, and *Globe*, Oct. 22, 1932.

28. James Farley recalled Smith's Boston Address as his most effective speech for Roosevelt, and felt it "helped us considerably in New England and all along the Atlantic seaboard." Farley, *Behind the Ballots: The Personal History of a Politician* (New York, 1938), p. 177.

29. *Globe*, Nov. 7, 1932.

30. Republicans had deplored Roosevelt's attempts to appear radical in the West and moderate in the East. "To my mind," wrote Henry Shattuck, "this is the weakest point in the Roosevelt candidacy, and is the strongest reason why he should not be President." Shattuck to John Richardson, Aug. 5, 1932, Shattuck MSS., Drawer 25.

31. Samuel I. Rosenman (ed.), *The Public Papers and Addresses of Franklin D. Roosevelt*, I (New York, 1938), pp. 842–855.

32. *Post*, Nov. 1, 1932. Frequent "We Want Beer" rallies at the Boston Common encouraged Curley to stress Roosevelt's position in favor of repeal. He told voters that the election of his candidate would allow them to enjoy "mellow Bourbon whisky, aged in wood, without hypocrisy," and urged F.D.R. and his advisers to exploit the issue. *Globe*, Oct. 1, 1932, and Curley to Roosevelt, Aug. 2, 1932, DNC-Mass., Box 265.

33. *Globe*, Nov. 5, 1932. The belated efforts of the Progressive League for Roosevelt attracted almost no attention from the Boston press, and the liberal organizers spent little money on the campaign. Although the group at the City Club played but a minor part in the 1932 election, the role of those who shared the podium with Hapgood—Felix Frankfurter, David K. Niles, Mrs. Arthur Rotch—was to become vital thereafter. See Chapters 6, 7.

34. *Globe*, Sept. 5, 1932. Catholic voters had been receiving conservative advice all year long from Cardinal O'Connell, whose pique toward the radio priest, Father Charles Coughlin, led him to criticize those "uttering demagogic stuff to the poor," and to defend wealthy bankers. " 'Demogogy' in the Pulpit," *Literary Digest*, CXIII (May 7, 1932), p. 18. *The Pilot* in September and October was repeating this theme and was emphasizing the need for Christian charity to the exclusion of other considerations.

35. "Annual Report of the Election Department," *Documents of the City of Boston*, No. 11, 1933; and Jerome Clubb and Howard Allen, "The Cities and the Election of 1928: Partisan Realignment?" *American Historical Review*, LXXXIV (April, 1969), pp. 1205–1220.

36. Computed from Eugene Roseboom, *A History of Presidential Elections* (New York, 1964), pp. 428, 441.

37. All comparisons have been calculated from raw totals given in "Annual Report of the Election Department," 1929, 1933. A more detailed analysis of voting patterns in national elections may be found in Chapter 12. See especially Table 12.1.

38. Clubb and Allen, "The Cities and the Election of 1928," p. 1211. This statistic is,

of course, less dramatic than it appears because of the resounding Democratic vote in 1928. Nevertheless, as Massey has pointed out, ". . . Massachusetts was no longer in the forward ranks of the national Democracy." Because of the Democratic schism, "the Commonwealth had forsaken her role as a Democratic harbinger; she was, instead, a Democratic laggard." Robert K. Massey, Jr., "The Democratic Laggard: Massachusetts in 1932," *New England Quarterly*, XLIV (December, 1971), pp. 554, 574.

39. *Italian News*, Nov. 11, 1932, clipping, JMC-SB, unnumbered.

40. Roosevelt to Curley, Nov. 21, 1932, Box 261. As an inveterate Brahmin-baiter, Curley especially coveted the possible appointment as Secretary of the Navy. To have succeeded Boston's Charles Francis Adams would have represented the quintessential triumph of the Irish over the Yankees. Russell, "The Last of the Bosses," p. 87.

41. Kelly, a master showman, appeared at the auditorium on February 9 flanked by husky bodyguards to create the impression that Curley planned to do him violence. *Globe*, Feb. 10–11, 1933. Two weeks earlier, he had challenged Curley to a fistfight in the Boston Garden with proceeds going to the unemployed. *Globe*, Jan. 24, 1933.

42. Virtually the sole report of new economic activity was made on February 25, 1933, when Tom Yawkey purchased the Boston Red Sox and started refurbishing Fenway Park. His lavish expenditures for players would soon lead reporters to refer to the team as the "Gold Sox."

43. Eva Whiting White, "Public Welfare Explained," *North, East, West, South*, II, No. 1 (1933), White MSS., Box 1, Folder 5.

44. Shattuck to Lippmann, Feb. 18, 1933, Shattuck MSS., Drawer 12.

45. *PCCB*, Jan. 16, 1933, p. 20; *Transcript*, Jan. 16, 1933; *Globe*, Jan. 26, 1933; Rosalind Brill, "The Rise of Urban Liberalism: Boston City Politics, 1926–1933," unpublished honors thesis, Brandeis University, 1967, p. 89; and Robert Lincoln O'Brien, COHC, No. 81, pp. 75–76.

CHAPTER 6

1. Rosenman (ed.), *Public Papers and Addresses*, II, pp. 11–12.

2. *Globe*, March 6, 1933.

3. *Ibid.*, March 6–7, 1933.

4. Quoted in Cabell Phillips, *From the Crash to the Blitz, 1929–1939* (New York, 1969), p. 107.

5. *Globe*, March 9, 1933.

6. Both the rich and the poor were caught short of ready cash. The *Crimson* disclosed that the average Harvard student had only twenty-two cents on hand, municipal employees waited vainly to cash checks, and men brought to the Charles Street jail found bail money impossible to obtain. *Ibid.*, March 6–13, 1933; Caroline Bird, *The Invisible Scar* (New York, 1966), p. 118; and Deposition of First National Stores to Boston City Council, *PCCB*, April 24, 1933, p. 149.

7. *Herald* and *Globe*, March 14, 1933. That more money was brought to banks than

was taken out duplicated what happened in many other cities, including New York. *The New York Times*, March 14, 1933. All banks in Boston resumed activity except those that had been in receivership prior to the bank holiday, but thirty-two institutions within the Boston Federal Reserve District remained unlicensed as late as September 1933, and ninety still faced limitations upon deposit withdrawals. Miscellaneous records of the Reconstruction Finance Corporation, National Archives, Record Group 24, box unnumbered but designated "Bankruptcy-Banks, Part I."

8. *PCCB*, March 13, 1933, p. 87.
9. *The New York Times*, March 31, 1933. This quotation also appears in Arthur M. Schlesinger, Jr., *The Coming of the New Deal* (Boston, 1958), p. 13.
10. Shattuck to Walsh, March 24, 1933, Shattuck MSS., Drawer 10.
11. *Globe* and *Post*, April 8, 1933. Some of the merrymakers were, in fact, shortchanged. Jake Wirth's German Restaurant, late in applying for a new license, served "near beer" to a crush of customers. Those who bellied up to the bar, however, never knew the difference. Morton, "Lean Times in Boston," p. 54.
12. Rosenman (ed.), *Public Papers and Addresses*, II, p. 13.
13. *City Record*, May 20, 1933, p. 488.
14. Federal Emergency Relief Administration Records, Massachusetts Files, National Archives, Boxes 128–130, hereafter cited "FERA-Mass.," and *Globe*, May 13–Nov. 20, 1933. Chapter 7 elaborates upon impediments to successful intergovernmental cooperation.
15. *Evening Globe*, Aug. 30, 1933, and *City Record*, Sept. 2, 1933, pp. 979, 981.
16. Rosenman (ed.), *Public Papers and Addresses*, II, p. 300; *Globe*, July 25–Aug. 2, 1933; and *Post*, July 26, Aug. 2, 1933.
17. *Globe*, Aug. 7, 11–12, 15, 28–Sept. 2, 1933; *Post*, Aug. 28–29, 1933; and BCLU Minutes, Aug. 18, 1933. For a larger perspective on the use of war rhetoric, personnel, and organization in the NRA, see William E. Leuchtenburg, "The New Deal and the Analogue of War," in John Braeman *et al.* (eds.), *Change and Continuity in Twentieth-Century America* (Columbus, O., 1964), pp. 81–143.
18. Bigelow was "Biggles" to Roosevelt, and the President was "Frank" to him. Not until 1935 did the two men quarrel through the mails. Wadsworth, the dominant figure in the Chamber of Commerce, recognized that things were "not as in the olden days," but the old school ties kept his public utterances about Roosevelt under restraint. Bigelow letters in DNC-Mass., Box 273, and PPF 2088, especially the angry exchange of June 3, 10, 1935; Wadsworth letters in PPF 1335, especially March 11, 1934.
19. Shattuck to Rogers, June 8, 1933, Shattuck MSS., Drawer 10.
20. *Globe*, May 4, 1933.
21. Arthur Rotch to Roosevelt, Nov. 12, 1932, DNC-Mass., Box 280.
22. E. A. Filene to Roosevelt, Nov. 9, 1932, PPF 2116.
23. Kirstein to Carl Dennett, June 17, 1932, Louis Kirstein MSS., Baker Library, Harvard School of Business Administration, Case 2, hereafter cited "Kirstein MSS."

24. Louis Kirstein, "Mind Your Own Business," *The Atlantic Monthly*, CL (October, 1932), pp. 403–410.

25. In 1932, Ely's fiscal retrenchment had worried progressives, but they nevertheless had perceived him as a champion of social justice. In the opinion of Niles and his cohorts, Ely had made excellent use of his pardon power and opposed capital punishment, he had prosecuted labor-law violators and exposed sweatshops, and he had interested himself in child welfare and in enforcing the Massachusetts minimum-wage law. To corroborate impressions of Niles and his friends gained from a variety of sources, use was made of the Niles MSS., Goldfarb Library, Brandeis University. I am indebted to Dr. Abram L. Sachar for permission to inspect these materials.

26. Florence Brennan to Roosevelt, March 22, 1933, President's Official File, Roosevelt Library, Hyde Park, No. 5434, hereafter cited "FDR-OF." Miss Brennan hit on what may have been Curley's greatest weakness: his mercurial temperament. A Boston columnist once depicted him as he still appeared to many members of the Ely-Walsh segment of the party: "[Curley] has unlimited political potentiality, that is, if he curbs his torrential spirit. In him are all the dangers of the electric current, which when harnessed drives the trolley but which in storms runs amuck, wounds and destroys." "Bob Washburn Says," *Transcript*, July 13, 1931.

27. *Sunday Post*, April 23, 1933. Also, Thomas H. Connelly to Walsh, March 15, 1933, David I. Walsh MSS., Dinand Library, Holy Cross College, Worcester, Mass.

28. The loss of the Italian ambassadorship was especially aggravating, since newspapers on several occasions reported he had been offered the appointment. The *Italian News* backed Curley for the post, and even Colonel House, who had deplored Curley in 1931, favored him for the Italian assignment. Rollins, *Roosevelt and Howe*, p. 204n. Cardinal O'Connell's objections may also have been decisive. William S. Braithwaite, COHC, No. 345, p. 200.

29. Russell, "The Last of the Bosses," p. 87.

30. "Press Conferences of the President," I, April 14, 1933, pp. 148–149, Roosevelt Library, and *Globe*, April 13, 1933. Curley subsequently embellished the story, telling senators in Washington that when Mayor Murphy of Detroit had decided to go to the Philippines as Governor General, his duty was to act as "the ambassador from the American cities to the Congress of the United States." U.S. Senate, Hearings on S. 1539, May 3, 1933, p. 7.

31. Dinneen, "The Kingfish of Massachusetts," p. 351. Roosevelt himself, according to one deposition, played up to this sort of cutting humor. "When friends went to Franklin D. Roosevelt to say that in Boston all the better people like Andrew J. Peters did not look with favor upon the appointment of James M. Curley as Ambassador to Poland, Roosevelt looked up with the query, 'What is there in Poland that Curley could steal?' " Robert Lincoln O'Brien, COHC, No. 81, p. 162.

32. *Globe*, Aug. 10, 1933.

33. *Ibid.*, Sept. 22, 1933.

34. Harold Gorvine, "The New Deal in Massachusetts," unpublished doctoral dissertation, Harvard University, 1962, pp. 127–138.

35. Harold Gorvine has stated that through September 1933 "all of the major appointments were made without [Curley's] approval." Mayor Murphy, appointed to the post of U.S. Marshal, would stand as an exception. *Ibid.*, p. 143.

36. Massey, Jr., "The State Politics of Massachusetts Democracy," p. 155, quoting from his interview with Brown, Sept. 7, 1967.

37. E. A. Filene to Howe, Nov. 7, 1933, PPF 2116. Filene spoke and wrote in defense of the NRA on any number of occasions. At the same time, he labored tirelessly for consumer cooperatives and credit unions. Indeed, he received one of the pens used by Roosevelt in signing the Credit Union Act of 1934.

38. "We in Massachusetts have never acquired either the art or the habit of carrying our troubles to the President or to the Congress," Ely continued. "We still cling to the theory that Massachusetts is a sovereign state responsible for the exercise of sovereign rights. . . ." Joseph B. Ely, "How Massachusetts Has Kept Her Costs Low," *National Municipal Review*, XXII (July, 1933), pp. 320–322.

39. The impact of the Great Depression and the New Deal upon ward leadership over a ten-year span is examined in detail in Chapter 12.

40. Mullen, "Poor Old Boston," p. 234, and Curley, *I'd Do It Again*, p. 192.

41. To anyone schooled in deciphering the shorthand peculiar to Boston, the generalizations made in this paragraph are confirmed by the campaign oratory of 1933. Mansfield, said Curley's man William Foley, was a tool of the Goo-Goos who believed that "money and flattery can employ backsliders and lickspittles to slander and abuse the regular Democratic nominee." (Translation: Mansfield had high Tory, Ward 5 support, and was no friend of the Irish.) Mansfield, said Curley, had sold out to "the motley aggregation of payroll patriots and pseudo reformers." (Translation: Mansfield was a pawn of taxpayers' associations dedicated to fiscal retrenchment.) Curley and his candidate were anti-Jewish, said Mansfield, since Curley had been entertained by Hitler's Cabinet. (Translation: Mansfield wistfully yearned for New Immigrant support, but could only make hyperbolic appeals.) *Globe*, Oct. 20, Nov. 3, 1933; and *City Record*, Nov. 4, 1933, pp. 197, 202.

42. Quotations respectively from *Globe*, Nov. 8, 1933; *Documents of the City of Boston*, 1934, No. 1, p. 6; *City Record*, May 19, 1934, p. 473; and Kierman, "Jim Curley, Boss of Massachusetts," p. 151.

43. Quoted in Shannon, *The American Irish*, p. 226, and in Curley, *I'd Do It Again*, p. 301.

44. William Shannon has written that Tobin can be best understood as an Irish Catholic desiring security in a period of economic decline and as part of "the ethos of a civil service city." But whereas Curley "to the end of his days . . . remained a self-crippled giant on a provincial stage," Tobin showed more inclination to work with New Deal programs. Shannon, *The American Irish*, pp. 187, 226–232; Vincent A. Lapomarda, "Maurice Joseph Tobin, 1901–1953: A Political Profile and an Edition of Selected Public Papers," unpublished dissertation, Boston University, 1968; and Vincent A. Lapomarda, "A New Deal Democrat in Boston: Maurice J. Tobin and the Policies of Franklin D. Roosevelt," *Essex Institute Historical Collections*, CVIII (April, 1972), pp. 135–172.

45. *PCCB*, Jan. 1, 1940, p. 1.
46. In 1929, a fellow Republican had denounced Saltonstall as a man "born with a diamond-studded spoon in his mouth. He knows only one side of life—the coupon-clipping side." Arthur Bartlett, "Leverett Saltonstall," *Scribner's*, CV (May, 1939), p. 7. But after the Roosevelt landslides Saltonstall and many other Massachusetts Republicans moved in more progressive directions. See Chapter 12.
47. Diary of John Ihlder, entry for Jan. 1, 1934, John Ihlder MSS., Franklin D. Roosevelt Library, Hyde Park, Box 56.

CHAPTER 7

1. Robert Kelso to Harry Hopkins, Sept. 17, 1933, FERA-Mass., Box 130.
2. *Ibid.*
3. H. F. Crozier to Hopkins, Aug. 11, 1933, FERA-Mass., Box 130. Boston compounded this offense by paying an emergency relief wage of $15 a week to workers on regular city projects, a stipend below the standards established by the NRA for municipal employees.
4. Congressman John McCormack eventually expressed sympathy with FERA for giving disproportionate aid to the South, but few Bostonians, especially political officials, sided with him. McCormack to Aubrey Williams, Aug. 29, 1934, telephone transcript, FERA-Mass., Box 134.
5. *City Record*, Dec. 23, 1933, p. 1713.
6. *Ibid.*, Sept. 9, 1933, pp. 1001,1004, and *Globe*, Sept. 7, 1933.
7. The initial city council opposition to PWA, ostensibly to halt "an orgy of expenditures," came from among those who had most ardently backed Al Smith in 1931 and 1932: John I. Fitzgerald (Ward 3, West and North Ends), John Dowd (Ward 8, Roxbury), Clement Norton (Ward 18, Hyde Park), and Francis Kelly (Ward 15, Dorchester).
8. Harold L. Ickes, *The Secret Diary of Harold L. Ickes: The First Thousand Days, 1933–1936* (New York, 1953), pp. 96–97. By 1936, Ickes was referring to Curley as "that hardened, old political reprobate." *Ibid.*, p. 681.
9. *Ibid.*, p. 73, and *Globe*, Aug. 3, 1933. A week later Ickes wrote the Governor that while a veto over "a purely federal function" might be convenient "for political purposes," Title II of the NIRA did not allow him to grant Ely the power to nullify decisions made in Washington. *Ibid.*, Aug. 9, 1933. Meanwhile, Roosevelt told Ickes that the Ely fracas was "the best story that had come out of Washington since March 4." Ickes recorded in his diary, "He [F.D.R.] said it was grand." *Secret Diary: The First Thousand Days*, p. 80.
10. *PCCB*, Jan. 4, 1937, p. 5.
11. See, for example, Charles N. Glaab and A. Theodore Brown, *A History of Urban America* (New York, 1967), pp. 299–305; Paul Conkin, *The New Deal* (New York, 1967), pp. 62–63; Leuchtenburg, *Roosevelt and the New Deal*, pp. 133–136; and Mark I. Gelfand, *A Nation of Cities: The Federal Government and Urban America, 1933–1965* (New York, 1975), pp. 59–65.

12. While the men on Beacon Hill fiddled, Chicago received $20 million and New York City $25 million. "We have been asleep or unintelligent," a city-council member lamented. "It is not the former," he added, "because the proposed law has been offered to the Legislature and has been dangling there like the inanimate Sacred Cod that hangs over the House of Representatives." *PCCB*, June 11, 1934, p. 229.

13. Congressman McCormack, believing that property owners had been inadequately compensated for such valuable land, filed bills in Congress for their relief. McCormack to Roosevelt, June 21, 1938, and Marvin McIntyre to McCormack, June 29, 1938, PPF 4057.

14. *PCCB*, Jan. 24, 1938, p. 27. Allowable incomes of Old Harbor Village tenants ran as high as $2,290 per year, double the average annual wage of blue-collar workers in the city. Boston Housing Authority, "Rehousing Low Income Families of Boston: A Review of Activities of the Boston Housing Authority, 1936–1940," Ihlder MSS., Box 108.

15. James Roosevelt to Maurice Tobin, Jan. 18, 1938, J. Roosevelt MSS., Box 22.

16. Wards 12 (Roxbury), 18 (Hyde Park), 19 (Jamaica Plain), and 20 (West Roxbury) returned a 30,685 to 14,170 vote verdict against federal housing.

17. The council should not be hasty and say "Yes, Yes," declared Henry Shattuck, just because money was temptingly placed before the city. "Cooperation as understood in Washington," Shattuck stated, "means 'Sign on the dotted line.' In Germany it is 'Heil Hitler.' The Washington equivalent is 'O.K. Chief.'" *PCCB*, Oct. 17, 1938, pp. 310–311, and *Globe*, Oct. 18, 25, 1938.

18. Of the first federal units to open, Old Colony, like Old Harbor Village, was located in South Boston, and both were by far the best-designed, best-built projects the city was to see in the next thirty years. The third cluster went up in Irish Charlestown, and the next two, Lenox Street and Mission Hill, were constructed in Irish sections of Roxbury. Negroes could look forward to the Orchard Park development, a block from Dudley Station in Roxbury, and East Boston's Italians awaited a small complex of 414 apartment units, but projects for both groups were still on the drawing board when World War II began. I am grateful to Stephen Demos for a tour of all projects constructed from 1938 to 1945, and to tenants of Old Harbor Village who shared their recollections.

19. Memorandum of Jan. 19, 1934, Hopkins Conference with Donald Stone, WPA-Mass., File 660.

20. *PCCB*, Dec. 11, 1933, p. 397.

21. Donald Stone to Corrington Gill, Jan. 6, 1934, both telegram and letter, Civil Works Administration Records, National Archives, Box 21, hereafter cited "CWA Records." Also, "CWA Project Records" filed in *ibid.*

22. Kelso to Hopkins, Jan. 17, 1934, Harry Hopkins MSS., Box 52, Franklin D. Roosevelt Library, Hyde Park. The Kelso Report is also in FERA-Mass., Box 130.

23. *Herald*, March 3, 1934.

24. Robert Lansdale to Aubrey Williams, March 21, 1934, telegram; "Report of Field Representative R. T. Lansdale, Visit to Massachusetts, March 20–23, 1934"; and

Lansdale to Williams, March 26, 1934, memorandum, all in Hopkins MSS., Box 52.

25. In 1935, President Roosevelt ordered Hopkins to keep Martin Davey, Democratic governor of Ohio, away from any relationship to the Works Progress Administration. Leuchtenburg, *Roosevelt and the New Deal*, p. 270, and Arthur M. Schlesinger, Jr., *The Politics of Upheaval* (Boston, 1960), pp. 354–355. But for over a year only Texas, Louisiana, and Georgia had paralleled the Bay State's circumstances.

26. Robert Lansdale to Aubrey Williams, May 22, 1934, WPA-Mass. 660 (NA), Box 1539.

27. *Globe*, April 4, 1934.

28. Only 7,800 laborers out of a quota of 113,000 were on the job in all of Massachusetts.

29. R. C. Branion to Hopkins, Nov. 11, 1935, telephone transcript, Hopkins MSS., Box 65.

30. R. C. Branion to Hopkins, April 16, 1935, FERA-Mass., Box 130.

31. Hopkins to Howard Philbrook, Aug. 19, 1935, telephone transcript, Hopkins MSS., Box 65.

32. In fairness to Sullivan and Rotch, some culpability must be assigned to the city council, which did not always appropriate money for materials and equipment. The federal government also contributed to delays by its vagueness about dollar quotas, and even by seemingly trivial oversights such as failing to supply the forms on which project applications had to be made. After the blanks arrived and were filled out, WPA wage rates changed so that the forms had to be redone.

33. McCormack to Hopkins, Sept. 13, 1935, WPA-Mass. 693, Box 1515. McCormack's rage stemmed in part from his desire to have a longtime friend appointed director of the Massachusetts WPA. The Congressman described his complaint as "the strongest I have ever written in my life."

34. Hopkins phone conversation with David Niles, Nov. 8, 1935, Hopkins MSS., Box 65. Five weeks later Curley's pique intensified because the WPA refused to certify his multimillion dollar proposal for installing paved sidewalks along all state highways. The governor warned of "riots and bloodshed in Massachusetts" if Rotch was not removed. "A change is necessary because hungry people know no law," he said. *Globe*, Dec. 11–13, 16, 1935.

35. Massachusetts Women's Political Club, Resolution of thanks to David K. Niles, Dec. 3, 1935, WPA-Mass. 660 (NA), Box 1539.

36. Hopkins to Edwards, Jan. 31, 1936, telephone transcript, Hopkins MSS., Box 65.

37. Quotations are, respectively, from the *Globe* of Feb. 1, 1936; *PCCB*, Jan. 27, 1936, p. 25; and R. C. Branion to Hopkins, March 19, 1936, telephone transcript, Hopkins MSS., Box 65.

38. Quoted in Schlesinger, Jr., *The Politics of Upheaval*, p. 355.

39. R. C. Branion–Hopkins telephone transcript, May 1, 1936, Hopkins MSS., Box 65.

40. Carney to James A. Farley, Aug. 5, 1936, DNC 1936, "Correspondence of James A. Farley, Massachusetts," Box 4. Also, telegrams from library-project workers to

Roosevelt, and Nels Anderson to Sidney Rosenberg, May 29, 1936, WPA-Mass. 641 (NA), Box 1494.

41. Curley to Farley, Sept. 10, 1936, DNC-1936, "Correspondence of James A. Farley, Massachusetts," Box 4.

42. Prejudicial hiring which favored the Irish is treated in Chapter 8. See especially Table 8.2.

43. Massachusetts Works Progress Administration, *Annual Report: 1938,* p. 10, and Massachusetts Emergency Council Questionnaires of July 19, Sept. 19, 1938, National Emergency Council Records, Division of Field Operations, Box 295, Federal Records Center, Suitland, Md., hereafter cited "NEC Records."

44. "Eighty-first Annual Report of the Overseers of the Public Welfare," p. 24, and George Hyland to Edward Fitzgerald, March 23, 1942, WPA-Mass. 651.1 (NA).

45. Mayor's Annual Address, *PCCB,* Jan. 4, 1937, p. 4; Tobin to J. Roosevelt, March 26, May 12, 14, 1938, *et seq.,* J. Roosevelt MSS., Box 28; and B. M. Harloe to Denis Delaney, Sept. 29, 1939, WPA-Mass. 651.1 (NA), Box 1506. Even Mayor Tobin, although in better repute with Washington than Curley or Mansfield had been, was accused of holding back on the city's monetary contribution to WPA. Col. F. C. Harrington to Aubrey Williams, April 11, 1938, and suggested draft of Harrington's response, WPA-Mass. 640 (NA), Box 1492.

46. *PCCB,* Feb. 3, 1936, pp. 39–40.

47. Kerrigan to Roosevelt, Aug. 27, 1938, WPA-Mass. 641, Box 1495.

CHAPTER 8

1. (Name withheld by author) to Eleanor Roosevelt, April 4, 1935, FERA-Mass., Box 132. Prompted by Mrs. Roosevelt's interest in the case, a social worker visited the woman and put her on an ERA sewing project at $12 a week.

2. Martha Gellhorn to Hopkins, undated report, "Visit to Massachusetts, November 15–25, 1934," receipt date stamped Dec. 10, 1934, Hopkins MSS., Box 59.

3. Benedict S. Alper and George E. Lodgen, "Youth Without Work," *The Survey,* LXX (September, 1934), pp. 285–286. Also, Lucile Eaves, "Discrimination in the Employment of Older Workers in Massachusetts," *Monthly Labor Review,* XLIV (June, 1937), pp. 1359–1386.

4. Robert Washburn to Hopkins, Nov. 3, 1934, Hopkins MSS., Box 59.

5. Federal Writers' Project, *Massachusetts: A Guide to Its Places and People* (Boston, 1937), p. 137.

6. At the end of 1932, the eight included Baltimore, St. Louis, Chicago, Philadelphia, Milwaukee, Los Angeles, San Francisco, and Pittsburgh. Buffalo ranked second to Boston but averaged only $27.12 for each case aided. All figures from U.S. Department of Labor, Children's Bureau Bulletin No. 237 (1937), *Trends in Different Types of Public and Private Relief in Urban Areas, 1929–1935,* by Emma Winslow, pp. 72–85, 96–100.

7. In 1935 combined municipal and federal relief payments per case aided (excluding WPA, August–December) averaged from $35 to $40 in New York, Philadel-

phia, Detroit, Pittsburgh, and Buffalo; from $30 to $34.99 in Chicago, Los Angeles, San Francisco, and Milwaukee; while Cleveland and St. Louis averaged $29.03 and $25.87 respectively. Boston's combined federal-municipal case load (again excluding WPA) averaged 553 cases per 10,000 population. Buffalo, Los Angeles, Pittsburgh, and Cleveland all topped six hundred, while Detroit ranked last with 248. *Ibid.*

8. *PCCB*, April 29, 1940, p. 172; *City Record*, Dec. 11, 1937, p. 1409, and Jan. 18, 1941, p. 51. As federal and state legislation allowed the city welfare department to change its emphasis, the portion of aliens on municipal relief, 1935–1940, climbed from 20 to 32 percent.

9. Robert Washburn to Harry Hopkins, Nov. 3, 1934, Hopkins MSS., Box 59.

10. *City Record*, Jan. 19, 1934, pp. 57, 60.

11. Bauman, "The City, the Depression, and Relief: The Philadelphia Experience, 1929–1933," pp. 193–223.

12. If a family of four remained on city welfare for a year they would have received $520 plus a small amount of supplemental aid, and the largest families would have taken in $780. According to a mid-decade State of Massachusetts reckoning, a family of four needed $767 to live, and in 1940 the federal government set a $1,430 "maintenance level" for the same size welfare household. If those on federal work relief had managed to put in a full year with no layoffs (and almost no one did), they would have earned $624 with ERA and $660 with WPA. *Globe*, Nov. 26, 1935; *PCCB*, Feb. 10, 1936, pp. 49–50; and *Monthly Labor Review*, LI (December, 1940), p. 1563.

13. *PCCB*, May 3, 1937, p. 202.

14. *Ibid.*, Aug. 3, 1936, pp. 261–262, and March 4, 1940, p. 81.

15. *Ibid.*, April 8, 1935, p. 156, and Jan. 4, 1937, *passim*.

16. *Traveler*, editorial, Aug. 4, 1938.

17. *Globe*, Aug. 12, 1936.

18. For the opening night of *Uncle Tom's Cabin* the ERA Civic Theater invited the eighty-four-year-old Mrs. Cordelia MacDonald of Belmont, the original Little Eva, to attend. Mrs. MacDonald first played the role at age four in 1852. Promotional attempts such as this helped lure capacity crowds—to the discomfiture of private theater companies.

19. Martha Gellhorn to Hopkins, "Visit to Massachusetts, November 15–25, 1934," Hopkins MSS., Box 59.

20. *PCCB*, Nov. 20, 1933, p. 369. Curley ingenuously responded, "Well, there is quite a lot of that being done now, but I don't think it is a good course to pursue." *Ibid.*

21. Employees of the Boston Public Library Civil Works Service to Hopkins, Jan. 27, 1934, telegram, CWA Records, Box 21.

22. *Globe*, Nov. 29, 1934.

23. Robert Washburn to Hopkins, Nov. 3, 1934, Hopkins MSS., Box 59.

24. Among fifty-nine cities studied in 1935, Boston ranked as the seventh most expensive place to live, and food costs topped every city with a population above

50,000 except New York. WPA, Division of Social Research, "Inter-City Differences in the Cost of Living," Series I, No. 20 (Washington, May, 1936).

25. Society of St. Vincent de Paul, "Annual Reports of the Metropolitan Council of Boston for Years Ending September 30, 1930–September 30, 1938"; *The New York Times*, Dec. 11–12, 1934; Arthur Rotch to Aubrey Williams, telephone transcript, Jan. 24, 1935, FERA-Mass., Box 128; and *City Record*, April 20, 1935, pp. 417, 420.

26. Each kettle of WPA chowder contained eight pounds of fish fillets, thirteen quarts fish broth, twenty-two pounds diced potatoes, two pounds diced onions, twelve ounces salt, and one and a half ounces pepper. *City Record*, Nov. 30, 1935, pp. 1141, 1143.

27. Spelling and punctuation are uncorrected. (Name withheld by author) to Roosevelt, Oct. 5, 1935, WPA-Mass. 641 (NA), Box 1494.

28. *Globe*, Dec. 16, 1935.

29. Federal writers were also subjected to Red-baiting, especially with the publication in 1937 of *Massachusetts: A Guide to Its Places and People*. Forty-one lines had been given to the Sacco-Vanzetti case but only nine to the Boston Tea Party and five to the Boston Massacre. Industry received no space, while labor got a chapter. Governor Charles Hurley told the writers to "go back where they came from" if they did not like America, and Joseph B. Ely was of the opinion that "they ought to take the books to the Boston Common, pile them in a heap, set a match, and have a bonfire." *Ibid.*, Aug. 19–22, 1937; *The New York Times*, Aug. 20–22, 29, Sept. 19, 1937.

30. Robert Washburn to Hopkins, Nov. 3, 1934, Hopkins MSS., Box 59.

31. Florence Birmingham to Roosevelt, May 12, 1936, WPA-Mass. 660 (NA), Box 1539.

32. See March–April 1938 correspondence of George Goodman, executive secretary of the Urban League, WPA-Mass. 693 (NA), Box 1546. The NAACP also denounced the Boston WPA for failing to imagine the Negro in anything more than the most menial capacities. That Colonel John McDonough, state WPA director, kept a Negro clerk outside his door was widely regarded as grotesque tokenism. NAACP Records, Box C-186, and WPA-Mass. 641 (NA), Box 1495.

33. (Name withheld by author) to Col. F. C. Harrington, June 5, 1939, WPA-Mass. 610.2, Box 1484.

34. Of 6,840 federal workers let go in Boston during July and August of 1939, only 8.7 percent were privately employed three months later, compared to 12.7 percent in other large cities. "Economic Status of WPA Workers Dismissed Under 1939 Relief Act," *Monthly Labor Review* (March, 1940), p. 623.

35. E. Wight Bakke, *The Unemployed Worker: A Study of the Task of Making a Living Without a Job* (New Haven, 1940), and *Citizens Without Work: A Study of the Effects of Unemployment Upon the Workers' Social Relations and Practices* (New Haven, 1940).

36. (Name withheld by author) to Harold Ickes, Sept. 23, 1935, WPA-Mass 641 (NA), Box 1494.

37. The connection between unemployment and emotional instability was seen by almost all caseworkers in the 1930s. Philip Eisenberg and Paul F. Lazarsfeld, "The Psychological Effects of Unemployment," *Psychological Bulletin*, XXV (June, 1938), pp. 358–390.

38. "A downward progression in standards set for the jobs the men were seeking was noticeable," Bakke observed in New Haven. Bakke, *The Unemployed Worker*, p. 239. For expenditure adjustments, see *ibid.*, pp. 253–281.

39. Alice Webber (Regional Social Worker) to Aubrey Williams, Aug. 30, 1935, WPA-Mass. 640 (NA), Box 1492. In Chicago, families on municipal relief showed a similar determination to stay off the dole—much more so than those unemployed families not on relief. Helen R. Wright, "The Families of the Unemployed in Chicago," *Social Service Review*, VIII (March, 1934), p. 27.

40. (Name withheld by author) to Works Progress Administration, March 6, 1936, WPA-Mass. (NA), Box 1494. That the unemployed made emphatic distinctions between municipal welfare and work for the federal government is confirmed in a number of studies. See, for example, Dorothy Mack, "Psychological and Emotional Values in CWA Assignments: A Study of Sixty-one Families on Relief Before and After C.W.A.," *Social Services Review*, IX (June, 1935), pp. 256–268.

41. Robert Washburn to Hopkins, Nov. 3, 1934, Hopkins MSS., Box 59.

42. (Name withheld by author) to Hopkins, Nov. 20, 1934, FERA-Mass., Box 133.

43. (Name withheld by author) to Roosevelt, June 21, 1936, WPA-Mass. 660 (NA), Box 1539.

CHAPTER 9

1. Charlotte Perkins Gilman, "To Labor," in 25th Anniversary Program of the Boston Women's Trade Union League, 1929, BWTUL Records, Schlesinger Library, Radcliffe College.

2. Jerold S. Auerbach, "New Deal, Old Deal, or Raw Deal: Some Thoughts on New Left Historiography," *Journal of Southern History*, XXV (February, 1969), p. 22.

3. Unless otherwise noted, union membership statistics in Chapter 9 have been derived from *Annual Directories of Labor Organizations in Massachusetts*, 1929–1941, and Troy, *Trade Union Membership, 1897–1962*. Also, Barbara Warne Newell, *Chicago and the Labor Movement: Metropolitan Unionism in the 1930's* (Urbana, Ill., 1966), p. 198.

4. Sidney Lens and Milton Derber, among others, have argued that worker spontaneity led to the awakening of the labor movement even before the NIRA was passed. Lens, *Left, Right and Center: Conflicting Forces in American Labor* (Hinsdale, Ill., 1949), pp. 272, 285, and Derber, "Growth and Expansion," in Derber and Edwin Young (eds.), *Labor and the New Deal* (Madison, Wisc., 1957), p. 9. The Boston story would confirm their views.

5. Henry Steele Commager (ed.), *Documents of American History* (New York, 1949), pp. 453–454, and Irving Bernstein, *Turbulent Years: A History of the American Worker, 1933–1941* (Boston, 1970), pp. 172–173.

6. LaRue Brown, Dr. Ben Selekman of the Associated Jewish Philanthropies, James T. Moriarty of the Sheet Metal Workers, Robert Watt of the State Labor Federation, and Professors Sumner Slichter and Calvert Magruder of Harvard were included, in part because of the political promptings of Louis Kirstein and Lincoln Filene.

7. Samuel E. Hill, *Teamsters and Transportation: Employer-Employee Relationships in New England* (Washington, D.C., 1942), pp. 87, 99.

8. James Nelson, *The Mine Workers' District 50* (New York, 1955), *passim.*

9. George Clifton to author, interview, Dec. 30, 1970, and Lawrence Sullivan to author, interview, Aug. 26, 1971.

10. From its inception in 1933 through its termination in mid-1934, the New England Regional Board held only eleven elections. Just three contests involving eight firms took place in Boston, and only two of these three elections resulted in union victories. National Labor Board Records, Record Group 25, National Archives, Drawers 86, 122, hereafter cited "NLB Records"; National Labor Relations Board Records, Record Group 25, Boston Administrative Files, National Archives, Box 32, hereafter cited "NLRB-Boston"; and FMCS 170-9620.

11. It has been estimated that 60 percent of all company unions in the United States were founded under NRA. Richard C. Wilcock, "Industrial Management's Policies Toward Unionism" in Derber and Young (eds.), *Labor and the New Deal*, p. 288.

12. Bernstein, *Turbulent Years*, pp. 200–205.

13. Docket No. 17, NLRB-Boston, Box 32; typescript reports in Labor-SF, General Subject File, 1933–1940, Box 66; and National Labor Relations Board, *Decisions of the National Labor Relations Board, December 1, 1934–June 16, 1935*, II (Washington, D.C., 1935), pp. 53–56.

14. This diverse group protected workers ranging from egg inspectors and theatrical wardrobe attendants to cigar-box finishers and sleeping-car porters.

15. Albert A. Blum, "Why Unions Grow," *Labor History*, IX (Winter, 1968), pp. 39–72.

16. *Globe*, Aug. 12, Sept. 5, 1933, and BCLU Minutes, Sept. 1, 1933.

17. Interview in 1936 by North Bennett Street Industrial School on behalf of the Consumers' League of Massachusetts, CL-Mass., Folder 462.

18. *Globe*, Feb. 24, 1934.

19. National Recovery Administration, Release No. 9764, NRA Records, Box 1074.

20. Chapter 10 includes a more detailed discussion of code evasion. A few Boston unions participated in the subversion of NRA provisions. An NRA field adjuster reported: "I am finding a new and dangerous situation whereby the unions are notifying the manufacturers not to pay any attention to the minimum wage requirements of the code. In order to spread work among piece workers the unions are refusing to assist in the keeping of any time system." C. S. Whittier to Leigh Orr, autumn of 1934, NRA Records, Box 1084.

21. *Globe*, Oct. 1, 1934. Watt, a fiery Scotsman from the Lawrence Central Labor Union, lived in Boston during much of the Great Depression, serving the Massachusetts Federation of Labor in a variety of ways. Beginning in 1936, Watt

became the American delegate to the International Labor Organization in Geneva.

22. Massachusetts State Federation of Labor, *Proceedings* (August 6–9, 1934), Resolution Nos. 16, 51, 68–69, pp. 54, 78–79, 85–93.

23. *Globe*, May 30, 1935.

24. *Ibid.*, June 16, 1933. Trade unionists issued a more formal call for government construction in August. Massachusetts State Federation of Labor, *Proceedings* (Aug. 7–10, 1933), Resolution No. 52, p. 62.

25. Massachusetts Building Trades Council to John Carmody, Jan. 8, 1934, CWA Records, Box 21.

26. John Carroll to James Myles, undated, but filed in January 1934 correspondence, *ibid.* The Society of Master Painters and Decorators, on the other hand, argued that the CWA threatened private business because its $15 wage for the unskilled was *too high.* The petition (CWA Records, Box 21) contended that the CWA wage was causing "tremenduous [*sic*] dissatisfaction which will take years to readjust."

27. R. C. Branion to Hopkins, July 19, 1935, telephone transcript, Hopkins MSS., Box 65.

28. In the crucial roll-call vote which prompted the split, the Boston delegate from the Upholsterers International Union abstained, and the head of a local union representing stenographers sided with Lewis. All other Bostonians voted "Nay" to industrial unionism. Those loyal to President Green included representatives of the Boot and Shoe Workers, Postal Clerks, Railway Clerks, Coopers, Firemen and Oilers, Hod Carriers, Hotel and Restaurant Workers, Street Railwaymen, and the Newspaper Writers. *Report of the Proceedings of the Fifty-Fifth Annual Convention of the American Federation of Labor* (1935), pp. iii–xx, 574–575.

29. *Justice*, Feb. 1, March 15, 1936. The ILGWU praised "the splendid militancy of the girl strikers" and the "matchless spirit in repulsing police brutality and hired thuggery." Also, *Advance*, January–April, 1936.

30. Three thousand workers in the silk-dress industry won a closed shop agreement, an objective which more than fifteen hundred cotton-garment and cloak-and-suit workers failed to obtain. All employers agreed to a $13 minimum wage and a forty-hour week. Given the total breakdown of labor standards after the death of NRA, the wage gain amounted to at least a 25 percent increase in every shop, while hours in each case were reduced from twelve to as much as sixteen per week. FMCS 182-1209 and 182-1713; *Globe*, April 2, 15, 1936; and *Justice*, April 1, 1936.

31. Calculated from "Industrial Disputes," *Monthly Labor Review*, XLII (May, 1936), pp. 1303–1306, and XLIV (May, 1937), pp. 1226–1227. The massive rallies on May Day, 1934, in cities like New York and Detroit, eviction riots in Chicago, the violence of the Pacific Coast dock strike, the Great Textile Strike which inflamed the Atlantic Seaboard in September 1934—Boston missed them all.

32. *Globe*, Aug. 13, 1935, *et seq.* "We know that radicalism flourished more in the wake of the New Deal reforms of 1933 and 1935 than in anticipation of them,"

Jerold Auerbach has written. "A sense of possibilities, elicited by the Roosevelt administration, repeatedly galvanized the Left." Auerbach, "New Deal, Old Deal, or Raw Deal," p. 24. This observation, if applied to Boston, is more true for 1935 and 1936 than for the two previous years.

33. *Globe*, Sept. 10, Oct. 7, 1936.

34. *Ibid.*, Aug. 28, Sept. 7–8, 1936; *Post*, Sept. 8, 1936. The American Liberty League, to which the union banners made reference, had been founded in 1934 and served as a haven not only for Republicans but for anti-Roosevelt Democrats. Joseph B. Ely was one of its most prominent members.

35. *Justice*, Feb. 1, 1937.

36. During its first full year, the Boston Labor Relations Board processed just 63 unfair labor practice complaints, but the number jumped to 298 in its second year and then to 563 between July 1, 1937, and June 30, 1938. Thereafter, the number of so-called "C" cases dipped slightly. In 1935 to 1936, the Boston Board superintended just 6 representation cases in the entire Northeast and held only 2 elections, but from July 1, 1937, to June 30, 1938, the NLRB in Boston took on 174 cases involving the certification of bargaining units and held 74 elections, 73.7 percent of which resulted in victory for a noncompany union. *First-Sixth Annual Reports of the National Labor Relations Board for Fiscal Years Ended June 30, 1936–June 30, 1941, 6 vols.*

37. *Myers et al. v. Bethlehem Shipbuilding Corporation, Limited,* 303 U.S. 41.

38. Tabulated from *Twenty-Ninth and Thirty-Ninth Annual Directories of Labor Organizations in Massachusetts* (1930, 1940), pp. 23–35, 21–39 respectively. Although the BCLU voted in 1936 to support the Randolph Resolution condemning union discrimination against Negroes, the ten craft locals with the highest percentage of skilled workers averaged just one black Bostonian each in 1938. Those blacks who belonged to unions tended to remain in segregated locals representing redcaps, musicians, and sleeping-car porters. Although a Negro was quoted to the effect that the CIO was "the best thing that has happened to the labor movement not only in Boston but throughout the rest of the country," few "salt and pepper" CIO locals existed in the capital of Massachusetts. Massachusetts State Federation of Labor, *Proceedings* (August 3–7, 1936), p. 124; *The Black Worker* (October, 1939, and March, November, 1940); and Seaton Wesley Manning, "Negro Trade Unionists in Boston," *Social Forces,* XVII (December, 1938), pp. 256–266.

39. Boston in 1939 and 1940 had 20.2 percent of all CIO locals in the state. The city's AFL locals, in contrast, made up 26.1 percent of all the federation's units in the Commonwealth.

40. Hillman to Louis Kirstein and Hillman message to Kirstein's office, March 24, 1937, telephone transcripts, Kirstein MSS., Case 7. "It would be a mistake," Hillman added, for organizers "to get public opinion against them" in Boston.

41. Massachusetts Federation of Labor, *Proceedings* (August 5–9, 1940), p. 94.

42. Quotations respectively from Amalgamated Clothing Workers of America, *Proceedings of the Twelfth Biennial Convention* (May, 1938), pp. 526–527, and *Globe*, March 4, 1940. Also, *CIO News*, Feb. 13, 1939, and March 11, 1940. By

the fairly comfortable margin of 135 to 93 delegates at the CIO's 1940 session in Worcester defeated an anti-Communist resolution backed by the National Maritime Union and the Packinghouse Workers.

43. Local No. 9, Stone Masons' and Marble Setters' Union to John Gleason, Jan. 21, 1937, WPA-Mass. 641 (NA), Box 1494; and letters to Hopkins of Jan. 4–5, 1937, with attached briefs, signed by officers of the American Federation of Government Employees, Lodge 294, *et al.*, *ibid.*, 651.3 (NA), Box 1511.

44. Hill, *Teamsters and Transportation*, p. 83. On the national level, too, the Fair Labor Standards Act proved to be of limited scope. Leuchtenburg, *Roosevelt and the New Deal*, pp. 261–263.

45. The way to an endorsement was smoothed by striking a clause from the original resolution which stated that Wendell Willkie was "Wall Street's personal representative." Massachusetts Federation of Labor, *Proceedings* (August 5–9, 1940), pp. 91–92. Quotations from *ibid.*, pp. 92–94, and *Globe*, Aug. 10, 1940.

46. Massachusetts State Federation of Labor, *Proceedings* (August 5–9, 1940), p. 93.

CHAPTER 10

1. James J. Irwin to James Farley, Oct. 18, 1932, DNC-Mass., Box 268.
2. Rosenman (ed.), *Public Papers and Addresses*, II, pp. 12, 14.
3. *Globe*, June 9, 1933, and Federal Reserve Bank of Boston, *Proceedings of the Eleventh Annual Meeting of Stockholders of the Federal Reserve Bank of Boston* (November 10, 1933), pp. 19–21.
4. "Confidential Report—April 26, 1934," P. A. O'Connell to Frank Walker, NEC Records, Box 181.
5. "Address of Hon. Joseph P. Kennedy," Nov. 15, 1934, pamphlet, Chamber of Commerce Records, Drawer 8, 358–370, and clippings covering his visit, *ibid.*
6. *Globe*, Aug. 11, 1933.
7. *City Record*, Sept. 2, 16, Oct. 14, 1933, pp. 979, 981, 1029–1030, 1117, 1120. As Curley lambasted foes of NRA, his own administration violated federal codes by working employees in hospitals and welfare institutions for more than forty hours a week.
8. Frankfurter to Kirstein, Dec. 19, 1933, Kirstein MSS., Case 3. The future Supreme Court justice advised his friend not to be intimidated by "the familiar methods of panic-mongering on which the Republican Party has lived ever since Mark Hanna brought the technique of panic-mongering to a high state of perfection." *Ibid.*
9. Kirstein to Felix Frankfurter, Nov. 28, 1933, *ibid.*
10. W. W. Walter (Chairman, Boston Compliance Board) to William Davis, Feb. 16, 1934, NRA Records, Box 1010.
11. Henry Bergson to Roosevelt, May 23, 1935, PPF 1669, and NRA Regional Office Number One, "Weekly Report," No. 20, May 18, 1935, NRA Records, Box 4753.
12. "Address of Robert Amory to the Harvard Economic Society," Nov. 18, 1933, typescript, and Amory to Louis Kirstein, Nov. 23, 1933, Kirstein MSS., Case 7.

A terror of price-fixing stimulated executives in other industries to resist the NRA.

13. *Globe*, March 27, 1935. In the precode month of July 1933, southern males earned 28 percent less than their northern counterparts, and in August 1934, a year after the codes took effect, they earned 29 percent less. George Sloan, "The First Year Under the First Code," typescript, Kirstein MSS., Case 7.

14. *Globe*, April 18, 1935.

15. *Ibid.*, April 24, 1935. Also, "Report of Semi-Annual Coordination Meeting of the Federal Agencies and Departments in Massachusetts," Dec. 5, 1935, typescript, p. 4, NEC Records, Box 359. In a *Globe* poll of New Englanders published January 5, 1936, 78 percent opposed the AAA, the most lopsided opinion sample reported in the nation. It was estimated that New England was on the paying end of AAA by a 16 : 1 ratio. *Globe*, Jan. 7, 1936.

16. *Ibid.*, April 22, 24, July 17, 1935, and *Herald*, July 17, 1935. Judge Elisha Brewster willingly granted injunctions, and the stakes ran high. Pacific Mills, operating out of Boston and Lawrence, blocked payment of $321,472, and in the largest lawsuit of all, the John P. Squire Meat Company of Boston filed a bill in equity seeking a refund of $5,225,227 from the processing tax on hogs. *Globe*, July 23, Aug. 1–2, 1935.

17. NRA Regional Office, Region No. One, "Weekly Report," June 7, 1935.

18. E. A. Filene, "Statement Before Senate Finance Committee," April 10, 1935, typescript, PPF 2116. Also, *Globe*, May 28, 1935.

19. Calculated from *Statistical Abstract of the United States* (1935), pp. 742–743, 781–782; *ibid.* (1940), pp. 839, 868–869, 875, 882–884; and "Statistics of Manufactures in Massachusetts, 1920–1938," p. 20.

20. Rosenman (ed.), *Public Papers and Addresses*, II, pp. 67–68, 81.

21. Byrd to Howe, Aug. 17, 1933, and Howe to Byrd, Aug. 19, 1933, telegrams, FDR-OF 666. As a token of how things had changed by 1937, Byrd once more requested funds from the Roosevelt administration to support his explorations, and this time Harry Hopkins complied. "That's the most modest request I've had in a long time," Hopkins told the Admiral. Telephone transcript, Jan. 5, 1937, Hopkins MSS., Box 65.

22. Dennett to Shattuck, May 10, 1933, Shattuck MSS., Drawer 10.

23. Hannah Connors and the Massachusetts Real Estate Owners' Association to Roosevelt, Oct. 20, 1934, telegram, FDR-OF 5434.

24. J. Roosevelt to F. D. Roosevelt, May 7, 1934, PPF 3, Box 1.

25. "Address by Joseph P. Kennedy," Oct. 24, 1936, typescript, PPF 207.

26. Robert Washburn to Hopkins, Nov. 3, 1934, Hopkins MSS., Box 59.

27. Boston Real Estate Owners' and Tenants' League to Hopkins, April 2, 1935, FERA-Mass.

28. Herman Loeffler, "Relief Problems of Local Governments: Boston," *National Municipal Review*, XXVII (January, 1938), pp. 30–33.

29. A textile employer complained that WPA sewing projects had left him without qualified stitchers, and he also had the temerity to tell Hopkins that his domestic servants had departed for better-paying WPA jobs. Hopkins sarcastically retorted

that the employer would not "have to look very far to find any number of earnest men very anxious to obtain good private employment." Samuel Eliot to Hopkins, April 27, May 6, 1936, and Hopkins to Eliot, May 1, 1936, WPA-Mass., Box 1545.

30. Dorchester Citizens' Association to Congressman McCormack, Feb. 15, 1939, *ibid.*, Box 1498. The campaign against shabby construction, in the view of WPA, reached a low in 1937 when the agency accused the conservative *Boston Herald* of printing doctored photographs which stigmatized the federal projects. *Works Progress Bulletin*, Aug. 16, 1937, WPA-Mass. 650 (NA), Box 1505.

31. Tinkham to ERA, Boston, June 12, 1934, FERA-Mass., Box 132.

32. Quotations respectively from *Globe*, Jan. 31, 1935; *ibid.*, Oct. 2, 1935; and National Emergency Council Report, Sept. 19, 1938, NEC Records, Box 295. Real-estate interests were favorably impressed with the stricter income limitations which the USHA imposed on its tenants, and they also liked the new loan-grant arrangement which was more generous than the PWA's 45 percent contribution. Still, the Massachusetts director of the National Emergency Council continued to count Boston bankers and realtors as opponents. Frank Foy to NEC, letter of April 5, 1939, and "Housing Report" of April 7, 1939, NEC Records, Box 323; and *City Record*, Oct. 26, 1940, pp. 1137, 1142–1143.

33. *Herald*, July 19, 1935. In condemning "the proposed vicious and un-American tax bill" of 1935, Minute Women gathered at the Old South Meeting House in the very room where colonials had condemned British tyranny in 1773. "The Horse and Buggy Helped Build This Nation with Sanity, Security, Safety," a banner proclaimed. The equine phrase had been used by Roosevelt in castigating the Supreme Court.

34. Based on a comprehensive survey undertaken by the National Emergency Council in the Hub, Jan. 28, 1938, NEC Records, Box 295. Also, *The New York Times*, April 12, 1937.

35. Address by Frederic H. Curtiss in *Proceedings of the Fourteenth Annual Meeting of Stockholders of the Federal Reserve Bank of Boston* (November 12, 1936), pp. 7–9.

36. Massachusetts Branch of the National Emergency Council, Report of Jan. 28, 1938, NEC Records, Box 295.

37. *Globe*, Jan. 8, 1932.

38. Frank Buxton to Louis Kirstein, Aug. 9, 1937, Kirstein MSS., Case 3.

39. Marguerite Le Hand to Frankfurter, Nov. 17, 1937, in Freedman (ed.), *Roosevelt and Frankfurter: Their Correspondence*, p. 440.

CHAPTER 11

1. *The Nation*, CXXXI (August 6, 1930), p. 139.

2. *PCCB*, May 25, 1936, p. 201.

3. *The New York Times*, Sept. 30, 1936.

4. *PCCB*, Jan. 3, 1939, p. 1. Boston's reversals, 1929–1939, also exceeded national losses in respect to wages earned (37 percent vs. 22 percent), value of products

(32 vs. 19), number of workers engaged in manufacturing (25 vs. 11), and unemployment rate (19.9 vs. 11).

5. Pittsburgh suffered a 22.2 percent unemployment rate in 1940, while 20.1 percent of Cleveland's labor force had no jobs. St. Louis (15.3), Chicago (15.2), and Detroit (14.7) were among those with smaller unemployment percentages than Boston (19.9). Computed from *Statistical Abstract of the United States* (1942), pp. 55–56.

6. One Bostonian sent President Roosevelt a cartoon showing Uncle Sam clutching a fistful of dollars. "Cheerio—$$ for Britain," Uncle Sam was saying, while next to him a haggard worker with a cup in hand said, "No help wanted." Philip Diehl to Roosevelt, Dec. 16, 1941, WPA-Mass. 641 (NA), Box 1499.

7. Despite the many shifts, portions of the labor force remained constant. Occupations related to the basic needs of the city—food supply and personal service, for example—held steady, and so did the number of men classified as laborers. Banking, insurance, and real estate also witnessed little change. Bureau of the Census, *Fifteenth Census of the United States, 1930: Population*, II, Part 3, p. 675, and "New England Community Abstracts," May 15, 1937.

8. Only the infusion of Tom Yawkey's dollars kept the Red Sox afloat, for in 1933 the team's attendance reached a low which never since has been equaled. Soon, the purchase of stars such as "Lefty" Grove and Jimmy Foxx, and the arrival of Ted Williams in 1939, helped considerably. On the other hand, not even the attraction of Babe Ruth in the lineup saved the Boston Braves from falling into receivership. Temporarily rechristened the Boston Bees in 1936, the baseball club managed to field a team while their nominal owner, Judge Emil Fuchs, moved into a new office during that year. Appropriately, Fuchs served as state chairman of the Social Security Board.

9. From 1920 to 1930, the population in the four rings extending outward from Boston jumped by an average of 23.8 percent. During the Depression, the increase in these areas amounted to a paltry 4.8 percent. Calculations from data in Leo F. Schnore and Peter R. Knights, "Residence and Social Structure: Boston in the Ante-Bellum Period," in Thernstrom and Sennett (eds.), *Nineteenth-Century Cities*, pp. 247–257.

10. The distinction between use of land for reasons of prestige—as opposed to any more practical consideration—is a central idea in Firey's exhaustive study, *Land Use in Central Boston* (Cambridge, 1947). While it is impossible to know much about the transient population that floated in and out of Boston, the number was substantial. In 1934–1935, the Federal Transient Service cared for 20,000 destitute itinerants. Thernstrom, while acknowledging that "the migratory currents sweeping through the community were running less strongly after about 1920," nevertheless sets the 1935–1940 total of comers and goers at 131,972. *The Other Bostonians*, pp. 26–28.

11. Bernard Sternsher (ed.), *Hitting Home: The Great Depression in Town and Country* (Chicago, 1970), pp. 267–268, and Clark Johnson, "Burlington Since the 1930's: Change and Continuity in Vermont's Largest City," in *ibid.*, pp. 269–281.

12. *Globe*, May 11, 1936. Italian chauvinism collided with the intense nationalism of

Boston's tiny Albanian community when Mussolini invaded their fatherland in 1939. Albanians, the WPA reported, also drew apart during the Great Depression, whereas Boston's Armenians displayed a greater tendency to assimilate. Federal Writers' Project, Massachusetts, *The Albanian Struggle in the Old World and the New* (Boston, 1939), pp. 81, 86, and *The Armenians in Massachusetts* (Boston, 1937), *passim*.

13. The failure of Italians to rise to skilled occupations as nimbly as other groups (their record in many respects was even more dismal than that of the Irish) is amply documented in Thernstrom, *The Other Bostonians*, pp. 135–144, 172.

14. Bruner and Sayre, "Shortwave Listening in an Italian Community," pp. 641–643. The tightness of community and family structure in the North and West Ends is traced in two well-known studies. See William Foote Whyte, *Street Corner Society: The Structure of an Italian Slum* (Chicago, 1943), and Herbert J. Gans, *The Urban Villagers: Groups and Class in the Life of Italian-Americans* (New York, 1962).

15. John P. Diggins, "The Italo-American Anti-Fascist Opposition," *Journal of American History*, LIV (December, 1967), pp. 579–598.

16. Robert Morss Lovett, "Witch-Hunting in Massachusetts," *New Republic*, LXXXXIII (December 1, 1937), pp. 96–97, and "Red Purge, Boston Style," *ibid.*, LXXXXV (June 22, 1938), p. 173.

17. *PCCB*, May 6, 1940, p. 202.

18. The St. Vincent de Paul Society's Boston headquarters raised $242,000 in 1938, more than double what it got in 1930, and the annual expenditure of the Catholic Charitable Bureau exceeded $400,000 in the post-1935 period, also a distinct gain from the first years of the decade. Virtually every other private welfare organization in the city fell off during the same interval. Society of St. Vincent de Paul, *Annual Reports*, and *Pilot*, April 9, 1938.

19. Quotations are, in order, from O'Connell to Roosevelt, March 4, 1933, telegram, PPF-148; *Globe*, July 5, 1934; *The New York Times*, Nov. 2, 1934; *ibid.*, Nov. 14, 1934; and Father Robert Barry, quoted in Robert Washburn to Harry Hopkins, Nov. 3, 1934, Hopkins MSS., Box 59.

20. At a meeting on the Boston Common, the secretary of the Boston Painters' Union wondered out loud whether the conservative Cardinal, by "crack[ing] the whip" over state legislators to get their vote against the Child Labor Amendment, was in fact trying to protect the church's money—funds which, the unionist alleged, were invested in sweatshops. *Globe*, Feb. 19, 1937, and *The New York Times*, Feb. 20, 1937.

21. *The New York Times*, Jan. 2, 1936. For development of the theme that the nation's leaders had succumbed to "evil counsel," see *The Pilot*, Jan. 8, 1938.

22. On the occasion of the fiftieth anniversary of O'Connell's ordination, James Farley urged extravagant praise which included the statement that the Cardinal's service had been "a benediction on our national life." Other aides toned down the fulsome message. Stephen T. Early, for one, understood the sarcastic implications of phrases which pointed to O'Connell's "inspiring patriotism." Farley to Marguerite Le Hand, May 23, 1934; Early's draft of Roosevelt to O'Connell, June 2, 1934; and Roosevelt to O'Connell, Nov. 14, 1934, PPF-148.

23. *Globe,* March 18, July 19–20, 1938; *The New York Times,* March 18, 1938; and Donald F. Crosby, "Boston's Catholics and the Spanish Civil War: 1936–1939," *New England Quarterly,* XLIV (March, 1971), pp. 82–100. Crosby particularly emphasizes O'Connell's fixation upon what he took to be Loyalists' "persecution" of the Church. The Spanish Civil War, argues Crosby, had "a most unfortunate effect on Boston's Catholics, for it intensified their minority feelings, it made them appear reactionary and undemocratic, and it postponed the day when Boston's Catholic citizens would seek the common good just as enthusiastically as they sought their own." *Ibid.,* p. 100.

24. *Globe,* Feb. 15, 1935. Any Catholic who might testify in favor of the bill, said Corrigan, was the possessor "of a sinister mind" and was guilty of "gross treachery unworthy of a true Catholic." "Statement by Reverend Jones I. Corrigan . . . Before the Committee on Constitutional Law of [the] Massachusetts Legislature, March 4, 1936," broadside, Alexander Lincoln MSS., Schlesinger Library, Radcliffe, Folder 6.

25. Francis L. Broderick, *Right Reverend New Dealer: John A. Ryan* (New York, 1963), pp. 67, 156–159, 202, and Neil Betten, "The Great Depression and the Activities of the Catholic Worker Movement," *Labor History,* XII (Spring, 1971), pp. 243–258. A few Bostonians participated in the CWM's back-to-the-land movement by founding St. Benedict's Farm in Upton, Mass. The group also started a House of Hospitality which sponsored a breadline, and it supported strikes by Boston fishermen and Massachusetts textile workers.

26. *Pilot,* Nov. 2, 1940. Also, *ibid.,* April 24, 1937, and Oct. 12, 19, 1940.

27. The percentage increases of nonwhite population registered by some other representative northern cities during the 1930s include those of New York (28.7), Indianapolis (25.6), Detroit (18.7), Chicago (14.3), Pittsburgh (12.2), and Philadelphia (11.8). Calculated from *Statistical Abstract of the United States* (1941), pp. 30–31.

28. (Name withheld by author) to Eleanor Roosevelt, June 17, 1936, WPA-Mass. 642 (NA), Box 1502.

29. Juanita Jackson to Rev. Richard Owens, March 26, 1936; "Remittances to National Office"; and Membership Lists in NAACP-Boston, Box G-89.

30. Walter White in New York, after years of chastising the Boston Branch, expressed delight that the organization was at last "getting the masses." White to Irwin Dorch, Feb. 9, 1937, NAACP-Boston, Box G-90.

31. Minutes of the Executive Committee, Feb. 24, 1938, *ibid.*

32. Thernstrom, *The Other Bostonians,* pp. 136–144.

33. *Globe,* Oct. 2, 1935. It has often been pointed out that Jewish culture—learning (Torah), Charity (Zedekeh), and "this-worldliness"—dovetailed with the liberalism of the thirties. Lawrence H. Fuchs, "American Jews and the Presidential Vote," *American Political Science Review,* XLIX (June, 1955), pp. 385–401. To attend to "the well-being of the masses," said Rabbi Silver, was not only a matter of "social wisdom," but also "one of the prime mandates of our religion." *Globe,* Oct. 21, 1935.

34. *Ibid.,* April 24, 1933, and Sept. 29, 1934.

35. On August 1, 1941, Roosevelt wrote Kirstein a note of thanks: "These ties are a real joy and some day I am going to tell you whose neck one of them will adorn.

The other two are very definitely for me." Two days later, Roosevelt left New London, ostensibly for a fishing trip, and on August 9 the fateful shipboard meeting with Churchill took place off the coast of Newfoundland. Felix Frankfurter later told Kirstein the President had mentioned that the Boston necktie had gone to Churchill. Letter and memorandum in Kirstein MSS., Case 5.

36. Halliday Witherspoon to Editor, *The New York Times*, Oct. 1, 1935.

37. *Back Bay Ledger and Beacon Hill Times*, Jan. 11, 1940, quoted in Firey, *Land Use in Central Boston*, p. 273.

38. In tracing 1,265 real-estate transactions between 1935 and 1939 in central Boston, the Urban Land Institute discovered that the aggregate sale price amounted to just 54.6 percent of assessed valuations. Urban Land Institute, *A Survey in Respect to the Decentralization of the Boston Central Business District* (Boston, 1940), p. 17, cited in Firey, *Land Use in Central Boston*, p. 272.

39. "NorthEastWestSouth," III (December, 1934), Denison House Records, Folder 22. Settlement-house workers in the rest of the nation also showed a tendency to turn from charity to an emphasis upon prevention (reform). "There was no talk among them of erosion of character that presumably attended Federal relief." Otis L. Graham, Jr., *Encore for Reform: The Old Progressives and the New Deal* (New York, 1967), pp. 103–108.

40. *Transcript*, Dec. 11, 1931, clipping, WEIU-Hqs.

41. R. L. Duffus, "Things That Make Boston What She Is," *The New York Times Magazine*, Feb. 16, 1930, p. 7.

42. Quotations respectively from *Globe*, March 28, 1935, and *PCCB*, Dec. 16, 1940, p. 461.

43. *Globe*, April 3, 1934.

44. *Ibid.*, May 22, 1935. The Committee on Moral and Social Welfare's 1935 call for a new analysis of "our whole capitalistic system," and the favorable vote on government ownership, represented a turn to the left from 1933. Even at that point, however, Congregationalist ministers had endorsed strong regulatory controls over business and national unemployment insurance.

45. In 1934 the Rev. Augustus Boyden had led a successful effort to block resolutions favoring the New Deal. A year later, however, Unitarians endorsed government ownership of public utilities, transportation, banking, and coal. They further resolved support of taxes that would redistribute wealth.

46. *Globe*, Feb. 4, 25, 1935.

47. Quotations from *Globe*, Sept. 30, 1935, and Rev. Dwight J. Bradley, "The Church of Christ Challenges the City," *The Missionary Review of the World*, LXI (July–August, 1938), pp. 333–335.

48. Rosenman (ed.), *Public Papers and Addresses*, V, p. 553.

CHAPTER 12

1. Van Nostrand, "The Lomasney Legend," p. 43.

2. *PCCB*, Jan. 3, 1939, p. 1.

3. Edwin O'Connor, *The Last Hurrah* (New York, 1956), pp. 326, 374.

4. A symmetrical comparison, one that would pit four pre-Roosevelt ward elections against four post-New Deal races, would obviously be desirable. But the twenty-two–ward system went into effect in 1925, and hence the first election for which the turnover rate can be calculated is 1927. All compilations are derived from "Annual Reports of the Election Department," 1926–1940.

5. In Chicago, only thirteen of five hundred ward leaders lost a contested election between 1929 and 1936, a 97.4 percent retention rate, which contrasts with Boston's 53.6 percent from 1929 to 1935. In Pittsburgh, the Roosevelt landslides breathed new life into the city's regular Democratic organization. Gosnell, *Machine Politics*, pp. 27–50, and Stave, *The New Deal and the Last Hurrah, passim.*

6. Samuel Lubell, "Post-Mortem: Who Elected Roosevelt?" *Saturday Evening Post,* CCXIII (January 25, 1941), pp. 9–11ff., and Whyte, *Street Corner Society,* pp. 194–198.

7. A high rate was not, of course, an unmitigated evil since it in part reflected Boston's greater willingness to spend for relief. Typically, though, Boston's rate exceeded by some $8 the second most heavily taxed city (usually Chicago) and doubled the least taxed city (usually San Francisco).

8. Chicago, Philadelphia, Cleveland, Baltimore, Pittsburgh, and Milwaukee boasted lower indebtedness in 1940 than in 1930. *Statistical Abstract of the United States* (1932), pp. 217–220, and *ibid.* (1940), pp. 264–265.

9. Russell, "The Last of the Bosses," pp. 21–25, 85–91, especially 87–88. "No such turmoil had occurred on Beacon Hill since cynical, droop-eyed Ben Butler had been governor fifty years before," Russell added.

10. *Globe,* Feb. 13, 1936. The '36 state budget of $69 million topped '35's by $7 million, and it exceeded the all-time Massachusetts high (1930) by $3,700,000. Budget increases were, of course, what liberals were calling for throughout the country and did not in and of themselves prove that Curley was a rogue.

11. Russell, "The Last of the Bosses," p. 88, and *Globe,* Sept. 19, 1936.

12. The four quotations in order are from Kierman, "Jim Curley, Boss of Massachusetts," p. 137; a radio address by Mayor Mansfield printed in *City Record,* Sept. 19, 1936, p. 1120; Dinneen, "The Kingfish of Massachusetts," p. 343; and *ibid.*

13. Louis M. Lyons, "Jim Curley and His Gang," *The Nation,* CXLII (April 29, 1936), p. 540; Dinneen, "The Kingfish of Massachusetts," p. 353; and "Sleepy Hollow," *The New York Times* editorial, Jan. 18, 1937.

14. Added "Silk Hat," "I still have the two mitts I left Ireland with seventy-two years ago this month." *The New York Times,* May 15, 1936. Curley's "plan" went through a number of versions. Finally, a moderate bill—one allowing judges with at least ten years of service to opt for voluntary retirement at age seventy on 75 percent of their salaries—failed in both the Senate and the House.

15. Perkins to Curley, Jan. 14, 1935, Labor-SF, Box 132; Eddie Dowling, COHC No. 532, p. 430; and Marion Frankfurter to Roosevelt, Nov. 15, 1938, in Freedman (ed.), *Roosevelt and Frankfurter,* pp. 465–466.

16. Attempting to recoup from the $500 per week payments necessitated by the court decision, Curley eventually became involved with a wartime "five percenter,"

and after a protracted legal battle he was sentenced to eighteen months in the Federal Correctional Institute in Danbury, Connecticut. But by the time the sentence was handed down, Curley had sat in Congress and had won another term as mayor of Boston. After serving five months of his sentence, Curley was pardoned by President Truman.

17. *PCCB*, Jan. 6, 1941, p. 1.

18. On the last loan of 1939, Boston achieved its record low interest charge, a mere .29 of 1 percent. The Depression high had come in 1933—5.75 percent.

19. The budget for all purposes, however, increased every year from 1929 through 1938, moving from roughly $71 million to a high of $83,800,000, and it then trailed off to $81,400,000 in 1940. Absence of home rule handcuffed the mayor: some 55 percent of the budget items (debt requirements, schools, police, the state tax, pension funds, county expenses) were outside his control. To His Honor's chagrin, most of these costs went up.

20. *Globe*, May 18, 23, 1934.

21. Boston in 1940, ninth in population, still employed the sixth greatest number of municipal workers and topped the larger cities of Cleveland, Baltimore, and St. Louis. *Statistical Abstract of the United States* (1942), p. 270. The most drastic cuts occurred during the Mansfield administration—a move which James Michael Curley likened to "the individual who endeavored to extinguish a fire in his home by pouring gasoline upon it." *Globe*, April 4, 1934.

22. Mullen, "Poor Old Boston," p. 235.

23. *City Record*, Sept. 19, 1936, pp. 1117, 1120. Terms such as "Curleycrat" and "Smithocrat" made sense, for, as Harold Gorvine has noted, even though "the Massachusetts Democracy was touched by the New Deal, it did not become a genuine New Deal party." "The New Deal in Massachusetts," p. 524. Also, Massey, Jr., "The State Politics of Massachusetts Democracy," pp. 203–207.

24. Curley to Farley, Sept. 10, 1936, DNC-1936, Box 4.

25. Congressman William Connery, for example, predicted that Alfred M. Landon would beat Roosevelt in Massachusetts by a 60-40 margin. Connery to James Farley, Aug. 12, 1936, DNC-1936, Box 4.

26. *Globe*, June 15, 1936.

27. O'Brien, a resident of Ward 22 (Brighton), had been a product of the Boston Latin School, Harvard College, and the Harvard Law School.

28. Coughlin had, of course, visited Boston several times, and during a stop in August 1935 he had addressed the state legislature and the city council. From both he had received standing ovations. At that time Coughlin maintained that only Waterloo, Iowa, had higher per capita membership in the National Union of Social Justice than Boston. *Globe*, Aug. 13, 1935, and *PCCB*, Aug. 12, 1935, p. 341.

29. "Radio Address Given by His Excellency Governor James M. Curley over Station WAAB, Sept. 30, 1936," typescript, FDR-OF 5434. Curley is said to have offered Coughlin $10,000 to remove O'Brien from the Massachusetts senatorial contest. Charles J. Tull, *Father Coughlin and the New Deal* (Syracuse, 1965), pp.

149–150. The Governor also instituted legal proceedings to remove the Union Party aspirant from the ballot.

30. Rosenman (ed.), *Public Papers and Addresses*, V, p. 518, and McGrath to Farley, Oct. 23, 1936, DNC-1936, Box 11. "Never in the history of Massachusetts," added McGrath, "has there been such an outpouring of sincere enthusiasm." After the electrifying reception, predictions of a Roosevelt victory were sent to Farley, although most thought the margin for the state would be close.

31. Los Angeles, Pittsburgh, San Francisco, and Detroit were among the other large cities where Roosevelt's percentage moved ahead of Boston's. Clubb and Allen, "The Cities and the Election of 1928," p. 1211, and "Annual Reports of the Election Department," 1929, 1933, 1937.

32. Only three other cities (Dubuque, Cincinnati, St. Paul) handed Lemke more than 5 percent of their vote. Tull, *Father Coughlin and the New Deal*, p. 170.

33. The nine in which the Union Party topped 10 percent included Ward 1 (East Boston), Wards 10–11 (Roxbury), 15–17 (Dorchester), 18 (Hyde Park), 19 (Curley's home district of Jamaica Plain), 20 (West Roxbury), and 22 (Brighton, O'Brien's ward of residence). "Annual Report of the Election Department," 1937.

34. *Pilot*, Feb. 1, 1936, quoted in George Q. Flynn, *American Catholics and the Roosevelt Presidency, 1932–1936* (Lexington, Ky., 1968), p. 201. Samuel Lubell has attributed the Union Party vote to hardcore isolationist sentiment and to Irish hatred of England. While Boston Catholics were saturated with archdiocesan concern about anticlericalism in Mexico and Franco's crusade in Spain, the Irish who supported the Coughlinites were reacting to more than just foreign affairs, as William Leuchtenburg has noted. Lubell, *The Future of American Politics*, pp. 143–146, and Leuchtenburg, *Roosevelt and the New Deal*, p. 195n.

35. "Hats in the Ring: Monsignor Jim," *New Republic*, CII (March 11, 1940), p. 334.

36. Roosevelt had told a columnist, Ernest K. Lindley, that in the event of a Cordell Hull–Farley ticket, people would construe Hull "as a stalking horse for the Pope." "Mr. Farley Announces," *Time*, XXV (April 1, 1940), pp. 13–14.

37. Italians also bristled at Roosevelt's famous remark at Charlottesville after Mussolini had fulfilled his promises to Hitler. "On this tenth day of June, 1940," Roosevelt snapped, "the hand that held the dagger has struck it in the back of its neighbor." *Globe*, June 11, 1940.

38. Margaret Weisman to Dorothy McAllister, Oct. 10, 1940, DNC-Women's Division, 1937–1944, Box 223.

39. *Globe*, April 6, Oct. 11–13, 1940; *Post*, *The New York Times*, Oct. 12, 1940; and "Lodge on Willkie," *Life*, IX (October 28, 1940), pp. 116ff.

40. "Address of Hon. James M. Curley at Democratic State Convention Rally, Municipal Auditorium, Springfield, Saturday, September 28," typescript, FDR-OF 5434, and *Globe*, Sept. 27–29, 1940.

41. Rosenman (ed.), *Public Papers and Addresses*, IX, pp. 514–524; *Globe*, *Post* and *The New York Times*, Oct. 31, 1940; Burns, *Lion and the Fox*, pp. 448–449; and Leuchtenburg, *Roosevelt and the New Deal*, pp. 320–321.

42. *Boston Chronicle*, Oct. 17, 1936, clipping, JMC-SB, No. 490.

43. *City Record*, Jan. 13, 1940, p. 23.
44. *Globe*, Oct. 5, 1936; "Birds of a Feather" and "People's Platform for Peace-Security-Jobs-Civil Liberties," Communist party pamphlets, 1940, WPA-Mass. 610.2, Box 1484; and Gerhardt Reder to author, interview, September 1968.
45. Designated as "wards not shown in table" (Table 12.1), these sixteen voting areas, which supplied almost exactly two-thirds of Boston's return, obviously contained substantial variety. But except for Ward 2 (Charlestown and part of East Boston) and portions of the South End, all exceeded the city's median rental. They included solid working-class portions of Irish Roxbury and Dorchester as well as the Irish-Yankee wards to the west and southwest of the urban core.
46. Shattuck to John Gebhardt, Jan. 7, 1939, Shattuck MSS., Drawer 10.
47. Norton to J. Roosevelt, Oct. 11, 1938, J. Roosevelt MSS., Box 22.
48. Mrs. Roosevelt, said the president of the Boston Ladies Auxiliary of the Sleeping Car Porters, was "the First Lady of the Negro people." *The Black Worker* (October, 1940), p. 2. Many Catholics, on the other hand, deplored her frequent departures from a conventional woman's role.
49. In his investigation of the 1936 and 1940 elections, V. O. Key estimated that 25 percent of Republican voters in the United States were likely to shift, but only 3 percent of Democrats were suspectible to crossing over. V. O. Key, *The Responsible Electorate: Rationality in Presidential Voting, 1936–1940* (Cambridge, 1966), p. 27.

CONCLUSION

1. *City Record*, March 8, 1930, p. 257.
2. John Winthrop, "A Modell of Christian Charity," quoted in Darrett Rutman, *Winthrop's Boston: Portrait of a Puritan Town, 1630–1649* (Chapel Hill, 1965), p. 4.
3. Benjamin Labaree, "Microanalysis," in Edward Saveth (ed.), *American History and the Social Sciences* (New York, 1964), pp. 370–378, especially p. 371.
4. David M. Potter, "Explicit Data and Implicit Assumptions in Historical Study," in Louis Gottschalk (ed.), *Generalization in the Writing of History: A Report of the Committee on Historical Analysis of the Social Science Research Council* (Chicago, 1963), pp. 178–194, especially p. 191.
5. Although Boston "has often been viewed as a deviant, stagnant, caste-ridden community, . . . in sheer size, ethnic diversity, economic importance, cultural contributions, and a variety of other ways, [it] was and is one of the great American cities." Thernstrom, *The Other Bostonians*, pp. 5–6. Precisely!
6. Mark Gelfand has correctly observed that Roosevelt's "program was urban only in the sense that it assisted people who lived in cities. . . ." Roosevelt and the New Deal, he adds, "rescued local government from financial ruin . . . but never came to grips with the city as an economic and social entity." *A Nation of Cities*, pp. 68–69.
7. After reviewing the relationships between the forty-eight states and the New Deal, James Patterson detected "conflict as well as cooperation, conservatism as

well as progressivism, reaction as well as reform." When writing about the "gloomier side" of the role of the states during the Depression, Patterson noted tendencies which were especially strong in Massachusetts—penurious spending for relief, little cooperation with the NRA, frequent federal-state conflicts, an inadequate administrative apparatus for receiving New Deal programs, suspiciousness of the WPA, "incorrigible factionalism of state Democratic parties," and few signs of "a dramatically new state progressivism." James Patterson, "The New Deal and the States," *American Historical Review*, LXXIII (October, 1967), pp. 70–84. Also, James Patterson, *The New Deal and the States: Federalism in Transition* (Princeton, 1969), *passim*.

8. *Globe,* Dec. 31, 1941.

9. *Post,* June 21, 1941, clipping, Kirstein MSS., Case 2.

A Note on Sources

PRIMARY

I. SPECIAL COLLECTIONS

Bostonians, among the most atavistic Americans by reputation, have on the whole been careless about records of the Depression period. Few who belonged to the city's power matrix have deposited papers, and local archives tend to reveal more about the 1730s and 1830s than they do about the 1930s. Happily, there are some notable exceptions. The Boston Chamber of Commerce Records at Baker Library, Harvard University School of Business Administration, for instance, contain excellent material on the city's economic difficulties and the response of local entrepreneurs. Useful, too, are the Louis Kirstein MSS., also at Baker Library, for what they disclose about the business community, Jewish philanthropy, and several of the city's liberal spokesmen. For the outlook of politically active Brahmins of a more conservative stripe, the Henry Lee Shattuck MSS., Littauer Center, Harvard University, and the George Read Nutter Diary at the Massachusetts Historical Society are of considerable value, while recollections of ward politicians of

366

the 1930s may be found in the Boston Public Library's oral history holdings. At the Schlesinger Library, Radcliffe College, the substantial collection of the Consumers' League of Massachusetts is excellent on Yankee reformers in the age of the Great Depression and on working conditions in Boston.

But, mainly, local materials in aggregate, rather than the special richness of any one collection, have aided this study. A picture of private social and charitable agencies during the Depression decade, for example, can be pieced together from annual reports and records of the St. Vincent de Paul Society; the Women's Educational and Industrial Union (the WEIU records are divided between the Schlesinger Library and the organization's downtown headquarters); the Associated Jewish Philanthropies of Boston; the Catholic Charitable Bureau; the Catholic Information Center; and the records of Elizabeth Peabody House, Denison House, and the Eva Whiting White MSS., all three at the Schlesinger Library. Miscellaneous material pertaining to Protestant churches and their welfare agencies is available at the Congregational Library, the Unitarian Universalist Association, the Massachusetts Diocesan (Episcopal) Library, and the New England Methodist Library at Boston University. Political activities of a rightist organization are recorded in the Alexander Lincoln MSS. (the Sentinels of the Republic) at the Schlesinger Library, and a small collection pertaining to the Boston Women's Trade Union League is also lodged in the Schlesinger Archives. Handwritten minutes of the Boston Central Labor Union are to be found at the offices of the Greater Boston Labor Council. In addition, the J. Donald Comer MSS. (also called the Avondale Mill Records) at the Baker Library contain scattered correspondence of Boston textile manufacturers and wholesalers during the Depression.

Farther away from Boston but still within Massachusetts, two collections stand out. At the Dinand Library, Holy Cross College, Worcester, more than six hundred scrapbooks pertaining to the career of James Michael Curley are shelved, and the vast majority of these volumes cover Curley's activities in the 1930s. And at Brandeis University's Goldfarb Library the David K. Niles MSS. were made accessible for purposes of corroboration by Dr. Abram L. Sachar to whom I am indebted. The David I. Walsh MSS. at Holy Cross and the Joseph B. Eastman MSS. at Amherst College proved disappointing.

Materials at the National Archives, Washington, D.C., and at the Federal Records Center, Suitland, Md., on the other hand, were of inestimable assistance. While the local historian searching for correspondence from his designated city is at the mercy of cataloguing systems, it is nevertheless the case that when agency records are filed by state, the yield in each box is often disproportionately high for the state's principal city. And though agency files tend to be cluttered with considerable housekeeping memoranda, they at the same time lay bare the successes and failures of intergovernmental cooperation. Agency files, containing letters and telegrams from a seemingly limitless variety of individuals and organizations, reveal as do no other collections the hardships suffered during the Great Depression, as well as the remedies proposed by Bostonians. The most significant records proved to be those of the President's Emergency Committee for Employment and the President's Organization on Unemployment Relief; the Federal Emergency Relief Administration (State Files, 1933–1936); the Civil Works Administration; the Works Progress Administration (State Series, Massachusetts, 1935–1944); the National Recovery Administration; and the Federal Mediation and Conciliation Service. Other federal records containing material of worth included those of the Reconstruction Finance Corporation; the Department of Labor (Office of the Secretary, General Subject Files, 1933–1940, and the Chief Clerk's File); the National Emergency Council; the National Labor Board; and the National Labor Relations Board (Administrative Files, Boston).

At the Franklin D. Roosevelt Library, Hyde Park, materials of great value were also tapped, particularly the Democratic National Committee Papers (Massachusetts, 1928–1944; Women's Division, 1933–1944); the President's Personal File, his Official File, and his private correspondence with James M. Curley, 1928–1932; the

Harry Hopkins MSS. (especially the transcripts of Hopkins's telephone conversations with state relief directors and the narrative field reports from Massachusetts); and the John Ihlder MSS. (especially Ihlder's revealing diary about public housing in Boston). To a lesser extent, the James Roosevelt, Louis M. Howe, Mary W. Dewson, and Aubrey Williams MSS. also proved helpful.

In addition, papers of the Boston Branch of the National Association for the Advancement of Colored People at the Library of Congress furnished material on the city's black community, and recollections by and/or about Bostonians in the Columbia Oral History Collection have been consulted. These include the depositions of William Braithwaite (No. 345), Eddie Dowling (No. 532), Arthur Krock (No. 54), James M. Landis (No. 551), Robert Lincoln O'Brien (No. 81), and James T. Williams, Jr. (No. 246).

II. NEWSPAPERS

Every issue of the Boston *Globe*, 1929–1940, has been examined. Throughout the Depression period, the *Globe* published both morning and afternoon editions. The *Evening Globe*, however, has been used only for events of special importance since it was less complete than the morning issue. Boston in the 1930s had many competing newspapers but the *Globe* offers most to the historian. The paper, more detailed than any of the others, represented no special group in the city and generally avoided controversy. In contrast, the *Transcript* served Boston's more aristocratic elements, and the *Herald* was aimed toward the newer wealth. Both were aggressively Republican. The *Traveler* contained the *Herald*'s evening news; the *Post* acted as the traditional Irish Democratic newspaper and is especially good on political topics; the *American* gave Boston a Hearst entry; and the *Record* was a wretched tabloid which contained little of local character. These newspapers, particularly the *Transcript, Herald,* and *Post,* have been read selectively as a check upon the accuracy of the *Globe*. To gain a broader perspective, virtually every entry in *The New York Times Index* under "Boston" has been traced to the appropriate issue of *The Times*, 1929–1940. In addition, scattered issues of newspapers which served Boston's ethnic neighborhoods have been located. These include the *Jewish Advocate*, the *Italian News*, the *Gazetta del Massachusetts*, and the Boston *Chronicle*. Every fourth issue of *The Pilot*, the weekly which relayed news of the city's Catholic Archdiocese, has been sampled for the 1929–1940 period.

Labor newspapers have also been a valuable source. Every issue of *The CIO News*, 1938–1940, has been checked for Boston items, and every fourth issue of the American Federation of Labor's *Weekly News Service* has been scanned. Both *Advance*, published by the Amalgamated Clothing Workers, and *Justice*, put out by the International Ladies Garment Workers Union, have been extensively surveyed. Other labor newspapers consulted include *The Black Worker*, *The Brewery Worker*, and *The Catholic Worker*.

III. GOVERNMENT DOCUMENTS: CITY, STATE, FEDERAL

Three sources merit special emphasis. The *City Record*, the mayor's newspaper, gives a detailed picture of municipal policies, not only those of Malcolm Nichols, James Michael Curley, Frederick Mansfield, and Maurice Tobin, but also those of the city's principal departments, including public welfare. Every issue, 1929–1940, has been combed. In the *Proceedings of the City Council of Boston* (*PCCB*), the Hub's ward representatives can be seen in action. Communications between both the mayor and the council and the municipal departments and the council, are inserted in the *Proceedings*. The minutes of every council meeting, 1929–1940, have been inspected. In addition, the published annual reports of Boston's municipal departments (*Documents of the City of Boston, 1926–1941*) have been extensively investigated, particularly those of the Overseers of the Public Welfare, the Election Department, the Soldiers' Relief Department, the Department of Public Works, and the City Collector's Report. Moreover, the annual reports of the Boston Port Authority and the Boston Finance Commission, as well as the pamphlets of the Boston Housing Authority, were of more than passing interest.

State sources also proved helpful. Reports emanating from the Bureau of Labor and Industries, for instance, were indispensable, especially the *Annual Directory of Labor Organizations in Massachusetts, 1929–1941; Report on the Census of Unemployment in Massachusetts, 1934; Statistics of Manufactures in Massachusetts, 1920–1938;* and *Time Rates of Wages and Hours of Labor in Massachusetts, 1929–1941.* The annual reports of the Massachusetts Department of Public Welfare, 1929–1941; *Massachusetts Legislative Documents,* 1929–1941; and The Commonwealth of Massachusetts, *General Laws* (Tercentenary Edition, 1932), 2 vols., were extensively mined.

Moreover, federal publications illuminated several aspects of Boston's experience. The reconstruction of a city's social geography in any era, of course, depends heavily upon the U.S. Bureau of the Census, and the standard volumes resulting from the Fifteenth and Sixteenth Censuses of the United States were profitably used. For more detailed work, "Population and Housing, Statistics for Census Tracts: Boston, Mass." [Washington, D.C., 1942 (?)] was invaluable. Comparisons to other cities were greatly facilitated by the Census Bureau's *Statistical Abstract of the United States* (1929–1944), while the Federal Reserve Bank of Boston's *Proceedings of the Annual Meetings of Stockholders* and *Annual Reports* (1930–1942) furnished helpful data on the city's economy. So, too, did the *Annual Reports* of the Federal Home Loan Bank (1932–1941). Congressional hearings on a variety of bills often contained depositions by Bostonians and turned out to be a useful way of understanding what both elites and nonelites expected of Washington: the pre-Roosevelt La Follette-Costigan Committee Hearings had high yield, and the hearings on virtually all major New Deal bills were also explored with varying degrees of profit. For urban labor history, the National Labor Relations Board's *Annual Reports* and *Decisions and Orders* (1935–1941) helped immeasurably, and so, too, did the U.S. Department of Labor's *Monthly Labor Review* (1929–1947). Federal Emergency

Relief Administration and Works Progress Administration studies of self-help cooperatives, slums and blighted areas, housing, and unemployment provided important information, but three studies merit special mention: Works Progress Administration, *Urban Workers on Relief: Part I—The Occupational Characteristics of Workers on Relief in Urban Areas, May 1934,* by Gladys L. Palmer and Katherine D. Wood (Washington, D.C., 1936); Works Progress Administration, *Urban Workers on Relief: Part II—The Occupational Characteristics of Workers on Relief in 79 Cities, May 1934,* also by Palmer and Wood; and Federal Writers' Project, *Massachusetts: A Guide to Its Places and People* (Boston, 1937). A study also of great use, especially for comparative purposes, is that of the U.S. Department of Labor, Children's Bureau, *Trends in Different Types of Public and Private Relief in Urban Areas, 1929–1935,* by Emma A. Winslow (Washington, D.C.: Children's Bureau Bulletin No. 237, 1937).

IV. MISCELLANEOUS

Three editions of Franklin D. Roosevelt's speeches and correspondence contain useful material—Elliott Roosevelt (ed.), *F.D.R.: His Personal Letters, 1928–1945,* 2 vols. (New York, 1947–1950); Max Freedman (ed.), *Roosevelt and Frankfurter: Their Correspondence, 1928–1945* (Boston, 1967); and Samuel I. Rosenman (ed.), *The Public Papers and Addresses of Franklin D. Roosevelt,* Vols. I–IX (New York, 1938–1950). The voluminous recollections of New Dealers include portions on Boston and, far more, place Boston within a larger framework. James A. Farley, *Behind the Ballots: The Personal History of a Politician* (New York, 1938), and *Jim Farley's Story: The Roosevelt Years* (New York, 1948); Harry L. Hopkins, *Spending to Save: The Complete Story of Relief* (New York, 1936); the reminiscences of Harold L. Ickes; and the works of Hugh Johnson, Raymond Moley, Rexford G. Tugwell, and Frances Perkins all provided helpful insights.

For Boston, Edward A. Filene, *Speaking of Change: A Selection of Speeches and Articles by Edward A. Filene* (New York, 1939); William Cardinal O'Connell, *Recollections of Seventy Years* (Boston, 1934); and James Michael Curley, *I'd Do It Again: A Record of All My Uproarious Years* (Englewood Cliffs, N.J., 1957) filled in important dimensions. In attempting to disinter the record of blue-collar Boston, the annual or biennial proceedings of the Massachusetts State Federation of Labor, the Amalgamated Clothing Workers, the International Ladies Garment Workers, the American Federation of Labor, the Congress of Industrial Organizations, and other unions were highly useful. Demographic work was aided by the *Boston City Directory* (1929–1940); Boston Council of Social Agencies, "Social Statistics by Census Tracts in Boston," 2 vols. (Boston, 1935); and United Community Services of Metropolitan Boston, "Social Facts by Census Tract, 1950" [Boston, 1953 (?)].

SECONDARY

If pleas for a consistent methodology in urban history have not always been followed in the course of this study, they have at least been heard, especially Sam Bass Warner, Jr.'s "If All the World Were Philadelphia: A Scaffolding for Urban History, 1774–1930," *American Historical Review*, LXXIV (October, 1968), 26–43. Other methodological promptings which in varying degrees influenced portions of this study include Louis Gottschalk (ed.), *Generalization in the Writing of History: A Report of the Committee on Historical Analysis of the Social Science Research Council* (Chicago, 1963); Oscar Handlin and John Burchard (eds.), *The Historian and the City* (Cambridge, 1963); Edward Saveth (ed.), *American History and the Social Sciences* (New York, 1964); and Leo F. Schnore, *The Study of Urbanization* (New York, 1965). Sensitivity to urban demography was greatly heightened by Sam Bass Warner, Jr.'s *Streetcar Suburbs: The Process of Growth in Boston, 1870–1900* (Cambridge, 1962); by Walter Firey's *Land Use in Central Boston* (Cambridge, 1947); by Peter R. Knights's *The Plain People of Boston, 1830–1860:*

A *Study in City Growth* (New York, 1971); by Stephan Thernstrom's *The Other Bostonians: Poverty and Progress in the American Metropolis, 1880–1970* (Cambridge, 1973); and by the essays of Knights and Thernstrom in Thernstrom and Richard Sennett (eds.), *Nineteenth-Century Cities: Essays in the New Urban History* (New Haven, 1969).

Nevertheless, *Boston, the Great Depression, and the New Deal* is more concerned with sociopolitical issues of the 1930s than with the so-called "new urban history." For a general overview of cities in this period, Mark I. Gelfand's *A Nation of Cities: The Federal Government and Urban America, 1933–1965* (New York, 1975), is a welcome addition to the recent literature. Urban political questions raised in Bruce Stave's *The New Deal and the Last Hurrah: Pittsburgh Machine Politics* (Pittsburgh, 1970) seemed especially worth pursuing, while inquiries into the New Deal's impact were in part shaped by Richard Kirkendall, "The New Deal as Watershed: The Recent Literature," *Journal of American History*, LIV (March, 1968), 839–852; Jerold S. Auerbach, "New Deal, Old Deal, or Raw Deal: Some Thoughts on New Left Historiography," *Journal of Southern History*, XXXV (February, 1969), 18–30; the closing chapter of William E. Leuchtenburg's *Franklin D. Roosevelt and the New Deal* (New York, 1963); and by the introductory essay in Bernard Sternsher's *Hitting Home: The Great Depression in Town and Country* (Chicago, 1970). In helping to establish a line of inquiry in the area of labor history, Albert A. Blum, "Why Unions Grow," *Labor History*, IX (Winter, 1968), 39–72, and Milton Derber and Edwin Young (eds.), *Labor and the New Deal* (Madison, 1957), were most helpful.

Care was taken to place Boston within a national context. For images of the Great Depression across the United States, Gilbert Seldes's *The Years of the Locust: America, 1929–1932* (Boston, 1933), a book now out of print, seemed particularly worth revivifying. Also helpful was John Kenneth Galbraith's *The Great Crash, 1929* (Cambridge, 1954); Arthur M. Schlesinger, Jr.'s magisterial trilogy, *The Age of Roosevelt* (Boston, 1957–1960); Cabell Phillips's *From the Crash to the Blitz, 1929–1939* (New York, 1969); Studs

Terkel's *Hard Times: An Oral History of the Great Depression* (New York, 1970); and Caroline Bird's *The Invisible Scar* (New York, 1966). The broader story of unemployment can be gained from Frances Fox Piven and Richard Cloward, *Regulating the Poor: The Function of Social Welfare* (New York, 1971), and from the older studies of Grace Abbott, especially *Public Assistance* (Chicago, 1940); Joanna Colcord, particularly *Cash Relief* (New York, 1936); the excellent review-of-the-literature essay by Philip Eisenberg and Paul F. Lazarsfeld, "The Psychological Effects of Unemployment," *The Psychological Bulletin*, XXXIV (June, 1938), 358–390; and E. Wight Bakke, *Citizens Without Work . . .* (New Haven, 1940) and *The Unemployed Worker: A Study of the Task of Making a Living Without a Job* (New Haven, 1940).

A partial list of the voluminous literature on national politics during the 1930s should be headed by the previously mentioned books of Leuchtenburg and Schlesinger, Jr., and should most certainly include James T. Patterson, *The New Deal and the States: Federalism in Transition* (Princeton, 1969); Patterson's essays in the *Journal of American History*, LII (June, 1965), 757–772 ("A Conservative Coalition Forms in Congress, 1933–1939"), and the *American Historical Review*, LXXIII (October, 1967), 70–84 ("The New Deal and the States"); Samuel Lubell, *The Future of American Politics* (New York, 1951); James M. Burns, *Roosevelt: The Lion and the Fox* (New York, 1956); Searle F. Charles, *Minister of Relief: Harry Hopkins and the Depression* (Syracuse, 1963); Paul K. Conkin, *The New Deal* (New York, 1967); J. David Valaik, "Catholics, Neutrality, and the Spanish Embargo, 1937–1939," *Journal of American History*, LIV (June, 1967), 73–85; George Q. Flynn, *American Catholics and the Roosevelt Presidency, 1932–1936* (Lexington, 1968); John P. Diggins, "The Italo-American Anti-Fascist Opposition," *Journal of American History*, LIV (December, 1967), 579–598; Frank Freidel's magnificent biography of F.D.R., especially the third and fourth volumes, *The Triumph* (Boston, 1956) and *Launching the New Deal* (Boston, 1973); Otis L. Graham, Jr., *Encore for Reform: The Old Progressives and the New Deal* (New York, 1967); Ellis Hawley, *The New Deal and the Problem of Monopoly: A Study in Economic Am-*

bivalence (Princeton, 1966); Alfred B. Rollins, Jr., *Roosevelt and Howe* (New York, 1962); Alfred Romasco, *The Poverty of Abundance: Hoover, the Nation, the Depression* (New York, 1965); and Charles J. Tull, *Father Coughlin and the New Deal* (Syracuse, 1965).

General developments in labor history are especially well-traced in Irving Bernstein's two volumes, *The Lean Years: A History of the American Worker, 1920–1933* (Boston, 1960), and *Turbulent Years: A History of the American Worker, 1933–1941* (Boston, 1970); Walter Galenson's *The CIO Challenge to the AFL: A History of the American Labor Movement, 1935–1941* (Cambridge, 1960); Milton Derber and Edwin Young (eds.), *Labor and the New Deal* (Madison, 1957); and in Sidney Lens's older but still stimulating *Left, Right and Center: Conflicting Forces in American Labor* (Hinsdale, 1949). More specialized studies worth singling out include Daniel J. Leab, " 'United We Eat': The Creation and Organization of the Unemployed Councils in 1930," *Labor History*, VIII (Fall, 1967), 300–315, and Neil Betten, "The Great Depression and the Activities of the Catholic Worker Movement," *Labor History*, XII (Spring, 1971), 243–258. Leo Troy's *Distribution of Union Membership Among the States, 1939 and 1953*, and his *Trade Union Membership, 1897–1962* (New York: National Bureau of Economic Research, Occasional Papers 56 and 92, 1957, 1965) facilitated comparisons between Boston and other parts of the nation, as did Barbara Warne Newell's *Chicago and the Labor Movement: Metropolitan Unionism in the 1930's* (Urbana, 1961).

While the *Statistical Abstract of the United States* permitted a number of quantitative comparisons to other major cities, more qualitative assessments of how Boston fared in relation to large urban centers rested on periodicals of the 1930s, as well as more recent journal articles, books, and dissertations. Sternsher's previously mentioned *Hitting Home* is a useful anthology (essays by Bonnie R. Fox on Philadelphia and Raymond L. Koch on Minneapolis stand out), as is Robert C. Cotner *et al.*, *Texas Cities and the Great Depression* (Austin, 1973). Older but still helpful books on single cities include Elin L. Anderson, *We Americans* (New York, 1937); Lillian Brandt, *An Impressionistic View of the Winter of 1930–31 in New York City* (New York, 1932); Robert S. and Helen M. Lynd, *Middletown in Transition: A Study in Cultural Conflicts* (New York, 1937); and Clarence Ridley and Orin Nolting (eds.), *What the Depression Has Done to Cities* (Chicago, 1935). Two recent dissertations, still unpublished, have been valuable—John F. Bauman, "The City, the Depression, and Relief: The Philadelphia Experience, 1929–1939" (Rutgers, 1969), and Leonard Leader, "Los Angeles and the Great Depression" (UCLA, 1972). Of the books on big-city mayors of the 1930s, Arthur Mann's *La Guardia Comes to Power: 1933* (Philadelphia, 1965), and Sidney Fine's *Frank Murphy: The Detroit Years* (Ann Arbor, 1975), are superb. Politics apart from City Hall are especially well-treated in Jerome M. Clubb and Howard W. Allen, "The Cities and the Election of 1928: Partisan Realignment?" *American Historical Review*, LXXIV (April, 1969), 1205–1220; Harold Gosnell, *Machine Politics: Chicago Model* (Chicago, 1937); and in Stave's previously mentioned *The New Deal and the Last Hurrah*. The big-city relief experience is the subject of Charles H. Trout, "Welfare in the New Deal Era," *Current History*, LXV (July, 1973), 11–15ff., while single cities are viewed in William H. Chafe, "Flint and the Great Depression," *Michigan History*, LIII (Fall, 1969), 225–239; Roman Heleniak, "Local Reaction to the Great Depression in New Orleans, 1929–1933," *Louisiana History*, X (Fall, 1969), 289–306; and Sidney Tobin, "The Early New Deal in Baton Rouge as Viewed by the Party Press," *Louisiana History*, X (Fall, 1969), 307–337.

In addition to placing Boston within a national framework, it also seemed important to put the city in its regional setting. For shifting economic flow, Otis Dudley Duncan *et al.*, *Metropolis and Region* (Baltimore, 1960); Simon Kuznets and Dorothy Thomas, *Population Redistribution and Economic Growth, United States, 1870–1950*, 2 vols. (Philadelphia, 1957, 1960); and Harvey S. Perloff *et al.*, *Regions, Resources, and Economic Growth* (Baltimore, 1960) were employed. Other regional dimensions were added by Duane Lockard, *New England State Politics* (Princeton, 1959); Walter Prichard Eaton, "New England in 1930," *Current History*, XXXIII (November, 1930), 168–173; and Samuel E. Hill, *Teamsters and Transportation: Employee-Employer Relationships in New England* (Washington, D.C., 1942).

Besides locating Boston within nation and region, pains were taken to place the city within the Commonwealth of Massachusetts. Valuable historical background is provided in Oscar and Mary F. Handlin, *Commonwealth: A Study of the Role of Government in the Economy—Massachusetts, 1774–1861* (New York, 1947); J. Joseph Huthmacher, *Massachusetts People and Politics* (Cambridge, 1959); and Murray B. Levin and George Blackwood, *The Compleat Politician: Political Strategy in Massachusetts* (Indianapolis, 1962). The Federal Writers' Project, *Massachusetts: A Guide to Its Places and People* (Boston, 1937), as well as its studies of Massachusetts' Albanians and Armenians, proved of great interest, and three unpublished dissertations also stood out—Harold Gorvine, "The New Deal in Massachusetts" (Harvard, 1962); William J. Grattan, "David I. Walsh and His Associates: A Study in Political Theory" (Harvard, 1958); and Robert K. Massey, Jr., "The State Politics of Massachusetts Democracy, 1928–1938" (Duke, 1968). Of the dozens of periodical articles on Massachusetts consulted for this study, the most helpful included Francis Bardwell, "Public Outdoor Relief and the Care of the Aged in Massachusetts," *Social Service Review*, IV (June, 1930), 199–209; Lucille Eaves, "Discrimination in the Employment of Older Workers in Massachusetts," *Monthly Labor Review*, XLIV (June, 1937), 1359–1386; William Haber and Herman Somers, "The Administration of Public Assistance in Massachusetts," *Social Service Review*, XII (September, 1938), 397–416; "Census of Unemployment in Massachusetts, January 2, 1934," *Monthly Labor Review*, XXXIX (December, 1934), 1332–1337; "Federal Receiverships in Massachusetts, 1929–1932," *Harvard Law Review*, XLVII (March, 1934), 828–840; and Robert K. Massey, Jr., "The Democratic Laggard: Massachusetts in 1932," *New England Quarterly*, XLIV (December, 1971), 553–574.

the city's travails and triumphs. The major contribution to ethnic history coming out of Boston during the 1930s is William Foote Whyte's *Street Corner Society* (Chicago, 1943). Also helpful is Jerome S. Bruner and Jeanette Sayre, "Shortwave Listening in an Italian Community," *Public Opinion Quarterly*, IV (Winter, 1941), 640–656. Joseph F. Dinneen, *The Purple Shamrock* (New York, 1949); Edwin O'Connor, *The Last Hurrah* (Boston, 1956); and Francis Russell, "The Last of the Bosses," *American Heritage*, X (June, 1959), 21–25ff., capture the flavor of Boston's brawling politics. More scholarly studies include John D. Buenker, "The Mahatma and Progressive Reform: Martin Lomasney as Lawmaker, 1911–1917," *New England Quarterly*, XLIV (September, 1971), 397–419; Vincent A. Lapomarda, "Maurice Joseph Tobin, 1901–1953: A Political Profile and an Edition of Selected Public Papers," unpublished doctoral dissertation (Boston University, 1968), and Lapomarda, "A New Deal Democrat in Boston: Maurice J. Tobin and the Policies of Franklin D. Roosevelt," *Essex Institute Historical Collections*, CVIII (April, 1972), 135–152; Jerome S. Bruner and Sheldon J. Korchin, "The Boss and the Vote: Case Study in City Politics," *Public Opinion Quarterly*, X (Spring, 1946), 1–24; Murray B. Levin, *The Alienated Voter: Politics in Boston* (New York, 1960); Lawrence H. Fuchs, "American Jews and the Presidential Vote," *American Political Science Review*, XLIX (June, 1955), 385–401; and Samuel Lubell, "Post-Mortem: Who Elected Roosevelt?" *Saturday Evening Post*, CCXIII (January 25, 1941), 91–92. Lawrence M. Jones, "Legislative Activities of the Greater Boston Chamber of Commerce . . . ," unpublished doctoral dissertation Harvard Graduate School of Business Administration, 1960), is best on the city's business community, while the Federal Writers' Project, Massachusetts, *Boston Looks Seaward: The Story of the Port, 1630–1940* (Boston, 1941) is also helpful on economic change.

Finally, approximately two hundred periodical articles were consulted. In addition to those already mentioned, a half dozen others of special use on a variety of topics were "Boston," *Fortune*, VII February, 1933), 26–36ff.; Seaton Wesley Manning, "Negro Trade

Boston, though, is the "hero" of this book, and the
the city's Depression experience is aided beyond recl
standing studies of earlier epochs. In *Streetcar Suburb*
1962), Sam Bass Warner, Jr., has bequeathed a ser
Boston's growth, while Walter Muir Whitehill, *Bosto*
phical History (Cambridge, 1968, 2nd ed.) provides
plement. In addition to the previously me
nodemographic work of Firey, Thernstrom, and Knig
ethnic history are admirably treated in Oscar Handlir
migrants: A Study of Acculturation (Cambridge, 1941
From Plotzk to Boston (New York, 1899); Barbara M
Ancestors and Immigrants (Cambridge, 1956); Will
The American Irish (New York, 1963); and Francis
Coming of the Jews," *Antioch Review*, XV (March,
Pre-Depression tribulations of Boston's Negroes are
Stephen R. Fox, *The Guardian of Boston: William M*
(New York, 1970), and William B. Hixon, Jr., "Moorfie
the Struggle for Equality," *Journal of American Hist*
cember, 1968), 553–554. For late–nineteenth-centur
philanthropic traditions, Arthur Mann's *Yankee Refc*
Urban Age (Cambridge, 1954), and Nathan I. Huggin:
Against Poverty: Boston's Charities, 1870–1900 (Wes
1971) are notable. Donna Merwick's *Boston's Priests,*
Study of Social and Intellectual Change (Cambridge,
study of the city's dominant religious ethos, and Dona
"Boston's Catholics and the Spanish Civil War: 1936
England Quarterly, XLIV (March, 1971), 82–100, sho
in action. Arthur Mann (ed.), *Growth and Achiever*
Israel, 1854–1954 (Cambridge, 1954), and Barbara Mil
Pioneers in Service: The History of the Associated Je
thropies of Boston (Boston, 1956) deal with a vital religi

Elizabeth M. Herlihy (ed.), *Fifty Years of Boston:*
Album (Boston, 1932), is the only attempt at a compr
ture of Boston in the 1930s, but the student of the D
cade has innumerable published sources for more limit

Unionists in Boston," *Social Forces*, XVII (December, 1938), 256–266; Paul Boyer, "Boston Book Censorship in the Twenties," *American Quarterly*, XV (Spring, 1963), 3–24; Charles W. Morton, "Lean Times in Boston: Depression and the Drys," *The Atlantic Monthly*, CCXI (February, 1963), 47–54; Joseph F. Dinneen, "The Kingfish of Massachusetts," *Harper's*, CLXXIII (September, 1936), 343–357; and Robert R. Mullen, "Poor Old Boston," *The Forum*, CIII (May, 1940), 232–237.

Index